THE AMERICAN DIPLOMATIC GAME

★ ★

THE
AMERICAN
DIPLOMATIC
GAME

By DREW PEARSON *and*
CONSTANTINE BROWN

DOUBLEDAY, DORAN & COMPANY, INC.
GARDEN CITY, NEW YORK
1935

★ ★

PRINTED AT THE *Country Life Press*, GARDEN CITY, N. Y., U. S. A.

*To the Pawns in
the Game*

CONTENTS

THE AMERICAN DIPLOMATIC GAME

THE WORLD RENOUNCES WAR

1. OUR INSTRUMENT OF NATIONAL POLICY

IT WAS hot in the Salle de l'Horloge. The August sun spread its slanting rays over the Seine, penetrated the deep curtained windows of the Quai d'Orsay, and danced among the great crystal candelabra of Louis XVI. The klieg lights added to the heat. Their intermittent glare cast shadows round the cadaverous eyebrows and great drooping mustache of M. Briand, making him appear more the stage villain than Europe's foremost exponent of peace. Perspiring camera men elbowed for position. A compact army of spectators stood on tiptoe, craning their necks to see over the cameras. They could catch the light glistening on a huge golden pen held in the hand of Gustav Stresemann. Four years later his successor was to help wreck a disarmament conference with demands for increased armament, but to-day Dr. Stresemann scratched his name on an ornate parchment pledging Germany to renounce war as an instrument of national policy. Across the table from him sat Eduard Beneš of Czechoslovakia. Four years later his country's munition plants at Skoda were to be working twenty-four hour shifts supplying the Far East, South America, Europe with instruments of war. But to-day M. Beneš' face glowed fervently as he scratched his name on the beribboned parchment. On it went around the table. It received the signature of August Zaleski, Foreign Minister of Poland, whose crack cavalry regiments later were to be concentrated along the German border in Upper Silesia. It received the blessing of Viscount

31386

Yasuya Uchida, whose imperturbable face gave no hint that four years later he, as Foreign Minister of Japan, would be snapping his fingers at the treaty he had signed.

The representative of a group of American religious weeklies spoke in an awed whisper of the scene he was witnessing—a climax to years of effort on the part of American peace societies toward disarmament. An American lady who had given many years to the cause of peace dabbed her eyes with happy, overbrimming emotion. The correspondent of the *Osaka Mainichi*, short of stature and flushed from welcoming American colleagues at Maxim's, put his hands on her shoulders and endeavored to hoist himself to a better view.

The pen scratched on. It was a great golden pen, given Mr. Kellogg by the city of Havre when he landed there en route to Paris. But it was top-heavy and awkward. Its point was new and did not hold ink; so that once when the klieg lights and the photographers focused upon it as it reached the chief author of the Pact, the pen balked— almost deliberately, it seemed—and for one fleeting instant it looked as if Mr. Kellogg was not to renounce war, after all.

But the pen struggled on.

Two Americans watching Mr. Kellogg's flushed face from the outskirts of the crowd, reminisced over the accident by which the statesmen of the world had stumbled on the Pact, the consternation with which Mr. Kellogg had greeted M. Briand's first proposal that the United States and France agree to outlaw war, the dismay of M. Briand when, after six months of worried deliberation, Mr. Kellogg had suggested that the outlawry of war was too great a privilege to be confined to two nations and should be offered to the entire world.

But if the fifteen plenipotentiaries remembered those early reactions, no trace now appeared in their faces to mar the solemnity of the scene. They were sedate, serene, and impressed with the gravity of the step they were taking. A British journalist, equally impressed, remarked that it was the League of Nations all over again, even to the same ceremony under the same ornate mantelpiece in the same room ten years before. The United States, he told a French friend, could never remain isolated. The Pact of Paris was the bridge by which it came back to coöperate with the world once again.

"But," came the skeptical French reply, "suppose America throws over the Pact of Paris as it did the League of Nations."

The pen at this point had scratched its last signature, and the plenipotentiaries filed out into the sunshine of a Paris afternoon, the flower-beds, the fountains, the terraces of President Doumergue's garden and the satisfaction that war had been renounced as an instrument of national policy forever.

Just a few weeks before that warm August afternoon in Paris, an enterprising American newspaper man, Harold Horan, had unearthed and published a secret memorandum between France and Great Britain. The contents of this memorandum had caused a shiver of surprise to run round the world. In the United States the surprise turned to righteous indignation, then pique—in some high quarters even wrath. Mr. Coolidge, spending his summer in the coolness of the Minnesota woods, sent for his Chief of Naval Operations, Admiral Charles F. Hughes, and exchanged telegrams with his Secretary of State, about to leave for the ceremony in Paris. As a result, Mr. Kellogg announced that he had changed his plans and would not visit London after the signing of the Pact. All he had wanted to do in London anyway, he said, was to see his tailor and play a few holes of golf. Instead, he would visit Dublin as the personal representative of President Coolidge in order to return the call of William T. Cosgrave, President of the Irish Free State.

The change was meant as a deliberate snub of Great Britain.

For the secret memorandum, so inconsiderately published by Mr. Horan, disclosed the fact that Great Britain and France had concluded a provisional understanding on naval strength whereby each was to advocate the reduction of those types of ships most useful to the United States, at the same time increasing the ratios in those types of ships most useful to them.

Exactly one year before, this same question had come up before the Geneva Naval Conference and had wrecked it. The admirals of the United States and the admirals of Great Britain had been in irreconcilable disagreement. The former had wanted a large number of big-gun, long-radius cruisers, while the latter wanted a larger number of small-gun, short-radius vessels. And, unable to break the deadlock, they had gone home.

Following which Great Britain was revealed by Mr. Horan to have been secretly negotiating with France to secure that country's support for a united disarmament front against the United States.

And what made pique and indignation beat more poignantly within the breast of Calvin Coolidge was the fact that these secret naval negotiations followed a period during which relations between the United States and Britain had been increasingly conducive of friction.

For some reason or other much of this friction had come to a head in the specific years 1927 and 1928—just as the Kellogg Pact was being negotiated.

There was, first of all, the row over oil.

Oil at that time was the weapon by which many Englishmen thought a haughty America could be brought to her knees, by which war debts could be repaid, by which the naval fuel sources of the world could be cornered. To this end Britain had quietly acquired most of the world's potential oil-fields, while watching the United States run through its oil supplies like a drunken sailor.

It was at the height of the oil controversy and at the climax also of the bitterness between Great Britain and the United States, that the State Department rubbed its eyes one morning to find the British-government-owned Anglo-Persian Oil Company negotiating for a large tract of land paralleling the Panama Canal in Colombia. And on a subsequent morning it awoke to find a group of high Tory officials with a gold company organized, in possession of another strip paralleling the Canal, this time in Panama. Since the first area was not known to contain oil and the second area was not known to contain gold, an atmosphere of suppressed expectancy settled over the State Department. This atmosphere was in no way dispelled a short time later when two British cruisers suddenly dropped anchor in the harbor of Corinto, where several thousand American marines were endeavoring to force upon Nicaragua a President amenable to the United States.

The appearance of two British warships in any other part of the world where His Majesty's subjects were in danger would have attracted a mere ripple of attention. But Nicaragua was the exception. Nicaragua not only was within that area made sacred to the State Department by the Monroe Doctrine, but also it was in the even more sacred waters adjacent to the Panama Canal. No agreement ever had been put in writing, but it was generally recognized that the Caribbean was a strictly American preserve on which there was to be no British poaching; and that the same exclusive privileges were accorded to the British in that area of "special and vital interest" around Suez, Egypt, and the Red Sea.

In view of which it was not at all surprising that when the British Ambassador informed the slightly deaf Joseph

C. Grew of the cruisers' arrival, that gentleman, then Acting Secretary of State, thought his hearing had deceived him. And when the *note verbale* was repeated to Mr. Grew, the Ambassador later reported to his staff that the news almost took the Secretary's breath away.

It seemed hardly a coincidence that all of these things should have come to a head in the year 1927. Moreover, it seemed hardly a coincidence that in that same year the State Department should have chosen to invade the British sphere of "special and vital interest" in North Africa.

Not since Thomas Jefferson fought the Barbary Wars in the early youth of the Nation had the United States paid any real attention to North Africa. In Abyssinia, for instance, the State Department had been quite content to put American interests under the protection of the British Minister. The nearest American vice-consul at Aden, across the Red Sea, considered himself extra energetic if he managed to get up to Addis Abeba, the Abyssinian capital, once a year.

But suddenly in 1927 the State Department established its own legation in Addis Abeba. Suddenly in the same year Ras Tafari, Prince Regent of Abyssinia, began flirting with the idea of getting American interests to develop his country.

This was anything but pleasing to the British. A secret understanding had been signed between London and Rome dividing Abyssinia into two spheres of influence. And what irked the Foreign Office most was the discovery that the J. G. White Engineering Corporation of New York had secured a provisional contract to build a dam at the mouth of Lake Tsana in the British zone of influence.

When the news finally leaked out the London press screamed in protest.

Lake Tsana, it raged, is the life-blood of the British

Sudan! It is the key to irrigation along the Blue Nile! It means life or death to the cotton-fields along the Nile! To have such a dam in American hands is a direct blow at the Empire!

The State Department smiled complacently. It remembered the Anglo-Persian negotiations in Colombia, the Panama gold-mining project, the two cruisers sent to Nicaragua. Never before had an American firm received such unyielding official support as the J. G. White Corporation.

Thus while Frank B. Kellogg was negotiating his pact to outlaw war, Anglo-American friendship was enjoying anything but a period of tranquillity. In fact, Anglo-American friction, still raw from the British attempt to corner the world's rubber supply, the struggle over Latin American markets, and the race for cable and radio channels, probably had reached its bitterest peak in many years of sometimes bitter history.

This was not a new condition either in regard to relations with Great Britain or in regard to relations with the rest of the world.

We have never claimed to be a pacific nation. According to John Bassett Moore, "our War of Independence was generally regarded in Europe as an act of rebellion against a lawful authority." In 1812, according to the same authority, we appeared as aggressive asserters of the freedom of the seas. General Grant pronounced our war with Mexico an act of unjust aggression. Our Civil War still stands out as the most carnal in history. At the Pan-American Conference of 1889, the United States was the only nation to refuse to renounce "conquest." Nine days before our formal declaration of war against Spain, the Spanish Minister of Foreign Affairs called in the American Minister to Madrid and promised "either such autonomy as the insurgents (Cubans) may agree to accept, recognition by Spain of the independence of the island, or cession of the island to the United States." All three of these we refused.

So, while the United States, on a sultry afternoon in Paris, was renouncing the instrument which molded it into a nation, the economic rivalries which make for war were just as vitriolic, just as unfettered, and just as instinctive as at any time in our history.

2. Mr. Kellogg Stumbles upon Fame

No Secretary of State succeeding William Jennings Bryan approximated his record for using the mailed fist with one hand and extending the olive branch with the other—until the advent of Frank B. Kellogg.

Frank B. Kellogg, during the year 1927, was not one whom any leader of the peace movement would have recognized as a fellow member. In fact, Mr. Kellogg, during the year 1927, was not a prepossessing figure. Appointed Secretary of State chiefly because he had been kind to Calvin Coolidge when that individual, as Vice-President, was a silent and somewhat snubbed presiding officer of the United States Senate, Mr. Kellogg inherited many problems and had no obvious qualifications for solving them. In Nicaragua he let an incipient revolt drift into civil war on such a scale that fifteen warships and five thousand marines were sent to keep in office the President chosen by Mr. Kellogg's bright young advisers. In South America a plebiscite between Peru and Chile to settle the sovereignty of the disputed provinces of Tacna and Arica threatened to involve the entire continent in bloodshed. In Mexico, a dispute between American oil companies and the new revolutionary government had brought tension between the two countries to a point where the breaking off of diplomatic relations was expected daily.

In China, a vigorous Nationalist Party from the south had overrun the Yangtze Valley, looting the American consulate at Nanking, murdering missionaries, pillaging American business establishments, and drawing a bombardment from American gunboats lying in the Yangtze river.

Probably at no time between the World War and the sultry day in August when the world outlawed war were the international relations of the United States more snarled, more hectic, and more smeared in blood.

Mr. Kellogg, during these feverish months, never would have been suspected as one in whose breast beat a passionate desire to renounce war. He was nervous and belligerent. When anyone asked a question, he jumped like a gangster on the spot. His method of solving problems was to stride up and down his office, hands behind his back, shoulders hunched forward, demanding action from a group of career diplomats whose advice invariably led him into deeper water. At the daily conferences where he was set upon by a merciless mob of newspapermen wanting to know when he was going to bombard Nanking, whether he would break with Mexico, how he ever expected to bring peace to Nicaragua, and if there was even the remotest chance of settling Tacna-Arica, he sputtered, fumed, denied, made himself the best punching-bag the press had ever had. His manner was very much as if the entire world had him in a corner and he was fighting for his life. Which was almost true. For there was a time in the middle of that hectic period when Mr. Kellogg's resignation probably was avoided only by a retreat for ten days' rest at the South Carolina shooting estate of ex-Senator Joe Frelinghuysen.

In view of all this, it was perhaps not unnatural that when Aristide Briand issued a statement in Paris on April 6, 1927, suggesting that the United States and France had now reached a stage of friendship and international sanity where they could outlaw war between themselves for ever and a day, Mr. Kellogg was inclined to view this as just another of his many troubles.

How was he to know that in this Briand statement there was the germ of an idea which was to mark a milestone in the lives of men, that was to write his name in large gold letters in the annals of history? How was he to know that behind that Briand statement were an American college professor, a Jewish lawyer, and a member of the United States Senate who never were to rest until they saw war outlawed?

Mr. Kellogg, unfortunately, was not blessed with psychic powers. And besides, the Briand statement, although made to commemorate the tenth anniversary of America's entrance into the World War, happened to follow fourteen days after Kuomintang had forced the fire of American gunboats at Nanking, ten days after some highly embarrassing documents had disappeared from the American Embassy pouch in Mexico City, and on the very day that Henry L. Stimson, subsequent successor to Mr. Kellogg, departed for Nicaragua to rescue the fifteen warships and the five thousand marines which Mr. Kellogg had sent there.

No wonder, then, that Mr. Kellogg shrugged his shoulders and gave M. Briand's idea of outlawing war not even a passing thought.

There were in Paris and Chicago, however, two men who had spent a good part of their lives interfering with things which usually are reserved for the rarefied realm of diplomacy, and whose persistent insistence eventually caused Mr. Kellogg's name to be scratched among those on the honor roll of time.

No two men could have been wider apart in character, personality, temperament, and method of approach, but no two men were more responsible for forcing the outlawry of war into the reluctant hands of statesmen than

James T. Shotwell, a Columbia professor, and Salmon O
Levinson, a Chicago lawyer.

Shotwell was a Canadian. Born in Canada, educated in
Canada, married to a Canadian wife, he moved to New
York just after the turn of the century and settled down
on Morningside Heights, where for thirty years he taught
history to the unimpressed youth of Columbia, directed
the international relations of the Carnegie Endowment,
wrote voluminous tomes, pamphlets, and magazine articles on peace and war, and in a quiet, unostentatious way,
pushed the idea that the United States must play its part
in the world of international affairs and that that part
must be dynamically for peace.

Levinson sprang from a more complex background.
Born in the metropolis of Noblesville, Indiana, of ambitious
Jewish parents, Levinson graduated from Yale in the same
class with Henry L. Stimson, Irving Fisher, and other New
York blue-bloods who came to appreciate him more after
he amassed wealth as a reorganizer of big corporations
than they did when he was a bumptious, irrepressible and
sometimes obnoxious youngster from the Middle West.

It was about the time he sent two sons to France that
Levinson's restless mind first delved into the question of
outlawing war. Levinson had no real objection to their
going, but it made him look a little more thoughtfully on
the spectacle of 120,000,000 people enthusiastically throwing themselves into a thing called war, and he began to
wonder where the demon got its power. Why, his legalistic
mind asked, should an entire nation so unanimously obey
the call? Was the call legal? Were submarines legal? Or
poison gas, dumdum bullets, the violation of the rights of
neutrals? Could those responsible for these things be punished?

He searched the law libraries for an answer.

There he found, somewhat to his amazement, that for
century after century war was the recognized method of

settling international disputes. Not only was it legal, but it was the authorized court of last resort. Francis Bacon called it the "highest Trial of Right." Later Levinson saw the Commission on Responsibilities at Versailles report that "a war of aggression cannot be considered an act contrary to positive peace. . . . No criminal charge can be made against the Kaiser."

In other words, Levinson reasoned, it was not the Kaiser who was to blame, but the system, the war system. As long as war was recognized as legal there was no punishment for those responsible for it; in fact, the Kaiser was the only man in Germany who legally could declare war. Furthermore, Levinson concluded, as long as war was legal, the steps leading toward its accomplishment—submarines, gas, the bombing of civilians—were legal, being merely the most modern methods in a perfectly legal system of warfare, to be made more modern and equally legal as other agencies more destructive are developed.

So even before the Versailles Treaty was signed, Levinson started his campaign to outlaw war. At first his ideas were vague, and his proselyting received as the irrational perambulation of an overwrought mind. Not many friends gave him encouragement. Among the few exceptions were Philander C. Knox, who had stepped from the office of Secretary of State into the Senate, and William E. Dodd, now Ambassador to Germany, who at that time was an itinerant college professor trying to organize a Chicago committee in support of Woodrow Wilson and his League of Nations. Levinson persuaded Dodd to include the outlawry of war as one of the goals of his committee and also to cable Colonel House in Paris, urging that the Versailles Conference go on record for the abolition of war.

At that time the League of Nations and the principle of sanctions upon which it rests were not anathema to Levinson and it was because of this that he was not able to get the support of his two good friends, William E. Borah and Raymond Robbins. They disagreed with him on his theory that behind the nations outlawing war must be a police force, a sort of international sheriff to bring the culprit into court.

"With that provision in there—nothing stirring," snapped Borah. "You'll have to figure out some way to eliminate it."

Levinson did. He finally stumbled upon James Madison's speeches before the Constitutional Assemblage in Philadelphia, where Madison had opposed the use of federal troops to enforce decisions of the Supreme Court upon the several states. Public opinion, Madison argued, is much stronger than force, and to settle any dispute by force merely lays the foundation for the next war. Levinson adopted the same reasoning. The outlawing of war, he decreed, must have behind it only the pledge of the individual nations which accept it.

From that point on Levinson had the unqualified support not only of Senator Borah, but also of a small but distinguished "Committee for the Outlawry of War," which included John Haynes Holmes, Charles Clayton Morrison, Judge Florence Allen, Robbins, and, while he was alive, Senator Knox.

But he did not have, except for one brief interval, the support of the other man chiefly responsible for foisting outlawry of war upon its unwilling parents. Professor Shotwell and Levinson seldom agreed, did not particularly like each other then, and entertain much less mutual admiration now that they are rivals for a certain amount of immortality. The chief point which kept them at arm's length at that time was identically that which first had prevented Borah from giving his support to the outlawry of war. Levinson had swung around to the Borah thesis of eliminating force; Shotwell had not. Levinson claimed that by clinging to the League of Nations' system of enforcing sanctions against an aggressor nation, Shotwell was outlawing war only against an aggressor, in fact was legalizing war as a method of settling disputes. Shotwell, in turn, claimed that by permitting nations the right of self-defense, Levinson was making every war legal.

So Shotwell built up his little New York group of World Court, League of Nations, and Locarno advocates, while Levinson built up his Chicago group of outlawry of war devotees; and like most people with great ideas they were entirely intolerant of surrender or compromise.

There was only one occasion when the two groups, both having as their common aim the peace of the world, ever were able to find common ground. This was in 1925, when they decided to come together on what they called a "Harmony Agreement" for both the outlawry of war and the World Court.

The Levinson group, because of its power with Borah, had achieved much more political success than Shotwell, and the latter wanted to take advantage of it. Raymond Robbins, for instance, had gone to see Harding just after the Chicago convention which nominated him in 1920 and got him to put the outlawry of war into his acceptance speech. In the 1924 campaign Robbins and Levinson also were active with a plan to make Borah the vice-presidential candidate on the Coolidge ticket, and would have succeeded had not Borah refused to have anything to do with what he called the "peanut-pusher from New England."

Later Dwight W. Morrow came to Robbins and asked him to support the ticket even though Borah had jumped it. Robbins replied:

"There's only one thing I'm interested in, and that is the outlawry of war. If Coolidge will mention it in his acceptance speech, I'll back him."

"But he's trying to get such things out of his speech."

"Then I'm not interested."

So Coolidge, a very practical man, inserted the outlawry of war in his speech, got the benefit of Robbins' powerful oratory, and after the election put to Robbins, with his usual bluntness, the question, "What do you want?"

"I want the outlawry of war, and I want you to work with Borah on it."

"Can anyone work with Borah?" asked Mr. Coolidge.

Nevertheless, Levinson and Robbins stood well with both Coolidge and Borah, and the Shotwell group knew it. So, to take advantage of the Robbins-Levinson political prestige, Shotwell and his friends signed a log-rolling agreement by which both factions agreed to support the World Court on condition that a world conference be called within two years to outlaw war. If the conference was not called, the United States would leave the Court.

This was called the Harmony Agreement. It was to be short-lived. For just two months later Calvin Coolidge came out for the World Court without the outlawry-of-war reservation, and the Shotwell group, no longer needing the support of Levinson and Robbins, tore up the compact.

But with all their petty rivalry, the first outlawry-of-war proposal never would have been made, or, if made, never would have been accepted, without the tireless tenacity of both James T. Shotwell and Salmon O. Levinson.

For despite the acceptance speeches of Calvin Coolidge and Warren G. Harding, despite the fortunes spent from the funds of the Carnegie Endowment by Shotwell and from his own pocket by Levinson, the principle they were promoting had made no very great dent on the public mind until April 6, 1927. In fact, not even on that date, when one of the most outstanding statesmen of Europe threw out the suggestion that France and the United States had reached a state of understanding where they might outlaw war one with the other, did the American public wake up to the events which were in store for them. The nineteen days which followed Briand's olive branch brought not a single chirp from the editorial commentators of our leading papers, not a sign of welcome or even recognition from our statesmen.

Judged by the standards applied to other first nights, Briand's initial performance was a flop.

But there is at least one thing which international statesmen enjoy in common with the theater, and that is build-up men. And during the first nineteen days following Briand's message to the American people and the first sign of ballyhoo it received in the American press, the two build-up men for the outlawry of war were on the high seas, both scuttling in different directions, and both working, entirely unknown to each other, to save their life's ambition from becoming nothing more than a dream.

On April 6th, the day after Briand made his proposal for the bilateral outlawing of war, Salmon O. Levinson read the message in the Chicago newspapers and got on a train to New York en route to Paris. Just two days before, Big Bill Thompson had been elected mayor of Chicago. Levinson had helped lead a bitter fight against him, was sick and disgusted with the result, and above all saw in the Briand statement an opportunity to make his dream come true.

Simultaneously Professor James T. Shotwell was boarding a boat in Europe, bringing him back to the United States.

Working behind the scenes, Shotwell had been responsible for that first barrage by Aristide Briand. He had spent the winter in Berlin as professor at the Hochschule für Politik, and on March 1st had proposed to the German Institute of Politics, including Chancellor Marx and most of the German Cabinet, that the Locarno treaties be expanded into a World Locarno for the outlawry of war. Later—March 22nd—Shotwell approached Briand with the suggestion that he lead the world toward the renunciation of war. The exact details of what Shotwell proposed to Briand, whether he suggested a multilateral pact or a treaty only between the United States and France, are not definitely known. Professor Shotwell has written an account of his conversations in a book deposited in the vaults of Yale University, to be published only after his death, and meanwhile is extremely loath to discuss the incident. It is known, however, that Shotwell urged Briand to time his proposal so that it would fall on the tenth anniversary of American entrance into the World War and also it is apparent that Briand seized on the idea not as a means of outlawing war throughout the world, but as a neat device for bringing the United States into a virtual alliance with France.

Having waited until Briand actually delivered his pronouncement, Shotwell hurried back to the United States, where he found that the Briand message had hit only page 12 in the *New York Times*, page 5 in the *New York Herald Tribune*, and had been ignored by virtually all save the metropolitan press. This omission Shotwell strove diligently to correct. He got his friend and superior, Nicholas Murray Butler, president of Columbia University, to lunch with the editors of the *New York Times*; following which, Butler wrote a letter calling upon a bored and *blasé* world to awaken and take note of the fact that the dawn of a new era had arrived. On the same date the *New York Times*, always coöperative where Nicholas Murray Butler and Shotwell are concerned, turned out an editorial supporting the Briand proposal.

And from that point on, Shotwell and the *New York Times* on one side of the Atlantic, with Levinson on the other, were working in perfect unison, although in complete ignorance of each other's efforts, for the renunciation of war for all time to come.

Levinson had arrived in London on April 15th, one day before Shotwell landed in New York. There he endeavored to arrange an interview with Sir Austen Chamberlain, then Secretary for Foreign Affairs. The interview was refused. Sir Austen was very busy. He had other things to do than listen to the "crazy ideas of American cranks," the Foreign Office explained.

So Levinson, highly indignant and threatening to denounce Chamberlain as one who still believed in war, went on to Paris, where on May 5th, Paul Scott Mowrer, of the *Chicago Daily News*, took him to see Alexis Leger, confidential secretary of M. Briand.

Leger was polite but skeptical. He was used to having all sorts of Americans storm Paris, but an American of Levinson's overpowering type seeking to tell him how and why the world should dispense with its chief weapon of the centuries, was almost too much even for a French diplomat. So despite a letter of introduction from Senator Borah to Ambassador Myron T. Herrick which Levinson showed Leger and which Leger surreptitiously sent out to be copied, the Frenchman remained skeptical. The one definite thing he told Levinson was that France had made the first move in proposing to outlaw war, and could not very well make another until there had been some demonstration of public opinion in America. He suggested that Levinson help to create such a demonstration. And after the latter had promised to do so, Leger promptly cabled Shotwell to find out who the burly Chicago lawyer was who had bothered him.

Levinson never knew the cable had been sent until six years later, but it would not have phased him if he had known. For in Levinson are combined all the fearsome, uplifting, irritating, idealistic, aggressive qualities which enabled the Jewish prophets to lead the tribes of Israel out of the wilderness. Nothing stopped him. He did not even know when people attempted to be rude to him. A strange mixture of dreams and of dollars, he spent a small fortune during the hectic month of May entreating his friends by cable to rise up and outlaw war.

On the day he saw Leger, Levinson reported by cable to Senator Borah, Raymond Robbins, and his old classmate, Irving Fisher. The reports were long enough to have caused a managing editor to fire the average foreign newspaper correspondent, but they brought results. Borah delivered an address in Cleveland four days later in which he put all the power and appeal of his eloquence behind the cause of outlawing war. He welcomed the Briand proposal, but urged that it be multilateral in form and that all the world be invited to participate.

This was the first important public pronouncement for the treaty in the form in which eventually it was written, and Borah himself evolved the multilateral formula. The French were not at all enthusiastic about it. Levinson, hitherto, had been working for a bilateral agreement between France and the United States, with the idea that once this initial puncture had been made in the legality of war, the movement could be increased to embrace other nations. Briand and Leger, on the other hand, had been working on the same plan of a bilateral pact with the idea that no other nations save the United States and France would dare to outlaw war, and that the Franco-American agreement, therefore, would serve as a warning to Germany that whenever France found it necessary to defend her Treaty of Versailles and her Little Entente, the United States never would join her enemies. Shotwell, meanwhile, had been working toward a multilateral pact, but with the idea of bringing the United States into the League of Nations machinery for punitive measures against an aggressor nation.

And of all those proposing the outlawry of war at that time, the only individual who saw the goal in clear perspective and stuck consistently to it was the senior Senator from Idaho.

Despite the length and expense of Mr. Levinson's cablegrams, it is doubtful if he would have been successful in

arousing the demonstration of American opinion demanded by the French, had it not been for the quiet wire-
pulling of Professor Shotwell.

Thanks to Shotwell, the obliging *New York Times* had
followed up President Butler's letter and its editorial of
April 25th by wiring its Washington Bureau for senatorial
reaction, and came out the next day with glowing anti-
war tributes from such statement-makers as Senator Cope-
land of New York, Senator King of Utah, Senator Shipstead of Minnesota, and Senator Norris of Nebraska.
Simultaneously, the faithful *Times* also had wired its Paris
Bureau to dig up French reaction to Butler's letter. The
epistle of an American college president published in a
newspaper three thousand miles away does not usually
stir into frenzy the placid population of France, but the
New York Times employs faithful, enterprising reporters,
many of them extremely close to the Quai d'Orsay, so the
reaction they cabled back to a somewhat indifferent American public was that France was ready to sign the treaty
for the outlawing of war, but felt that since Briand had
initiated the idea, common courtesy required the next
move to come from Washington.

By that time Levinson had received so much cabled encouragement from his friends in the United States—something which for him was not at all necessary—that he was
tackling his mission with all the irrepressible fervor of a
howling dervish. On May 10th he saw Leger again. This
was one day after Senator Borah had delivered his Cleveland speech, just after the late Senator Tom Walsh of
Montana had delivered a somewhat similar address at the
Sorbonne, and a few days after the *New York Times* had
printed additional letters and reactions, all tending to
force the outlawry of war on the hitherto silent Mr. Kellogg. Leger said he was satisfied with the reception given
the idea in America, and in another meeting the next
day, suggested to Levinson that he draft the outline of a

treaty outlawing war between France and the United States forever.

Leger, however, had spoken without consulting the man who eventually was to become co-author of the Pact. M. Briand did not feel so ebullient about the idea of outlawing war—at least not enough so to leap the bounds of ordinary diplomatic protocol. Such a proposal, he thought, was somewhat like a proposal of marriage, and in France, at least, one did not make such advances unless one had definite assuranccs of recceptibility and a proper dowry from the person courted.

Accordingly, Mr. Levinson, who had motored to Geneva with Senator Walsh, got this telegram from Paul Scott Mowrer, his chief intermediary: "Briand refuses to act without Washington approval. Fears reaction of French opinion against us if proposal made and officially ignored. Essential to smoke out Coolidge."

That gentleman, however, refused to be smoked.

It was one thing to mention the outlawry of war in his acceptance speech before election, but quite another to translate words into action three years after that election had been won by an overwhelming majority. So when Raymond Robbins came to see him in response to a cable from Levinson, he found Coolidge peeved and in no mood to coöperate. He was peeved first at the way the outlawry of war had been proposed, and second at the fact that the French, who were proposing it, had boycotted his own pet project for reducing war costs—the Geneva Naval Conference, scheduled to start in just a month.

So in reply to Levinson's suggestion that he get Coolidge to make a speech on Memorial Day recognizing the common bond between France and the United States, Robbins had to reply: "Had interview. Found resentment against public appeal. Matter must follow regular channels. Declined commitment."

And in a press conference, one day after Levinson had

wanted him to deliver the world-wide appeal for the renunciation of war, Coolidge made the following laconic comment:

"I am aware that certain individuals, particularly in New York—including Professor Shotwell of Columbia—are preparing proposals for treaties between this government and other countries which are usually referred to as treaties for outlawing war. I have directed these individuals to take up the matter with the State Department."

Had this brief bombshell been allowed to explode on the French threshold without advance warning, probably the Pact of Paris would have had to look for other parents. But Levinson, by an intuitive stroke, had cushioned the shock.

When he received the negative wire from Raymond Robbins, he was crestfallen.

"For God's sake, don't show that to the Quai d'Orsay," was the reaction of Harrison Brown, his assistant.

"That's exactly what I shall do," Levinson replied. "I've got to show them that we are playing square. This will prove it."

So Robbins' telegram reporting that Mr. Coolidge refused to be smoked out, was shown to Briand and Leger. Probably it not only prepared them for the later negation from the White House, but, what was more important, spurred them into taking the initiative. The spring-board of that initiative was Charles A. Lindbergh, who had just catapulted himself into fame, and the people of the United States and France into enthusiastic frenzy, by making the first non-stop flight across the Atlantic. In honor of that feat, Aristide Briand was giving him a luncheon. At the luncheon Leger planned to have Briand say a word or two suggesting that the ancient friendship between France and the United States, now so happily reëmphasized by the Lindbergh flight, should be permanently cemented by outlawing war between the two nations.

The luncheon was held. And Briand, his voice dripping friendship, did his stuff. Later, in an aside to Ambassador Myron T. Herrick, on his right, he suggested that he sound out the State Department regarding the renunciation of war between the two countries.

This was on May 26th.

Several days passed. Briand and Leger took a trip to London on other matters, and while there talked with Ambassador Alanson B. Houghton, who said he was going to the United States soon and would use his influence for the peace pact.

Levinson, who had received a suggestion from Ambassador Stahmer in London that Germany did not want to be left out of the renunciation-of-war move, went to Berlin. Arriving back in Paris, he found the Quai d'Orsay distinctly cool. The dream that he had concocted with Briand and Leger seemed to have floated out of the window. They would not even see him. Meanwhile disheartening reports came from Washington. First there was Coolidge's icy blast already quoted. This was followed a day later by a statement from the belligerent Mr. Kellogg, who, put on the defensive in a press conference, said he had "not given any consideration to the proposals of certain professors. Of course," he added, "if these proposals are submitted to me, I will consider them very carefully."

Not the slightest hint did the future co-author of the Pact give that M. Briand, the Foreign Minister of France, had suggested through the American Ambassador in Paris that the United States inform the French Government regarding its wishes in this matter.

No wonder Briand and Leger were cool.

The next day the same thing happened. Mr. Kellogg, heckled in press conferences, replied rather peevishly that he "simply had had no time to look into this subject," as he "had been busy with navy officers every day."

And two days later—June 4th—there was another burst

of peeve. Mr. Kellogg, again questioned by the press regarding his reaction to the proposal to outlaw war, replied that he had been "so busy with the Geneva Conference he had not had time to examine the matter."

Briand, reading these reactions in the Paris press, became more provoked than ever. But Leger, having had some experience with Ambassador Herrick in the past, started a personal investigation. Herrick, during these days, had been patting Levinson on the back and telling him he was rendering a great service to Franco-American friendship. But on at least one occasion he had told Briand privately that Levinson was "just a crank."

So Leger, making sub-rosa inquiries at the American Embassy, found that Herrick never had transmitted Briand's inquiry at the Lindbergh luncheon as to whether or not the United States would entertain a proposal from France to outlaw war. Herrick apparently either did not understand, or else did not think the inquiry was worth bothering about.

So Briand finally yielded to Leger's persuasion and made his inquiry all over again. This he did with punctilious routine, summoning Ambassador Herrick to the Quai d'Orsay and asking him if the United States would have any objection to entertaining a proposal from France that the two nations sign a treaty outlawing war.

Apparently the United States did. For the day after Briand made this move, William R. Castle, Jr., Under Secretary of State, had this to say about the subject in which the French Government seemed so interested:

"I think that people overlook the fact that our treaty with France on arbitration [the Root Treaty of 1908] and also the treaty with France on the advancement of peace of 1914 both cover the situation fairly well. They appear to come about as close to a treaty between any two nations to prevent war as could be obtained. It is a thing that seems to have been more or less overlooked in the excitement caused by Briand's proposal."

A reply like this, however, could hardly be given officially to a nation proposing—on the surface at least—one of the most friendly gestures in history; so Mr. Castle and Mr. Kellogg framed a gingerly-worded telegram which they dispatched to Ambassador Herrick two days later, stating that the United States "would be pleased to engage in diplomatic conversations on the subject."

As a result, Aristide Briand handed Ambassador Herrick, on June 20th, the text of a treaty which, except for the preamble, eventually was to serve as the instrument by which the world united in the renunciation of war.

Most of that text had been scrawled on the back of an envelope by Salmon O. Levinson, meddling Jewish evangelist from Chicago.

Exactly six months and eight days elapsed between the day M. Briand submitted that text and the day he got a reply.

During those six months every indication points to the fact that the other eventual co-author of the pact felt that the Briand proposal had put him in extremely uncomfortable diplomatic hot water. Mr. Kellogg's friends, of course, deny this. They point out that at the time Briand delivered the text of his treaty, President Coolidge was in the Black Hills for the summer and there was no opportunity for consultation on so important a move. They also point out that Levinson was promoting Senator Borah as the next Republican presidential candidate and had tried to get Ambassador Stahmer in London to have the German Government instruct all German Americans to vote for him. Finally, they point out that Mr. Kellogg was extremely busy with the Geneva Naval Conference, that the Senate had adjourned and could not be consulted, and finally that a treaty to outlaw war with France alone

meant nothing less than an alliance with France and that
the old fox, Briand, knew this.

All of this was true.

But when Levinson stopped in to see Kellogg on his
way back from Europe in early July, the reaction of that
fretful statesman was: "What is Briand driving at? What
is he trying to do? What does he mean by trying to outlaw war?"

While the report of Senator Borah, who stopped off
in Chicago to see Levinson on his way to Idaho a little
later, was this: "I had a hell of a time with Kellogg, but
I think I finally made a dent. I explained it from the legal
side—why not have a law on it, I said. This seemed to
strike home."

Later in the summer Borah wrote Levinson: "The
whole thing is dead. Kellogg will never act. We will never
hear of it again."

And it looked as if he were right.

As the summer wore on the Briand proposal for the
outlawry of war continued to gather dust in the files of
the State Department. The Diplomatic Corps came back
to the Capital, members of Congress started trickling in
to tackle pressing problems of politics and patronage. The
State Department threw off its summer lethargy and began to revamp its policy in Mexico and China. But the
Briand proposal lay buried—as mute as the tomb of Tut-
ankh-amen. And the State Department seemed anxious to
keep it that way.

On November 19th, Secretary Kellogg, questioned by
newspapermen regarding the effectiveness of the Pact
which he was about to sire, declined to comment. On
November 25th Calvin Coolidge, being asked the same
question, remarked: "There is no short cut to peace or
any other kind of salvation. The matter must be worked
out with fear and trembling." The next day Secretary
Kellogg, again questioned regarding Briand's foundling

child, said that he "did not wish to go into the subject of outlawing war."

"Some people might think it was very simple," the petulant Mr. Kellogg continued. "And perhaps it is. But I do not wish to discuss it."

In the face of these obstructionist tactics, Nicholas Murray Butler, one of the earliest supporters of Professor Shotwell, dared brave the wrath of the President on December 9th by defending the Briand proposal. The next day Senator Frazier of North Dakota introduced a resolution proposing that it be made impossible for the United States to enter a war for any purpose whatsoever. A few days later the mercurial Mr. Hamilton Fish of New York introduced an outlawry-of-war proposal in the House of Representatives. Finally, on December 22nd Secretary Kellogg appeared before the Senate Foreign Relations Committee.

This meeting was fated to go down in history.

The ostensible reason for Kellogg's appearance was to get the committee's reaction to an arbitration treaty which he proposed to negotiate with France. The treaty, which replaced the expiring arbitration agreement negotiated by Elihu Root in 1908, went much farther than any previous arbitration pact to which the United States had been willing to subscribe and also included in its preamble a sentence "condemning," but not "outlawing," war as "an instrument of national policy" by the two nations. This sentence had been inserted for obvious reasons. In the first place it gave an "out" to Mr. Kellogg. In the second place, it gave an "out" to the French. The latter had become increasingly alarmed at the way the American people had picked up M. Briand's perfectly safe proposal for a Franco-American alliance outlawing war, and with characteristic naïveté, opened its arms to include the entire world.

Without going into these details, Mr. Kellogg explained

his arbitration treaty to the Foreign Relations Committee. The members showed no very great interest in it, and Chairman Borah said that he assumed their silence meant consent.

"But, Mr. Secretary," he added, "all this does not dispose of the proposal to outlaw war."

Mr. Kellogg looked nervous and displeased. He replied that a treaty outlawing war between the United States and France meant nothing more than an alliance between the two countries.

"But, Mr. Secretary," persisted Borah, "the American counter-proposal should be a pact to outlaw war between all the nations of the world. We should point out that this is too important to confine only to this country and France."

And Borah began to poll the leading members of the committee.

"That's the best way to get rid of the damn thing," growled the irreconcilable Senator Moses. "Extend it to all nations. France would never consent to outlaw war with Germany."

The others were either definitely affirmative or else non-committal.

"I think, Mr. Secretary, you may consider it the sense of this committee that you go ahead with the negotiation of a pact to include all countries," finally decreed Borah.

Six days later Aristide Briand got the long-awaited reply to his proposal that the United States and France outlaw war. Mr. Kellogg had been jarred into action.

As Secretary of State, Frank Billings Kellogg was a peculiar mixture of vacillation and determination. Few men occupying that post in recent years have experienced more ups and downs, more hitches and false starts in seeking a definite line of foreign policy; but likewise few

Secretaries of State have stuck more persistently to their path once it was charted.

Kellogg is not a prepossessing person. But there is something about him—a sort of bulldog tenacity—that worries him through almost any job he tackles. Probably his own physical handicaps have contributed toward that tenacity. Undoubtedly, also, so did the experiences of his early youth.

For the story of that youth is the legendary one of the farm boy who goes out to conquer; except that in the case of Frank Kellogg the hero was a rather puny youngster who had migrated with his parents from New York State to Rochester, Minnesota, just after the Civil War, and who deserted the farm for a village law office because he was not strong enough to follow the plow.

That law office was Kellogg's education. He never attended a real grade school, a high school, or a college— a loss which even in his seventy-sixth year occasionally is noticeable in his speech. Moreover, even his months in the village law office were interrupted in the spring and fall when he had to stop for seeding or harvesting. The thirteen dollars a month he earned there, together with a little money he picked up doing stable chores and tending fires, paid his entire expenses through the winter.

Four years passed before young Kellogg was ready to be admitted to the bar. They were grueling years—years which developed fighting qualities—years which later made him such a fearsome "trust-buster," which made him refuse to quit when he was under devastating fire as Secretary of State. They were also years during which Kellogg acquired a tremendous facility for getting a mental picture of a written page and holding that picture in his mind indefinitely, a facility which enabled him, as Secretary of State, to reel off gun calibers, cruiser tonnages, and naval ratios with such accuracy and speed that the admirals could not keep up with him.

Kellogg always has shown qualities of being a better student than a performer before multitudes. When, at the age of twenty-two, he came up before a committee of local lawyers for admittance to the bar, he was rattled and nervous. It was one of those moments from which he suffered many times in later life—in his press conferences at the State Department, at the crowning moment of his career when the golden pen refused to work in the Salle de l'Horloge in Paris.

In this, the most crucial test of his youth, Kellogg floundered and made a bad impression. One lawyer opposed his admission to the bar. But a Judge Mitchell, later of the Minnesota Supreme Court, argued that the youngster knew more than he was able to give expression to, and thus Frank Billings Kellogg was started on his career to wealth and fame.

Kellogg spent all of his early life in championing the under dog. He first attracted attention when he fought through the Supreme Court of the United States a case on behalf of two Minnesota villages against powerful rail lines—and won. After that he was the Justice Department's choice in many big anti-trust suits. He fought the Paper Trust, the Union Pacific, Southern Pacific, and forced the Standard Oil to dissolve. He made a name for himself even in a period famous for trust-busting. Old Teddy Roosevelt called him "The best trust-buster of them all."

And then, like many others, Kellogg deserted to the side which paid the biggest fees.

Seven years later, when he entered the Senate, Kellogg was so permanently branded as a corporation lawyer that in 1922 a naïve dentist named Hendrik Shipstead was able to convince enough people in the State of Minnesota that Kellogg was a tool of big business to retire him from office.

Shipstead's allegations were not, however, entirely true.

Kellogg's record shows that he retained a sneaking inclination toward the under dog even in the august and sometimes conservative upper body of Congress. He voted for women's suffrage, for the maternity and infancy law, for all pension and temperance legislation, and vigorously supported the cause of the Chinese in the Japanese steal of Shantung. Furthermore, he was probably the most tireless and meticulous member of the Senate in attending all committee meetings, and, perhaps most important of all, was one of the few Senators who went out of his way to be decent to that snubbed and silent little under dog, Calvin Coolidge, when he was Vice-President and presiding officer of the Senate.

It was this which sent Kellogg to London as American Ambassador to the Court of St. James's and which subsequently brought him back to be Coolidge's Secretary of State.

As already described in these pages, Mr. Kellogg's first two years in the State Department were featured by a deluge of international catastrophes and personal ineptitudes, most of them avoidable, during which the betting odds were all to the effect that the new Secretary of State would be swept off his feet and down the gutter of retirement. During this period anything which added to the burden of the harassed Mr. Kellogg was treated with petulance and repulsion. If the Angel Gabriel had offered Mr. Kellogg an advance ticket through the golden gates, properly stamped and authenticated, his reaction would have been very similar to that which he experienced when Aristide Briand suggested the pact which later was to make him famous. He just didn't want to be bothered!

But as the hectic year 1927 drew to a close, Mr. Kellogg enjoyed more peace and composure. Mexico he had entrusted to the human hands of the late Dwight W. Morrow. Nicaragua had been pulled out of its crisis by Henry L. Stimson. China was more pacified and exceedingly grateful for American support. The Geneva Naval Conference, although a complete fizzle, was at least finished and out of the way.

So that by December, 1927, Frank B. Kellogg enjoyed, for perhaps the first time during his hectic career in the State Department, a breathing space.

What finally induced him during that month to push the plan for outlawing war, probably Mr. Kellogg himself has never completely analyzed. Undoubtedly the pressure of public opinion plus the Senate Foreign Relations Committee meeting of December 22nd had much to do with it. Undoubtedly also the fact that Mr. Kellogg, for the first time in two years, felt less harassed had its effect on the fate of the Pact. Finally, Mr. Kellogg at that time was being advised by two of his young assistants, Spencer Phenix and J. Theodore Marriner, to reply to M. Briand; and probably it was the culmination of all these things—plus a few days' rest at Christmas— which finally induced Mr. Kellogg, on December 28, 1927, to answer Aristide Briand.

It was characteristic of diplomacy that when Mr. Kellogg finally screwed himself up to the point of action, his reply was vastly displeasing to the French. In fact, the French got more and more lukewarm over the idea of outlawing war during every minute they were weaned from the overpowering presence of Mr. Levinson. And the thing that chilled their ardor most was the stark generosity of the American public. To outlaw war with a nation separated by three thousand miles of ocean with which France always had enjoyed a sentimental friendship was one thing, but to extend one's arms in a loving embrace to the whole world was something else again.

So that long before Mr. Kellogg sent his reply to M. Briand on December 28th, suggesting that the outlawry of war was too good a thing to be limited to two nations, the French had begun to hedge on their original offer.

And being among the world's most astute diplomats, they had carefully prepared a cushion on which to fall.

That cushion was the American arbitration treaty upon which Mr. Kellogg himself had leaned rather heavily during the Senate Foreign Relations Committee meeting when Senator Borah goaded him into a real treaty for the renunciation of war. Into the preamble of that treaty the French had written some references "condemning" war as an instrument of national policy and it was undoubtedly their intention—probably also of Mr. Kellogg at first—to give the world the impression that the antiwar talk at last had borne fruit. Certainly the French made a definite effort to this end.

They selected for the date of signing the treaty February 6, 1928—one hundred and fifty years after the first treaty between France and the Thirteen Colonies had been signed by Benjamin Franklin in Paris. And after the klieg lights and the moviemen had done their work and everyone thought the ceremony was over, Paul Claudel, poet Ambassador of France, rose and addressed these totally unexpected words to the assembled dignitaries:

"The first treaty [between France and the United States] gave the start to a new nation; the second treaty gives the start to a new idea.

"Outlawry of war is a specifically American idea, not because it was born in America, but because it shows two marks of your country—it is great and it is practical. 'Outlawry of war' is one of those well-coined words which not only have a striking meaning but a working power; one of those words which have a great future because they are cautioned by a glorious past."

Claudel acted on explicit instructions from Paris. That little speech, from the French point of view, ended their explorations into the field of outlawing war. They had flirted with the idea, made a polite gesture toward it, and that was to be the end.

But they had figured without the irascible Mr. Kellogg. That gentleman, one of the hardest persons in the world to set in motion, was much more difficult to stop. All of the tenacity which he had acquired as a youngster determined to hew out a career in law rose up at that moment to plague the Quai d'Orsay.

Mr. Kellogg had the bit between his teeth. The story of how he ran away with the negotiations and forced the world to outlaw war some twenty-five years too soon has been written many times and requires no detailed repetition.

There were, however, three important points in these negotiations which have some bearing on future history. One was an attempt to attach peace machinery to the Pact; the second was Mr. Kellogg's insistence on limiting the treaty to few and simple words, and the third was the manner in which Mr. Kellogg conducted his negotiations under the spotlight of complete publicity.

The attempt to attach peace machinery to the Pact was suggested by Spencer Phenix, who worked out a plan for a conciliation or consultation commission to be set up whenever war threatened. Many times in the years which followed, Mr. Kellogg's successor was to regret the failure of that proposal. Many times, also, attempts were to be made to set up a similar plan for consultation—to put teeth in the Kellogg Pact. But Secretary Kellogg, himself, was personally responsible for turning the proposal down. He argued that it was going to be hard enough to get the Senate to ratify his treaty under any circumstance, and that to load it up with a complicated peace machine— sure to be looked upon with suspicion and downright dread by certain irreconcilable Senators—meant almost certain death when it came to ratification.

Undoubtedly, Mr. Kellogg was right. Having served six years in the United States Senate, he knew its temper. Furthermore, he was almost daily in touch with Borah, who warned him that the Senate would stand for nothing which smacked in the slightest degree of entangling alliances. Finally, Kellogg himself was convinced that the treaty he was negotiating must be couched in the simplest language, not cluttered up with conditions, reservations, or appendages, must be a brief statement that the world renounced war as an instrument of national policy.

Mr. Kellogg also believed it absolutely essential to restrict the original negotiation of his treaty to a small group of nations. Inclusion of a larger number, he reasoned, would necessitate endless delay and bickering. Starting with the five great world powers as the original negotiators, Kellogg yielded gracefully and immediately to British and French suggestions that the Dominions and the Locarno nations—Poland, Czechoslovakia, and Belgium—be brought into the discussions, but after that refused to budge another inch. Not even when that punctilious old monarchist, Ambassador Alejandro Padilla of Spain, came down to the State Department and almost wept because his country was not permitted to become a charter member of the Outlawry of War Society, was Mr. Kellogg's heart moved. Nor would he listen even to that starched and soulful figure, Ambassador Gurgel do Amaral of Brazil, a negation which probably was directly responsible for the fact that the last two important countries in the world to adhere to the Pact were Brazil and Argentina —the former because its pride was hurt, the latter because it argued that an Argentina fettered by an anti-war treaty might not so easily defend itself against a Brazil which was not.

Mr. Kellogg in those days was adamant and victorious. He rode rough shod over all obstacles. His victory in pushing the Pact to a successful conclusion he now attributes in large part to his policy of pitiless publicity. After many months of mistakes in Mexico and the Caribbean, Kellogg had learned that it is not difficult to have public opinion with you if, first of all, you are in the right, and, second, the public knows exactly what you are doing. And in the case of his anti-war treaty he used the latter principle with tremendous success. Each note, almost the minute it was received by the recipient nations, was made public. And each note received by the United States was treated likewise. Mr. Kellogg even went to considerable expense to publish his dispatches abroad. Confident that his arguments could not be rebutted, if understood, Kellogg cabled the full texts to American diplomatic missions in the world's chief capitals and ordered an immediate release to the press. The effect on world opinion was one which no statesman could resist. Even the staid and crusty Sir Austen Chamberlain was forced to give at least lip service to the idea which a year before he had described as "pure American bunk."

The American author of the Pact, during this period, was the exact antithesis of what he had been a year before. He became a fervent enthusiast. He was as radiant as a small boy who, after days of disappointment, finally goes to the head of his class. He lived and slept with his problem. He bobbed in and out of the office of Spencer Phenix, his chief assistant, half a dozen times a day. He acquired much of that spiritual passion which causes Catholic priests to spend their lives on an island of lepers or Indian fakirs to lie on a bed of nails. His fervor was contagious. He sold others as he sold himself. And although he was never able to sell some of those immediately around him, who up until the end referred to the Pact as "the old man's folly," he did sell the foreign Ambassadors who visited him almost daily. In fact, he sold them so successfully that Ambassador Paul Claudel found himself much more enthusiastic about the treaty than its original author in Paris and was somewhat embarrassed to find himself expressing to Mr. Kellogg certain views of his government with which he did not agree at all.

Thus an enthusiastic and irascible old man, after fretting for six months at the diplomatic impasse in which Briand had put him, finally pushed, goaded, and cajoled the rest of the world into the renunciation of war supposedly for all time to come. The final acceptance came on July 20, 1928, with the note of Baron Giichi Tanaka, prime minister of the nation which later was to become the most grievous violator of the Pact.

Frank B. Kellogg sailed for Paris on August 17th, a very happy man. He had restored his prestige. He had turned what looked like a complete rout of his policies in Latin America and the Far East into complete triumph, and he had done it by focusing world attention on a great emotional move to bring peace to a war-weary people. And so on the S.S. *Ile de France* Mr. Kellogg dozed in a steamer chair with a slouch-cap over his eyes, paced the deck with all the vigor of a fourteen-year-old boy, and felt complacent and happy about the state of the world.

But even while Mr. Kellogg was on the high seas, radio messages from his State Department gave him weather warnings that the nations which he had persuaded to outlaw war had no more intention of forgetting their hereditary intrigues than the United States had of abandoning its tradition of isolation.

A list of countries had been prepared in the State Department which were to be invited to outlaw war immediately the Pact was signed by the original fifteen signatories in Paris. It was a comprehensive list. Mr. Kellogg wanted the benefits of his Pact to be extended to the entire world, including Russia (which he did not then recognize), Iceland, a subsidiary of Denmark, Afghanistan (where we had no minister), and even Morocco and the Free City of Dantzig. The latter two were included at the behest of Prentiss Gilbert, acting chief of the Western European Division, who claimed that they were sovereign states and therefore capable of both waging war and outlawing it.

This reasoning immediately struck a snag. In the case of Morocco, the snag was France. In the case of the Free City of Dantzig the snag was Poland. Both brought Mr. Kellogg face to face with the inference that as far as these two areas were concerned, France and Poland had no great intention of outlawing war, treaty or no treaty. The Quai d'Orsay volunteered no explanation for its opposition to a new era of peace in Morocco. But none was necessary. Obviously France considered Morocco a protectorate capable of waging no wars without the permission of France, except possibly guerilla wars against France.

The United States, on the other hand, had concluded a treaty of peace and friendship with Morocco in 1787. This was the first treaty the United States signed with any country, and it has considered Morocco quite capable of signing its own treaties ever since. However, when the American Embassy in Paris radioed the Secretary of State on the high seas suggesting that he treat the invitation to Morocco as a mistake, Mr. Kellogg was much too contented with life and his steamer chair to do anything but acquiesce.

Almost simultaneously he got a radio notification of Poland's objection to the fact that the Free City of Dantzig could make no treaties without Polish permission, and that when Poland waged war Dantzig would be in that war on the same side whether she liked it or not. The League of Nations by a ruling of November 7, 1924, had held the opposite, but Mr. Kellogg, advised of the Polish objection, ordered the name of the Free City crossed off the list.

Life was too complacent just then, and the cherished

goal of August 27th too near to be marred by such diplomatic gnats as Dantzig and Morocco. So Mr. Kellogg
steamed serenely on.

With two possible exceptions—when he temporarily
misplaced the gold pen presented him by the City of
Havre, and when the bandmaster of the U.S.S. *Detroit*
forgot to secure scores of the Irish National Anthem—
the entire trip was serene.

Mr. Kellogg was the hero of Paris. He won over the
most cynical group of newspapermen in the world when,
at a press conference at the American embassy, he remarked, "I am sorry I am so small you can't all see me."
He won the boulevards when he visited the Tomb of
the Unknown Soldier and, instead of merely decorating
it with the conventional wreath, fell upon his knees and
remained there—a small, solitary, white-haired figure who
had led the world in outlawing war.

Paris, during those brief days, belonged to Kellogg.
His only worry was that his beloved and beribboned
parchment would not suffer the same temporary fate
as had his golden pen, with the result that he personally
supervised the deposit of the Pact in the safe aboard
the U.S.S. *Detroit* on which he went to Dublin, in the
strong-box of the American Legation at Dublin, and in
the purser's safe on the S.S. *Leviathan* on which he returned to the United States.

The Kellogg reception in Ireland was even more inspiring. Hundreds of Irishmen in small boats swarmed
about the *Detroit* as she dropped anchor in Kingstown
Harbor. Thousands more shouted to him as he whirled up
the long Dublin road past high-wheeled jaunting-cars,
double-deck trams, and donkey-pulled grocery carts, past
lines of gray tenements, their windows packed with cheering humanity, past green parks, and the government
offices, which only then had begun to remove their barri-

cades—ugly reminders of the days when the Irish used war as a grim instrument of internal policy.

Scores packed the small and stuffy reception-room of Mansion House, heard Seumas Murphy say: "There are many names on the world's register of fame, placed high by deeds of courage and acts of wisdom. But with you, the angels of peace have come to minister to men again. With your advent in Europe has come the birth of what may be termed the second era of peace—peace on earth to men of good-will."

Scores saw Mr. Kellogg try to reply—scarcely heard his words because of his emotion.

Not until he was two days out of New York on the homeward trip did Mr. Kellogg's troubles—through no fault of his own—begin again.

Mr. Kellogg had repeatedly stated in his private conversations that his cherished Pact belonged to no political party. It was the achievement, he said, of the entire nation—Democrats and Republicans alike. From the point of view of getting his treaty ratified by a two-thirds vote in the Senate, this was extremely wise philosophy. But from the point of view of partisan politics and the approaching campaign to put Herbert Hoover over the top as President of the United States, it was bad business, and those around Mr. Kellogg on his homeward voyage realized that a G.O.P. drive would be made immediately to make the Pact the football of politics. Furthermore, they feared that Mr. Kellogg, being a good party man, might let this pressure sway his better judgment.

So a conspiracy took place in which the oblivious and complacent Mr. Kellogg was destined to play the major rôle.

One of the conspirators—Drew Pearson—represented the *New York Times*. His part in the plot was to send to Frederick T. Birchall, managing editor of the *Times,* the following radio:

Suggest sending me following query. Quote. Ask Kellogg whether he intends to let his treaty become football of politics or whether he believes it should remain completely non-partisan issue. Unquote.

Mr. Birchall radioed as suggested. A copy of the radiogram was shown to Mr. Kellogg, and that unsuspecting gentleman gobbled the bait. The Pact of Paris, he said, with some passion, was not to become a political issue in the presidential campaign. His eyes snapped when he said it. Should the Republicans claim it as theirs, the Democrats would immediately use it as a target, and ratification by the Senate would be out the window. He planned, he said, to issue a statement to that effect when he landed in New York. Furthermore, he believed in, and was prepared to advocate, a greater continuity in American foreign policy. In evidence of this belief he had incorporated the Bryan conciliation treaties, verbatim and without the change of a single word, in his newly negotiated arbitration treaties. Peace, concluded Mr. Kellogg, is too fundamental to the welfare of the nation and the world to be made the issue of partisan politics.

When he spoke, Mr. Kellogg did not know that on the day previous Herbert Hoover, recently chosen by a Kansas City convention as his party's candidate for the Presidency, had made a speech in which he claimed the Kellogg Pact as one of the great achievements of the G. O. P. The *New York Times* correspondent, however, did know it. And the dispatch which appeared on the front page of the *Times* next morning carried this lead:

Aboard the SS *Leviathan*:
Secretary of State Kellogg does not approve the attempt of Mr. Hoover to claim the renunciation of war treaty as a great achievement of the Republican party, and he has decided to do his best to prevent the treaty from becoming a political issue in this presidential campaign.

Herbert Hoover, in Washington, saw red.

And no sooner did Mr. Kellogg set foot in Washington next day than he got a message from the Republican nominee, asking him to come and see him.

Hoover had always considered Kellogg a bungler. He had been vigorous and virulent in his criticism of Kellogg's Latin American policy. He had glowered at him when the two men sat opposite each other in the Coolidge Cabinet. Kellogg reciprocated this dislike.

But even had Mr. Kellogg wanted to reverse himself, it was too late.

As he left the slower *Leviathan* in lower New York Harbor and steamed toward the Battery in a special tug, Mr. Kellogg was interviewed by the press.

"Well, have you got the paper in your pocket?" queried a ship reporter.

"What paper?"

"You know, that paper you signed over in Paris."

Mr. Kellogg, a little stunned by the contrast between his reception abroad and this homecoming, fumbled in his pocket and pulled forth, not the treaty, but several little slips of paper. They had been carefully prepared by Spencer Phenix, his assistant, and typed by William H. Beck, his secretary, who knew something of the political barrage awaiting their chief when he landed. Slowly he handed them to each reporter.

They read:

> I do not think the treaty for the renunciation of war should be made a party issue either in the campaign or in the Senate, and I cannot conceive that it will be.

The session which followed between Herbert Hoover and Frank B. Kellogg was a stormy one. But it got nowhere. Kellogg stuck by his guns. And in the campaign which followed he made five speeches, each of them containing a careful and pointed reference to the fact that the Pact of Paris was as much a Democratic victory as it was Republican.

A few months later his strategy was rewarded. The Senate ratified his treaty, with only John J. Blaine of Wisconsin dissenting.

3. KELLOGG WINS THE FIRST SKIRMISH

Frank B. Kellogg returned from his pilgrimage to Paris and the signing of his Pact in September, 1928. Simultaneously there was under consideration in his State Department a loan which eventually was to bring the first declaration of war violating his treaty.

Dillon, Read & Company proposed to advance $23,-000,000 to Bolivia, and in conformity with the State Department's request to all bankers, brought the loan to the attention of its officials in Washington. In reply, Francis White, Assistant Secretary of State in charge of Latin American affairs, stated that the State Department had no objection to the loan.

Mr. White, however, did not take this position without some thought and without considerable opposition from the Department of Commerce. Financial experts in the latter pointed out that Bolivian finances were in a chaotic state, that the loan was sure to be defaulted, that the American bond-buyer would be left holding the bag. One other point was emphasized by the Department of Commerce. This was the fact that out of the $23,000,000 to be loaned to Bolivia, $5,060,000 was to pay for arms and ammunition previously ordered from the famous British munitions firm, Vickers, Limited, while $1,500,000 was to pay for building military roads near the Paraguayan border.

The fact that $5,060,000 was to pay for munitions was

known and so stated in the prospectus. What was not known to the general public, however, but certainly must have been known to a State Department with trained observers in Bolivia and Paraguay, was that the military forces of those two countries at that very moment were jockeying for position to begin hostilities. The scene of their maneuvering was the Gran Chaco, 100,000 square miles of wilderness which had been the bone of contention between Paraguay and Bolivia since the days when their colonial titles were granted by the Spanish Crown. The Chaco is one of the least habitable areas in South America. Its chief attributes are poisonous snakes, malaria, a vast chain of swamps which make it impassable in the rainy season, evidences of oil on the strength of which the Standard Oil Company of New Jersey has staked out an important concession, and finally an outlet to the sea. For the last named, Bolivia has struggled desperately during most of her national existence. Turning first against Chile in the war of the Pacific and then against Paraguay near the Atlantic, she had beaten against the mountains of the Andes and the swampland of the Chaco in an effort to break her landlocked border.

And in preparation for a new effort, she had cut in 1928 a zigzag line of *fortinas*, or little forts, across the bosom of the Gran Chaco, matched like pawns on a chessboard by similar Paraguayan *fortinas*, their juxtaposition made doubly dangerous by the fact that Paraguayan *fortinas* frequently had been pushed inside the Bolivian lines, with Bolivian *fortinas* vice versa.

The alignment of these forts was a known fact in South America, had been published in the local press.

Their existence, however, apparently meant little to Francis White. For many years he had been promoting a State Department policy of backing the bankers in all their Latin American enterprises. So when Dillon, Read argued that they had loaned Bolivia $14,000,000 in 1927 and that this would be defaulted unless it were refunded through a $23,000,000 loan in 1928, the argument fell upon sympathetic ears. Apparently it made no difference to Mr. White that Bolivian finances were such that the default could only be postponed a year or two.[1] Apparently also it made no difference that Mr. White's chief had just taken the initiative in negotiating a treaty to outlaw war.

So in the same month that Mr. Kellogg arrived home from signing his treaty, the loan was O.K.'d.

Two days later, the Bolivian representative in Buenos Aires, negotiating with Paraguay for a straightening out of the boundary, packed up his bags and went home.

Two months later a Paraguayan patrol cruising through the Chaco jungle before sunrise, bumped into Fort Vanguardia, opened fire, and leveled it to the ground.

The Kellogg Pact was on the firing-line.

When the news leaked out of the jungle and trickled back to La Paz three days later, the Paraguayan *chargé d'affaires*, Elio Ayala, was taken from the Legation under armed guard and put on a train headed for the Peruvian border. The next day—December 10th—the Bolivian *chargé d'affaires*, B. Mercado, was given safe conduct from Asunción. Four days later, a Bolivian patrol, seeking revenge for the destruction of Fort Vanguardia, razed Fort Boqueron, a Paraguayan stronghold. In La Paz, the crowds milled around the palace demanding President Siles and war.

Scheduled to meet in Washington on the day Bolivia and Paraguay severed diplomatic relations was a conference of Pan-American states charged with formulating arbitration and conciliation treaties which would make war impracticable and impossible in the Americas.

Probably this was the luckiest break Mr. Kellogg's Pact ever got. The conferees arrived in Washington to find

[1] Bolivia defaulted two years later.

the cause of peace definitely on the spot. Either they had to act or become the world's funniest spectacle. Most of them had come fresh from adhering to the Kellogg Pact. All of them were pledged to take new and important steps toward preventing war. And here were two of their own members staging a cat-and-dog fight in their own back yard.

The effect was electrifying.

It was especially electrifying considering the fact that Pan-American conferences hitherto had studiously avoided any subject less innocuous than the protection of trade-marks, the exchange of students, and the promotion of good roads for the purpose of selling North American road machinery.

Their agendas in the past had been meticulously fixed by the United States, and the precedent for innocuous-ness dated from 1826, when the United States Senate debated so long over the danger of participation in the first Pan-American conference that it adjourned while our delegates were en route to the scene of action. Innocuous conferences to us were such a virtue that we even boasted of them. With pride in his voice Elihu Root told the Rio de Janeiro Conference: "According to your program no great and single impressive thing is to be done by you; no political questions are to be discussed; no controversies are to be settled."

But now, faced with the prospect of disgraceful and ignominious retreat before the puny fistics of the two most backward nations in South America, this particular Pan-American Conference took on an unprecedented de-gree of boldness. The sleepy patio of the Pan-American Union, which for years had witnessed nothing more ex-citing than the lamb-stew lunches of Director-General Leo S. Rowe, suddenly became charged with activity. Telegraph instruments were set up in improvised press-rooms, newspapermen thronged the corridors. Even the varicolored parrots drowsing for decades under the bust of Bolivar screamed with excitement. And a battery of press typewriters began pounding out the story of how the Pan-American Union had deviated at last from its time-honored program of unveiling monuments of South American patriots and distributing stereopticon slides to women's clubs, by tackling one of the most contentious disputes on the South American continent.

The conference was plowing virgin soil and it had to plow rapidly. In a series of plenary sessions and secret committee meetings it proposed that the two hostile countries accept the good offices of the Pan-American Conference to settle their dispute, following which every conceivable form of pressure was used to force acceptance of the offer.

Paraguay yielded first. In fact, there was reason to believe that Paraguay had precipitated the conflict by drawing first blood at Fort Vanguardia because she knew Bolivia was arming. Bolivia not only had purchased the $5,000,000 worth of munitions to be paid for by the Dillon, Read loan, but also had hired a German army officer, General Hans Kundt, to train her troops. Confronted with a nation of vastly superior man power, Paraguay knew that she had to act quickly or be swallowed. So the good offices from Washington came as a life-saver.

Bolivia was more difficult. She considered herself the aggrieved party. Moreover, President Siles faced a precarious political situation and had to make a reasonably bloodthirsty showing if he was to stay in office. Diplomatic pressure, therefore, was concentrated on La Paz.

Mr. Kellogg dispatched instructions to David E. Kauffman, American Minister in the Bolivian capital, to exert all possible influence. The Chilean Government, which controls the most direct line of communication between La Paz and the sea, did the same. But more effective than either was the consistent, unrelenting pressure of public opinion being molded by eighteen sister republics, all represented in Washington and all sitting in judgment against the nation which refused to submit its dispute to their good offices. Each day that passed, the press dispatches reaching La Paz from Washington, Santiago, Buenos Aires, Rio de Janeiro, Lima, became more caustic and more critical. Each day that passed Bolivia felt more isolated.

At one plenary session she suffered agonies of indecision. The Paraguayan delegate, Eligio Ayala was seated with the others. The Bolivian delegate, Diez de Medina, had received instructions to shun all meetings dealing with the Chaco. So while his colleagues sat in the Hall of the Americas, Minister Medina paced up and down the corridor outside. As he passed the open door of the conference, he paused and cocked one ear. Each time he passed the door he paused a little longer. Finally Francis White rushed out, took him by the arm, and escorted him into the conference hall.

But as they appeared on the threshold, Secretary Kellogg, not realizing that the prodigal was returning to the fold, rapped his gavel and adjourned the meeting. Mr. White rushed up to point out that an important act of conciliation had been frustrated. But it was too late.

Finally, however, Bolivia yielded.

And on New Year's Day the Pan-American Union celebrated the most momentous achievement of its innocuous career. It compelled the representatives of Paraguay and Bolivia to sign a protocol for the mediation of their dispute.

The victory was not so complete as it might have been. The protocol did not provide for the settlement of the basic issue—division of the 100,000 square miles of Chaco swampland. It provided merely for fixing responsibility for the clash at Fort Vanguardia, for a temporary period of peace between the two nations, and for the appointment of a neutral commission with a life of six months in which to bring the two countries together.

Probably the conference could have increased this scope had it insisted. At that particular moment it had a stronger hand over Bolivia and Paraguay than any body of neutrals ever were to have for many years to come. But at the time its victory seemed stupendous. It was hailed as one of the major triumphs of Pan-Americanism and as such it was celebrated on that New Year's night.

On that night was born the Neutral Commission. It was to consist of five members; and the original plan was to select them from the countries bordering Paraguay and Bolivia. Chile, however, refused to serve. She sent a note to that effect to Secretary Kellogg, following a slurring remark made by the Bolivian Minister, Diez de Medina, who resented the strongly worded note Chile had sent his government urging acceptance of the Conference's good offices.

That one move proved a momentous one. For following the Chilean withdrawal, other neutral neighbors did the same. Brazil felt that she was a little too close to the scene of action—some of the fighting had been on her territory. Argentina, following the mandate of the isolationist Irygoyen, was not represented at the conference. And the result was that, with the exception of Uruguay, the five neutrals chosen to make up the Commission were those farthest away from the Chaco and probably the least interested in it. The United States was chosen because it was the United States. Cuba, Mexico, and Colombia were chosen not because their foreign offices were the worst informed about the Chaco—which was the case —but because their representatives at the Conference were among its most outstanding and ablest jurists.

Thus was born the Commission of Neutrals, whose persistent efforts to bring peace to the Western Hemisphere were to weave intermittently and at times ingloriously through Pan-American history for the next five years.

Many things, including a declaration of war, were in store for it. But Mr. Kellogg and his Pact had won the first skirmish.

4. MR. STIMSON GETS SLAPPED

Midsummer in the year 1929 promised to be reasonably peaceful, and Henry L. Stimson felt that he really deserved it.

He had only recently become Secretary of State.

He had gone from the Philippines, which he thought at that time were hot, into the maelstrom of Mr. Kellogg's State Department, and found that he had jumped from a comparatively cool frying-pan into an insatiable fire. And having dealt as best he could with a dying revolution in Mexico, the travail of Europe in giving birth to the Young Plan, the fulminations of the Senate over Elihu Root's attempt to bring the United States into the World Court, the beginning of negotiations with Great Britain for a naval treaty, and the outcry of outraged "wets" at the sinking of the Canadian rumrunner, *I'm Alone*, 215 miles off the Louisiana coast, Mr. Stimson crossed off the hectic months of April, May, and June and looked forward to July with a sense of relief and the hope that it was to bring him a vacation.

The one definitely scheduled event for the month of July was the ceremony of putting the Kellogg Treaty into full and final force. Almost one year had passed since the Pact was signed by fifteen nations in Paris. All of these, plus many others, had ratified it, and their plenipotentiaries were now invited to leave their cool vacation resorts, shake the moth balls from their cutaways, and brave the heat of Washington on July 24th to put the Pact into official effect. Some of them demurred a little about this. But when it became known that Frank B. Kellogg was coming all the way from St. Paul and that even Calvin Coolidge was deserting his front porch at Northampton for his first and only visit to the White House since March 4th, the Diplomatic Corps decided to make the best of it.

No sooner had these plans been made when one prominent signatory of the Kellogg Pact seized the railroad and telegraph lines belonging in part to another signatory, and booted its officials out of North Manchuria. Following which, Russia and China broke off diplomatic relations.

No wonder that Henry L. Stimson felt the fates were against him!

The crux of the trouble which caused Mr. Stimson such consternation was the Chinese Eastern Railway, which cuts a thousand miles and about two days from the long route of the Trans-Siberian across the steppes of Asia between Moscow and Vladivostok. Behind that rail line and all its difficulties is a background of conflict between a supine China and an aggressive Russia dating back nearly a century.

Supreme in Manchuria in the summer of 1929 was Chang Hsueh-Liang, a war lord of only thirty-one, who had spent his adolescence in the bridge-playing atmosphere of the Anglo-American Mukden Club, who preferred his Martinis dry with pickled onions, and who had inherited from his ex-bandit father $10,000,000, the precedent of taking more than one wife, and an intense antipathy for all things Russian.

Faced with the action of this strenuous young man in seizing the jointly-owned Chinese-Russian Railway, Moscow mobilized 28,000 men on the eastern side of the rail line, gave orders for its 6,000 crack cavalry troops to be in readiness on the western border, and sent up reinforcements from the Trans-Baikal.

It looked as if Mr. Kellogg's treaty, despite all its travail, still would die aborning.

The days crept closer to the momentous date of July 24th. The Diplomatic Corps held its breath. Mr. Kellogg fidgeted in St. Paul.

On the surface, at least, Henry L. Stimson remained calm and unperturbed. On July 18th, six days before the proclamation of the Pact, he went about the ordinary routine of making public an interesting report from the American consul in Seville regarding the International Exposition there, approved the details for the funeral of an American Minister who had died in Liberia, sent some congratulatory telegrams to Bolivia and Paraguay over their exchange of prisoners, continued his conversations with Ambassador Dawes regarding a naval agreement, and appeared to be haughtily oblivious to the fact that there was such a thing as a threat to the Kellogg Pact.

Beneath the surface, however, Mr. Stimson was worried. He could foresee the possibility of his carefully planned ceremony becoming the laughing-stock of the world. And in his own slow and methodical manner he was working on moves which he might make to head off disaster.

Finally, on July 19th he announced them to the world. His program was threefold. First he called in the Ambassadors of Great Britain, France, and Japan and reminded them that they were signatories of the Four Power Pact of 1921 for preserving the peace of the Pacific. Second, he reminded China and Russia that they were signatories of the Pact for the renunciation of war. And third, he informed these same two countries that as far as he could ascertain from the information before him, their dispute over the Chinese Eastern railway was justiciable and therefore could be submitted to arbitration.

Communication with Russia, still a pariah nation as far as the United States was concerned, was carried on through the channel of the French Ambassador, *via* the Quai d'Orsay, *via* the Soviet Ambassador in Paris, thus keeping Mr. Stimson's hand unreddened and immaculate.

Mr. Kellogg, now arrived in Washington, looked on and approved. So did the rest of the world. There was no question that Mr. Stimson had scored. Public opinion was with him one hundred per cent. By acting energetically he had turned what looked like a major defeat for the newborn Pact into a victory. He had shown that the United States, despite a change of administrations, stood flat-footed behind Mr. Kellogg's child. In fact, he had shown that the new administration went much farther. It had forsaken the Kellogg-Hughes era of power without responsibility, for at least one deliberate and definite assumption of an international obligation.

This conviction became deeper when the British Government sent an immediate reply supporting Secretary Stimson, and when Aristide Briand of France followed suit. In a second telegram the same day, Briand informed Stimson that he had interviewed the Russian Ambassador in Paris and had received assurances that the Soviet Government wished to respect the Kellogg Pact. Simultaneously, Mr. Stimson got a call from Dr. C. C. Wu, urbane Chinese Minister, informing him of the same desire on the part of China. Finally, came a message from Katsuji Debuchi, diminutive Ambassador of Japan, that his government also would coöperate. The message was a little slow in coming and had been preceded by intimations from Tokyo that Japan resented American intrusion at her own back door even though in the cause of peace. Conciliatory Baron Shidehara still was Minister of Foreign Affairs at that time, but even his message of complete coöperation contained the significant reminder that he had talked with the Russian Ambassador and the Chinese Minister "last week," had urged them to respect the Kellogg Pact, and had been assured that in the absence of any attack upon them they would do so.

Japan, in other words, was quite capable of keeping its own eye on its own sphere of influence.

July 24th came and went. The Kellogg Pact was put into full force and effect. The only incidents which marred the ceremony were Calvin Coolidge's insistence upon giving one of his own unique and caustice press conferences, thereby diverting part of the flood-light away from his successor in the White House; plus the failure of the radio stage-hands to connect the microphones, so that Herbert Hoover's somewhat feeble voice scarcely was heard even within the limits of the Blue Room, being entirely missed therefore by the waiting world outside.

Despite these blemishes, however, the morning of July 25th found the Kellogg Pact in full force and Henry L. Stimson faced with the much more difficult problem of translating the lip service given to it by Russia and China into an actual agreement to prevent hostilities.

Mr. Stimson had not been unaware of these realities and had a plan to deal with them. So promptly on the morning of July 25th, before the plenipotentiaries who had come to Washington for the ceremony could return to their summer resorts, Secretary Stimson summoned five of them to the State Department. They were Sir Esme Howard, the British Ambassador; Ambassador de Martino of Italy; Ambassador Paul Claudel of France; Ambassador Katsuji Debuchi of Japan, and Rudolph Leitner, *chargé d'affaires* of the German Embassy.

They were summoned singly, and none of them knew until they arrived that it was a joint occasion or why it was they had been called. Ushered into the office of the Secretary of State, very much like a group of schoolboys, they listened intently while Mr. Stimson read to them his plan for settling the dispute between Russia and China.

He proposed a conciliation commission very much after the precedent already established by the Neutral Commission for the Paraguayan-Bolivian dispute. The commission was to be composed of six members—Great Britain, France, Italy, Japan, Germany, and the United States— and was to undertake the ironing out of the Manchurian controversy.

Ambassador Claudel did not understand Mr. Stimson very well and asked him a question. Mr. Stimson, in turn, could not understand M. Claudel. Ambassador Martino came to the rescue. But Mr. Stimson had precluded any misunderstanding. He had carefully typed his proposal on different sheets of paper and now passed them out, one by one, to his diplomatic visitors. Whereupon they filed out, the diminutive de Martino waving his copy excitedly above his head as he scampered down the corridor toward his Embassy and the cable codes.

Beyond any reasonable doubt, Henry L. Stimson's proposal was the most practical one possible. He had proposed, just one day after the Pact had come into force, a complete piece of machinery for making it effective. His proposal was exactly what Spencer Phenix had urged upon Mr. Kellogg during the days when the Pact still was in embryonic form, but which Mr. Kellogg had vetoed because of the Senate. It was exactly the plan of "consultation" or "putting teeth" in the Kellogg Pact for which Europe subsequently clamored, which subsequently disrupted the London Naval Conference, and which the world now rejected.

For that rejection Mr. Stimson, himself, was almost entirely to blame. It was in the method of his proposal, rather than its content, that Mr. Stimson went wrong. He had not profited by the example of Frank B. Kellogg in forcing the chancelleries of Europe to accept his Pact.

Kellogg had not learned that pitiless publicity, used when a nation unquestionably is in the right, can mold a public opinion more powerful than any private negotiation, any secret note exchange. And not having learned this, Mr. Stimson did not publish his *aides mémoires*. Nelson T. Johnson, Assistant Secretary and his chief adviser on the Far East, urged him to do so; but Mr. Stimson was too much the gentleman, had too much regard for the feelings of others, thought he would wait until he saw what reaction he got from the five powers addressed. Therefore, when the five envoys left Mr. Stimson's office, clutching their slips of paper like schoolboys their report cards, no one except these five and, later, their foreign offices, knew what these slips of paper contained.

The result was that the Stimson proposal was at one and the same time the most worth-while and yet the flattest dud of his entire career.

What Mr. Stimson did not know, in fact never did learn, is that no move in foreign relations, no matter how carefully guarded, ever long remains secret. Therefore the best rule of diplomacy is to get your own version of the story out before the other chancellery does, because the version imbedded in the public mind first, is the one which sticks. Mr. Stimson had many opportunities at many different times to learn this, but he never did.

And being particularly green at that time, Mr. Stimson sat at his desk, complacently awaiting answers to his proposal—a proposal, incidentally, which so shattered the Republican post-war policy of power without responsibility that Henry Cabot Lodge must have turned over in his grave.

Mr. Stimson waited from July 25th, when the proposal was made, for a period of nearly two weeks. Then suddenly there burst from Vienna a newspaper story which sent his plans completely haywire.

The story stated that the United States had sent a secret

note to the five world powers proposing a capitalist plot
to rob Russia of her historic Chinese Eastern Railway. According to the version in the first pages of Moscow newspapers, the United States had asked Great Britain, France,
Japan, Germany, and Italy jointly to form a peace commission, meanwhile appointing a neutral manager to operate the coveted and controversial Chinese Eastern.

"This news uncovers the unmeasured falsity and hypoc-
risy of the 'pacifist efforts' of the American Foreign Minister, Stimson," stormed *Pravda*, official organ of the
Soviet. "It displays in all their ugliness the anti-Soviet
plans of the imperialist powers trying to ignite a conflagration in the Far East."

There was just enough truth in the story to make it
appear absolutely plausible. Stimson *had* summoned the
diplomatic envoys of the countries mentioned in the
Vienna story. He *had* proposed that they set up a six-
power conciliation commission. But instead of intriguing
to secure control of the Chinese Eastern for the United
States or any other neutral power, he had gone farther
than diplomatic intercession really warranted in demanding that the road be turned back to its original status of
one-half Russian ownership and operation. He had
pounded on the table and "talked like a Dutch uncle"
to the urbane and blinking Dr. Wu in demanding that
China return the railroad to its *status quo ante*.

But since Mr. Stimson had scrupulously refrained from
making public his proposal, there was no way in which
the Vienna story could be denied. And to this day no
official evidence ever has been put forward to show that
it was false.

Undoubtedly the story was a "plant." The fact that
it originated in Vienna in itself was suspicious. Vienna,
since the days of the Hapsburgs, has not been a sounding-
board for important international news, except when the
German Foreign Office wants to make something public

without focusing suspicion on Berlin. The two nations most interested in planting such a yarn were Japan and Germany. France and Italy, after some hesitation, had accepted Mr. Stimson's conciliation proposal. Great Britain had indicated its acceptance, but showed some deference to the reaction of her ex-ally, Japan—a deference, incidentally, which presaged the position of complete Anglo-Japanese sympathy she was going to take when the Manchukuo controversy broke with genuine seriousness two years later.

Germany at that time had a completely platonic interest in Manchuria. But because of an unofficial understanding she had worked out with Tokyo, was tacitly supporting the Japanese. And the Japanese military had watched with increasing concern the peace efforts of Henry L. Stimson. The intrusion of any foreign power into their own self-delineated domain, even on an act of peace, was to them a thing to be viewed with suspicion and horror. So after they had partially recovered from Stimson's quick intervention, the Japanese began to try to steal for themselves his rôle of pacifier.

It was just after they sent out their first olive branch to the two belligerents, that the Vienna news report, having all the ear-marks of a German-Japanese plant, exploded in the face of Henry L. Stimson.

From that time on he was estopped. Not only did he lack the coöperation of the Germans and the Japanese, but, most important of all, one of the two chief parties to the dispute—Russia—was profoundly suspicious and decidedly unanxious to coöperate.

During the weeks that followed, therefore, Mr. Stimson's attitude toward the Manchurian dispute was much akin to that of the average individual toward a hot potato. And since he was continually absorbed in the initial spade work for his approaching London Naval Conference, and in a half-dozen other international incidents which were always bobbing up to bother him, he was quite content to leave the Chinese Eastern Railway to the conciliation efforts of the slightly ruffled Japanese.

Three months passed. The Chinese and Russians held a desultory conference at Manchuli, which broke up when the former flatly refused to reinstate the Russian manager and assistant manager of the Chinese Eastern before formal peace negotiations started. The Russians increased their cavalry concentration along the border. There was more dickering, more futile calls by Dr. C. C. Wu at the State Department, more Chinese notes written for the sole purpose of trying to monopolize space in the newspapers.

Then, finally, the soft gumbo soil of North Manchuria having frozen, and the attention of the world being diverted to other things, the Russians reverted to the argument which they had found from centuries of experience is the only one which counts with the Chinese.

They attacked.

They sent their Cossack cavalry across the Amur and did not stop until they had reached the Khinghan Mountain range where the Chinese Eastern dives through a tunnel to emerge on the wind-swept Manchurian plain beyond.

A howl that could be heard clear across the Pacific and which reverberated and reëchoed along the Siberian steppes to the capitals of western Europe, went up from the Chinese. Mr. Stimson, busy at that time with final preparations for his naval conference, heard it, and recognized in it the wail of his long-lost child.

The attack had started in mid-November. By November 20th Soviet troops had captured Dalanor, a famous market-place on the Manchurian-Mongolian border. By November 24th they had taken Hailar, another important Manchu-Mongol trading town. By November 25th a good portion of North Manchuria between Manchuli and the

Khinghan Mountains was in the hands of the Red Army.

So fast did the Red Army operate that it was not until approximately the latter date that Secretary Stimson heard the wail from prostrate China and realized that something was decidedly wrong with the conciliation move he had started in July. November 25th, however, was the day on which Mr. Stimson planned to go to his Long Island estate, Highhold, to inspect his hounds and his hunters over the Thanksgiving week-end. And despite the reverberations from the Far East, he went.

It was not until November 30th, five days later, that he returned, and plunged immediately into the conflict. The Ambassadors of the major powers were summoned to the State Department. Mr. Stimson discussed with some of them the revival of his old plan for a conciliation commission similar to that which had functioned between Paraguay and Bolivia. But it was too late. Not only had the plan been rejected by Germany and Japan, and severely criticized by the Russians, but equally important, public opinion, once mobilized and volatile, had been allowed to become inert and impotent.

Mr. Stimson, therefore, chose a different method of attack. He drafted an appeal to the fifty-three other adherents to the Kellogg Pact—or, as he expressed it, "substantially the entire world"—asking them to unite with the United States in bringing moral pressure against China and Russia to prevent war in Manchuria. Additional notes also were cabled to the two recalcitrant nations.

The Stimson appeal was strong and well worded. In it he placed special emphasis upon the weapon of public opinion which he had neglected to use when he made his conciliation proposal in July.

> The efficacy of the Pact of Paris [he said] depends upon the sincerity of the governments which are a party to it. Its sole sanction lies in the power of public opinion of the countries constituting substantially the entire civilized

world, whose governments have joined the covenant. If the recent events in Manchuria are allowed to pass without notice or protest by any of these governments the intelligent strength of the public opinion of the world in support of peace cannot but be impaired.

But while Mr. Stimson was drafting this appeal, in fact while he was still enjoying his Thanksgiving turkey on Long Island, events in Manchuria had moved far ahead of him. On November 26th Marshal Chang Hsueh-Liang, Governor of Manchuria, had decided that discretion was the better part of valor where the Red Army was concerned, had provisionally accepted Soviet terms for a truce, and had sent a personal representative to Nikolsky-Ussuriisky, just across the Siberian border, to sue for permanent peace. This delegate, Tsai Yun-shen, arrived at his destination on December 1st—the very day that Secretary Stimson was dispatching his world-wide appeal—and on December 3rd he signed a protocol with M. Şimanovsky, agent of the Soviet Foreign Commissariat, for a peaceful reorganization of the Chinese Eastern Railway. Meanwhile, all Russian troops had been evacuated from Chinese territory.

Mr. Stimson, however, completely ignored this. Either his agents in the Far East had failed to advise him, or he had failed to take their advice.

Whatever may have been his reasons, however, Mr. Stimson not only acted after the horse had been stolen, but made his position particularly vulnerable by stating that Russian troops were on Chinese soil.

The come-back from Moscow was instantaneous and left nothing to the imagination. Foreign Commissar Maxim Litvinoff, its author, has an international reputation for diplomatic invective. In the note to Stimson, he outdid himself.

Pointing out that Russia never had used armed force externally, reminding the world that the Soviet had set

62   THE AMERICAN DIPLOMATIC GAME

an example by relinquishing her extra-territorial rights
in China which other nations had not followed, Litvinoff
arched an accusing finger at Stimson for trying to upset
peace negotiations between Russia and the Mukden Government just as they were being successfully concluded.

> The Government of the United States [he said] has ad-
> dressed its declaration at a moment when the Soviet and
> Mukden Governments already had agreed to several con-
> ditions and were proceeding with direct negotiations
> which would make possible prompt settlement of the
> conflict between the Soviet Union and China.
> In view of the fact, the above declaration cannot but
> be considered unjustifiable pressure on the negotiations
> and cannot, therefore, be taken as a friendly act.
> The Soviet Government states further that the Pact of
> Paris does not give any single state or group of states
> the function of protector of this Pact. The Soviet, at any
> rate, never expressed consent that any states themselves
> or by mutual consent should take upon themselves such
> a right. . . .
> In conclusion, the Soviet Government cannot forbear
> expressing amazement that the Government of the United
> States, which by its own will has no official relations with
> the Soviet, deems it possible to apply to it with advice
> and counsel.

The graveyard of international relations is dotted with
catastrophes caused by much milder notes than this. A
secret session of the Senate and the instantaneous passage
of the Japanese Exclusion Act in 1924 was the result of
a note from Ambassador Hanihara informing Charles
Evans Hughes that the contemplated legislation, if passed,
would be considered "unfriendly." Other uses of the term,
on occasion, have provoked or preceded war.

Neither Litvinoff nor Stimson, however, had any such
intention. The Russian had seen his chance to take a slap
at what Moscow considered the smuggest representative of
the smuggest government in the world, and that was all

he wanted. Mr. Stimson received the news with quiet and dignified calm. It was read to him over the telephone while he was shaving for a White House dinner. He replied, "I care to make no comment whatsoever."

The next day he took stock of the situation.

He had on his desk favorable replies from three of the countries—France, Italy, and Great Britain—which he had sounded out in advance and which had given him a pledge of support. He also had unfavorable replies from Germany and Japan, the latter still stubborn in her opposition to peace efforts in her own back yard. In addition, he had supporting telegrams from Cuba, the Netherlands, and from Mexico, which promised to whip into line all her Central American neighbors.

It was not a great number out of a total of fifty-three.

For ten years the United States had been importuned by Europe to take a more active part in world affairs. For ten years the United States had been urged especially to coöperate with Europe in maintaining world peace. The United States had been told that Europe could not reduce her armies and navies until she received that coöperation. And now the United States for the first time had taken a highly important step toward that coöperation; a clumsy step, to be sure, and one which did not follow the familiar ruts of Old World diplomacy—but the steps of all beginners are beset with pitfalls.

Fifty-three nations had been invited! Only eight had deigned to reply! Six expressed their willingness to coöperate![1]

At the ceremony in the Salle de l'Horloge one year before, a Frenchman had said: "But suppose America throws over the Pact of Paris as it did the League of Nations?"

Mr. Stimson is a man capable of extreme personal temper, but also of extreme perseverance. At times he has been known to let his temper mar his effectiveness. But he

[1] Other replies were received, but after December 4th.

did not on this occasion. He sat down and penned a statement which represented the peace policy he intended to follow—and did follow in disarmament, in war debts, in Latin America, regardless of international rebuff. That statement represents the highwater mark of American cooperation in world affairs, a mark which may not be attained again for many years to come.

> I have seen [he said] the text of the Russian memorandum as reported in the press.
>
> Between co-signatories of the Pact of Paris it can never be rightly thought unfriendly that one nation calls to the attention of another its obligations or the dangers to peace which from time to time arise.
>
> The message of the American Government was not sent from unfriendly motives but because this Government regards the Pact of Paris as a covenant which has profoundly modified the attitude of the world toward peace, and because this Government intends to shape its policy accordingly.
>
> In the language of the joint statement issued by the President of the United States and the Prime Minister of Great Britain on October 10th last, "both our governments resolved to accept the peace pact not only as a declaration of good intentions but as a positive obligation to direct national policy in accordance with its pledge."
>
> The present declaration of the authorities of Russia that they are now proceeding with direct negotiations which will make possible the settlement of the conflict is not the least significant evidence to show that the public opinion of the world is a live factor which can be promptly mobilized and which has become a factor of prime importance in the solution of problems and controversies which may arise between nations.

The Pact of Paris was still preserved.

Chapter II

THE WORLD THROWS DOWN THE WEAPONS OF WAR

1. ANGLO-AMERICAN COURTSHIP

As HERBERT HOOVER steamed north from his good-will trip to Latin America he had every reason to be a very happy man. He had escaped the politicians. He had enjoyed a good rest. He had been only slightly seasick. He had learned something about the ports and Presidents of South America. And he had created the impression in North America that all Latin Americans loved us and that this was entirely his doing.

The trip, it is true, had been marred by one or two unfortunate episodes. George Barr Baker had run off with the top-hat of the Foreign Minister of Ecuador, who probably never knew that later it was raffled off to a crowd of newspaper correspondents as the prize trophy of the voyage; an American sailor had shot a Peruvian policeman in the leg; Mr. Hoover's chief Secret Service man had had his pocket picked of $300 in the crowd at Buenos Aires; and Costa Rica, apparently under the impression that the President-elect was on a mission to investigate American imperialism, had asked him to keep his eye on the United Fruit Company. But all of these things were so carefully hushed up by George Barr Baker's efficient censorship that they did not detract from the gaiety of good will; in fact, were more than compensated for by the sight of half the population of Latin America crowding down to its seaports on muleback, in ox-carts, and in wheezing banana trains to see the great and good President-elect of the Colossus of the North.

Many prominent potentates have visited South America—Elihu Root, Orlando, Clemenceau, the Spanish Infanta, the Prince of Wales; but none of them got a reception equal to Hoover's.

Despite this, Mr. Hoover, pacing the deck of the U.S.S. *Utah* en route to the United States, was not a happy man. For on his trip he had come face to face with the most important conflict in the development of the post-war world.

It was the economic struggle between the two most powerful nations in the world—Great Britain and the United States.

Mr. Hoover, himself, as Secretary of Commerce, had contributed materially to that conflict. He had been the leader of the attack on the British rubber monopoly. He had been the spearhead of the drive to capture world markets—the majority of them British—for the United States. He had pushed this drive so successfully that during the period between the start of the World War and the year Mr. Hoover went to Latin America, American exports had increased forty-eight per cent, while British had declined five per cent. He had watched the influx of American capital into the British Dominions until they became competitors of the mother country and less and less receptive to her exports. He had encouraged mail subsidies for American merchant ships, equipped with reinforced decks to carry six-inch guns and engine-rooms located with the greatest protection from gun-fire—all as an answer to British supremacy of the seas. He had witnessed the efforts of the Navy Department to set up a radio network to break the British cable and wireless monopoly, and had seen the navy order a cruiser to patrol the Florida coast to prevent the Western Union-British combine from laying a cable from Miami to South America. Finally he had pushed the idea of air routes linking the United States with Latin America, all as a part of a great system of ship lines, motor highways, radio and cable circuits tying the Western Hemisphere into one vast economic and cultural unit.

It was a great dream, but it clashed, more than he had realized before his good-will trip, with the future of the British Empire.

Great Britain, left with an antiquated industrial plant on her hands, in a world of too many factories and too many factory hands, was in a desperate position. She had eliminated Germany as her chief economic rival only to face two factors even more dangerous. One was the growing trend toward nationalism—the tariff barriers, the infant industries of Europe and the Dominions which whittled her markets down to mere shadows. The other was the emergence of an Anglo-Saxon rival which had developed mass production and scientific commercial technique to a degree unprecedented, and which in addition depended upon foreign markets to dispose of only six per cent of her production.

As a result, the United States and Great Britain found themselves glaring at each other across two oceans for possession of the only lucrative and unindustrialized markets left in the world—the Far East and Latin America.

Although Herbert Hoover had contributed materially to the bitterness of the British-American economic conflict, his friends indicate that he was not acutely aware of that bitterness prior to his trip to South America. Mr. Hoover had been the foremost pusher of North American trade in Latin America. He had complained because Mr. Kellogg's policies in Nicaragua militated against that trade. He had sat in the Coolidge Cabinet while the State Department had tried to wring from the British an agreement to limit auxiliary vessels at the Geneva Naval Conference. And he had been aware of the Coolidge-Kellogg consternation when the French and British hatched a secret naval agreement just a few months before he started on his good-will trip. But that he, or most of those complacently holding the reins of the Coolidge Bull Market, had any acute realization of the fundamentals of Anglo-American economic rivalry is highly doubtful.

No similar lack of realization existed on the other side of the Atlantic. British Tory leaders, sons of peers who had carried the power and prestige of the Union Jack to every corner of the world, suckled on the belief that power and prestige could be maintained only by complete supremacy over the markets and trade routes, were acutely aware of the challenge thrown out to them by the new empire across the Atlantic. Lord Haldane, discussing this with one of the writers during the year Mr. Hoover took his good-will trip, suggested that it was not naval rivalry which worried him so much as "our relations in regard to South America."

"Europe can no longer be considered an adequate market for British over-production," Lord Haldane explained, "so we are turning to South America. And here is where the interests of Great Britain and the United States come into direct conflict.

"At present you are using your Monroe Doctrine for the benefit of your industrialists and merchants. When you feel threatened in your domination of that continent, you do not hesitate to use the political weapon to intimidate and force some of the weaker Latin American states to obey you. You are mixing yourselves, indirectly, in the internal politics of all those states and want to choose your own men as Presidents. We cannot remain indifferent to this forceful penetration of that vast continent. We have to safeguard our interests and adopt, if necessary, your system. And here lies the danger.

"What will happen in case both Britain and the United States are firm and unyielding? Don't forget that economic rivalries are the underlying motives of most, I should say all, wars. I shudder to think of the possible consequences."

Tory leaders echoed Lord Haldane.

Among the foremost of these was Sir Austen Chamberlain, destined to do more to arouse the United States over British rivalry than any other one man. Sir Austen once was described by Lloyd George as a stork standing on one leg in the middle of Lake Locarno, having caught exactly one fish and with an air of ineffable self-satisfaction spread over his face. That Sir Austen's one fish was the Locarno Agreement is not exactly true. His other fish— the one which in the end swallowed him—was the secret Franco-British naval agreement negotiated in the summer of 1928.

That the agreement caused such furore was partly due to the unique personality of its author. It was negotiated in Sir Austen's own apartment under conditions of strictest secrecy. Sir Austen regarded foreign affairs as a sacred cult of which he was the high priest. When questioned on the floor of Commons regarding his stewardship of the Foreign Office, he answered with pained surprise and a note of bland superiority. Never did his answers or the cold stare from behind his monocled eye give the slightest hint of the Franco-British edifice he was erecting.

The foundation of Sir Austen's edifice was the thesis that Britain's days of splendid isolation were over and that with her most important stake on the Continent she must take a powerful initiative to maintain its peace. With this many Englishmen agreed. But Sir Austen went one step farther. He argued that in order to maintain the peace of Europe, Britain must have an ally, and that that ally could be none other than France.

"France," he once said, "I love as a lover loves his mistress."

So into the arms of France this great lover proceeded to throw British destinies in 1928.

What prompted the deed at that specific time was a move on the part of German and French industrialists to coöperate in the formation of steel and chemical cartels, a move which caused immediate reaction from those two stanch defenders of the *status quo*—British industry and the French General Staff. Their consternation played directly into the hands of Sir Austen Chamberlain's love for France; and after some preliminary conversations between the two foreign offices, Philippe Berthelot, Secretary General of the Quai d'Orsay, made a secret visit to London.

Sir Austen's French is so perfect and he uses it so frequently that Stanley Baldwin once reminded him of old Dr. Johnson's advice not to speak French, "since it puts the rascals at too great an advantage." On the occasion of M. Berthelot's visit, however, his advice was completely ignored. Not more than half a dozen people knew Berthelot was in London. Perhaps fewer than that number had a chance to talk with him. For an entire week he was closeted in Chamberlain's apartment. There the two men spoke French to Sir Austen's heart's content and put down in black and white what later became known as the Franco-British naval agreement.

Actually the agreement contained much more than an understanding on navies. In it were some sections dictated by the French General Staff which had a very direct bearing upon the eventuality of war on the Continent. But the naval sections alone were quite sufficient to cause sputters of extreme indignation from Messrs. Coolidge and Kellogg and a storm of resentment from the American press.

Mr. Kellogg, incidentally, did not begin to sputter immediately. At first he did not read Mr. Horan's exposé of the Franco-British alliance. The dispatch was published in the Hearst press, and Mr. Kellogg did not and would not read the Hearst press, until William P. Flythe, one of its correspondents, took the exposé to Mr. Kellogg and urged him to read it. After that, and after he had come back from signing his Pact, Mr. Kellogg directed a note of protest, written in the iciest and most incisive language of his assistant, Mr. Castle, to the two conspiring powers. And they, never intending their amours to receive public attention, and already perturbed over the scandal created, called off the deal.

Sir Austen Chamberlain, greatly upset, suffered a slight stroke and started on a trip around the world. Before he left he issued an explanation to the effect that Britain and France merely were planning a step toward disarmament which they could present to the rest of the world. But he had no explanation for the fact that in their anxiety for disarmament Britain and France had gone out of their way to spike every item on the American naval program.

Despite Sir Austen's explanation, the barometer of Anglo-American relations indicated stormy weather.

Herbert Hoover paced the deck of the U.S.S. *Utah* thinking these things over. In South America he had got a close-up of British and American commerce at bay. He had seen at first hand something of the British propaganda campaign covertly supported by the Foreign Office to discredit North American intentions in the Americas. He had seen the United States depicted as the Colossus of the North eager to seize the entire Western Hemisphere. He had heard the slogan of the British colony in Buenos Aires, "Buy from those who buy from us." And finally he recalled the Armistice Day speech of Calvin Coolidge, who, still piqued by Sir Austen Chamberlain's covert alliance with France, had sounded a virtual trumpet-call for the American nation to build up the fleet.

So Mr. Hoover sent a messenger to the port side, reserved for newspapermen, and asked that Edward Price Bell of the *Chicago Daily News* come to see him. Bell had been stationed in London for more than thirty years and had come to know both England and Hoover intimately.

"I don't like the situation between us and the British," Hoover said with his usual petulant bluntness. "Do you think something could be done to change British public opinion so we could talk business with the British Cabinet about navies?"

For an hour the two men, seated on a coil of rope, discussed Anglo-American rivalry. In the end, Hoover suggested working through the British press to influence public opinion, and after that starting naval negotiations. He asked Bell, who had many influential British newspaper friends, to go to London with this in mind and Bell promised to do so.

Subsequently Mr. Hoover invited the late Walter Strong, then publisher of the *Chicago Daily News,* to visit him in Florida, where he was waiting impatiently for March 4th and the exit of Calvin Coolidge. Simultaneously Bell had gone to Ottawa to talk improved Anglo-American relations to Prime Minister Mackenzie King. The upshot of these two trips was that Strong readily agreed to lend Bell to Mr. Hoover for an indefinite period, while the Canadian Prime Minister was enthusiastic over the idea of clearing up Anglo-American misunderstandings.

Bell sailed for London shortly thereafter, but en route stopped in Washington for a final talk with Hoover. His mission he understood to be twofold. First, he was to influence the British public through his friends among the British press. Second, he was to sound out Stanley Baldwin on the possibility of a trip to the United States during which Baldwin and Hoover could have an informal and intimate discussion of their mutual problems. Bell had no authority to invite Baldwin to come to Washington, but was instructed to reconnoiter and communicate with the White House if the Prime Minister reacted favorably.

It was a safe attempt. A newspaperman always can be disavowed.

Bell arrived in England toward the end of March and began working on the London press. At first his success was meager. The *Times* was lukewarm and the other papers could not be bothered. But in the *Sunday Observer* Bell found at least one enthusiastic disciple. Its editor, J. L. Garvin, never had visited America, but had been a stanch advocate of Anglo-American coöperation. So he, alone in the entire field of London newspapers, started booming the idea of a rapprochement.

The other part of Bell's mission also met with qualified success. Baldwin listened with much interest to his suggestions and said he would think over the idea of going to the United States for a talk with the President. For the time being, however, he said it was useless to make definite plans since he might be turned out of office by the May elections—a possibility which had not occurred to Bell and Hoover.

Chamberlain, his health recovered, also was sympathetic to the idea of improving Anglo-American relations. Britain was in a bad way economically, and anything to stop the construction of a powerful American navy was welcome even to the man who loved France like a mistress. But Sir Austen had his own ideas about how Britain could eradicate the friction between the two countries, and put forward the suggestion of dismantling British fortifications at Jamaica and in waters adjacent to the United States. Such a gesture, he thought, would be of no consequence to the British navy, but might have a tremendous effect on the people of the United States. Chamberlain even went so far as to ask the foreign editor of the *Times* for his editorial support whenever the time was ripe for such a move.

But for Sir Austen Chamberlain, at least, that time never came.

During all this reconnoitering Bell had not for one instant envisaged the possibility of a Labor Government. Toward Ramsay MacDonald, with whom he had no particular sympathy, he had made no approach whatsoever. MacDonald, on the other hand, had taken up the idea of Anglo-American rapprochement entirely on his own initiative and probably was doing more than any other one man to attain that objective. His campaign speeches not only influenced his own Labor colleagues, but also had the effect of forcing the Conservative opposition onto the band-wagon; so that even dyed-in-the-wool Tories like Lord Cushenden, hitherto an obstinate pole-sitter for complete British sea supremacy, were forced to advocate an end of the naval race with America.

MacDonald went farther than this. He wrote a syndicated article for American newspapers in which he warned that it was a "hopeless and dangerous task to build ships against the United States" and proposed an international conference to decide the chief question which has confronted the American navy during countless European wars—the rights of neutrals on the highseas.

This olive branch not only received a most favorable reaction in the United States, but was answered tit-for-tat a few weeks later by Ambassador Hugh Gibson. Gibson proposed to the Preparatory Commission for Disarmament the principle of the naval "yardstick." This meant that the United States would not insist upon matching cruiser for cruiser with Great Britain, but would be willing to work out some scheme whereby the fighting strength of a 6,ooo-ton cruiser was measured against the fighting strength of a 10,ooo-ton cruiser, so that three of the big cruisers, for instance, might equal five of the smaller ones. In this way, Gibson suggested, parity might be attained.

Thus no matter what the political results in Great Britain, the stage was set on both sides of the Atlantic for rapprochement between the estranged cousins of the Anglo-Saxon race.

The decisive victory of the Labor Party in May took Edward Price Bell completely by surprise. Also it left him uncertain of his next move. Only once since the World War—when he had joined the pack which hounded the pacifist Labor leader into exile—had he spoken to Ramsay MacDonald. And this was when MacDonald for the first time became Prime Minister of Great Britain. MacDonald did not like Bell and Bell knew it. So Bell approached Constantine Brown, who in turn asked the late Lord Thomson, one of MacDonald's most intimate friends, if he could get the new Prime Minister to have a talk with Hoover's unofficial envoy. A day or two later Thomson replied that MacDonald flatly refused to see Bell. He was, however, tremendously interested in the idea of a trip to the United States and wanted Thomson to make sure that Bell had definite authority to make such a suggestion.

In order to establish the authenticity of Bell's mission Bell and Lord Thomson lunched at the United Service Club. Bell exhibited letters he had received from Hoover congratulating him on his success with the *Sunday Observer* and thanking him for his talks with Stanley Baldwin and Sir Austen Chamberlain. Lord Thomson seemed satisfied, and the next day reported that the new Prime Minister would be delighted to come to the United States for a conference with President Hoover when and if Mr. Hoover invited him.

At this point Mr. Hoover's diplomacy suddenly shifted to more formal channels. Bell had cabled the President immediately upon getting MacDonald's favorable response. In reply he received a letter thanking him for his "valuable services" and saying that the Ambassador to the Court of St. James's, Brigadier-General Charles Gates Dawes, U.S.A. retired, was en route to his new post and would take up the question of Ramsay MacDonald's visit.

The effulgent Mr. Dawes landed in England on June 14th—just nine days after MacDonald had formed his new Cabinet—and it was difficult to say whether Dawes or the British public was looking forward with greater anticipation to his arrival. Charley had just finished four hectic years as Vice-President of the United States and loved it. He had been a turbulent wielder of the gavel before a somnolent Senate. He had amazed Washington by giving a dinner to Buster Keaton. He had aroused the wrath of Calvin Coolidge by sleeping through the vote on the confirmation of the latter's Attorney-General. He had led a highly exciting and amusing life, and the idea of going back to sit in the high-ceilinged and stodgy offices of his Chicago bank bored him beyond words. So Charley had gone about the preparation for his conquest of London with much the same gusto that he went about his studies of *Nize Baby, Snowshoe Al,* or the history of Maya civilization. He made frequent visits to the State Department. He puffed his underslung pipe, struck countless matches, and said absolutely nothing to crowds of interviewing newspapermen. He made a dark mystery of the kind of pantaloons he would wear at court *levées* at St. James's Palace. And he made an even greater mystery of the part he would play in the impending naval negotiations and the much-discussed visit of Ramsay MacDonald to the United States.

The British public meanwhile awaited the arrival of the new Ambassador with the same mingled curiosity which might have attended the visit of Mary Pickford married to the Dalai Lama of Tibet. No other diplomat ever had stirred up anything like it. For days the London press had carried the most minute descriptions of the new Ambassador. His "Hell 'n' Maria" blasphemy before a Congressional committee, his shaking of a broom under the bewhiskered chin of the august Charles Evans Hughes, his berating the Senate for frittering its time away, all had been plastered on the front pages. The mere fact that President Hoover had selected a former vice-President of the United States to represent him in Great Britain made a tremendous impression in the British Isles. "It is just as if Mr. Hoover had come to England himself," the editorial writer of the *Daily Chronicle* proclaimed.

Thus was the state of British opinion when the new "Ambassador of Peace and Good Will" stepped off his ship at Plymouth.

Charley Dawes is not one to fumble his cues when he steps before so dazzling an array of footlights. He was equal even to this occasion. No envoy ever rushed through the rigmarole of being accredited to a new government with as much speed and as much resultant publicity as the new Ambassador to the Court of St. James's. He arrived on a Friday. On Saturday he presented his credentials to King George. By Saturday night he was aboard the Flying Scotsman en route to Lossiemouth to talk naval negotiations with a Prime Minister who had been in office only nine days.

Surely matters of great importance were at stake. Surely the new Ambassador carried with him carefully-worked-out proposals for a new basis of friendship—perhaps even an alliance—between the two English-speaking peoples. Above all, Mr. Dawes must be anxious to consummate the Washington pilgrimage of Ramsay MacDonald, already so much discussed in the press.

"Ambassador Dawes is the man who is bearing an in-vitation which may well mark the beginning of a great new era in the history of the English-speaking peoples and of the world," reasoned the *London Daily Express*.

And most of the people of Great Britain and of the United States reasoned as well.

Their reasoning, however, was without an intimate knowledge of the character of Charles Gates Dawes. Mr. Dawes has spent a lifetime aiming at big things but never quite getting there. Consummation is something he either does not appreciate or else does not understand. The thrill of the chase to Mr. Dawes is more important than the kill.

And so to those who knew him it was not at all sur-prising that he should have a very pleasant visit with Ramsay MacDonald, that he should discuss any number of puerile subjects, and that he should depart without having fulfilled any of the public expectations which he had deliberately fanned to such a fierce flame.

Mr. MacDonald, however, was not one who at that time fully understood the complexities of the Dawesian character. So when newspapermen pounced upon him at the end of the conference and asked whether the new Ambassador had extended an invitation for him to come to Washington, the new Prime Minister of Great Britain almost hit the ceiling.

From that point on, the position of Ramsay MacDon-ald in relation to the Anglo-American rapprochement which he had stressed so vigorously became increasingly similar to that of the young lady left waiting at the altar. Mr. Dawes, who obviously controlled the groom, con-tinued to remain silent. Mr. MacDonald continued to look forward hopefully for definite overtures. But al-though he saw Mr. Dawes frequently in the weeks that followed, got to the point where it was "Mac" and "Charley" between them, still the Ambassador said nothing about the visit to America.

This was most embarrassing. MacDonald had welcomed Bell's suggestion with tremendous enthusiasm. He had even thrown aside his usual Scotch caution and told newspapermen before Dawes arrived that the President of the United States wanted to discuss important matters with him.

Meanwhile the London press, taking its cue partly from the Foreign Office, partly from the lead set by the *Sunday Observer*, had launched a pro-American campaign with powerful and far-reaching effects. Under Bell's prompting, the *Sunday Observer* even attempted to explain the complexities of Herbert Hoover to the British public.

> In this country [J. L. Garvin wrote] Mr. Hoover has been ridiculously represented as an economic monster of a standardized continent and as a passionless intellectual of organized materialism, devoted ruthlessly to the sacred egoism of America, with little human feelings for other countries and less good will for our own. Mr. Bell dispelled these misrepresentations. Here is what he says: "A genuine feeling for Great Britain and the whole British family of nations characterizes the new administration in Washington."

Coupled with this press campaign was the feeling that through coöperation with the United States lay Britain's economic salvation. The financial position of Great Britain during the summer of 1929 was difficult. Unemployment was increasing, trade was decreasing. India was in turmoil and Lancashire cotton-mills were feeling the effects of the Gandhi boycott. Even Tory diehards had got tired of singing "Britannia Rules the Waves" and welcomed the idea of avoiding a naval race with the mighty power across the Atlantic.

The culmination of all this was a British public more friendly to the United States than at any time in years. England was keyed up and awaiting dramatic events.

But they failed to materialize.

Mr. Dawes continued silent. Washington appeared to have folded its once welcoming arms. From it came an officially inspired statement that Mr. MacDonald had invited himself to come and see Mr. Hoover. The call of Cecil Carlisle Burns, close friend of MacDonald's, upon Senator Borah strengthened this idea. It was interpreted as a move by the British Premier to secure an invitation.

As June gave way to July, Mr. MacDonald's position became increasingly awkward. He feared that some of his political opponents might ask embarrassing questions from the floor of Commons. He feared especially that "that trouble-maker," Winston Churchill, might want to know what had become of the much-heralded trip to America. MacDonald had just averted defeat on a minor finance bill by securing the support of the Liberal party, and he could not risk another immediate embarrassment.

So he expressed his fears to his friend, Lord Thomson, who in turn went to Constantine Brown, then London correspondent for the *Chicago Daily News*. Thomson said that MacDonald was suspicious of Bell, remembered his attacks during the World War, and thought Bell now was trying to harass him a second time.

"Did he have any real authority to talk for Hoover?" MacDonald had asked Lord Thomson.

The substance of MacDonald's fears was relayed to Ambassador Dawes, who exploded.

"You newspapermen should mind your own business," he said. "Mac will get his invitation when I'm good and ready to give it to him and not before."

This was reported back to MacDonald and made the now increasingly nervous Prime Minister suspect even his friend Charley.

And, as a matter of fact, his suspicions were justified. Charley Dawes, anxious as he was to be an Ambassador, had certain very positive ideas about diplomacy, and these ideas he had outlined to Mr. Hoover in no uncertain terms before accepting the job. One of them was that he was not to be a rubber-stamp Ambassador. He was not to serve merely as an errand boy to trot messages back and forth between Downing Street and the code-room of the American Embassy. Moreover, he was not to leave naval negotiations to naval experts and the white-spat boys of the career corps. He was to do the negotiating himself.

Mr. Dawes had once made a speech along these lines. He had timed the speech just three days after the Geneva Naval Conference disbanded in abject failure, and he had delivered it in the presence of the sponsor of that Conference, Frank B. Kellogg, at the dedication of the International Bridge at Buffalo. The speech consisted chiefly of a scathing denunciation of diplomacy for failing to prepare for the Conference in advance of its convocation.

Having placed himself thus on record, Charley Dawes was determined not to let another naval conference fail for lack of preparation. And he had laid down the law to Herbert Hoover, before accepting his ambassadorial post, that such informal diplomats as Edward Price Bell be eased out of the official picture. The next naval conference must be preceded by adequate spade work, he argued, with him, Dawes, as the chief spader.

This spade work was taking place spasmodically during the weeks of June and July, when Ramsay MacDonald was fidgeting about his invitation and not realizing that it was his friend Charley who was sitting on the lid.

It was in mid-July that the harassed Mr. MacDonald had approached Lord Thomson. A code cable was sent immediately to Walter Strong, publisher of the *Chicago Daily News*. The cable explained the embarrassing position in which MacDonald had been placed and warned that through this newspaper-diplomatic meddling there was some possibility that the Labor Cabinet might fall.

Two days later a cable from Strong reported that "the gentleman [in the White House] expresses high appreciation and gratification for Bell's actions and results and says something will be done to get the other out of the hole."

Something was done, and immediately.

Dawes called the next day upon MacDonald to say that while it was not propitious for him to come to Washington before the fall, his visit would be most welcome then, provided the two countries had worked out a provisional understanding on cruisers. Mr. Dawes had received instructions from the White House.

MacDonald was relieved but not satisfied. In order to save face politically, he insisted on some sort of official announcement. Dawes agreed to this, provided no date was set for MacDonald's departure. So on July 17th the Foreign Office "let it be known" unofficially that the Prime Minister would visit President Hoover, that no date had been set, and that Mr. MacDonald would choose his own time. And in order not to offend the susceptibilities of the Ambassador whom the Foreign Office was now beginning to understand, it was added that Mr. MacDonald would go to Washington with no idea of settling anything in particular, least of all naval questions, which would be carried on through usual diplomatic channels and Charley Dawes.

From that date in mid-July until early September, when it was finally decided that Mr. MacDonald should make his trip, Charley Dawes had a clean track for his naval negotiations. But during that period two things happened. The differences between American and British naval needs, which Charley thought so easily solved if only out of the hands of experts, became more and more intricate and finally were removed from his hands altogether. Second, his idea of holding up MacDonald's trip until there was some semblance of naval agreement proved to be a stroke of genius. At first regarded as the fetish of an eccentric ambassador, his strategy was finally adopted as a definite policy by Hoover and Stimson. And without that diplomatic club held over the head of an harassed Prime Minister the naval negotiations might have strung out forever.

Discussions during the remainder of the summer divided themselves into two categories. There was, first of all, the ballyhoo about Anglo-American friendship which reverberated with tremendous volume when both Hoover and MacDonald announced the suspension of cruiser and submarine construction. And there was, in the second place, the day-in and day-out haggling of the admirals over the most trivial advantage in gun caliber or cruiser tonnage which one navy might gain over the other.

It was this haggling over details which so got on the nerves of Charles G. Dawes. His hatred of naval experts was so deep-rooted that when Captain William Galbraith, his naval *attaché*, came in one day with a sheaf of clippings gathered during the régime of Ambassador Alanson B. Houghton, Dawes flung them into the fireplace. Captain Galbraith's face turned purple, then white. He rang the Ambassador's bell, told the office boy to take the file from the fireplace, placed it on the Ambassador's table, and stalked out.

That was the last Dawes ever was to see of American naval experts.

But the British admirals, perhaps in retribution for the insult to their American colleague, were to plague His Excellency for many months. Dawes had explained his anathema for admirals to Ramsay MacDonald, and his friend Mac had expressed profound agreement. All discussions of cruisers, destroyers, and submarines would take place directly between them, he said, and with no other aid than ordinary common sense—plus, of course, the advice of the First Lord of the Admiralty.

To fill that post, MacDonald had picked a good safe party man. Albert V. Alexander was a person of humble origin who had gained an important position in the Labor party through his management of the coöperative movement; and many an arch-Tory shuddered at the idea of a "grocer" heading His Majesty's navy. But the high officers in the Admiralty only smiled. They had had more difficult First Lords than Alexander to win over, and they had never failed. Their strategy was to be particularly gracious to the former grocer. There was nothing they could not do for him. He was escorted on a round of the navy-yards. He was taken out to inspect his battleships. He was piped up the companionway—a new sensation for an ex-grocer clerk. Guards of honor presented arms. Guns boomed. Admirals saluted. Within six weeks A. V. Alexander had become more naval-minded than his most dyed-in-the-wool admiral and was eating out of their hands.

The result was that the MacDonald-Dawes plan to leave the admirals on the side lines struck a snag. During every conversation at No. 10 Downing Street, Alexander either participated or was called in afterward. And he, in turn, served as a glorified messenger boy between No. 10 Downing Street and the Admiralty. The sea lords were consulted on everything.

Dawes, who soon discovered how he was being thwarted, used to storm and rage.

"To hell with the experts!" he once shouted, shaking his fist in the face of Britain's pacifist Prime Minister. "Haven't we got good will? Don't we want to get together?"

Invariably MacDonald agreed. But, he added, after all the navy is the navy and it is rather difficult to get around these fellows without rousing the entire Empire against you. So, on more than one occasion Dawes summoned Hugh Gibson from his comatose Embassy in Belgium, and Gibson would endeavor to pacify his irate colleague by showing him how the proposals which he, Dawes, had made in 1929, were identical with those made by him, Gibson, in 1927; and that not even the most incurable optimist could expect the British Admiralty to change its view in less than a decade.

But the British Admiralty had changed.

It was preserving a completely open mind on the most important policy affecting the two great sea powers of the world, only to find that this policy was the only thing which the United States was not willing to discuss.

The principle of Freedom of the Seas had dragged the United States into one war with Great Britain in 1812. It had come close to causing a break between Britain and the North during the Civil War. It had caused Secretary Lansing to direct even more vigorous notes to Great Britain during one period in the World War than the United States sent to Germany. And the British Admiralty dreaded it as the one thing which might draw the British and American fleets into another conflict. More than anything else the Admiralty feared that its fleet might be called upon to enforce a League of Nations blockade against an aggressor nation, and that the United States, outside Geneva's pale, might attempt to break that blockade. Contemplation of this was bad enough with the American fleet in its present condition, but with parity achieved through the brand-new 10,000 ton, eight-inch-gun cruisers proposed by the Navy Department, American opposition to a blockade would constitute a challenge almost inevitably leading to war.

The Admirals also asked the hypothetical, but to them very real, question of the effect on British trade should the United States put into practice the British principle of the search and seizure. What they particularly had in mind was the drive of American imperialism toward Latin America, the struggle for oil, the fight for markets.

"Suppose," the Admirals argued, "that the United States should become involved in a conflict in Nicaragua, in Mexico, in any part of the Western Hemisphere. In the blockade which would be sure to eventuate, British shipping either would require the militant protection of His Majesty's navy or else British shipping would be driven from Latin American waters.

"Therefore, the only sane solution to the whole naval question of naval rivalry," the Admirals told MacDonald, "is to revise the world's outworn interpretation of the Freedom of the Seas."

All of this struck a most responsive cord in the heart of Britain's emotionalist Prime Minister. Being one who invariably acts more on impulse than reason, MacDonald had not gone into the ramifications of the Admiralty's arguments, but, prompted chiefly by the sentimental belief that no nation should deprive another of the essentials of life, had arrived at the same conclusion.

These ideas, when presented to Ambassador Dawes, however, got nowhere. The Ambassador assumed his most hard-boiled manner and decreed that the moot question of Freedom of the Seas was not at all pertinent to the things he wanted to talk about. And because MacDonald by this time had come to be a little suspicious of how far his friend Charley was representing his own views or those of his government, he cabled Sir Esme Howard to do some informal reconnoitering in Washington.

Sir Esme had read in the newspapers that the Senate had passed a resolution requesting the President to call a conference on the Freedom of the Seas. He had also read that Senator Borah, chairman of the Foreign Relations Committee, was the author of this resolution. And having had a long and intimate friendship with the Senator.

Sir Esme went up to his office one afternoon to find out just what he and other Senators thought regarding the question.

Probably no one ever would have considered anything wrong with this had not Albert W. Fox written an article in the *Washington Post* next morning charging the British Ambassador with going over the State Department's head and meddling with the legislative branch of the government. Poor Sir Esme read about his misdemeanor at breakfast and hastened to make official explanations to Secretary Stimson. The latter issued a ponderously worded statement denying that the British Ambassador ever had discussed Freedom of the Seas with Senator Borah.

But the denial only served to make important an otherwise trivial incident.

Senator Borah had stated that Freedom of the Seas was discussed. Secretary Stimson stated that it was not. A controversy is always news, and this particular controversy had as its only result the shrouding of the State Department in a complete veil of secrecy as far as Freedom of the Seas was concerned.

The reason for the mystery was not so much that Mr. Hoover and Mr. Stimson opposed the thesis of the British Admiralty, but that they did not know whether they opposed it or not. Nor was there any solidified body of opinion in the United States to guide them. There was the Borah-Swanson group in the Senate which wanted the United States to hold out for the traditional right of the United States to trade with any enemy despite a blockade. There was also the Shotwell-church-peace group which wanted the United States to agree not to trade with an aggressor nation against which the League of Nations was enforcing a blockade. And finally there were those in and out of the State Department who pointed to American trade and American investments now as far-flung as those of the British Empire, and argued that American policy, therefore, should be molded closely after the British.

This multiplicity of American views resulted in an absolute zero. Mr. Stimson and his State Department were convinced only of one thing: that under no circumstances could they afford to risk a discussion of Freedom of the Seas. Such a discussion, they reasoned, not only would result in a cleavage of domestic opinion, but also would throw any international conference into inextricable confusion.

So that Charley Dawes, in refusing to discuss this question with his friend Mac, for once at least was obeying instructions.

In the end, the only thing that Charley was willing to discuss was the concrete, hard-and-fast question of how many 10,000 ton, eight-inch-gun cruisers the United States was going to have, as compared with the number of cruisers for Great Britain. Regarding this also, Dawes was acting on instructions. Mr. Stimson had evolved the idea that big oaks out of little acorns grow, and had decided that sweeping naval limitation could be obtained only by isolating one germ in the disease of naval rivalry, killing it, and then isolating another.

So he began with cruisers.

In doing this, however, Messrs. Hoover and Stimson ran headlong into the naval experts whom Mr. Dawes had sought to avoid. At first the Admirals, despite a considerable gnashing of teeth, were kept on the sidelines. The President and his Secretary of State concurred in this just as heatedly as did their Ambassador to the Court of St. James's. But before they had realized it, a tremendous hue and cry, instigated by the Admirals themselves, went up from the jingo press.

"The United States is giving away its shirt!" screamed the *Chicago Tribune*, the *New York Herald-Tribune* and the Hearst newspapers. "Naval officers are being side-

tracked for ignorant diplomats. The only people qualified
to pass on naval disarmament are naval officers themselves."

So the Admirals woke up on the morning of August
14th to find themselves invited to breakfast at the White
House. Several breakfasts followed, each interspersed by
periods of sometimes acrimonious debate between the State
Department and the Navy, during which the naval experts completely justified all that Charley Dawes ever had
said about them, and during one of which the belligerent
Secretary of the Navy gave vent to an explosion of New
England expletives against all diplomats, turned on his
heel, and walked out.

The chief haggling-point in the debate was the "yardstick."

Mr. Hoover had discovered this to be a word beautifully adapted to the headlines. It was easy for newspaper
copy desks to handle. It was something which made the
man in the street think that naval negotiations really were
getting somewhere. But when it came down to actually applying the yardstick to the fighting strength of an eight-
inch-gun cruiser as against one carrying six-inch guns, Mr.
Hoover found more varieties of opinion among his Admirals than barnacles on one of their ships. There was
only one point on which they agreed. If Britain was to
have a larger number of six-inch-gun cruisers than the
United States, then the United States, in turn, must have
a larger number of eight-inch-gun vessels than Great
Britain.

The six-inch-gun cruiser, the Admirals repeated in
monotonous sing-song, is peculiarly suited to the needs
of the far-flung British Empire. It carries ample fuel for
the short distances between Britain's many naval bases.
It carries a gun powerful enough to cope with Britain's
recalcitrant colonies. It is cheaper and more efficient to
operate. But for the United States, with only three naval

bases at widely scattered points in the Pacific, the six-inch-gun cruiser carries much too little fuel. Furthermore, the Admirals continued, its gun is no match for the giant passenger liners of the British mercantile fleet already equipped with reinforced deck plates for mounting six-inch guns in wartime. Therefore, the Admirals concluded, a large number of eight-inch-gun cruisers is absolutely essential, in fact imperative and indispensable to compensate for British superiority in smaller vessels and to prevent the United States from committing strategic suicide.

But when it came to measuring the fighting strength of an eight-inch-gun vessel against a six-inch, the Admirals got so tangled up in details, that gun calibers, cruising radii and armor plate completely obscured the major issue of Anglo-American friendship. In the middle of this they allowed themselves to be goaded into frenzied fury by Joseph P. Cotton, Under Secretary of State, who reminded them that the eight-inch-gun vessel was totally untried as far as the American navy was concerned, and that perhaps they should build one and sail it around a bit before putting all their eggs in one basket.

The Admirals did not know at the time how close Cotton, came to hitting the nail on the head. They did not know that the first five of their prize eight-inch-gun cruisers were to crack their stern-posts and be sent back to the shipyards for repairs at $30,000 each. Nor did they know that these same cruisers were to roll so badly that the aim of the brand new eight-inch guns danced up and down against the horizon like jo-jo tops, necessitating a return trip to the shipyards for bilge keels and rolling tanks.

And not knowing that they would have to eat dirt, some of the Admirals got so bitter against Mr. Stimson that they started dishing out subterranean propaganda against him, and even cast aspersions on his war record.

In the end, the American Admirals proved just as great a stumbling-block to Mr. Stimson as the British Admiralty did to Mr. MacDonald. The latter gentleman, caught between his own desire to achieve something substantial in the field of disarmament and the insistence of permanent British officialdom on "gaining something for Britain," knew not which way to turn.

Upon one thing, however, MacDonald had definitely made up his mind. Regardless of British officialdom, he was going to carry out the long cherished plan of a trip to America.

But as the summer dragged on and the telegrams between Washington and London over cruiser tonnages became longer and more complicated, it became increasingly apparent that this trip was going to be difficult to make. British public opinion, stirred up by Edward Price Bell's subtle prodding of the press, was for it one hundred per cent. But two other important factors stood in the way. One was the leading members of MacDonald's own Cabinet. The other was those members of Mr. Hoover's Cabinet who had anything to do with naval negotiations. MacDonald's chief Cabinet advisers were convinced that the trip should not be made unless Mr. Hoover granted advance concessions to Great Britain. Ambassador Dawes and Mr. Stimson, on the other hand, wanted a cruiser agreement virtually signed, sealed, and delivered before letting the British premier make the pilgrimage to Washington.

In taking this stand they were motivated by two things. One and perhaps least important was an anxiety lest American public opinion let its hopes soar during MacDonald's coming, only to have them dashed by naval failure afterward. The other was the realization that MacDonald had his heart set on making the trip, that he was in a tight place politically, and that they could squeeze almost anything they wanted from him before they let him set foot on American soil.

The main thing which they wanted to squeeze from MacDonald was tonnage reduction; and Mr. Hoover wanted this badly. He had made the mistake of announcing to the press that one of the main achievements of his naval-limitation program was economy, and the taxpaying public, always in quest of relief from its burden, had received the announcement with huzzahs. As the negotiations progressed, however, it became as plain to Mr. Hoover as the nose on his face that parity with Great Britain could be attained only by building up to the British fleet or else persuading the British fleet to scale down. The first alternative meant the sacrifice of Mr. Hoover's economy program. The second meant the sacrifice of good British ships. Both were difficult of accomplishment. To build up to the British meant the construction not only of all fifteen of the eight-inch-gun cruisers authorized by Congress—of which only eight had been appropriated for—but also the construction of several smaller cruisers in addition. This was anything but economy, and Mr. Hoover shrank from the task of breaking the news to an economy-expectant public. The second alternative was the almost impossible one of persuading an imperialistic British Admiralty to scrap vessels already built and allegedly vital to Empire defense—all to help a rival navy achieve the two incompatible goals of parity and economy.

How impossible was the latter can be gathered from the fact that several leaders in MacDonald's Cabinet still were urging their Premier to sell naval parity for something more substantial than a mere reduction of tonnage; to ask as his price at least a settlement of that vexing problem—the Freedom of the Seas. Such materialists in his Cabinet as Philip Snowden and A. V. Alexander were openly opposed to their Premier's good-will aspirations. Arthur Henderson, a dreamer and pacifist of the MacDonald type, was a little hurt that he had been left in the background, and joined the chorus who demanded that Hoover at least be required to express himself on the question of Freedom of the Seas. Even Lord Thomson, MacDonald's most intimate friend, when asked to accompany him to the United States for a general disarmament discussion, threw up his hands.

"Qui trop embrasse, mal étreint," Thomson replied. "You have done a big thing so far; for God's sake don't spoil it by wanting too much. People like to talk peace and disarmament, but the moment you try to pin them down to real accomplishment, you will get the strongest opposition in every country—even the United States. Every admiral, general, and air marshal will be against you, as will the munitions and steel manufacturers, and in the long run the press.

"If you are satisfied with moderate results, do what the American capitalists desire. Place American and British relations on a new basis of coöperation and let it go at that. As far as I am concerned I would rather resign from the Cabinet than go with you to Washington for a general disarmament discussion."

It was now late August. The MacDonald pilgrimage, if ever to be consummated, had to take place within the next six weeks. An immediate decision was necessary.

But the naval negotiations still were in complete deadlock.

The American Admirals were holding out for twenty-one big-gun cruisers, against fifteen for the British, giving the British a dubious supremacy in small-gun cruisers in return. Mr. Hoover and Mr. Stimson were as vigorously opposed to this as was the British Admiralty. The idea of building more than fifteen cruisers looked to them like political suicide. The British, after considerable pressure from MacDonald, were willing to accept fifteen big-gun cruisers for both fleets and said that it was entirely up to the United States whether its navy built up to British strength in small-gun cruisers or whether it didn't.

To the ordinary individual, the British thesis did not look like an unfair proposition. The British had their vessels built and in action. The United States was bargaining with mere blueprints. Many British admirals deemed it highly unlikely that the American navy would ever persuade Congress to appropriate the money for parity even if granted, and subsequent events proved that they were right.

Obviously the British had the best of the bargaining position as far as ships were concerned. But—and this for the moment was much more important—Mr. MacDonald wanted to come to the United States. He wanted to come to the United States so badly that during the last week in August he secretly booked reservations for himself and his daughter Ishbel on the S.S. *Berengaria* sailing from Southampton September 28th, and made arrangements with Sir Esme Howard for his program in Washington.

Apparently there was no doubt in Mr. MacDonald's mind that he was coming to the United States.

But on August 30th, when the *Baltimore Sun* published these secret plans, they received Mr. Stimson's prompt and unqualified denial. Mr. Stimson knew how badly Mr. MacDonald wanted to come to Washington. He knew how much it meant to MacDonald's political future. And he knew that he still did not have from the British Admiralty cruiser figures which would satisfy both the American navy and the American public.

So naval negotiations dragged on for twelve more days.

Finally at one o'clock in the morning of September 12th,

after an all day and most of the night argument between Secretary Stimson's diplomats and Secretary Adams' admirals, the State Department sent a code cable to Ambassador Dawes, by which the two countries came close to naval agreement. The cable was in reply to one received from MacDonald in which the Admiralty, prodded by their Prime Minister's desire for transatlantic travel, set forth the most favorable terms they had yet propounded. With the exception of one point, they were acceptable to the United States. The terms included:

Lengthening the age-limit of battleships.

Reduction of battleship tonnage by failure to replace certain ships when they reached their age limit.

Fixation of a gross tonnage limit for destroyers and submarines, leaving each nation free, within certain broad limits, to build the type of vessel best suited to its own defense.

Provision that in case no naval agreement was reached with France and Italy, the other countries could increase their tonnage proportionately in the event of French and Italian increases.

A tie-up between the Kellogg Pact and the naval agreement.

Parity between the American and British fleets.

The one point which remained undecided was the exact number of eight-inch-gun cruisers to be built by Great Britain and the United States.

"This means," said Under Secretary Cotton, "that we are near enough to an agreement to have Mr. MacDonald come over here."

Mr. MacDonald wasted no time in confirming this. A few hours after the receipt of the State Department's cable he announced that he would sail for the United States on September 28th.

The long period of Anglo-American courtship was bearing fruit.

2. ON THE LOG AT THE RAPIDAN

When Ramsay MacDonald tried to book passage to Stockholm in order to attend a Socialist Peace Conference in 1915, no ship's crew could be found willing to man a boat on which he set his pacifist foot.

But now that he was Prime Minister of Great Britain, it was different. Aboard the *Berengaria* thirteen years later, nothing on that gigantic liner was too good for him. The Prince of Wales' suite was at his disposal. The chef had gone to great pains to familiarize himself with the Prime Minister's favorite Scotch dishes. The steward, learning of MacDonald's weakness for port wine, had stocked up with the best London could offer. For to every member of the ship's crew, to every workman in Great Britain, to many Laborites in other parts of the Empire, the pilgrimage of Ramsay MacDonald was one in which they played a vital part. "Mac" was their man. Like them, he had roamed the streets of London without a shilling in his pocket. Like them he was suckled in a bleak stone cottage, had wrung his boyhood living from a rocky soil, had struggled through the vicissitudes of a sometimes unkind fate until finally he had become the incarnation of their own hopes and dreams.

Mac was their man. They had put him in office. They had brought him to America. They were proud of him, proud of themselves for achieving him. And as he boarded the welcoming ship *Macom*, and stood on her deck in top-hat and cutaway, hundreds of the *Berengaria's* crew stood at the portholes.

"Good-by," chorused three stewardesses, scarcely a yard from their Prime Minister's elbow.

"Good-by," echoed a dozen cooks and dishwashers amidships. They were Cockneys and Scots and Irish and there was something in their voices—something that must have made Ramsay MacDonald know how proud they were of the man whom they had made the leader of their Empire.

"Good-by," he called back, and his voice was very low, very distinct, and very personal.

Twenty minutes after Ramsay MacDonald set foot on the tip end of lower Manhattan he had completely won the city which then made a specialty of welcoming transatlantic fliers and Channel-swimmers, kings and queens, premiers and potentates and which had become a little fed up with doing it. MacDonald met every hazard put in the path of a distinguished visitor and took them beautifully. He stood on the bridge of the *Macom* as it steamed up the bay, gave a message to the American people through the microphone, waved good-by until his arm ached, gazed into a glaring sun and in general won his way into the heart of the most exacting photographer. He stood in the *Macom's* steaming cabin facing a hundred newspapermen who wanted to know about unemployment, the Scotch heather in his buttonhole, a message of greeting for Canada, what he would talk about with President Hoover, and the time he came to America last to thank the eighty-three-year-old lady in Concord, Massachusetts, who had been so kind to his wife during the MacDonald honeymoon.

And although MacDonald once had been deported from Belgium as a pacifist, was expelled by his golf club, and had the word "traitor" painted on the wall of his home at Lossiemouth, he did not bat an eye when the military aide of Secretary Stimson greeted him with all the military pomp and folderol of a European princeling.

Ramsay was even equal to the bibulous breathing of His

Honor the Mayor, the array of top-hats which crowded into the Aldermanic Chamber to give him the freedom of the city, and the speech of Master of Ceremonies Hector Fuller who addressed him as the "Prime Minister of the United States."

It was in his reply to all this that MacDonald really captured New York.

He began very simply:

"How is it possible for me by words to convey to you the deep emotions in my heart as a result of your welcome?"

This might have gone down as usual gush to the ordinary New Yorker to whom visiting celebrities have become mere commonplace. But there was something vibrant in the quality of MacDonald's voice which left no doubt as to his sincerity.

"I come on a mission of peace," he continued. "I believe that while I was still far away there was a desire in your hearts to bless the relations between Great Britain and the United States so that we together could be an example to a world in the pursuit of peace.

"Standing here with Secretary Stimson I think I can say that nation speaks to nation. We are not individuals. We represent our people. We stand here this morning speaking to each other—greeting each other. You represent the United States. I represent Great Britain."

Then the Prime Minister of Great Britain did what for anyone with less simplicity, less sincerity, would have turned his audience against him.

He was being welcomed in the wealthiest city in the world. He had in his audience some of the wealthiest men in the world. Facing him were Adolph Ochs, millionaire publisher; Edmond Guggenheim, copper king; Felix Warburg, wizard of finance; Jesse Isador Straus, the world's largest retail merchant; Patrick Crowley and Daniel Willard, presidents of two of the world's largest railroads.

To this assemblage the former Scotch school-teacher proceeded, as naturally as if he were addressing a classroom, to preach a sermon on wealth.

"Through the gateway of New York," he said, "millions of people have passed, seeking not only riches but nourishment to their minds and souls. The United States is not merely a geographical and material expression. My friends —I hope I may call you so since you have given me this scroll—among the traditions you will always cherish are the traditions of the exile—the seeker—those who lifted up their eyes and looked at the West, and finding the hand of the past too strong, set sail across the Atlantic, seeking peace and comfort for their bodies and souls.

"Your millions can be counted up to untold numbers of dollars, but that which is more precious than all else in your possession is your own soul.

"I have come here to meet your President, not to advance our material possessions, but in order that we two nations, most powerful in the present and more powerful in the future—may shake hands; not to pledge ourselves to any alliance, but to talk over our common aspirations, and in order that whenever the work of the world has to be done we will be found side by side doing it."

Judging from the reaction upon that sophisticated audience, the Prime Minister of Great Britain had won the American public even before he arrived in Washington.

There is a routine ceremony for the entertainment of distinguished visitors at the nation's capital and almost every Washingtonian knows it by heart. It begins with an assemblage of top-hats at Track 20 of the Union Station, a long streak of crimson carpet, a Marine Corps salute, a battalion of the 16th Field Artillery, two troops of the Third Cavalry, the "Star-spangled Banner" and a host of photographers outside the President's waiting-room. It includes a call at the White House at 5 P.M., a formal dinner at 8, a wreath laid on the Tomb of the Unknown

Soldier, a pilgrimage to Mount Vernon, a call on the Vice-President and another on the Chief Justice of the Supreme Court. Except to change the national anthem according to the nationality of the visitor, the routine never varies.

Nor did it in the case of J. Ramsay MacDonald. That magnetic gentleman went through it, however, with such enthusiasm, such charm, such appreciation for all those whom he met, that *blasé* Washington lined the sidewalks, stormed the corridors of the State Department, and followed him about as if this were the first time any visitor had received any attention from any administration whatsoever.

When he called at the "Throne Room" decorated with the Indian trophies of Charley Curtis, it was an event. When he addressed a luncheon of the Overseas Writers, he almost converted those hard-boiled minions of a capitalist press to Socialism. And when he appeared before the Senate, his victory was more complete than when his British forebears rolled barrels of tar under the gallery of the House and Senate and burned the Capitol to the ground. Rear Admiral Sir George Cockburn, the last British victor, had plumped his muddy boots upon the rostrum, brandished the Speaker's gavel, and shouted:

"Shall this harbor of Yankee Democracy be burned? All for it say aye!"

MacDonald had stepped before the rostrum as much at home as if he were in his own House of Commons, and, his voice vibrant with emotion, his words brimming with poetry, had wrung from his audience a greater response than the storm of "ayes" which greeted Admiral Cockburn.

It was Ramsay MacDonald's day. In fact, it was his six days. During the whole of his visit, particularly during his week-end with Mr. Hoover at the Rapidan, this son of a Scottish servant girl was the focal point of the entire United States.

The Rapidan meeting was the high-water mark in Anglo-American friendship. It was the climax of a long summer during which the United States and Great Britain climbed slowly up the hill of better understanding, attained the Hoover-MacDonald conversation, and shortly thereafter began slowly sliding down again.

What happened when the heads of the two English-speaking nations discussed their joint problems on a log in the Virginia forest has never been disclosed in detail. There was no stenographer present, in fact no member of either the Hoover or MacDonald party sat with the two men. No records exist in the State Department regarding the conversation, and if either Mr. Hoover or Mr. Mac-Donald made any notes as to what they said to each other, those notes have never come to light.

However, by piecing together information obtained from the associates of the two statesmen, it is possible to give a fairly accurate though not infallible picture of what they talked about at this historic meeting.

The talk began in the Hoover cabin which stands between Mill Run and Laurel Run in the fork where the two streams form the Rapidan. There the two men sat until eleven, when they decided to go outside and enjoy the brilliant sunshine of the October morning. Walking down the Rapidan, they found, according to Presidential Secretary Akerson, considerable water in the pools. They stopped to look at the fish, but did no fishing, the season having closed two months previously. A mile and a half downstream they found a log overhanging the creek, where they stopped and talked for the remainder of the morning.

The two men rambled through the whole gamut of Anglo-American relations, Mr. MacDonald being the aggressor in most of the conversation. One thing was particu-

larly on his mind, the very thing that Lord Thomson had
warned him must not be discussed—general world disarmament. MacDonald explained to Hoover the bitterness which existed between France and Germany, the
danger always facing Britain of war on the Continent.
He emphasized the ambition of his government—after the
restoration of Anglo-American harmony—to settle this
vexing problem.

Mr. MacDonald did not entirely forget, however, Lord
Thomson's warning. He proposed no sweeping solution
of disarmament, sought only to enlist Hoover's interest
in the problem, persuade him that the London Naval
Conference must be a part of the general scheme of disarmament and fit into the major problem later to be
solved at Geneva. In this Mr. Hoover heartily concurred.

Another question on Mr. MacDonald's mind was the
danger of alienating the French. The latter, he reminded
Hoover, were a suspicious race. Especially were they suspicious of too amicable relations between the United
States and Great Britain, particularly with a Labor Government in power. And since their coöperation was essential to any naval agreement, Mr. MacDonald urged that
every precaution be taken to placate French susceptibilities. This was a point which the Prime Minister himself
never would have thought of—and he promptly forgot it
afterward—had it not been drilled into him by his Foreign Office. Permanent officials of the latter, having to
deal with France during both the open amours of Sir
Austen Chamberlain and the cold aloofness of the Labourites, were worried over the French resentment against the
summer's passionate Anglo-American courtship, and to
dispel this they had prepared invitations to a five-power
naval conference to be issued to France, Italy, and Japan
the moment MacDonald had clinched this point with
Hoover. As a result, a cable from Washington that very
afternoon notified the British Foreign Office to release

the invitations. The Quai d'Orsay had a copy in its hands the next day.

These and many other things the two men discussed during that brilliant October morning on the Virginia mountain-side.

And then Ramsay MacDonald brought forward his *pièce de résistance.* It was one which he had worked out all by himself on the ship coming over, and he was convinced that it would put the final seal of sincerity upon British-American friendship and make his trip the most outstanding event in the history of Anglo-American relations.

He proposed to Mr. Hoover that Great Britain dismantle all her naval bases in American waters.

With this accomplished, he suggested, complete agreement on cruisers would be easy; in fact, the two countries might then settle their age-old controversy over the Freedom of the Seas. Great Britain, he said, was quite ready to revise her traditional policy of the right of seizure and search.

So far as is known, Mr. MacDonald did not ask for any *quid pro quo* from Mr. Hoover. He put forward his idea as a magnificent gesture, an offering upon the altar of Anglo-American friendship for which he asked nothing concrete in return.

Mr. Hoover, naturally, was delighted. Also he was not to be outdone. Once before when the British Prime Minister had announced delays in naval construction as a gesture toward Anglo-American understanding, Mr. Hoover had matched it with an announcement of similar American delays. So now he telephoned to Washington and asked Under Secretary of State Cotton, chief expert on cruiser negotiations, to rush to the Rapidan. Also he telephoned his secretary, George Akerson, that a joint *communiqué* would be issued shortly and that the newspapermen might expect a most important announcement.

Early the next morning the President of the United States and the Prime Minister of Great Britain motored back through the Virginia countryside. They had enjoyed a good rest. They had come to be rather warm friends. And after three months of hesitation and hectic negotiations they had brought their two countries to an understanding on all major differences.

And so, arriving in Washington, one went back to his desk and the other back to his round of ceremonies, both confident enough of their achievement to leave the remaining details of Anglo-American friendship to be mopped up by their subordinates.

But just as a precaution and because his secretary, Sir Robert Van Sittart, demanded it, MacDonald did get Philip Snowden on the transatlantic telephone and tell him of his offer to dismantle British naval bases in American waters.

Under Secretary Cotton, meanwhile, was putting pressure on the Admirals to rush through a final agreement on cruisers before MacDonald's departure.

Early the next afternoon it became apparent that all was not going well with the Hoover-MacDonald honeymoon. The magnificent gesture with which Mr. Hoover wanted to reciprocate had been checked at the elbow. First indication of disaster came when Charles Francis Adams, Secretary of the Navy, rushed up to Mr. Cotton's office. Ordinarily Mr. Adams did not rush. Ordinarily he did not come to see Mr. Cotton, no matter what his speed. Mr. Cotton was only an Under Secretary, and rather an obnoxious Under Secretary as far as the navy was concerned. But on this particular occasion Mr. Adams not only came to see Mr. Cotton, but also he rushed. For when Mr. Adams was fighting the cause of his Admirals, he was capable of doing many things, one of them being an exhibition of the most adamantine streak of stubbornness possessed by any member of the Cabinet.

Mr. Stimson, when he heard of Charley Adams' visit, came into Mr. Cotton's room, listened quietly to what he had to say, and then went across the street to tell the President about it. Mr. Cotton picked up his hat and went down to the Navy Department with Secretary Adams. He wanted to get the Admirals' story first hand. The story which the Admirals told him was rather long, but ran something like this:

The navy had no intention of surrendering its demand for twenty-one big-gun cruisers. It had no intention of surrendering even three of them. It had no intention of surrendering them even if Great Britain dismantled its naval bases in American waters.

These bases constituted no threat to the United States whatsoever. The American fleet could take them overnight. The dry dock at St. George, Bermuda, was built shortly after the Civil War and could not handle vessels larger than small cruisers. Bermuda's two old forts were manned by only four hundred British army regulars, plus sixty-three naval officers and engineers, and could be wiped out by a few volleys from a modern battleship. The Canadian dry dock at Halifax recently had been reduced, while that at Esquimault in Puget Sound was merely a skeleton organization. Canadian naval forces had been demobilized except for five hundred men belonging to the Naval College. The Canadian navy consisted of two destroyers, four armed trawlers, and a motor-launch. Jamaica, the nearest British naval base to the Panama Canal, had defenses no better than those of Bermuda. The harbor at Kingston would admit larger vessels, and had a fueling base for warships, but no dry dock. Seven hundred and fifty British regulars were stationed at the fort, which was armed with one heavy battery. Port Castries in the Windward Islands consisted only of a naval anchorage, and lacked defenses, dry dock, or even a fueling station.

The dismantling of these bases not only would remove no threat to the United States, but might create a dangerous precedent against all naval fortifications in the Caribbean. It might interfere with the navy's right to lease Great Corn and Little Corn Islands off the coast of Nicaragua. It might interfere with American treaty rights to establish a naval base in the Gulf of Fonseca. It might spoil the plan, long toyed with by the navy, of using Samaná Bay in Santo Domingo and the Mole of St. Nicholas.

No! The dismantling of British naval bases in American waters not only was valueless as far as cruiser bargaining went, but was something devoutly to be avoided.

Apparently Ramsay MacDonald was biting at a gnat.

How much the Admirals' opinion would have weighed with Mr. Hoover remains a question which never will be answered.

That night there was a reception at the British Embassy. It was the most grandiose occasion since the peak of war-time prosperity. The huge old building on Connecticut Avenue, since replaced by a gasoline filling-station, was packed with one of the most important conglomerations of personages ever found under one Washington roof. Alice Roosevelt Longworth, just returned from Cincinnati, laughed at the way she had sent regrets for the White House dinner the night before as a back-handed slap at Dolly Gann. Rosy-cheeked Ishbel MacDonald attracted more bachelors than the champagne buffet. In a side salon younger members of the Embassy staff showed gallant impartiality in amusing dignified dowagers and whirling débutantes of the season.

In the middle of one of these whirls, Sir Adrian Baillie, second secretary, suddenly stopped. He bowed to his partner, turned on his heel, and followed an embassy *attaché* who had tapped him on the shoulder. Upstairs in the Ambassador's study, where he was led, was a long code telegram from London. Sir Adrian and other secretaries set to work decoding it.

The telegram was from Philip Snowden, acting Prime Minister during MacDonald's absence, and was the written confirmation of a telephone conversation with MacDonald a little earlier. It stated that after receiving word of the proposed dismantling of all British naval bases in American waters, Snowden had called a meeting of War, Navy and Air Ministers, together with the Minister of Foreign Affairs. They listened in stark amazement as he unfolded the general plan of their chief.

Not one of them ever had heard of it before.

Probably, they concluded, it was something Ramsay had concocted while on the highseas. A. V. Alexander said the Admiralty never would accept it. Lord Thomson described the idea as "crazy." He said the British public opinion was not ready for it. Snowden and Arthur Henderson saw defeat and the end of the Labor Government if the proposal were put before the House of Commons.

So they telephoned and cabled Ramsay MacDonald to that effect.

The next morning there was a hurried conference between the two promoters of harmony at the Rapidan. The *communiqué* which they had drafted was rewritten. All mention of naval bases or the Freedom of the Seas was omitted. Instead the two statesmen reëmphasized the new era of peace ushered in by the Kellogg Pact. They underscored the importance of a naval agreement as a nucleus for general disarmament. They pumped additional diplomatic verbiage into their statement and let it go at that. To newspapermen who had been promised something spectacular the *communiqué* was a dud. To the man in the street, however, it was not. Ramsay MacDonald had won the American public. His victory began from the moment he set foot in New York, was in no way lessened by the petifogging red tape of an official Washington reception, and was considerably heightened when he entertained the Philadelphia physicians who had saved his life two years before.

American admirals and the British Cabinet had cramped a magnificent gesture. War debts, commercial rivalry, trouble in the Far East, were to tarnish the effect of the Rapidan. But when he sailed from New York, a great many people had come to take seriously the words of Ramsay MacDonald when he arrived.

"I have come," he said, "in order that whenever the work of the world has to be done, we will be found side by side doing it."

3. Mr. Stimson Embarks for London

When Henry Lewis Stimson boarded the S.S. *George Washington* on January 9, 1930, en route to the London Naval Conference, he made no effort to conceal the belief that he was undertaking the crowning achievement of his career. People who were inclined to underestimate the value of the conference, or who, perhaps, did not know Mr. Stimson, might have got the idea that his career prior to that date had been barren of achievement.

This, however, was not the case.

Henry L. Stimson had squeezed into his sixty-three years considerably more than the average young man born of aristocratic ancestry and with a silver spoon in his mouth. He had dabbled disastrously, though with deadly seriousness, in New York State politics. He had been defeated for Governor on the Republican ticket in the same election which saw Franklin D. Roosevelt, a dilettante youth just out of Harvard, win a seat in the state Senate; and he had been made Taft's Secretary of War as a reward for his political martyrdom. As Elihu Root's partner, he amassed a fortune at law, discovered that the accumulation of mere wealth can be the most empty occupation in the world, and in the past three years had stepped back into the public limelight, first as rescuer of Mr. Kellogg's marines in Nicaragua, then as Governor-General of the Philippines, and finally as Secretary of State.

During this career, Mr. Stimson had come to be a person of unique and sometimes conflicting character. As Secretary of War, for instance, he was one of the most slavishly militaristic executives ever to bring joy to the hearts of the generals who really rule the War Department. As a private citizen beyond the draft age when the World War broke out, he took a training course at Plattsburg, received a lieutenant's commission, and later, as a colonel in command of the 305th Field Artillery, he served gallantly in action under generals once his subordinates.

And yet, as Secretary of State, Henry L. Stimson completely flouted the militarist precedents laid down by his predecessor, Mr. Kellogg. He waived the oath to bear arms in granting a passport to Dorothy Detzer, militant pacifist leader. He admitted to the United States the hitherto ostracized Count Karolyi, and undertook a persistent policy of withdrawing American marines from the territory of Latin American neighbors.

Few Secretaries of State ever exhibited such a weird conflict of pacifist liberalism with militarist conservatism as Henry L. Stimson.

Probably the explanation for this conflict goes back to Mr. Stimson's aristocratic forbears. His fifth great-grandfather, John Stimson, came over on the *Truelove*. John's son, George, having settled in Ipswich, Massachusetts, took down his rifle and powder-horn to fight the Indians in King Philip's War. The latter's grandson, also named George, served as captain in the French and Indian and the Revolutionary Wars, later returning to Windham, New

York, in which state the Stimsons ever since have played at politics, made money, and been proud to live.

Henry Clark Stimson, grandfather of Henry Lewis, born in 1813, became a wealthy banker and railroad president just at the period when the Morgans, the Harrimans, and the Hills were making railroad history, and Stimson's father, although under no compulsion to make a living, coupled medicine with serving his country as a captain and aide-de-camp in the Civil War. Like most Stimsons, he served it well.

Young Henry Lewis Stimson was born into a stultifying world of wealth and luxury which might have submerged him had it not been for one member of the family. Henry Albert Stimson, uncle of Henry Lewis, and over ninety years old, spent a lifetime raising seven children and becoming the most liberal Congregationalist divine of his day. Like all his family, Uncle Henry believed in service, but his service in the work of the Lord had opened broader vistas than had been available to most Stimsons, and in young Henry Lewis, who saw much of his uncle, he planted certain ideals destined later to influence the course of nations.

One of these was American responsibility in respect to the rest of the world. The strong, young Stimson felt, were born to rule. And just as his grandfather George and his grandfather John and his grandfather Henry had not shunned responsibility in the affairs of the state and nation, so young Henry came to feel that the United States could not shun responsibility for the peace and ordered prosperity of its neighbors.

And at the moment he sailed for London the two brightest stars guiding Henry L. Stimson's policy as Secretary of State were, first, the belief that the path of the United States must be steered increasingly among its fellow nations, and, second, the conviction that that path must lead resolutely toward peace. As an instrument of fulfillment for both of these, Stimson had fastened upon the Kellogg Pact with greater enthusiasm and even more devotion than the gentleman for whom it was named. Stimson was inclined to think of Frank B. Kellogg as an ineffectual old man to be avoided when he returned to Washington. But in his Pact, Stimson saw a foundation on which could be erected an edifice of world disarmament. In Manchuria and in the Chaco he had already made important contributions to that edifice and he hoped that by continued building, the United States soon could be weaned from the Harding-Coolidge policy of "power without responsibility" and finally take its seat among the council of the nations.

And as he set foot upon the S.S. *George Washington,* Mr. Stimson felt that this day was fast approaching.

Toward the goal of the London Naval Conference Mr. Stimson had been working since the day he first learned he was to become Secretary of State. He made his first move while en route home from the Philippines, when he stopped in Tokyo to discuss the importance of further naval reduction. Later he braved the heat of Washington to iron out American difficulties with the British. As a climax to that summer he hovered over the Rapidan Conference between Herbert Hoover and Ramsay MacDonald. And during the month before sailing he closeted himself in his home at Woodley to the exclusion of all the pressing problems of his State Department, and concentrated on the task ahead of him at London.

So when Henry L. Stimson remarked to Dwight Morrow, "If other delegations are as well prepared as ours, this conference cannot fail of success," he really believed what he said.

There were, of course, certain discouraging factors which had arisen between the Rapidan and his embarkation which even Mr. Stimson realized did not augur well for the success of his conference. But in the white heat of his idealism he was inclined to sweep them aside.

There was, for instance, the stubbornness of the Japanese.

It had been decided at the Rapidan that further spade-work for the London Conference should be divided between Great Britain and the United States: Mr. Stimson taking over the task of reconciling Japanese and American naval views, Mr. MacDonald undertaking to whip the French and Italians into line. In accordance with this division, the Japanese delegation had stopped in Washington to explain with meticulous politeness that they would require a cruiser ratio of seven as against ten for the United States instead of their present six. Mr. Stimson and his associates listened to these statements, entertained the Japanese at dinner, and, confident of goodwill at London, sent them on their way. They arrived at no agreement.

There were also the French.

Mr. Stimson suddenly awakened to the existence of the French shortly after the Anglo-American honeymoon was consummated. As a result, he improvised a definite policy which, in the succinct language of Under Secretary Cotton, was, "Butter up the French." The only trouble with the policy was that it came too late. Already the French had come to the conclusion that, as far as the naval conference was concerned, the cards were stacked against them. Already they had discussed ways and means of sabotaging it. So that when that great friend of France, Norman Davis, called up his friend, Joseph P. Cotton, from New York, urging that Aristide Briand also be invited to come to Washington, the State Department would have jumped at the idea had it not been too late. The French were peeved and determined to stay that way. Even unofficial suggestions that the American delegation come to Europe early and spend a few days in Paris got no glimmer of appreciation from the Quai d'Orsay.

And just to make sure that the British and American publics knew how France felt about the Rapidan honeymoon, Foreign Minister Briand set forth the French case in three thousand words of blunt diplomatic language, published exactly two weeks before Mr. Stimson sailed for London. The gist of this note was that the League of Nations had set up machinery for the reduction of armament and that France intended to stick by the League. Briand did not exactly say so, but it was easy to read into his note the obvious fact that France, with her Little Entente allies plus Poland and Belgium, easily could control the disarmament attempts of the League, while she did not at all trust the new log-rolling combine between the English-speaking peoples.

Mr. Stimson realized rather vaguely that one of the problems he might face in London was some kind of political agreement. M. Briand certainly had indicated this. But after all, Mr. Stimson figured, this was something which he need not worry about until the question arose.

Much more worrying, though much less important to the success of the Conference, were certain violent differences of opinion among the experts in Mr. Stimson's own delegation. These had cropped out chiefly over the hackneyed but ever-present question of the relative merits of the eight-inch and six-inch gun. Both schools of strategy were almost equally represented among the naval advisers of the delegation. Admiral William V. Pratt, commander of the United States fleet and one of the two chief naval advisers, favored a cruiser fleet almost equally divided between the two types of gun. Rear Admiral Hilary P. Jones, one of the oldest navy experts on disarmament and co-naval adviser with Admiral Pratt, believed in putting nearly all of the navy's cruisers into the eight-inch gun basket.

With Admiral Jones stood all the members of the General Board, including those distinguished and recalcitrant gentlemen who, during the summer, had breakfasted intermittently at the White House and stuck steadfastly by their claim that the navy must have twenty-one of these eight-inch-gun, 10,000-ton cruisers. Even during the Rapidan they had not budged from their claim. But as the date of the London Conference approached and nothing more was said to them about eight-inch-gun cruisers, Admiral Jones and the General Board began to suspect that the State Department had settled this question behind their backs.

Admiral Jones approached Senator Reed on the subject; also Admiral Pratt. Both were staunch champions of adequate American defense, but for some strange reason they evaded the question.

Suddenly the light dawned upon Hilary Jones. He was being taken to London merely as a rubber stamp. He was the decoy to win the support of the eight-inch-gun school.

The twenty-one eight-inch-gun cruisers, he suspected, already had been bartered away.

As a matter of fact, this was not the case. But Hilary Jones, sensing that something was wrong, informed Mr. Stimson that he was not going to London. Mr. Stimson was irritated. He was especially irritated when the story leaked to the press. In fact, he was so irritated that he issued a categorical denial that Admiral Jones had told him any such thing. Lyle Wilson, United Press correspondent, who had written the story, threw the denial back at Under Secretary Cotton. The latter practised diplomacy with his tongue in his cheek.

"After this treaty is signed," said he, "it will be sent to the Senate. And the Senate will call Admiral Jones to testify. You can see that a Senator asks him the proper questions."

Six months later Admiral Jones told the Senate the truth.

But just on the eve of the London Conference the truth hurt, and in order to prevent a public break in his delegation, Mr. Stimson resorted to the expediency of making Charles Francis Adams, Secretary of the Navy, one of the delegates. Charley Adams, he knew, had the complete trust of the admirals. They could depend on him that the navy would not be sold out. Under these circumstances, Hilary Jones was persuaded to go to London.

All of these worries Mr. Stimson postponed or surmounted one way or another. But there was one factor which simply could not be surmounted and which still bothered him as he stepped aboard the *George Washington*. This was the fact that at London he could obtain no naval reduction.

Politically, this was not an inviting prospect. All summer long he and the President had drummed away on the advantages of reduction. As early as Memorial Day Mr. Hoover had dwelt upon the gains—both to the taxpayer and to world peace—which his naval negotiations envisaged. Mr. Stimson himself had re-emphasized this point the very next day. And during the long, hot summer that followed, few opportunities were missed in press conferences and in public speeches to hammer home the financial and political advantages of a smaller navy.

And now it had become apparent that this much-vaunted reduction could not take place. Instead of reducing from the fifteen cruisers already appropriated for, the navy would have to build at least three additional big cruisers and some smaller ones besides.

So about a week before Mr. Stimson embarked he decided to prepare the unsuspecting public for the inevitable. All during the summer he had been working on cruisers. Battleships, already limited by the Washington Conference, had not entered the picture.

But on January 5th, four days before he sailed, Mr. Stimson summoned the press to Woodley, and switched the emphasis to battleships. Back in 1927, at the Geneva Naval Conference which marked the peak of Anglo-American rivalry, W. C. Bridgeman, First Lord of the Admiralty, had made a proposal for postponing the replacement of battleships and the reduction of their size. His ideas were scorned by the United States. From that time on the same plan was offered periodically at Geneva disarmament sessions, and each time received the full force of the American cold shoulder.

But now, faced with the necessity of finding actual saving to the taxpayer, Mr. Stimson resurrected this three-year-old proposal, brushed off the distasteful label of the Geneva Naval Conference, and brought forward the first part of it as the real reduction to be expected at London.

Battleships, he pointed out, cost about $42,000,000 each. By 1942 they would cost about $50,000,000. And by 1942, the United States, under the terms of the Washington Treaty, would have to build fifteen battleships to replace those which soon would reach the age limit. Therefore, he concluded, prolongation of the life of these monsters of the sea would mean a tremendous saving.

Mr. Stimson at last had found the reduction for which he and Mr. Hoover had been groping.

With all this behind him, and much more ahead, Henry L. Stimson boarded the ship which had carried Woodrow Wilson to the ill-fated Paris Peace Conference.

4. THE LONDON NAVAL CONFERENCE

FIRST ROUND

The Naval Conference opened in a blanket of yellow fog for which London is famous.

Members of the American delegation looked out of their windows in the Ritz and wondered if this was symbolic. They groped their way down to the House of Lords where the Conference was to open. Buses thundered out of the murky emptiness. British heroes sitting astride bronze horses loomed up as big as Westminster. King George, preceded by a retinue of torch-bearers, made his way from Buckingham Palace at a snail's pace. Even slower was the progress of Ambassador Dawes, who did not slip into his seat with the American delegation until after His Majesty had finished speaking.

Stray wisps of fog penetrated the House of Lords and pervaded its sedate gallery. Bemedaled ushers in knee breeches escorted delegates to carefully designated places. Aristide Briand paced back and forth beneath the portrait of Lord Nelson. In a neighboring aisle André Tardieu, his one-time enemy, now chief, chatted with Ramsay MacDonald. Sir Austen Chamberlain, the man who loved France like a mistress and helped to steer Britain and America to their peak of sharpest rivalry, strode past them. Stanley Baldwin, who had supported Chamberlain's policy, joined him. En route he stopped to felicitate his Labour opponent, MacDonald, who had steered Anglo-American relations back to this friendly climax. Lord Cecil, tall, stoop-shouldered, and serious, slipped past the Tories and his elder brother, Lord Salisbury, to take a place near the ranks of Labour.

Then, as quiet suddenly descended on that vast assemblage, Ramsay MacDonald appeared in the doorway with George V of England and escorted him to a golden throne in the center of the hall.

And George V, looking down at the admirals with whom he had mixed hot toddies as a carefree ensign, read a brief address in which he urged the delegates assembled to reduce the "heavy burden of armament now weighing upon the people of the world."

Just across from him as he read, Richard the Lion-hearted leaned on a lance and looked down with disapproving bewilderment.

"Since the Great War, all people have determined that human statecraft shall leave nothing undone to prevent a repetition of that grim, immense tragedy," proclaimed his successor, apparently oblivious of the disapproval.

And having said what he had to say in a forceful, quiet manner, His Majesty stepped down from his throne, looked neither to the right nor to the left, traversed the long expanse of carpet to the door, and departed. The Conference paused a moment while his throne was carried out after him—somewhat haltingly and with one perilous moment when it almost dropped on Stanley Baldwin's outstretched legs—and then was ready to proceed with business.

In the words of Arthur W. Page, the American delegation "lit in London runnin'." Its arrival had been preceded by an advance crew of career diplomats which had not overlooked a single detail of preparation. The top floor of the Ritz Hotel had been transformed into an up-to-date, bustling business office. Beds had been removed, bathtubs piled high with documents. There were ice water and a separate telephone service, run by an American operator, in every room of the delegation. Typewriters and telegraph instruments were set up in a press room. Each delegate was handed a special set of calling-cards. Messengers hurried to leave them on all the lords and ladies of London. Delegates even were provided with a pocket directory informing them where to get the best American haircuts, where to buy American pies, where to obtain the most permanent waves, where to find a heart specialist, plus the friendly tip, "On Regent Street, just below Piccadilly Circus and next to the large building under construction, is a good Hungarian restaurant."

And, having adjusted all the machinery of the Conference with a speed that left London gasping, the American delegation looked around to begin the work of limiting navies—and found itself with absolutely nothing to do.

Apparently Mr. MacDonald and his Cabinet had forgotten that there was to be a naval conference. For up until the time that Secretary Stimson arrived at Paddington Station and rushed to No. 10 Downing Street, without even going to his hotel to wash away the cinders, there was not one visible scrap of British preparation. Ramsay MacDonald had been engrossed with many other domestic problems. Coal operators were threatening to lower wages. Cotton mills in Lancashire faced the same problem. Farmers all over England were making a drive on the Labour Government. Unemployment continued unabated despite the solemn pre-election pledges of the Labourites. A recalcitrant India was objecting more violently than ever to British rule. A delegation from Egypt was en route to London to work out a new treaty. And probably most important of all, a Parliament adjourned for the Christmas holidays was about to return in a ripe mood for asking embarrassing questions about all these complications and many others besides.

No wonder that Ramsay MacDonald was busy.

No wonder also that he opened the Conference by suggesting that there be no fixed agenda, but that the five delegations follow a hit-and-miss plan of meeting whenever they felt like it and on whatever question was current. This was exactly opposite to the program followed at the Washington and Geneva Naval Conferences, but its elasticity permitted MacDonald to keep one hand on the affairs of his Empire while he juggled naval tonnages with the other.

This plan—or rather lack of plan—also permitted MacDonald to sidestep temporarily the fact that the most important piece of preparation he had promised Hoover at the Rapidan had been completely neglected.

Five minutes' talk with Premier Tardieu on the afternoon he landed in London convinced every newspaperman covering the Conference that his influence for harmony at the naval parley was analogous to that of a bull in a china-closet.

M. Tardieu explained to his friend Dwight Morrow that he felt the French were being dragged to London in order to have their naval program ridiculed before the world and to receive a public spanking. And because they did not propose to be spanked, the French announced that before they could begin to talk about sacrificing an important branch of their armed security, they must insist on compensatory political security—preferably a Mediterranean Pact. Principles, they said with characteristic French logic, must come before naval tonnages.

This hit the American delegation in a vulnerable spot. Mr. Stimson had held class-room exercises for his colleagues on every conceivable detail which might arise under the all-embracing subject of sea strength, but had completely ignored the one point without which the Conference could not succeed. A political agreement for the neutralization of the islands of the Pacific had been the key factor in the success of the Washington Conference. A political agreement for the Mediterranean powers was going to be the key factor to success at London. The press of Europe had discussed this to the exclusion of all else and yet, as the Conference opened, there appeared to be no unified American realization that this was going to make or break their Conference.

There were, of course, one or two realists in the delegation who knew what was ahead of them and did not hesitate to say that, inasmuch as Mr. Kellogg and Mr. Stimson both had led the world toward consultation during the Chaco and Manchurian threats to the Kellogg Pact, there was no reason why the United States should decline to consult in case war threatened in other quarters.

But their realism proved disastrous. At that particular moment it was too advanced for Mr. Stimson. He was for world coöperation, but wanted to take his own sweet time about admitting it. So when press reports based upon the realism of his colleagues came to his attention, the Secretary of State emitted loud exclamations of horror and promptly clamped the muzzle of secrecy upon his entire delegation.

What made matters worse, as far as the French were concerned, was a Stimsonian denial that the United States even contemplated a political agreement.

Some London skeptics doubted the sincerity of the denial, but they were wrong. The tragedy was that the denial was genuine. Henry L. Stimson ardently believed in increasing the international responsibility of the United States, but even at that late date was still under the delusion that all he needed to do was sit on the side lines and listen to the persuasive eloquence of Ramsay Mac-Donald while he argued his neighbors across the Channel into a five-power naval treaty.

Dwight Morrow, however, shared none of Stimson's delusions, and from the first day in London he became the spearhead of the drive for greater American political coöperation with Europe. Morrow had known Tardieu back in the war days when the latter was French High Commissioner in Washington. He had known him again in the post-war days when Morrow's banking firm—J. P. Morgan and Company—had come to the rescue of the French franc. And with his unique capacity for putting himself in the shoes of the other fellow, Morrow realized how Tardieu jeopardized his own political position by almost anything he did at the Naval Conference. Tardieu's ministry held office by a majority of only one. In order to keep that majority, the Premier was playing ball with

Aristide Briand, a man whose efforts toward peace were almost the antithesis of his own strident idealism, but with whom he was now thrown by a Naval Conference which everyone in France viewed as an Anglo-American frame-up and which they all wanted to see scuttled—provided France did not get the blame for scuttling it.

Adroit sabotage was the French watchword, and Dwight Morrow, realizing it, divided his time between nursing the French and trying to convince Henry L. Stimson of the danger lurking in the French frame of mind.

This was no easy job. Mr. Stimson was doomed to spend an important part of his remaining three years as Secretary of State trying to straighten out the differences between France and Italy; but at the opening of the London Naval Conference he was totally oblivious to his fate. Also he was rather annoyed that two—in his opinion—relatively unimportant countries should stand in the way of the great step toward peace which he and Ramsay MacDonald had spent so much time working out. French recalcitrance, he was inclined to think, should be dragged out into the full spotlight of a plenary session and exposed to the world.

His friend, Ramsay MacDonald, was inclined to agree with him. He had come back from the Rapidan full of good intentions to whip France into line; but after one encounter with French unwillingness to compromise without security, the ever-optimistic MacDonald had decided that this question could easily be solved in the spirit of brotherly love bound to prevail at London, and had turned to more pressing problems at home.

Now, however, the opening days of the Conference were over. The spirit of goodwill and brotherly love had been turned on with all the volume of which the dulcet tones of George V, Henry L. Stimson, and Ramsay MacDonald were capable. Still the French remained just as recalcitrant, just as logical, and just as determined that there could be no limitation of their huge cruiser-building program without a compensating pledge of security.

Moreover, the French delegation appeared to be putting across its case with the press and the public. It was well equipped to do so. It contained the two most incompatible but ingenious negotiators in France. Tardieu, speaking perfect English, an excellent judge of men, a shrewd bargainer, a dynamo of energy, could be counted upon to surrender his life before he surrendered the dot of an "i" on the French naval program—without something else in return. Briand, veteran of a dozen peace conferences and a dozen cabinets, originator of Locarno and the Pact of Paris, played an opposite, though complementary rôle. While Tardieu was discussing tonnage and gun calibers, Briand's 'cello voice was booming consultation and Mediterranean Pacts.

The combination was so effective that after one week of bucking their heads against it, MacDonald and Stimson assigned Dwight Morrow to camp on the trail of the Frenchmen while they themselves went ahead with more tangible things.

The most tangible thing they could work on was the Anglo-American naval agreement, virtually completed long before Mr. Stimson came to London. Less tangible but perhaps more important was agreement with the Japanese. David Aiken Reed was delegated to that, Ambassador Hugh Gibson was asked to coöperate with the Italians, and Mr. Stimson himself set about the task of working out the few remaining details unsettled in the Anglo-American agreement.

The chief gap in this agreement was the long-debated question as to whether the United States navy should insist upon twenty-one of the big eight-inch-gun cruisers or only eighteen, plus compensatory six-inch-gun cruisers.

That two inches in the size of a gun could rend a navy

literally asunder is hard for the average layman to understand. Yet at London this rift became an acute actuality.

Before he went to London Admiral Hilary Jones, white-
haired champion of twenty-one big-gunned cruisers, was
convinced the cards were stacked against him. Yet despite
this, he put up a valiant fight. In fairness to both cruiser
cliques, and in order that the American delegates might
get a clear picture of the eight-inch-gun battle, Secretary
Stimson held hearings. Jones and Pratt each were given a
turn to tell their story. Pratt informed the delegation that
while the eight-inch gun was better adapted for the majority of American cruisers, the six-inch gun could shoot
faster and was more effective at close range, at night or in
foggy weather. He argued that at least some cruisers should
be armed with six-inch guns in order to balance the fleet.
He concluded that the fleet might well substitute for the
three additional big-gunned cruisers which Admiral Jones
wanted, four or five six-inch-gun cruisers which the British
wanted us to have, and that despite this the fleet would be
just as strong, perhaps stronger.

Admiral Jones, on the other hand, informed the delegation that the eight-inch-gun cruiser was the only type
which could cope with Britain's gigantic trans-Atlantic
liners armed in war time, and the only type which could
bridge the long ocean lanes of the Pacific between fueling
at Hawaii and fueling at the Philippines. To prove this he
read a long memorandum repeating arguments which the
delegates had heard often and which so bored even the Secretary of the Navy that he voted against the admiral whom
he had come over to defend.

Hilary Jones had inherited his militant patriotism from
a father who fought in Lee's army and from a mother who
was a great-granddaughter of John Marshall, Chief Justice
of the United States. He had been called "Admiral" ever
since the days when he had sailed his father's hencoops in
a Virginia cow pond. He had weathered a life at sea dating
back to the Samoan hurricane and the days when marine

guards had to be stationed over the hatches to prevent mutiny. This battle around the council table of diplomacy was the first he had ever lost.

Now when he failed to convince even his chief, Jones, a turbulent, broken old man, packed his trunk and sailed for home.

As a result of his defeat, the British and American delegations had three important points of agreement around which they were confident of building at least a three-power treaty. These points were:

> First, a decision to limit the treaty to only six years. This was a distinct defeat for disarmament realists, but it had the advantage of aligning the date of the treaty's expiration with that of the Washington treaties. Far more important, the British Council of Imperial Defense secretly had fixed 1936 as the last year the world would keep inviolate the Kellogg Pact. Resort to armed force was likely after that date, the Council decided, and because of that the question of naval strength would have to be reviewed. Finally, a six-year treaty pleased naval designers because they recognized that new types of ships in the interim might necessitate new standards of limitation.
>
> Second, a decision to reduce battleship tonnage by failing to replace those vessels reaching their age limit in the immediate future.
>
> Third, an optional agreement whereby the United States might build either eighteen eight-inch-gun cruisers plus 143,520 tons of six-inch-gun vessels, or the alternative of fifteen eight-inch-gun cruisers plus 189,000 tons of six-inch-gun vessels.

This, members of the American delegation unanimously agreed, provided for unequivocal parity with their ancient rival of the sea; and if all else failed at London, they could at least take this important victory back to the American people.

In a complacent frame of mind, therefore, they went

about the work of spurring on the French and Japanese
to bigger and better things.

On February 6th, however, this complacency disappeared. Arthur Sears Henning, correspondent of the *Chicago Tribune*, dropped in to see Ambassador Charles
Gates Dawes, also of Chicago.

"Mr. Ambassador," he said, "I understand that the
American delegation has surrendered the American fleet
to the British."

"Arthur," replied Mr. Dawes, "you're wrong."

"Yes," continued Henning. "I understand that we've
come back to the proposition the British held out to us
months ago and are going to take eighteen 10,000-ton
cruisers instead of twenty-one. In fact, I understand we
may go as low as fifteen."

Henning was right, but Dawes denied it vigorously.

"Arthur," he said, "you're crazy."

"Crazy or not," continued Henning, "I've got information to the effect that you've made this compromise."

Now there was no person anywhere in the vast city of
London whom the American delegation would have liked
less to have this information than Arthur Sears Henning.
Mr. Henning's stories, appearing in the Paris edition of
the *Chicago Tribune*, were read avidly by every member
of the delegation the minute the mail train arrived from
Dover. In these dispatches they saw old Admiral Jones pictured as the valiant fighter for American rights, Secretary
Adams as the Boston revolutionary who was "withholding
his fire until he could see the whites of the enemy's eyes,"
and Henry L. Stimson as the English-mannered aristocrat,
living on a baronial estate south of London and ready at
any cost to please the British. Mr. Henning decidedly got
under the delegation's skin.

When Ambassador Dawes, therefore, found that Arthur
Henning had the inside story of the British-American
agreement, he hastily called his chief, Mr. Stimson, and

Mr. Stimson, in turn, summoned a meeting of the entire delegation.

"This man Henning must be circumvented," Dawes told his colleagues.

So it was decided to scoop Henning on his own story. Henning meanwhile accepted Dawes' denial at its face value and had written nothing. The next night, however, he was surprised to receive an important press release from the American delegation. The details of the Anglo-American naval agreement, confirming his information, were being rushed to all newspapers.

The effect of the announcement was most favorable in Great Britain and the United States—for one day.

The next morning Mr. Stimson discovered that, in his haste to beat Mr. Henning to press, he had completely overlooked two highly important things. He had been scrupulously careful to ask permission of the British to make his statement, but he did not consult the French. The French, it is true, were not directly concerned with British and American naval figures, but they were nervous about them. Ever since the previous October, Mr. MacDonald and Mr. Stimson had been trying to dispel that nervousness, and now Mr. Stimson had undone everything. With this concrete evidence of an agreement made behind their backs, the French were more convinced than ever that what they had seen was not a bugaboo, but a firmly cemented Anglo-American understanding. M. Tardieu made a hurried trip to No. 10 Downing Street and complained bitterly. Mr. MacDonald attempted to smooth over the incident by explaining that a copy of the American proposals had been "purloined" by an American newspaperman who was about to publish them. This, of course, was a stretch of the MacDonald imagination, and helped to pacify neither the belligerent Frenchman who left for Paris, nor Mr. Henning, who was now more bent than ever upon bedeviling the American delegation.

The second thing Mr. Stimson overlooked in making public his emergency press release was the giant dreadnought which he proposed building for the American fleet. True, he had not exactly overlooked it. The fact was, he carefully expunged all mention of it from his statement to the press. But he had overlooked the fact that no state secret ever long remains a secret, and that his proposal that a conference for the limitation of navies should stamp with approval the construction of one superdreadnought in a day when dreadnoughts threatened to follow the path of dinosaurs, was simply too fantastic to be kept quiet.

Friends of the British Admiralty discreetly slipped the secret to the British press. London smiled. The American public roared. Newspapermen dubbed the proposed sea monster the *"U.S.S. Henry L. Stimson."*

Mr. Stimson has suffered some embarrassing moments in his long and varied career. He reproached Soviet Russia for its invasion of Manchuria after Soviet troops had been withdrawn. He proclaimed his crusading support of the Brazilian Government just one day before it fell. He was spanked by the spokesman of the Japanese Foreign Office for a press interview he had given on Manchuria. But none of these were so difficult to explain as his proposal to build a giant new battleship.

Mr. Stimson did try to explain it. The immediate and official explanation was that the new sea monster was needed to offset the superior speed and armor plate of the *Rodney* and the *Nelson*—two prizes of the British fleet, both completed after the Washington Naval Conference. Japan, he said, could build one, too. Later, Mr. Stimson gave a private explanation. He summoned the press to tea and talked in a very hurt tone about the difficulty of bringing the Japanese into line, and about the strategy he had evolved of clubbing them with the threat of this new battleship. The Japanese could not afford to build a new battleship, Mr. Stimson explained, and would submit to a 10-6 ratio on cruisers if the United States in turn surrendered its blueprint monster of the sea.

Unfortunately, the club had been rendered about as effective as an inflated sausage-casing. Aside from press-room quips, that was the last ever heard of the *U.S.S. Henry L. Stimson.*

The Conference, now nearly one month old, was almost back to the point at which it started.

The United States and Great Britain were in complete accord—but had been so on principal issues ever since the summer. The Japanese still were adamant for the higher ratio demanded when they passed through Washington, and the French and Italians were just as much at loggerheads as on the day the Conference opened.

And so the delegates, having tried to forget about Mediterranean pacts, consultative treaties, and the Italian demand for parity with France, wearily came back to this —the main problem of the Conference.

By this time political friction between the two dominating powers of the Mediterranean had drifted from bad to worse. Underlying their rivalry over navies was a rivalry for territory in Africa—a rivalry which had caused mighty battles to be waged round the rim of the Mediterranean since the days of Hannibal and Cæsar. Italy had infiltrated French Tunis with her citizens and demanded for them a privileged status. Other Italian immigrants to Nice urged its reconquest. South of Lybia in the Sahara, France and Italy both claimed vast undefined areas. And as if with malice aforethought, the Italians sent an expeditionary force into this region just as the Conference opened. On January 24th, only three days after George V made his plea for world peace at London, General Griziani hoisted the Italian flag over Murzak, the oasis capital of Fezzan, claimed by France. A few weeks later he captured the oasis of Ghat, key to north and south caravan routes and one of the most important watering-places in the vast Sahara. A little later he killed Souleimann Sef-en-Nessar, Arab ruler of that area.

While this conquest of the desert progressed, the Italian delegation at London was demanding absolute equality with the French fleet. It also harped continually on the Hoover thesis of "reduction." The London Naval Conference, monotonously repeated the Italians, was called in order to reduce, not increase. The French program, they pointed out, required staggering increases.

The French listened and shrugged their shoulders. They did not care if the Italians got parity, they said, if the Italians wanted to build up to parity. And the secret of this nonchalance, of course, was the belief that the Italians could not afford to build.

As far back as 1924 the French, still smarting from their diplomatic defeat at the Washington Conference, had passed their "Statut Naval," a construction program providing for ten modern 10,000-ton cruisers, two brand-new battleships, and 100,000 tons of submarines to be built whenever France had the funds. Now for the first time in years, the French treasury was flush, the cruiser program had been started and there was not an iota of opinion to be found from the Rhine to the Rhone in favor of sacrifices to appease either a belligerent Mediterranean neighbor or the personal ambitions of Messrs. Stimson and MacDonald.

The French delegation in London stood pat.

The impasse welded the two Anglo-Saxon delegations into an alliance firmer and perhaps more frantic than at any time since Mr. Stimson's fourth great-grandfather, George Stimson, took down his rifle and powder-horn and fought France and the Indians side by side with British regulars. George III of England, the recipient of certain American invective during the Revolutionary period which followed, and whose portrait hung just behind Secretary Stimson during the plenary sessions at St. James's Palace, must have been amazed as he looked down upon the feverish coöperation of his successors to save their Conference from failure.

Stimson and MacDonald tried every argument, every form of strategy ever known to 'diplomacy. M. Tardieu remained suave, smiling, immobile.

On one occasion Ramsay MacDonald resorted to his old tactics of the schoolroom. He delivered a lecture to the French Premier on the necessity of making sacrifices for the common good. Great Britain, with the most powerful navy in the world, said MacDonald, is willing to cut her cruisers to the small—the almost negligible—total of fifteen.

"Why," he asked, with pathos in his voice, "cannot France make a similar sacrifice and agree to build only six, or at the most seven?"

Tardieu bit his lip and listened. Then diplomacy deserted him. His face became crimson. His sangfroid disappeared. He told MacDonald that he did not care how many cruisers Britain wanted to build. That was no concern of France. But France needed ten cruisers and France was going to have them.

That, for the moment, ended that.

Perhaps because the French delegation seemed to take pleasure in being recalcitrant, perhaps because Messrs. Stimson and MacDonald were so inept, they failed to move the French even on the question of humanizing submarine warfare. This was one of Mr. Stimson's pet hobbies. Elihu Root, his old friend and law partner, the man who had made him Secretary of War under Theodore Roosevelt and helped to make him Secretary of State, had negotiated at the Washington Conference a submarine treaty which never had become effective due to failure of ratification by the French. And Mr. Stimson swore that if he did nothing else at London he would bring back French approval of a new submarine treaty similar to that concluded by his old friend Root.

The French, however, again showed signs of resistance. The submarine was their most inexpensive and effective weapon of naval defense. With it they were at least some match for Britain's superior fleet. With it they could play far greater havoc with British shipping passing through the jugular trade route of the Empire—the Mediterranean —than did the Germans during the World War. The submarine was something they wanted neither to humanize nor to surrender.

Informed of this position by George Rublee, his submarine expert, Mr. Stimson fumed and sputtered.

"We'll hold a plenary session," he declared. "We'll expose them to the world. They should be cowed into submission. They should be coerced, not persuaded."

And the French, seeing the fire in Stimson's eye and having some inkling of what was in store for them, prepared for public coercion. They dug up a report signed by Herbert Hoover, when he was Secretary of Commerce and an adviser to the Washington Naval Conference, in which he emphatically supported the French thesis for the retention of the submarine; and they prepared to throw it into the teeth of the American delegation if Mr. Stimson challenged them in public.

But it never came to that. Mr. Rublee advised persuasion and Mr. Rublee had his way. Finally he worked out a compromise acceptable to the French and acceptable to him, but not to Mr. Stimson. That loyal gentleman insisted on a treaty almost identical with that of his old friend Root. And he was immovable. So also were the French. Finally Rublee obtained Stimson's consent to cabling the important portions of the draft treaty to Elihu Root himself, also to Under Secretary Cotton and to John Bassett Moore in order to get their reaction.

All three cabled immediate approval. Only then did Mr. Stimson yield.

The major deadlock over high French naval tonnage, however, did not melt away so rapidly. And after many midnight hours spent in trying to outmanœuvre André Tardieu, Mr. Stimson finally came round to the conclusion reached by some of his own delegates even before the Conference opened, that the only way to bring a five-power treaty back from London was through American participation in a political agreement.

On February 17th, therefore, Mr. Stimson held a luncheon for part of the press. During its course he dropped word that there was no reason why the United States should not enter a consultative pact. Such a treaty, Mr. Stimson said, would be an almost exact replica of the Four-power consultative pact for the Pacific which the United States signed during the Washington Conference, and would go no farther than the policy of consultation he followed in Manchuria and the Chaco. And he said this with all the profundity of a pundit giving voice to a stirring dictum, apparently unaware that exactly the same thesis had been bruited about by the press for weeks.

Having thus unburdened himself, Mr. Stimson awoke the next morning to find that the government of M. Tardieu had fallen. The London Naval Conference was declared in recess.

5. THE LONDON NAVAL CONFERENCE

ROUND TWO

When M. Tardieu went back to Paris to repair his shattered political fences, many conferees sighed gratefully and looked forward to getting some London clothes and enjoying a few English week-ends. Nothing better, they thought, possibly could have happened. Actually no more serious blow could have been struck at the Naval Conference. For one month it had struggled, at times most unsuccessfully, but always consistently toward a climax. And then just as the American delegates came forward with the political key expected to bring that climax, the Conference folded in their faces.

For some, of course, the French holiday was a real vaca-tion. The American stenographers, whose thin ankles and scantiness of underwear had been so featured in the British press, immediately made the rounds of the Caledonian Market and the West End in search of bargains. Mr. Wakatsuki and his delegates started out to enjoy London systematically. Cameras and guide-books in hand, they scoured every corner of the British Museum, Westminster, the Tower of London, jotting down notes as if making a report to the Emperor. Secretary Stimson was able to spend more time at Stanmore, the baronial country estate which he had leased for the winter, while MacDonald was able to enjoy the gardens at Chequers, which the American wife of Lord Lee had sacrificed to all British premiers for the sake of her husband's ambition and a peerage.

Time dragged on. The Ritz was cold. Chambermaids were unsympathetic. "Why," they asked, "didn't the American delegation wear woollies?" When one of Adams' marines tried to light a fire in the grate of the conference room, the delegates were smoked out. The fireplace was ornamental only.

Time dragged particularly because word had been passed to leaders of British society that the American delegation would be too busy to dine out. And British society, per-haps glad of the excuse, took the delegation at its word. So the wives of the delegates watched the social whirl from the side lines, and bemoaned the fact that a Labour

Government was in power. Its official parties were so stodgy.

Sole relievers of this monotony were the vivacious Lady Astor and the caustic Bernard Shaw, whom she beguiled to Cliveden and sandwiched between Senator David Aiken Reed and Ambassador Dwight W. Morrow with the admonition: "Now say something amusing. These Americans expect it of you."

Shaw—on the spot—did his best.

"Instead of holding Olympic games every year," he began, bravely, "all the people who believe in war should get together and carry out their convictions. The rest of us could watch them. You Americans could bring over your Daughters of the American Revolution, the American Legion, and the Ku Klux Klan. Mussolini could contribute his Black Shirts, Hitler his Brown Shirts, and England would donate Lord Birkenhead and Winston Churchill. We could line them all up on Salisbury Plain, where they could march and drill and strut their rooster feathers and brandish their tomahawks, and then after plenty of warming up they could get down to real fighting.

"This would weed out enough fighters every year so that the rest of us could go on living fairly peacefully."

For four members of the American delegation the French holiday meant no more than any other day of the Naval Conference. They were Ambassador Hugh Gibson, who was in poor health; Ambassador Charley Dawes, who furnished the delegation's window-dressing; Charles Francis Adams; and Senator Robinson of Arkansas, whose job did not begin until the treaty faced ratification on the floor of the Senate.

Uncle Joe Robinson was a pathetic figure. An able politician, not a bad negotiator, he sat among the red-plush cushions of the Ritz waiting wistfully for something to do. Even during Easter which he wanted to spend in Paris, Uncle Joe remained in the dreary Ritz. Every day he waited. But always about three in the afternoon, having received no summons from Stimson headquarters, he gave up. With a sigh of mingled regret and satisfaction, he stole down the service elevator, avoided newspapermen in the lobby, and joined his old crony, Lloyd George, on the golf links.

Thus did the Senator from Arkansas push forward the cause of naval limitation.

It was not his fault. Too many delegates already were spoiling the broth. Charles Francis Adams was not one of these. During the first week of the Conference he had been appointed on a technical committee, struggled manfully with the French transactional proposals and global tonnage, and then tried to explain them to a press conference. After ten minutes of watching Charley flounder, Arthur Henning, who had touted Adams as the "Hope of the Naval Conference," remarked:

"My white hope has clay feet."

And Adams, sensing the futility of his efforts and watching the hectic gyrations of Henry L. Stimson, decided the most useful thing for him to do was merely to receive the salutes of his marines.

In the same category of usefulness, though not of modesty, was His Excellency the Ambassador Extraordinary and Envoy Plenipotentiary to the Court of St. James's. Charley Dawes' great passion in life was to keep in front of the footlights. And ever since his wild and fruitless dash to see MacDonald at Lossiemouth he had managed somehow or other to hold the centre of the stage. Sometimes, it is true, he resorted to weird tactics to hold it. Once he hired Leon Errol to pose as a drunken waiter and spill cold lobster into the lap of the Duke of Norfolk. Again, he made such a fad of lunching at Ye Old Cheshire Cheese that American tourists stood in line for a chance to sit near the American Ambassador. Finally, either by accident or by intention, he did not bow before Queen Mary during a Court levee at St. James's Palace.

All of which made him the talk of London.

During the Conference he tried desperately to retain that distinction. He entertained lavishly and wise-cracked when given the most meager opportunity. He gave a party in honour of Mr. Wakatsuki at which Will Rogers, cowboy comedian, kept most of the guests in convulsions, but during the middle of which the guest of honour arose, bowed stiffly, and left. Mr. Wakatsuki did not appreciate American humour.

Most of Dawes' strategy was like this. Instead of sitting patiently on the side lines as did Adams, or going out to play golf like Uncle Joe, Charley chafed constantly at the way the Conference edged him away from the footlights. Late one afternoon, Stimson called a sudden meeting of the delegation. Except for Dawes, who lived at the Embassy, all the delegates had rooms at the Ritz and were easy to summon. Young Henry Dawes, hearing of the meeting, asked Stimson whether he should send word to his uncle. Mr. Stimson hesitated a moment, and finally replied:

"Oh, you can if you want to."

The dynamos of the delegation were Messrs. Stimson, Morrow, and Reed. Of these the Senator from Pennsylvania was perhaps the hardest-hitting negotiator. He did not fret as did Stimson. He did not spend long hours conferring as did Morrow. He got to the point quickly. He did not butt his head against the stone wall of impasse. He retreated, planned new strategy, and attacked again. He worked intensely while in London, and relaxed on the country estates of British nobility while away from it. Reed's job was to persuade the Japanese to accept figures they did not want. Without his assistance both with the Japanese at London and with reluctant Senators at Washington, Mr. Stimson might have had no treaty at all.

The member of the delegation who worked all the time was Dwight W. Morrow. Yet he never lost his resilience or his optimism. In fact, he was too optimistic. Morrow's optimism got to be so noticeable during Conference doldrums that it became a barometer with newspapermen. They found that during the heights of Morrow optimism the Conference was in its lowest depths of depression. No matter how late Morrow sat in his room trying to inveigle French or Italian delegates to recede from their demands, he was up and at work early the next morning. He had the bounce of a rubber ball. His energy was like the non-stop flights of his famous son-in-law. His concentration on the problem in hand was so intense that he was completely oblivious to everything around him, and one of the main duties of the American marines stationed on the top floor of the Ritz was to keep the Ambassador from straying into someone else's room while en route to his own. Once while leaving his room, he opened what he thought was the exit door and walked into the closet.

Henry Lewis Stimson led his little band of delegates as a corporal marches his squad across the parade-ground. There was no moment during any part of the Conference when anyone was in doubt as to who headed the American Delegation. This, perhaps, was Mr. Stimson's chief trouble. He could not delegate responsibility. He turned the French over to Morrow and the Japanese to Reed, but he, himself, was not happy unless he had his fingers continually upon the details of almost everything they did. This would have been all right had it not been for the fact that Mr. Stimson was both so overburdened with details and took such a long time in deciding them that frequently the entire delegation had jumped far ahead of him and an hour or two was necessary to persuade its chief of the efficacy of its stand.

One of Mr. Stimson's greatest handicaps was that all of his diplomatic and executive experience in the past had been in fields where he was supreme. As Secretary of War, his word had been law. As mediator in Nicaragua, he had been able to write a letter to the rebel leader, Moncada, demanding that he lay down his arms or be disarmed—and when Mr. Stimson said that, he had the entire force of the United States army and navy behind him. Finally, as Governor-General of the Philippines he had been tolerant and coöperative with the Filipino leaders, but if they balked he always had the power of absolute veto.

In London, however, Mr. Stimson found himself sitting across the conference table from men who had behind them armies all larger than that of the United States, and, in two cases, navies as strong or stronger. It was a situation requiring fast thinking and lots of it.

In this situation Mr. Stimson fell down.

For months both in Washington and en route to London he had carefully rehearsed his lines. But now, during scenes when his lines were supposed to carry the drama up to a climax, Mr. Stimson sometimes discovered there was no one on the stage but himself.

The worst of it was that this got tremendously on his nerves. And lacking the resilience of Dwight Morrow or the strategy of Dave Reed, the chief of the American delegation became nervous, fretful, and at times almost ill.

This nervous fatigue contributed also to Mr. Stimson's difficulties with the press. Press relations always had been difficult for the Secretary of State, but at London he was convinced that he had a perfect set-up. Not only did he have the regular press officer of the State Department, but as a super-moulder of public opinion he had the services of Arthur W. Page, son of Wilson's famous war-time Ambassador to the Court of St. James's. Arthur Page was a neighbor of Stimson's on Long Island, also vice-president of the American Telephone and Telegraph Company in charge of public relations. What could be more fortuitous,

Mr. Stimson reasoned, than to have this expert in handling the press and him in London.

But as an added precaution for the proper press build-up, Arthur Page and his chief staged a dinner for the publishers of New York's foremost newspapers and held evening conferences for reporters in the children's dining-room of the *George Washington*.

Despite these precautions, everything about the press went wrong. His luncheon for publishers, Mr. Stimson discovered, was just so much wasted food. The reporters on the firing-line, not the men who own newspapers, can make or break conferences. The latter got very much on the Secretary's nerves. They dubbed his press conferences "Stimson's Bedtime-story Hour," and resented his unfortunate habit of passing out obvious truths wrapped in the strictest seal of confidence. Also, Mr. Stimson believed in patriotism and insisted upon setting himself up as the sole arbiter of what constituted that virtue. So it galled him tremendously when the *Chicago Tribune* or the Hearst newspapers would not admit that his patriotism reached a higher plane than theirs.

Mr. Stimson initiated press relations at London by informing several hundred newspapermen gathered in the Ritz bar that he was happy to be in London, was very tired and did not want to be questioned. On that occasion he was let off. On subsequent occasions he was not. Questions were no more blunt than usual, but Mr. Stimson, imbued with the belief that "unpatriotic" questions should not be asked, became cross and irritable and on one occasion stalked out of the room. And on another occasion he ordered out of the press conference William T. Stone, of the Foreign Policy Association, whom he accused of stirring up American sentiment for a consultative pact.

Finally press conferences ceased altogether. For weeks naval negotiations rocked along with American newspapermen getting their information chiefly from British,

French, and big navy sources. The resultant impression
upon the American public was not one calculated to make
smoother the task of treaty ratification. And one day
Herbert Hoover advised his Secretary of State to do
something about his press relations. Mr. Stimson's
luncheon for the publishers had helped not at all.

Simultaneously, Mr. Hoover himself took a hand. He
called to Washington that staunch and trusted Republican
publisher, John C. Martin, step-son-in-law of Cyrus Curtis.
To Martin he complained bitterly about the London dispatches of several leading correspondents. The three chief
culprits were Edwin L. James of the *New York Times*,
Paul Scott Mowrer of the *Chicago Daily News* and Frank
Simonds, at that time writing for Mr. Martin's *New
York Evening Post*. These men, said Mr. Hoover, had
lived so long abroad that they had become denationalized,
had lost their American point of view. And then to clinch
his argument he pointed out that all three had received
the French Legion of Honour.

Martin, himself, had just received the Legion of Honour. From that time on Frank Simonds had a freer hand
than ever to criticize the naval conference.

Meanwhile, Mr. Stimson in London struggled desperately to please.

His advisers told him he should be more human, more
malleable, more spontaneous. And to dispel the impression that he was an unbending New York blueblood,
they staged a motion-picture scene for him on top of the
Ritz Hotel. The shot was particularly designed for the
American public and opened with the Secretary of State,
his back to the camera—apparently oblivious to the fact
that his picture was being taken. He was looking off over
the sprawling city of London. Beside him stood an English friend.

"There you are, Mr. Secretary," pointed the friend, "the
famous Buckingham Palace where the King and Queen

live. You notice that the palace guard is just being changed. And to the left is Westminster with the famous Big Ben clock on the tower of Parliament. And farther to the left is the river Thames up which has come British shipping for hundreds of years."

At this point, the Secretary of State turned to get another view of London, faced the camera, and held up his hand in mock surprise.

"What," he exclaimed, "is my picture being taken?"

"Yes, Mr. Secretary," explained the cameraman. "We thought you wouldn't mind. And now that we think of it, Mr. Secretary, why not give us a message for the American people."

Whereupon the Secretary of State, always the human, spontaneous person, reached into his pocket and pulled out his message to the American people.

The Tardieu Government fell February 17th. It was not until March 6th that he could get a Cabinet functioning again and send M. Briand back to London at the head of the French delegation.

During those seventeen days the Naval Conference had registered not one tangible advance. Many of its delegates had struggled desperately. But the sole results of the French holiday were the shaken confidence of the American public plus the realization that agreement with the Japanese had become increasingly difficult.

The attempt to reconcile Japanese and American cruiser differences had begun immediately after the French deserted London. Obviously it was about the only thing that could be accomplished during the French holiday, and the American delegation went at it with the same easy optimism they had exhibited toward the Japanese in Washington.

They were in for cruel disillusionment. The Japanese

had come to London with a tacit understanding with the French to block the Anglo-American alliance. They also came with embryonic plans for the conquest of Manchuria in the minds of their more nationalistic naval officers. And finally they had come to London determined to secure a ratio in auxiliary vessels of 10-7—in other words, seventy per cent of the British and American levels, as against the sixty per cent given them at Washington for capital ships. Furthermore, their hand was considerably strengthened by the fact that they arrived in London with this ratio for cruisers more than an accomplished fact. Their own cruiser program was complete, while that of the United States was still chiefly a matter of blueprints. Even while on the high seas Mr. Stimson had received a confidential radio from Ramsay MacDonald expressing great concern regarding the Japanese demands and asking him to speed up the *George Washington* in order to help settle them.

Despite this, however, Messrs. Stimson and Reed started their negotiations on the assumption that the Japanese were asking for the moon and would be content with only a few minor constellations. In this they were sadly mistaken. The Japanese naval demands had been carefully worked out in Tokyo and submitted to the Emperor. They represented a compromise between the extreme nationalist views of the younger naval officers and the more conciliatory attitude of the Japanese Foreign Office.

But as the Conference dragged along, the attitude of the navy men stiffened.

Not until eighteen months later was the world to realize the grip of these young army and navy officers on Japan. Those who dealt with the Japanese delegation at London did not see peering over the shoulders of the suave Matsudaira and the staccato-worded Wakatsuki thousands of grim-faced patriots ready to go to any lengths—even assassination or war—to make their navy supreme in the

Pacific. And as the French sabotage of the Conference continued, these patriots saw an excellent chance to gain complete victory at London. The United States and Great Britain, they knew, would not quit the Conference until they had some form of treaty. Failing a five-power pact, they had to have an agreement between the United States, Great Britain, and Japan. For the political futures of both Ramsay MacDonald and Herbert Hoover this was mandatory. After all the goodwill ballyhoo, after all the promises of reduction, neither could face public opinion at home without some sort of treaty.

So the Japanese stood pat. Their price was high, but they stuck to it.

All during the French holiday when real progress might have been achieved, they held out. Ambassador Matsudaira, uncle-in-law of the Emperor, was the most suave and courteous of negotiators. He met with Senator Reed almost daily. The two men reviewed their positions microscopically. They sifted naval figures with a fine-tooth comb. But they got nowhere. And that was exactly where they were on March 6th when Aristide Briand finally came puffing back to London.

Another development, perhaps more serious than this, had taken place while the French were absent in Paris. The seventeen-day delay, during which the American delegation was pictured in the press as sitting futilely in London hotel lobbies, had shaken the disarmament morale of the American people. American newspapermen, disgusted with Secretary Stimson's secretive tactics, had gleefully contributed to this picture. So that the American public, once ready to swallow a consultative pact or almost any kind of treaty born of London, now was convinced that the American delegation was headed by a vacillating aristocrat futilely wasting the taxpayers' money for something he didn't know anything about. There were increas-

ing demands in the American press that the delegation
come home.

Aristide Briand returned to London realizing that hope
for a successful conference rested in his wily and altruistic
soul.

The eyes of all Europe focused upon him as he got off
the boat train and registered at the Carlton Hotel. Here
was the man who had established a reputation as Europe's
greatest pacifier; the man who, out of Poincaré's invasion
of the Ruhr, had pulled the Locarno Treaties; who had
dared propose a United States of Europe; who had
breathed first life into the Kellogg Pact; and who now, an
old man with little more to gain and much to lose, suddenly became the key to naval disarmament at London.

The betting odds were two to one that Briand would
produce the necessary miracle.

Why should he have come back to London otherwise,
the cynics argued. He had achieved almost everything in
life. His prestige could be enhanced but little more. Without certain success at London, he would have rested on his
laurels in Paris.

But Briand, old as he was, tired as he was, wise as he
was regarding the frailties of human nature, nevertheless
cherished one remaining ambition—to bring the United
States into the orbit of the League of Nations.

Briand returned exuding optimism, and the day after
his arrival staged one of his famous luncheons, this time in
honor of the American delegation. At a much more
famous luncheon at Thoiry, Briand once had laid the
foundation for Locarno, as he described it, "between the
pear and the cheese"; and at this luncheon in London he
tried to lay the foundation for closer American coöperation with Europe. His hospitality was a prelude for a
formal call on Mr. Stimson the next day, at which the old
question of a political agreement came back to the centre

of the stage again and held it. M. Briand presented Mr. Stimson with the tentative draft of a Mediterranean Pact. He also laid down a take-it-or-leave-it proposition that there would be no reduction of the French naval program without a security agreement in exchange.

Afterward the French Foreign Minister went over to see Arthur Henderson and made the same proposition to him. Neither visit gave him much encouragement. Mr. Stimson referred to the recent unfavorable reaction of American opinion and the difficulty of getting any sort of political treaty ratified by the Senate. Mr. Henderson replied that he would be willing to study the text of the pact, but felt that Britain should accept no additional commitments and that the French price was too high.

Mr. MacDonald's reaction was even more dour than that of his Foreign Minister. His party had just squeaked through a final vote on the coal bill with a majority of nine, and he had been criticized in private meetings of his party for his dilly-dallying diplomacy at the Naval Conference. His veto of a Mediterranean Pact, therefore, was flat and final.

Whereupon the mercurial M. Briand staged a meeting of the French press, at which he exuded as much pessimism as cigarette smoke and said that the United States and Great Britain might go ahead with Japan and a three-power treaty, but that was about all that would come out of the conference.

Almost simultaneous with these remarks, M. Briand laid down another of his many cards on the conference table. He proposed a consultative pact for the Atlantic. This had a definite precedent in the Four-power Pacific Pact, sponsored by the United States in 1921, and Briand's chief objective in proposing an Atlantic counterpart was to put Mr. Stimson on the spot.

By this time Henry L. Stimson had vacillated back and forth on the question of consultation as frequently as the

French had commuted between London and Paris. On the
S.S. *George Washington* he had ignored the idea altogether. On his arrival in London he had denied that the
United States had any intention of entering such an agreement. On the day the French Cabinet fell he had sent out
a trial balloon indicating that the United States might be
willing to enter a consultative pact. And as a result most
of the American people, fed a stream of variegated reports
by the press, had come to the general conclusion that
Henry L. Stimson was a naïve old gentleman being made
the goat by wicked European diplomats and that the consultative pact was a tool of the devil definitely to be
avoided.

It was not surprising, therefore, that just two days after
Briand put the consultative pact in the headlines again,
the American delegation received word from Washington
that any treaty mentioning the words "security" or "consultation" would have extremely difficult sledding in the
Senate. Accordingly, Mr. Stimson staged a newspaper tea
where he gave an involved and lengthy explanation as to
why the United States could enter no such treaty. Such
an agreement, he explained, meant a moral obligation to
use the armed forces of the United States against an
aggressor should consultation fail. Such an obligation,
Mr. Stimson said, was one which the United States, because of its traditions of aloofness, could not assume. However, should other powers, because of their proximity to
Europe, care to appease the French appetite for security,
the United States would be most happy to applaud from
the side lines.

The reaction to the Stimson press conference was immediate and resembled a cloudburst.

"I have finished my rôle," announced Aristide Briand,
"and tomorrow further matters will be handed over to the
French delegation. I am going home.

"I do not know what Secretary Stimson means by talking about moral obligations toward France if the United States entered into a consultative pact. We do not ask Mr. Stimson to guarantee our security.

"When I originated the Kellogg Pact I intended it to be a pledge only between the United States and France, but America extended it to include the entire world. Now it might be said that all the world is obligated to help America settle her disputes.

"I give the conference two more weeks to close its doors," he said, and ended the interview.

The Briand outburst took place on March 12th. The next day he planned to issue a polemic on the question of security and return to Paris.

But immediately after breakfast the next morning, M. Briand received two unexpected visitors. They were the diminutive Mr. Morrow in charge of American liaison with the French, and his chief of delegation, Henry L. Stimson. They had received a first-hand report of M. Briand's dolorous wail and came determined to prevent his departure from London.

They bore two arguments—one a threat, the other a bribe. The first was a warning that at future disarmament discussions in Geneva the United States would withdraw all the concessions she had made to France at London. The second was a promise to put pressure on the Italians.

Later in the day M. Briand received another caller— the irate and by this time highly nervous Ramsay Mac-Donald. MacDonald also bore two arguments—one a bribe, the other a threat. The first was the same promise made by Mr. Stimson to bear down on the Italians. Only in the case of MacDonald, this really meant something. The second was the warning that if Briand returned to Paris, he, MacDonald, president of the Naval Conference, would adjourn it immediately and announce to the world that the French were to blame. This would put in an extremely bad light the nation posing as Europe's chief champion of disarmament, and Briand knew it. So he decided to look at life from a rosier point of view.

The diplomatic rout caused by Stimson's veto of a consultative pact finally had been stopped.

That night Aristide Briand held another press conference. He had expected to issue a dirge on the question of security. Instead, he said:

"I wish to rectify a few details regarding which the British press has quoted me incorrectly, namely, that I was in a bad humour and ready to shake the dust of England from my feet. This, you must know from your own experience, could hardly be true of one who is such an old hand at international conferences and knows better than to lose his temper at delays. There are difficulties at all conferences. Frequently that is the way results come. So I expect to continue negotiating and still cherish the hope and conviction for success."

That same day Aristide Briand telephoned his Premier in Paris and arranged for him to come to London the next week-end. The job of squeezing the Italians had begun.

That job, however, proved even more difficult than that of security. Throughout the conference the Italian delegation had been treated like a stepchild. Although religiously attending every meeting, its members were largely ignored. Dino Grandi, young and enthusiastic chief of the delegation, was recognized as an able diplomat, but so closely tied down by orders from Rome that he won the nickname "HMV"—"His Master's Voice."

Grandi was only thirty-five and suffered from the fact that in order to conceal his youth he had grown a beard. And it so happened that his beard and general façade were almost identical with those of Herbert F. Wright, State Department historian, charged with keeping the delegation's documents in order. At more than one official reception, Wright was announced as "His Excellency the Foreign Minister of Italy," while at the most elegant recep-

tion of all—that given by the Lord Mayor of London—
Grandi made the mistake of treading so close upon the
heels of M. Tardieu that the heralds, glittering in
mediæval uniforms, got no opportunity to trumpet his
arrival.

This hurt Signor Grandi's feelings at times, but was not
nearly so great a diplomatic handicap as the fact that a non-
Fascist, non-Nationalist, semi-Socialist Government at the
helm of Italian affairs in 1921 had been able to bring back
from the Washington Naval Conference parity with
France. It was an achievement which a Fascist Government
boasting a rejuvenated Italy was compelled to equal.

So Dino Grandi and his colleagues sat on the Conference side lines without plan, program, or naval figures.
When asked what Italy wanted they croaked the parrot-
like refrain, "Parity with France." When MacDonald and
Stimson decided to bear down upon the Italians, they got
much the same answer.

"Italy is ready to reduce to the absolute minimum," the
smiling Grandi replied. "We are even willing to abolish
our navy—provided France does the same. You want me
to put down figures so that you can give France a larger
tonnage than Italy. I have had instructions from Signor
Mussolini not to do so."

The discussion got nowhere.

In fact, it was in this state of vacuum three days later
when M. Tardieu returned to London on the first visit
he had paid the Naval Conference since his Cabinet fell
one month before. He arrived on March 16th—a Sunday
—and after breakfasting with Dwight Morrow, Tardieu
motored direct to Chequers. With him went his colleague,
M. Briand.

The three men sat before an open fire for two and a
half hours before luncheon and an hour afterwards, during which they discussed every possible key to the naval
deadlock. They adjourned with no definite solution, but

with M. Tardieu obviously more delighted than at any
time since the Conference opened. What pleased him was
Ramsay MacDonald's promise to go over Grandi's head
and make a direct appeal to Mussolini through the British
Ambassador in Rome. MacDonald also promised that he
would speak to his friend Mr. Stimson and get him to exert the same pressure through the American Ambassador.
Because of Italy's somewhat precarious economic condition, diplomatic pressure by the two most powerful nations in the world might readily produce results.

So next morning M. Tardieu, still beaming with joy,
called on Secretary Stimson to thank him for his cooperation.

Mr. Stimson looked flabbergasted. Not only had he
never heard of MacDonald's pledge to Tardieu, but informed him that nothing could be farther from his mind.
It would be highly unethical to go over the head of the
Italian delegation in London, Mr. Stimson said. Moreover, it would get nowhere. Grandi, he concluded, was
following Mussolini's instructions to the last letter.

André Tardieu made an abrupt departure. He went
back to the Carlton, ordered his bags packed, and took
the first train to Paris. On the platform at Victoria Station
he met Paul Scott Mowrer of the *Chicago Daily News* and
invited him to ride as far as Dover. En route the French
Premier poured out a story of bitterness and rancour un-
equalled in a Conference featured by bitterness and rancour. He was bitter against MacDonald, who had deceived
him, against Stimson, who had lectured him. This trip,
Tardieu said, was the last that London would ever see
of him.

And it was.

The Conference dragged on for exactly one month
more, but André Tardieu never came back to London.

The imbroglio which he left behind now looked worse
than ever. Both the French and the Italian delegations

were frankly worried by the resentment which the naval discussions had aroused at home. The differences in London, fanned by the jingo press of Italy and France, had turned the Naval Conference into an international irritant rather than an avenue of peace.

Only one bright spot appeared on the Conference horizon and it at times flickered feebly.

This was the ratio dickering between the United States and Japan.

For weeks the Japanese had stuck to their demand for a flat ratio of seventy. Senator Reed had coaxed, cajoled, and wheedled. Ambassador Matsudaira, whom he had known in Washington, remained adamant. Mrs. Reed, an old friend of Mrs. Matsudaira's, brought her charm and hospitality into play. Still no results. At one time Matsudaira brought up the question of immigration. He suggested that if the United States should revise the Asiatic Exclusion Act, putting Japan on the same par with other countries, the effect on Japanese public opinion would be such that a lower cruiser ratio could be accepted.

In reply, Reed pointed out that to hitch an immigration agreement to a naval treaty would be the surest way to kill Senate ratification. But he indicated he would do his best as an individual Senator to have the immigration act changed.

As long as the Conference remained in the doldrums, the Japanese were unmovable. But with the first flush of enthusiasm which attended Briand's return to London in early March, the Japanese yielded. Apparently getting word from the French that the Conference had some chance of success, and not relishing the rôle of obstructionists, the Japanese delegation, on March 13th, accepted the Reed compromise.

As far as destroyers and six-inch-gun cruisers were concerned, this compromise gave Japan the 10-7 ratio she so ardently desired. It also gave her what she wanted in submarines, namely, parity with the United States and Great Britain. But in regard to the powerful 10,000-ton eight-inch cruisers, there was a real and rather intricate compromise. The United States held Japan down to a 10-6 ratio in theory, but gave her a 10-7 ratio in practice. This was due to the fact that Senator Reed agreed to delay construction of the three last big-gunned American cruisers so that they would not be completed until after 1936— the expiration date of the treaty. By that time Japan— if she did not like the treaty—would be free to build again.

Because it had to go back to Tokyo for final approval, the Reed agreement was the most carefully guarded secret of the entire Conference. What Reed and Wakatsuki both feared was that a leak regarding their compromise would be twisted in such a way as to arouse Japanese public opinion.

Their fears were more than justified. Japan's ultra-nationalistic naval officers were ready to move heaven and earth to get their complete demands, and to this end they quietly slipped word of the compromise to the press.

The leak almost killed the agreement completely. It caused a furore in Japan only equalled by the furore of the American admirals when they learned that Senator Reed, chairman of the Military Affairs Committee and one of the most militarist members of Congress, had "bartered away" three of their big-gunned cruisers.

In Tokyo Admiral Kato, chief of the General Navy Staff, recommended immediate rejection of the compromise. Younger naval officers demanded that Admiral Takarabe, a delegate at London, resign. Admiral Kato even took his protest direct to the Emperor. And for three weeks it looked as if not even an American-Japanese understanding would come out of London.

It was at this point in late March that the Naval Conference touched rock bottom. It had reached low depths before, but never quite the dismal abyss in which it now found itself. Tardieu had gone home. Briand was getting ready to follow. The drive to bludgeon the Italians into submission had got nowhere. In addition, embarrassing questions were being asked of MacDonald in Cabinet meetings. Philip Snowden on one occasion was caustic and critical. Lord Thomson pointed out that Britain's great commercial stake lay across the Channel, not across the Atlantic. He intimated that MacDonald was throwing away a tried and trusted friendship with France for a flirtation with fickle, high-tariff America which might change completely next election day.

Embarrassing questions also were asked regarding Mr. Stimson in Congress. The funds of the American delegation were running low. Representative Tinkham of Massachusetts toyed with the idea that the money had been spent on London gin. An investigation of the delegation's expense accounts was suggested. William Randolph Hearst was printing violent editorials demanding that the delegation come home. Just as his most vituperative editorial appeared, and as if in answer to it, three of the naval experts were sent back.

In London an air of discouragement descended upon the Conference. St. James's Palace was empty and deserted. Telegraph messenger boys lolled wistfully in the corridors. The soft-drink bar, set up in deference to the Americans, closed for lack of customers.

Spring was in the air. Palace guards had discarded their heavy uniforms. Daffodils along Rotten Row blossomed gloriously. The park beside the Ritz teemed with stout nurses and bonny babies. Members of the American delegation looking out of their hotel windows saw the spring, but enjoyed it not. Pearl Demaret, personal stenographer to Mr. Stimson, killed herself by jumping out of a window. People recalled the jinx of the ill-fated S.S. *George Washington*.

At the depth of this discouragement, Dwight Morrow

and Henry L. Stimson, walking up from St. James's Palace, passed their two chief critics, Arthur Sears Henning and Frank Simonds. Simonds bowed, lifted his hat. Henning did not.

"Why did you tip your hat, Frank?" asked Henning as the two delegates passed on.

"I always uncover," said Simonds, "while passing a funeral."

At this same time Mr. Stimson got a suggestion from his chief in the White House that he counteract the shaken confidence of the American public with an international broadcast. Mr. Stimson complied immediately. In fact, too immediately; for in his hastily written radio speech he made the preposterous claim that the Naval Conference would permit the scrapping of 200,000 tons of ships. And when newspapermen exposed the fact that 150,000 tons of these vessels had been rusting away in Philadelphia and San Diego shipyards for years, Mr. Stimson broadcast another pep talk condemning the pessimists who would disparage the work of the Conference.

"We stick in London until we sign a treaty," Mr. Stimson announced with his fists clenched.

But while he said this, many of his colleagues, both in the American and in the other delegations, were looking for the most expeditious and painless manner of adjourning the Conference. The French and Italians were willing to postpone the meeting *sine die*. The Japanese concurred. But the British and American delegations demanded at least a three-power treaty.

And up until this point they had been completely confident that a three-power treaty would be a relatively simple matter. Now, however, they suddenly woke up to find that it would be anything but simple.

Two obstacles stood in the way. One was the fact that a three-power pact was impossible without Japan. And so far Japan had refused to give its final O.K. Almost daily

Ambassador Castle cabled voluminous reports regarding the naval debate in Tokyo. Almost daily Senator Reed declined English dinner invitations and sat in his hotel room waiting for final word from Wakatsuki. But nothing happened.

The second obstacle was the British Admiralty. Its sea lords insisted that if France and Italy did not come into the treaty, British naval requirements must be raised over those agreed upon with the United States. France and Italy were now so aroused against each other, the Admiralty pointed out, that their naval programs had become a national issue. They were sure to build. And the British fleet, in keeping with the traditional two-power standard, must equal a combination of the French and Italians.

MacDonald's Labour colleagues tended to support the Admiralty. They said a three-power Anglo-American treaty was worse than no treaty at all. Ramsay MacDonald could not budge them.

Everything considered, it looked as if the determination of Mr. Stimson to remain in London until he got a treaty might keep him there the rest of his life.

At this point, Aristide Briand, tired of twiddling his thumbs in the Carlton Hotel, disillusioned regarding his cherished ambition of a security pact, announced that he at least was one who did not intend to rot in London. He announced once and for all that he was going home.

This was the last straw, and Ramsay MacDonald made a desperate effort to prevent disaster. He telephone Briand immediately and arranged a private dinner with him that night at the Carlton. The two men remained together all evening. A French naval expert sat in an adjoining room in case he was needed. But he was not. MacDonald left at ten o'clock, looking worried. Briand departed for Paris the next morning. Jacques Dumesnil, the French Minister of Marine and François Pietri, Minister of Colonies, followed him twenty-four hours later. Aside from a few experts, the French delegation had evaporated.

This occurred on March 21st.

Although only two men knew it, that day—the blackest on the Conference calendar—marked the beginning of a new move which eventually was to win for the London Naval parley at least a record of semi-success.

The two men who initiated the move were Dwight W. Morrow and George Rublee, his staunch friend and adviser. Rublee was variously known in Conference circles as "Morrow's shadow," "the mystery man," and Dwight Morrow's "Colonel House." One of those rare characters who can be successful corporation lawyers and yet retain the liberal leanings of their youth, Rublee found in Morrow a kindred spirit. The two men became acquainted when both were serving with the Allied Maritime Transport Council in London during the World War and had been inseparable ever since. When Morrow resigned from J. P. Morgan and Company to become Ambassador to Mexico, Rublee gave up his lucrative law practice in Washington to go with him. A tall gaunt figure, almost twice the size of Morrow, Rublee held no official position at London, but lurked in the shadowy background working long hours of the day and night to help his friend and the cause of disarmament.

As the Conference neared its crisis in mid-March, Rublee spent much time visiting with some of his friends in French and British liberal circles. And the reaction he got from them ran something like this:

> The key to the peace machinery of Europe lies in Article XVI of the Covenant of the League of Nations providing for sanctions against an aggressor nation. The most powerful factor in such sanctions would, of course, be a blockade of the recalcitrant nation by the British fleet. But now Britain, in agreeing to grant parity to the

United States, has robbed itself of the power to enforce a blockade without the risk of serious challenge from a fleet just as powerful as its own. And since the United States traditionally has insisted upon the right of trade with blockaded nations, and since the United States is not bound by the Covenant of the League of Nations, Article XVI of the Covenant is seriously weakened by British unwillingness to enforce it.

However, should the United States agree to consult in case of European war clouds, and should Great Britain know that the United States would at least listen to reason before using her fleet to break a blockade, then in this case, Britain might well consider giving greater security to France under Article XVI.

Thus the old question of the freedom of the seas, so carefully shunned by Hoover and Stimson throughout the previous summer, rose up to thwart the naval agreement for which they struggled so desperately.

Mr. Rublee turned this idea over in his mind. Then he discussed it with Dwight Morrow.

"It being specifically understood," Mr. Rublee reasoned, "that consultation in time of emergency does not obligate the United States to follow through with armed force, consultation is a perfectly praiseworthy principle against which no one can object. And if agreement on the part of the United States to consult would ease the qualms of the British fleet, thereby permitting Great Britain to ease the qualms of the French regarding security, then consultation is a small price to pay for a naval treaty."

All of this was virtually what the French had wanted from the beginning. It was what M. Briand had proposed to MacDonald during the week-end at Chequers on March 9th. It was what Mr. Stimson had been so hazy about during the early days of the Conference. It was what he had at one time accepted, then rejected. It was the same old question of putting the "why" of disarmament ahead of the "how" of disarmament, of establishing peace before scrapping the weapons of war.

Dwight Morrow listened to the idea and was for it.

He agreed, furthermore, to sell it to the chief of the American delegation and left that afternoon—March 22nd —for Stanmore. It took some time to get the idea into Mr. Stimson's cautious cranium and Morrow remained at Stanmore part of the week-end before he was successful. When he did succeed, however, Stimson became equally enthusiastic, and Morrow went back to London with the understanding that the momentous decision would be communicated to Ramsay MacDonald immediately.

It was Sunday, March 23rd when Morrow returned to London and began to discuss the new plan with other members of the American delegation. Then suddenly he remembered that he and Stimson had made no provision for cabling the President about their change of front. Mr. Hoover, he knew, felt very strongly on the subject of a consultative pact, viewed it as so many tons of political dynamite planted in the path of his reëlection. Probably, therefore, he would prefer to know about it first hand.

So Morrow tried to get Stimson on the telephone. He could not. The Secretary of State was out on the golf links. Finally Morrow motored back to Stanmore. This took an hour. Then he had to catch up with the Secretary of State on the golf links. Mr. Morrow's legs were short and this took another half hour. After that he left Mr. Stimson to send the telegram when and how he saw fit.

Mr. Stimson sent the message, but it was brief and did not fully set forth the complicated political position which caused the American delegation to right-about-face on consultation. Also it was late. The President did not receive the message until after he had read Paul Scott Mowrer's syndicated dispatch in the *Washington Star* and until after he had received various representations from the Foreign Policy Association urging him to support the delegation on consultation. All of which irritated Mr. Hoover infinitely.

And although Morrow drafted a second cablegram much more comprehensive than the first, Mr. Hoover at his March 25th press conference gave vent to a background statement calculated to kill any idea of "consultation."

What he said in substance was this:

> No security or consultative pact has been considered at any time during the course of the London Conference.
>
> No suggestion for such a pact has come at any time from any of the governments participating in the Conference and the character of such proposals as have come from outside sources do not interest the Governments represented.
>
> Only a security pact which would commit the signatories to military guarantees could be depended upon to reduce naval tonnage so much as one ton and that sort of guarantee is something that the United States will not give.

Simultaneously, Mr. Hoover communicated with Walter Strong, publisher of the *Chicago Daily News* and asked whether Paul Scott Mowrer or the American delegation was running the Naval Conference. He added that Mowrer's story that the United States was ready to enter a consultative pact was absolutely false.

Big things sometimes hinge on trifles. Had it not been for the fact that the sun sets in London five hours earlier than it does in Washington, plus the fact that there was a leak in the British delegation, the consultative pact which prevented the London Naval Conference from going on the rocks probably never would have been formally proposed.

Herbert Hoover was exceedingly wroth with his delegation. But before he had time to put his views in the form of a cablegram, the *London Herald*, organ of the British Labour party, published the report that the United States

was willing to enter a consultative pact. Obviously the report was a "plant" to force Mr. Stimson into the open. The
story appeared in an edition of the paper just before midnight of the day on which Mr. Hoover held his acid press
conference, and it was the first that London knew of the
startling proposal.

Naturally, there was an immediate clamor at the door
of Secretary Stimson to know if the report were true.

Mr. Stimson deliberated for an hour during which he
made a hasty call upon Ramsay MacDonald. Finally at
about one in the morning of March 26th he issued a carefully worded statement in which he announced American
readiness to consider a consultative pact if the French
"demand for security could be satisfied in some other
way."

Mr. Stimson purposely was vague about the "other
way" in which French security might be satisfied; but all
of Europe knew what he meant. If Great Britain would
secure the safety of France, then the United States would
have no objection to entering a consultative pact with
Britain and with other signatories of the treaty.

Chief responsibility for a five-power naval treaty, therefore, was shifted to the somewhat stooped but always willing shoulders of J. Ramsay MacDonald.

Next morning came a telegram from the State Department sent at the direction of the President. During the
entire Conference Mr. Hoover had given no direct orders
to his delegates and he did not do so now. He did not
directly veto a consultative pact but he was most petulant
about it. He complained bitterly that there had been a
leak in the American delegation permitting members of
the Foreign Policy Association to bombard the White
House on behalf of the consultative pact.

Probably if the telegram had been received one day
earlier, Mr. Stimson never would have made his announcement.

But it was too late.

The paralytic Conference had become electrified. Jaded delegates previously intent on making steamship reservations cancelled them. Aristide Briand, who had been sulking in Paris, returned to London. Arthur Henderson, who had abandoned all hope of attaining his cherished dreams of peace, came back into the discussions. And the Japanese, getting a tip from their friends, the French, that the Conference might be successful, after all, sent the long-awaited word from Tokyo virtually accepting the Reed compromise. Most important of all, from the American point of view, Henry L. Stimson took a new lease on life. The careworn, worried person who had been moping around the halls of the Ritz suddenly became a man of courage, vigor, and leadership.

"The Americans have changed everything," exclaimed M. Dumesnil after a meeting of chief delegates. And immediately the Conference started juggling additional pieces of naval puzzle—hitherto only a heterogeneous jungle of blocks—into something which began to resemble vaguely a five-power naval treaty.

Negotiations concentrated upon the problem of French security. Chief negotiators became Aristide Briand and Arthur Henderson, with Ramsay MacDonald looking nervously over the latter's shoulder. By this time there had been so much discussion of French security in the British press, that British public opinion approached a condition of skittishness very much like that of the American public regarding consultation. A Mediterranean pact, as first proposed by the French and once possible of acceptance, now would have wrecked the Labour Government.

Because of this, M. Briand and Mr. Henderson had to confine their labors to well-ploughed ground. They dug up a total of twenty-two formulas and recipes for security over a period of two weeks, but all of them suffered from one of two faults. Either they did not give enough security to France, or else they required too great commitments by Britain.

Finally, the discussions simmered down to the problem of interpreting the most controversial section of the League Covenant, Article XVI, and of trying to reconcile the differences between the Covenant and the Kellogg Pact.

For years the French had been skeptical regarding the support Britain would give the League if the Council should test the ominous words of this Article and require its members to sever "all trade or financial relations," prohibit "all intercourse between nationals," prevent "all financial, commercial, or personal intercourse," and take "effective military, naval or air force" action against an aggressor nation. France regarded these obligations as compulsory. Britain did not. France long had wanted to know in advance, and down to the last detail, just what Britain would do in case Article XVI of the Covenant was invoked. Britain, on the other hand, wanted to leave this just as vague as possible. She was inclined to fall back on the resolution of the Assembly voted in 1921 whereby each member of the League could judge individually whether the Covenant had been violated, and whether an army should be sent into the field and a navy across the seas to thwart the violator.

So now M. Briand, unswerving champion of the League of Nations, proposed that as a partial substitute for a Mediterranean security pact, Britain should put down in black and white just what she would do to support Article XVI. He also proposed that Great Britain adopt the findings of Viscount Cecil's committee for the reconciliation of differences between the Covenant of the League and the Kellogg Pact.

The crux of these differences lay in Article XV, which in two specific instances provides for war: first if one disputing country accepts the Council's report and the other does not; second in case the Council fails to agree unanimously regarding an international dispute. In either case, the alternative provided under the Covenant is war. And yet war under the Kellogg Pact is not legal.

Arthur Henderson, who had grappled with these problems during countless sessions at Geneva, was willing, in fact anxious, to grapple with them again. And probably there would have been agreement between the British and French at London had it not been for the political nervousness of Mr. Henderson's Prime Minister, J. Ramsay MacDonald. That mercurial gentleman vacillated back and forth between the demands of the French and the demands of his Cabinet like an animated shuttlecock. The chief stumbling-block in his own Cabinet was his Chancellor of the Exchequer, Philip Snowden. Snowden was adamant that no additional commitments be given to France. So was Lord Thomson. Their Tory opposition was even more adamant. And Lloyd George, whose little bloc of Liberals held the fate of the minority Labour party in the hollow of its hand, was equally hostile.

The result was that for one solid week Dwight Morrow spent most of his time dogging the erratic heels of the Prime Minister, trying to pick up the pieces of broken diplomacy which MacDonald scattered in his path. On the night of Sunday, March 30th, Mr. MacDonald returned to London from Chequers. And despite the fact that he had spent much of the day working with M. Briand toward agreement, he inspired an emphatic statement to the effect that Britain did not propose to surrender her political independence on the Continent.

What inspired the statement no one ever knew. But when the French Foreign Minister read it in the newspapers next morning, you could have knocked him over with his own ivory cigarette-holder. He staged another exhibition of Briand temperament, informed the press that both he and MacDonald had agreed to issue no public statements during the security negotiations, and once again threatened to go home. The tension became so great that it took a good hour of soothing palliatives on the part of Dwight Morrow and Henry L. Stimson to calm the feelings of the ruffled old Frenchman, after which they went over to Number 10 Downing Street and laid down the law to Mr. MacDonald for kicking over the international apple-cart. To retrieve the apples, they advised Mac-Donald to issue a statement in Parliament that France never had asked Britain to increase her commitments on the Continent.

MacDonald followed this advice.

After the speech next day, Briand felt better. So also did the Conference.

Thus the naval parley blew hot and cold, hot and cold.

Henderson and Briand by this time had got down to an understanding on Article XVI. Henderson had agreed to accept an interpretation previously outlined in Annex F of the Locarno Treaty, and Briand appeared satisfied. This interpretation stated:

> Each state member of the League is bound to coöperate loyally and effectively to support the Covenant and in resistance to any act of aggression to the extent which is compatible with its military situation and takes its geographical position into account.

This was not a new doctrine. Nor was it a new commitment for Great Britain. In 1925, when adopted, it was hailed as a great diplomatic achievement. Sir Austen Chamberlain, who negotiated it, was deluged with honors. Immediately after the announcement, King George presented Chamberlain with the Order of the Garter, highest reward that can be given anyone below the rank of duke. The Emperor of Japan and the Shah of Persia both had sought it. Balfour and Grey were the only commoners in twenty years to receive it. Its award to Chamberlain gave the stamp of royal approval to Locarno. Afterwards when the Locarno treaties came before Parliament, an efficient Tory machine jammed them through with clockwork precision. Baldwin, Churchill, and Chamberlain spoke in rapid succession. Labour opposition crumbled. Locarno was accepted despite the fact that it definitely increased the commitments of Great Britain on the Continent of Europe.

But now when it came to a mere reaffirmation of what Britain once before had promised, no steam-roller organization was available. The forces of Labour were scattered. Hundreds of newspapermen had been dishing up the debate over French security until the British public was hostile and weary. And to cap the climax, the man who had negotiated Locarno, who had been decorated by the King, who had been described by Lloyd George as a stork standing in the middle of Lake Locarno with one lone fish— the Locarno Pact—now was in opposition.

Sir Austen Chamberlain had become one of Mac-Donald's severest critics. The most embarrassing questions asked in debate came from Captain Anthony Eden, Chamberlain's former Parliamentary secretary.

To parry these, MacDonald once went even to Aristide Briand for help. He had heard Briand quote that staunch pillar of the Tory party, Disraeli, regarding Britain's obligations on the Continent during the period when British hesitation in supporting Turkey against Russia had led to the awful massacre of the Crimean War.

"I say it is extremely important that this country should take a step beforehand which would indicate what the policy of England would be," Disraeli had told Parliament, "that you should not have your Ministers meeting in the Council Chamber, hesitating and doubting and considering possible contingencies and then acting at last, but acting perhaps too late."

"That is all France asks of you now," Briand had told MacDonald; and MacDonald, impressed by Disraeli's words, asked Briand for the quotation for use against his Tory critics.

But it was no use. The Naval Conference had waited too long. It was too old to be entirely rejuvenated.

In the end, MacDonald made what were for him considerable concessions. After much backing and filling, he agreed to accept the Locarno interpretation of Britain's obligation under Article XVI. He also agreed to accept a compromise bridging the gap between the Covenant, which under Article XV permitted war, and the Kellogg Pact, which did not. He agreed that in case members of the Council should be at odds regarding the designation of an aggressor, the nations involved should not be released to have recourse to war, but should continue to be bound by the Kellogg Pact. This inferred commitments greater than apparent to the naked eye. It meant that Britain, under extreme circumstances, might be called upon to prevent war—perhaps use her fleet to prevent it.

But there was one all-important hitch in the agreement. Any amendment of Article XVI would have to be ratified by every member of the League. This might take years. Meanwhile Briand demanded a British pledge that she consider the amendment effective with the signing of the naval treaty.

Arthur Henderson was willing to give Briand the pledge. MacDonald was not. He saw political defeat, the end of the Labour Government staring him in the face. He refused to budge.

On this point the security discussions finally stalled. Aristide Briand returned to Paris to ascertain from his Cabinet just how much reduction of naval tonnage France was willing to give Britain in return for Britain's security definitions.

When he returned on April 8th, he brought, in effect, this answer:

France is not getting the security pact which she desired, but merely a reaffirmation of something already pledged. Moreover, there still remains the Italian claim to parity with France. In view of these facts the reduction of French naval tonnage cannot be appreciable. However, France sincerely appreciates the effort made by Great Britain to redefine her commitments on the Continent and the effort made by the United States to enter a consultative pact; and in view of this will give her blessing to a three-power naval treaty. Furthermore, France will resume naval negotiations with Italy in the very near future in order that both may sign the treaty. And as an evidence of good faith, France will even delay part of her building program in order to give time for a five-power treaty to be completed.

The British and American delegates now emerged from the cloud of security technicalities which tended to obscure their perspective. They took stock of their major achievements. Thanks to the tireless haggling of the dour-faced Senator Reed, plus the anxiety of the Japanese not to bear the stigma of being disarmament-wreckers, they had a three-power treaty. They also had French goodwill. This was all-important. There had been a time during the early days of the Conference when the American delegation—particularly its chief—did not give a tuppenny damn about the French. As long as Great Britain and the United States stood together, Mr. Stimson felt, it did not matter what the French said or did. There was a time also when this was the idea reflected by Ramsay MacDonald. But both had learned better. The unwillingness of Mr. MacDonald's Cabinet to divorce an old continental liaison for an untried and uncertain marriage across the Atlantic was what first brought the two upholders of the Rapidan against the hard wall of reality. The refusal of the British Admiralty to accept the original Anglo-American naval agreement if France stayed out of the picture added to their education. And finally Mr. Stimson, coached by that

indefatigable conciliator, Dwight Morrow, began to realize that the greatest inducement to disarmament was a
happy and satisfied France.

Apparently France was now satisfied. There had been
a ring of sincerity to M. Briand's message. Unquestionably
France was pleased that MacDonald had tried to redefine
British commitments under the League of Nations. Unquestionably, also, France would make an honest effort to
enter the naval treaty later. A new spirit of harmony pervaded the halls of St. James's Palace, and beyond any
doubt the last-minute willingness of the United States to
enter a consultative pact had been the cause of it all.

The end of the London Naval Conference came very
quickly after that. George Rublee, on his own initiative,
had been working on the draft of a three-power pact; and
after the decision to abandon a five-power treaty he quietly
produced it. Its most important provision was the "escalator clause," so christened by John Balderston because it
permitted the British Admiralty to lift up tonnage levels
in case any power outside the treaty—the French and
Italians—built beyond the water line of British safety. Because of Briand's pledge to delay French construction, the
escalator clause did not for the moment worry the Conference.

The treaty also contained a five-power section—signed
by France and Italy—setting forth humanitarian rules of
submarine warfare, an agreement extending the life of
capital ships, the regulations for the replacement, con-
version, and scrapping of war-vessels. It contained, however, none of Mr. Stimson's long-promised reduction.

For the United States, the naval construction bill was to
be $848,814,000.

The treaty was signed on April 22nd in the pleasant
drawing-room where Queen Anne once took tea, and
which on this particular day reflected the cheer of April
sunshine, scarlet damask, cut-glass chandeliers, the smile

of General Dawes, and yards and yards of red baize. The three King Georges of England looked down from their portraits immediately behind the American delegation, and it almost seemed as if the radiance of that morning had compelled George III to forget his scowl. A fire still burned brightly in the huge fireplace, but the scantily-clad American delegation which once had dreaded plenary sessions, did not need it now; and not even Dwight Morrow, who sat in a chair much too big for him, shivered. Senator Reed had cast off his sacrilegious sport suit for more formal attire, and M. Briand suggested to Senator Robinson that now was the time for him to make his long-promised speech on the naval sacrifices of the sovereign state of Arkansas.

But there was in that pleasant drawing-room a note not present at Versailles, nor at Washington in 1922, nor at Geneva in 1927. It was a note new to international conferences. The Versailles Treaty had been signed amid the fanfare of trumpets heralding a new era of peace. At the signing of the Washington Naval Treaty, Charles Evans Hughes had said: "This treaty absolutely ends naval competition for all time." Later, the last session of the Geneva Naval Conference was marked not by humility at failure, but determination to build.

But dominating even the smile of General Dawes on this balmy April morning was a note of humility, of appreciation for the work of naval reduction which still remained undone, a spirit epitomized by Ramsay MacDonald, Prime Minister of England and president of the Conference, when he said:

"This is just the end of the chapter. We are merely turning over a new leaf in naval negotiations."

A great many things—perhaps more than Mr. MacDonald or any of his colleagues realized—lay ahead.

On the voyage back to the United States, Dwight Mor-

row did not shave for four days. He was resting. Dressed
in a pair of baggy gray trousers and bedroom slippers, he
sat with his feet propped on a chair, talking to George
Rublee and dictating to his stenographer a personal diary
of the London Naval Conference. Perhaps the most important incident in the diary was Rublee's insistence that
the United States offer the Conference a consultative pact.

One day Henry L. Stimson dropped into Morrow's
cabin. He also had been dictating his Conference memoirs.
He also considered the Consultative Pact the high light
of the Conference.

"I've been trying to remember," he remarked, "how it
was I happened to propose that Consultative Pact."

Mr. Morrow did not reply.

6. IMPASSE IN THE MEDITERRANEAN

By the time Henry L. Stimson finally pushed his London
Naval Treaty through the Senate he felt that he justly deserved a vacation. For twelve months he had thought and
dreamed nothing but naval tonnages. All the preceding
summer, by long-distance telephone and cable, he had
hammered at naval reduction. All that winter he had
pounded on the tables of St. James's Palace. During the
heat of the early summer he had withstood the battering
cross-examination of Hiram Johnson, whom he hated, and
remained unruffled under the puny insults of Senator
Freddie Hale, whom he scorned.

So, as the summer waned, he took his military aide up
to Ausable, the most exclusive club in America, where he
cast for trout, tramped the pine-needle-strewn paths of
the Adirondacks, and ended with a motor trip through
Canada.

When finally Mr. Stimson returned to Washington in

September, he found that the world had made the most of his absence. Even during the few brief weeks that his back was turned, the worst that he had feared at London had happened. France and Italy, chief obstacles to a five-power naval treaty, had started a fast and furious naval race.

Mr. Stimson realized, of course, that the race actually started while Senator Morrow still was enjoying his four-day growth of beard aboard the *Leviathan*. On April 25th Italy had launched five new warships and laid the keel to a 45,000-ton transatlantic liner—all in the same day. The warships had been in the process of construction for more than a year, but there was something ominous in the fact that Mussolini rushed them to completion even before the American delegation had time to get home from London. There was something even more ominous in the fact that on May 1st—two days after the delegation landed—the Fascist Council of Ministers announced a 42,900-ton building program for that year. Ten days later, Il Duce, speaking at Leghorn, served notice of Italian insistence upon naval parity with France. One month later he laid down the keel of the cruiser *Bolzano*, following it with the keels of six destroyers, and the cruiser *Armando Diaz*.

By this time France, which at London claimed the Italian naval program was all bluff, got an attack of jitters. She rushed into effect her huge building program, the *Statut Naval*. Even Ramsay MacDonald, who during the London negotiations told himself so often that Italy did not have the money to build that he actually came to believe it, sent a note to his colleague in Washington warning that unless the race between Britain's two neighbors was checked, he would not be able to stop his rebellious admirals from invoking the escalator clause.

This worry finally resulted in a six months' Franco-Italian naval construction holiday, but it had little effect upon Mussolini. On September 19th, that gentleman found enough technical flaws in the truce to lay down the keel of another 10,000-ton cruiser, the *Luigi Cadorna*, following it in October with the keel of the *Montecuccoli*.

The full momentum of all this struck Mr. Stimson immediately after his return from the Adirondacks. Although he had described his London Treaty to the public in the most rapturous language, he knew all too well that it was deliberately evasive regarding the future of the battleship, had postponed the issue with Japan on cruisers, would cost the American taxpayer over $800,000,000 in any event, and meant nothing unless kept in cotton wool long enough for Italy and France to agree to its restrictions. Finally, Stimson realized that unless the precarious health of his treaty was improved, the chances of the general disarmament treaty for which the world had been waiting ever since Versailles, were about as valuable as the Armenian war debts.

This realization was corroborated by Hugh Gibson, who came back from Brussels simultaneously with Secretary Stimson's return and painted a picture distressingly similar to that which Mr. Stimson had seen but did not want to believe. Gibson served under Brand Whitlock during the occupation of Belgium, became an intimate friend of Herbert Hoover during his food-relief days, and was always a White House guest during his trips to Washington. On this visit Gibson sat with his host until a late hour describing the two armed camps into which Europe was divided: France and her satellites—Poland, Belgium, Czechoslovakia, Yugoslavia and Rumania—all profiting from the preservation of Versailles, and all facing Italy, which had thrust herself forward as champion of those profiting from revision of Versailles. Aligned with Italy were Germany, whose battles Grandi was fighting at Geneva; Austria with which Mussolini had patched up his old quarrel in the Tyrol; Bulgaria, whose King was wedding a royal Italian princess; Albania, which had become a protectorate of Rome; and Hungary, to which Italy was giving a free port on the Adriatic.

With Europe in this frame of mind, Gibson told Hoover, no disarmament conference could succeed. And in order to avoid disaster he urged that the General Conference be postponed until the statesmen of Europe could apply salve to some of its sore spots. The United States, he suggested, might take the lead in quietly getting these statesmen together.

The first part of this idea brought a frown from Mr. Hoover. He said the world was weary with waiting, should be asked to wait no longer. Public opinion, Mr. Hoover thought, would bring disarmament if only the world would settle down to the conference table. Besides, 1932 was a presidential-election year and, his host concluded, a successful conference held before election might be much-needed political ammunition during the campaign.

So postponement was ruled out. This, however, did not apply to Gibson's proposal of getting the statesmen of Europe to patch up their differences before the Conference; and as a starter to this, Hoover gave his friend permission to try his hand at the rôle of peacemaker between France and Italy.

For Gibson this was a big moment. Success meant the crowning climax of his career. Gibson had started at the bottom of the diplomatic ladder, and had gone far. Through a freak of circumstance—that of being hit over the head by an irate Cuban editor while sitting at a restaurant—he had been transferred from Havana to Europe just on the eve of the World War, where he had fought for the life of Edith Cavell, helped to break up the Austro-Hungarian Empire, married a Belgian wife, acted as Pershing's political adviser, and become the first American Minister to Poland. After the war he served in Switzerland, where he distinguished himself as chief advocate of closer coöperation between the United States and the peace efforts of the League of Nations. In fact it was Gibson who persuaded Coolidge to hold the 1927 Naval Conference under the League's friendly shadow at Geneva, bore the brunt of five long years on the Preparatory Commission for Disarmament, and who scampered back and forth across the Channel between Brussels and London whenever Charley Dawes had hemorrhages over his 1929 Anglo-American naval negotiations.

At the London Conference later, Gibson had been eclipsed by the more spectacular satellites which Stimson brought with him from Washington, and felt rather strongly that the Conference had rendered a definite disservice to the cause of disarmament by focusing the spotlight of public attention upon the bad blood between France and Italy. The more intense this spotlight, the more adamant became public opinion in both countries, and the more impossible for the delegations of either country to compromise. Therefore, if negotiations could be conducted within the cloister of the Foreign Offices, Gibson argued, there might be real chance of agreement.

To this end he worked out with Secretary Stimson a double-barrelled plan of attack. One was a barrage of sentimentality on the general question of naval limitation. The other was a series of secret disarmament conversations in Rome and Paris for which Gibson was to act as liaison officer.

On October 15th the first barrel was fired. The S.S. *Hikawa Maru,* arriving at Vancouver with the Japanese ratification to the London Treaty, was met by the American Consul-General, Ely T. Palmer, who handed the document to Lieutenants William M. Caldwell and Irvin A. Woodring, U. S. Air Corps, for an emergency flight across the continent in order to complete formal ratification of the London Treaty before the Preparatory Commission on Disarmament met in Geneva November 6th. Lieutenant Caldwell was killed in a snowstorm in the Rockies, but his co-pilot deposited the Japanese ratification in the hands of Pierre Boal, State Department disarmament expert, in time to catch the *Leviathan* to London. There he delivered the document to Ambassador Matsudaira.

The race across land and sea was to focus attention upon naval limitation. And although the Irish Free State spoiled Mr. Stimson's carefully laid plans by holding up British Empire ratification, nevertheless, Ramsay Mac-Donald and Mr. Hoover broadcast a radio appeal to the world on the night the treaty was supposed to go into effect, calling upon France and Italy to end their naval differences. That same night, under cover of the publicity barrage, Hugh Gibson was in Paris explaining his mission of bringing the two countries into the London Treaty.

Three days later he left for Rome.

Meanwhile, the French had been active in Washington. Commander Louis Sablé, naval attaché of the French Embassy, approached Constantine Brown with an idea which he thought might settle the controversy. He pointed out that while both Italy and France had a treaty right to parity in battleships, Italy was not interested in more battleships. On the other hand, France was. Let it be agreed, therefore, that France build three more battleships than Italy, in return for which France would scale down her cruiser program to a point approaching parity with the Italian fleet.

This plan, relayed to Secretary Stimson, caused him to exclaim, "Why didn't I think of that before!"

The next day he called Sablé and Ambassador Claudel to the State Department, discussed the idea in more detail, and cabled it to Hugh Gibson. In the end this became the basis on which Gibson built his Franco-Italian compromise.

Mussolini was definitely favorable to the compromise, despite his belligerent outbursts against France. But when

Gibson returned to Paris he struck a snag in the person of André Tardieu, most militarist-minded of recent French premiers. Apparently Sablé, although in communication with his Ministry of Marine, had not gone beyond to the Government itself. Tardieu objected vigorously. First and most important, he objected to France's building three new battleships. They were expensive, and in his opinion not worth the money. Three sea monsters would cost France about $100,000,000, while for only $70,000,000 France could build all eleven of the 10,000-ton cruisers contemplated in the Statut Naval. For a French politician perpetually bothered by budget-balancing, three battleships were something not to be kissed off with a smile. In the second place, even if France were to build the three additional battleships, Tardieu wanted something in the treaty specifying that Italy was not to build also. This was exactly what Mussolini sought to avoid. Il Duce didn't want the battleships, was ready to give verbal pledges not to build them, but couldn't risk the ignominy of putting this surrender down in black and white.

Tardieu remained adamant, and Hugh Gibson, tired of arguing, went back to Brussels for Christmas. Thus ended the American attempt to serve as a political intermediary for Europe.

The second chapter in the Franco-Italian naval mediation began shortly after Christmas and was conducted by the British. There were three reasons for this switch. One was British Labour alarm for the fate of the London Naval Treaty; another was the ending of the Franco-Italian naval holiday; and the third was a communication from the Council of the League of Nations asking the United States to participate in advance political discussions in order to clear away some of Europe's most contagious sore spots in preparation for the general disarmament conference. Coming at a time when Ambassador

Gibson had received only rebuff for trying to settle the Franco-Italian row, this invitation aroused considerable American peeve and caused Secretary Stimson to reply that the United States considered the disarmament conference primarily a European affair, and that the most it could do during the preliminary negotiations was cheer from the side lines. Regarding the particular problem of the Franco-Italian naval rivalry, so close to his heart, Stimson suggested to Ramsay MacDonald that he was nearest the scene and that it was his turn to assume the rôle of peacemaker.

Simultaneously, the naval construction truce between France and Italy came to an end. Actually the truce never had any real effect upon the building program of the two countries, but its formal conclusion served to emphasize in the public mind the importance of a Franco-Italian naval agreement.

This emphasis was borne home with particular force upon Ramsay MacDonald and his Labour cohorts, first because upon their shoulders rested all credit or blame for the London Treaty, second because the Admiralty and its Tory supporters were pointing to French and Italian naval programs and demanding that Britain invoke the escalator clause in order to preserve the two-power standard. In fact, it became obvious that some of the big-navy Tories actually were hoping that there would be no Franco-Italian agreement so that they might have an excuse to increase the power and prestige of His Majesty's fleet.

Realization of this caused MacDonald to send R. L. Craigie, chief of the American Section of the Foreign Office, back to Paris early in February to try to pick up the threads which Hugh Gibson had dropped in December. Craigie was a curly-haired Welshman who, despite an unassuming appearance which he tried to hide behind a monocle, had shown a certain canniness in dis-

armament negotiations. In Paris, however, he became lost
in a maze of naval technicalities, and got nowhere.

Finally, with the Admiralty bringing more and more
pressure upon the Labour Cabinet, and with A. V. Alexander, First Lord of the Admiralty, forced to inform Parliament that invocation of the escalator clause soon was
imminent, Arthur Henderson himself stepped into the
breach.

With an abruptness completely incompatible with his
life as a school-teacher, the British Foreign Minister telephoned Aristide Briand early in the morning of February
23rd, to ask when he could talk over the entire naval question.

"Immediately," replied Briand.

So the afternoon boat train found Henderson, Alexander, Craigie and two other experts en route to Paris. Never
had an important conference between two great nations
been arranged with such complete disregard for preliminary preparations.

The negotiations which followed continued to be
marked with abruptness and informality. Immediately
upon their arrival in Paris the British delegation went
to the Quai d'Orsay and remained there until late at night.
The next morning they conferred until noon, took time
off for one of Briand's famous luncheons, held an afternoon meeting—this time of experts—and caught the
5:20 P.M. train for Rome. Just before the train pulled out
they announced that sufficient agreement had been reached
to permit a concrete plan to be laid before Premier Mussolini. It seemed almost too good to be true. Skeptics said
there was a catch in it somewhere.

Meanwhile, Rome was consumed with curiosity and suspicion. The sight of the French and British Foreign Ministers arriving at an agreement in Paris looked to the
Fascist Government very much like a *fait accompli* which
Italy would be asked to swallow. In this they were mis-

taken. Mussolini found his belligerency punctured by the naïve charm of the blunt Mr. Henderson; and also Il Duce very much desired a naval agreement. The British proposal was similar to the formula André Tardieu had turned down just before Christmas. It provided for complete elimination of that patriotism-provoking word "parity," plus Commander Sablé's idea of additional battleships for France in return for a scaling down of the French big-cruiser program to seven—the Italian level. Both nations were to build 34,000 tons of airplane-carriers and were permitted only replacements of small cruisers and destroyers. Instead of three battleships, both countries had the nominal right to build two, but it was tacitly understood that Italy would not take advantage of that privilege.

Even two battleships, it is true, cost a great deal of money and Premier Tardieu's budget worries were still just as pressing in February as in December. But one important development had taken place in the interim. Germany had laid down a sister vessel to the pocket battleship *Ersatz Preussen*. And compared to the spectre of a German threat on the high seas, the cost of two battleships, even to the parsimonious André Tardieu, was as nothing.

For Arthur Henderson and the First Lord of the Admiralty the return trip to Paris resembled the return of Roman conquerors. All during the London Conference the most distinguished statesmen of Europe and the United States had endeavoured to settle the Franco-Italian naval deadlock. For additional weeks one of the shrewdest diplomats in the American service had striven to bring the two countries together. All had failed.

And now within three short days the direct and informal diplomacy of Henderson and Alexander had accomplished the unaccomplishable.

They were justly proud—even more so when they read the pæans of praise sung all round them.

"Mr. Henderson and Mr. Alexander have very happily crowned their efforts with success," remarked M. Briand.

"You have performed a real service and I am much pleased," said George V as he received his First Lord of the Admiralty at Buckingham Palace.

"We may take great satisfaction that the movement originally initiated by this country has finally apparently reached a complete solution and stopped all naval competition between those five powers," announced Secretary Stimson in a carefully mimeographed statement to the press.

"The peoples of the world owe a debt of gratitude to all who have collaborated so effectively toward the settlement," proclaimed Herbert Hoover.

Even the laconic *London Times* remarked that it was "a relief to be able to congratulate the Government on anything" and that the mission of Henderson and Alexander was "opportunely taken and ably performed."

But the statesmen of the world spoke too soon. Their hosannas rang forth on March 3rd and 4th. On March 6th Secretary Stimson planned to amplify his praise of the new-found love between France and Italy by a coast-to-coast broadcast over the *Washington Star* National Radio Forum. In fact, he had written his speech and sent out a draft for distribution when on March 5th, he suddenly recalled it.

The radio audience still is waiting for that address to be delivered.

Something had gone wrong in Paris. In fact, even while the plaudits of the statesmen were reverberating through Europe, the now worried Mr. Craigie had sent a telegram to Rome suggesting that some inconsequential changes would have to be made in the text of the agreement and that the naval experts of the three powers would meet in London to iron them out.

The trouble centered round 66,000 tons of French vessels which reached their age-limit before the treaty expired in 1936 and which the French admirals wanted to begin replacing before then. M. Massigli, the French expert, raised this question when Augusto Rosso and Don Fabrizio Ruspoli, the Italian experts, came up to confer with him.

"That's all settled," said Rosso.

"Not at all," replied Massigli.

Whereupon it developed that Mr. Craigie, the British go-between, had either misunderstood or deliberately ignored one of the important French demands. On their list of active vessels the French had retained several ships about to reach their age limit, others over-age, and even two, the *France* and the *Edger Quinet*, which had been sunk. But for bargaining purposes they were still listed as integral parts of the French navy, and the French insisted upon beginning replacements for them in 1934, two years before the treaty expired. Italy, on the other hand, had begun its construction program more recently, had new ships, and would reach the treaty expiration date of 1936 with a modern fleet, and ready to build against France on a more nearly equal footing.

But France upset the Italian strategy by insisting on beginning replacements before that time. In fact, she insisted with such tenacity that on this point, and this point alone, the much-vaunted Franco-Italian naval agreement was left dangling in mid-air.

Mr. Stimson, meanwhile, fretted helplessly in Washington. He, probably more than any other single person, had set his heart on the complete rounding out of his London Naval Treaty. Yet he sat on the other side of the Atlantic, powerless to move.

Also he had other worries. He noticed in the text of the agreement a reference to the fact that France and Italy

favored the limitation of battleships to only 23,333 tons
and the limitation of their guns to only a twelve-inch
diameter. He also noticed in the text a statement that "His
Majesty's Government in the United Kingdom will give
the French Government a written assurance that they
themselves favor a gun of a maximum calibre of twelve
inches and a reduction of the existing displacement of 35,-
000 tons." But despite these advance hints, Mr. Stimson
was not prepared for the information which the French
Ambassador, in his usual nonchalant manner, handed him
one day.

This information took the form of a telegram from the
French Government stating that "the British Government
had let the French and Italian Governments understand
that, should the Italo-French understanding of building
battleships not larger than 23,333 tons become a three-
power understanding, His Majesty's Government would
undertake to obtain the adherence of the Japanese and
the United States Governments as well."

This looked to Mr. Stimson very much like a frame-up.
It had all the earmarks of a revival of the old British attempt to put across what they had attempted at Geneva in
1927 and again at London in 1930—the reduction of the
monster dreadnaught which the American admirals
claimed to be indispensable for long-distance cruising to
the Philippines.

So Mr. Stimson radioed his most trusted negotiator,
Dwight Morrow, then en route to Sicily for a vacation,
asking him to go to London, sit down with the French,
British, and Italians, and try to straighten out the entire
naval mess.

This was March 16th. Senator Morrow arrived in London the next day, and called at the Foreign Office the same
evening. After forty-eight hours of strenuous negotiating
he thought he had persuaded the French that 66,000 tons
of replacements before 1936 was going to be rather an ex-

pensive proposition in addition to other French naval building, and believed he had worked out a satisfactory compromise. At any rate, this was what he reported to Mr. Stimson over the transatlantic telephone on March 18th. The telephone conversation lasted fifteen minutes, and immediately afterwards the Secretary of State let it be known that an agreement had been reached. Also he announced that his long-delayed radio address outlining the terms of the Franco-Italian agreement would now be made. It was scheduled for March 27th.

Mr. Stimson did not know, however, what fate had scheduled for March 20th. It was to be Europe's most important post-war development.

On March 4th, while the statesmen of western Europe had been singing hosannas over the new-found peace between Italy and France, the German Foreign Minister, Dr. Curtius, had slipped down to Vienna to discuss the common problems of Germany and Austria. And so busy was western Europe with its naval discussions that its diplomats, whose duty it is to ferret out every political development in the Germanic states, remained for two weeks blissfully ignorant of the momentous decision agreed upon in Vienna.

It was not until March 20th, two days after Senator Morrow had telephoned his encouraging news to Secretary Stimson, that the world suddenly became electrified by the news that Austria and Germany had negotiated a customs union.

Naval discussions immediately lapsed.

The French went into a huddle with their Little Entente Allies. The Anschluss at last was upon them! The long expected threat of German expansion had come!

The Italians also were busy. But their attitude was more aloof. Contrasted with the bitter denunciation of France, the position of Rome was lukewarm, almost friendly. There were even reports that Italy contemplated entering the customs union.

Suddenly the 66,000 tons of naval replacements loomed as large to France as the entire Italian fleet. French statesmen had visions of an Italy aligned with the traditional enemy across the Rhine, of an Italy whose warships France some day must face in the Mediterranean. And saying little more about it, these 66,000 tons of replacements became the *sine qua non*, as far as France was concerned, of any naval understanding whatsoever.

Negotiations dragged on for a short time. Statesmen went through the motions of continued hope, but only for the purpose of covering up the seriousness of the deadlock.

By April 1st, one month to the day after Arthur Henderson had announced success in Rome, his agreement was as dead as the cause of peace in Europe.

Once more—and for the last time—Mr. Stimson postponed his radio address.

To this day the only tangible result of the Franco-Italian naval negotiations is a bronze wreath on a grave in Arlington, paid for through an original donation of thirty-five cents by Shizeyoshi Fukushima, a Japanese schoolboy, who felt that the life of Lieutenant William Caldwell, in attempting to take the Japanese ratification of the London Naval Treaty across the treacherous Rockies, should not have been offered in vain.

7. Mr. Hoover Disarms the World

As President of the United States Herbert Hoover was a genuine man of peace. Most people attributed this to his Quaker ancestry plus his experience in feeding a war-starved Europe. In part, of course, they were right. Although reared in a "Friendly" atmosphere on an Iowa farm and in an Oregon boom town, Hoover had spent most of his life in parts of Australia, China, and Siberia, where the "Inner Light" dwindled at times to a scarcely discernible flicker. It grew brighter in later years when Mr. Hoover fell back upon the Society of Friends to feed the children of Germany and Russia, but even then he chafed and fumed at the pacific patience of his Quaker colleagues, and on one occasion stormed up and down the room because Quaker relief workers turned the other cheek to Soviet rebuffs. When he entered the White House some years later, he showed a greater devotion; also caus-ing, incidentally, a schism in the ranks of Washington Friends, some of whom wanted to build a new and stately Meeting House worthy of the President, while others felt that the simple meeting-place on I Street which had served them and their fathers for generations was adequate for any Friend, even though he be President of the United States. In the end, the modernists won. The new Meeting House was built on Florida Avenue, a preacher imported, and the Meeting rose in silent tribute as Mr. Hoover en-tered—much to the dismay of other Friends who recalled that William Penn had refused to take off his hat even to the king.

Despite the estrangement of the years, however, Mr. Hoover did owe part of his pacifism to his early Quaker upbringing; though more deeply rooted was another aver-sion to war which sprang from an entirely different source. If there was one thing in life which Herbert Hoover hated it was waste. His whole being rebelled at it. Much of his life had been spent in trying to eliminate it. As a mining engineer, as a conservator of food, as Secretary of Com-merce, he had taught the gospel of its elimination. Through the Bureau of Standards he persuaded the elec-tric industry to eliminate its wasteful manufacture of many different types of bulbs. He induced the saw industry to discard more than one hundred little-used types of saws. He negotiated with Canada to use the wasted water which flowed through the St. Lawrence. He juggled departments of the government to decrease top-heavy overhead. And one of the wastes which bothered him most was the sight of the navy's monsters of the sea costing $40,000,000 to build, and fulfilling no purpose more useful than to ride at anchor off Hampton Roads. This, to Herbert Hoover, was sheer, inexcusable waste, and his soul rebelled. It rebelled every time he went over the annual budget and saw listed thereon more money for the army and navy than all the other departments of the government together. It rebelled every time he thought of the nations of Europe spending billions on armament but pleading inability to pay their debts. And finally it rebelled every time he remembered the terrific, terrible wasted manpower of war.

So early in his term Mr. Hoover resolved that one achievement for which his administration would be notable was disarmament. The American people truly wanted disarmament, Mr. Hoover had concluded, and he was going to get it for them. It was an idealistic issue, and also it was good politics—which was the reason he so bluntly rejected Hugh Gibson's proposal in 1930 that the General Disarmament Conference be postponed until Europe was ready for it.

Mr. Hoover could not quite conceive of Europe not being ready for it. He had listened to the idealism that dripped from the lips of Ramsay MacDonald and Viscount Cecil. He had been impressed by the shrewd diplomacy of Briand and Grandi. He had become convinced that all war-burdened Europe needed was independent leadership and it would throw off the clutches of militarism. The masses of Europe, he was sure, were thirsting for peace. Disarmament, like prosperity, he believed, was just around the corner.

Henry L. Stimson felt just as keenly as his chief about the cause of disarmament, but for different reasons. To Stimson the world had reached a crisis where it could either build new and finer additions to the edifice of peace, or else retrograde to the time-honored doctrine of war. Unless the world showed confidence in the League of Nations, the Kellogg Pact, and all the other paraphernalia of peace by laying aside its arms, Stimson was convinced that the peace structure would crumble and decay.

How fervently he believed this, Mr. Stimson amply had demonstrated during the disputes between Paraguay and Bolivia, between Russia and China, and finally between China and Japan. Without batting an eye at Senate murmuring, he had delineated a militant policy of supporting the Kellogg Pact and led the world by the nose when it was reluctant to follow. He had gone farther in breaking down the traditional isolation of the United States than any man save Woodrow Wilson, and at times Herbert Hoover held his breath and almost deserted him. Theoretically, Mr. Hoover always favoured the Wall Street-Eastern intelligentsia doctrine of sharing world responsibilities, but never was he able to close his ears to the ranting of Hearst, Hiram Johnson, and other irreconcilables; with the result that the Hoover administration dabbled in Europe's political future under cover of a constant oratorical barrage lauding the isolationist policy of the Father of the Country.

But despite his desire for disarmament, Mr. Stimson was inclined to listen respectfully to the advice of Hugh Gibson. During a week-end at the Rapidan, Gibson hooked Toby, the pet rainbow trout of Peggy Ann Hoover, and cautioned her grandfather about starting a disarmament conference before Europe was ready for it. No disarmament was possible, Gibson argued, while the French and Germans remained at loggerheads. Almost equally difficult was any reduction of armament as long as the French and Italians continued their impasse. Even Great Britain, the great stabilizing power of Europe, was mistrusted by those whom she sought to stabilize, and the risk of inviting sixty nations, with a complexity of unsettled problems, to sit round a conference table with no guarantee they would

not jump at one another's throats was simply too great to undertake.

Mr. Hoover listened and remained unmoved. Aside from getting into a controversy with Assistant Secretary of the Navy Jahncke, over the propriety of "eating any kind of a trained animal, particularly one of Peggy Ann's pets," Gibson accomplished nothing.

Mr. Stimson, however, began to see that Gibson was right. A disarmament conference without advance political preparations, he finally decided, would be a calamity. And he made up his mind to go to Europe to act as personal intermediary in healing Europe's sore spots.

The Stimsonian strategy was simple. He was convinced that Europe's problems were not insoluble, that her statesmen suffered from lack of perspective, and that someone from the outside could contribute fresh ideas and inspiration. Stimson had made some genuine friends during the London Conference. He knew they trusted his honesty—though he did not know how much they distrusted his naïveté—and he felt that if he could get the heads of two or three governments together in an atmosphere of friendly coöperation, he might really smooth out some of the difficulties which bedeviled disarmament. If he could talk things over in the secrecy of a drawing-room, without the scrutiny of the public and the spotlight of headlines, Stimson was convinced he could get results.

So in order to preserve the myth of American isolation, Stimson arranged with the President to vacation in Europe. With him on that vacation, however, he took George Morlock, a code clerk, Allan Klots, his chief assistant and his class baby at Yale, plus that most indispensable of all encumbrances—his military aide.

In Italy Mr. Stimson had the time of his life. He was met in Naples by the bearded Signor Grandi, swept off his feet by the spontaneity of Latin enthusiasm, conferred sedately with Benito Mussolini in the Palazzo Venezia, and, as a climax, spent a seaside week-end with Grandi in the old castle of San Gallo where he planted the germ of an armament holiday, later to be sprung upon the world as a full-fledged Italian idea. Mr. Stimson was so busy he scarcely had time for an afternoon siesta. And it was while finally enjoying one that he was rudely awakened by word that the dictator of Fascist Italy himself was outside the castle in his speedboat, waiting to take the Secretary of State for a cruise. Mr. Stimson rubbed the sleep from his eyes, managed to hire a small rowboat, and went out to where Il Duce was anchored. Somewhat out of breath and wet with spray, Mr. Stimson was a little dismayed at Mussolini's greeting.

"But where is Mrs. Stimson?" he asked.

So the Secretary of State rowed all the way back to bring her.

Finally both got aboard. Except for a mechanic, Mussolini was his own crew.

"Shall it be fast or shall it be slow?" he asked, with a wave toward the open sea.

"Whatever you desire, Excellence," ventured Mrs. Stimson, and immediately wished that she hadn't. For the next hour she and her august husband clung to the gunwales of the boat and tried to look nonchalant while their pilot ploughed the Mediterranean at forty miles an hour, taking his hands off the wheel while he made orations in broken but voluble English.

After it was all over they said it was a great day and a fitting climax to a great visit in Italy.

The visit to France was less enjoyable. As commander of the 305th Field Artillery during the World War, Mr. Stimson had agreed with his doughboys that the French were a "peculiar race." But he did not understand, in fact, was somewhat hurt, by their failure to take notice of his visit. Their negligence was first apparent when he

arrived at the French border. No one, not even a high
official of the railroad company, was there to greet him.
This, Mr. Stimson excused as an oversight. His reception,
he thought, would come later in Paris. But when his train
pulled into the Gare de Lyons and he saw on the platform
only the usual crowd of porters, a fat newspaper woman,
and the staff of the American Embassy, he had to admit
he was disappointed. While he had not expected President
Doumer to be there in person, he had expected at least
the Chef de Protocol.

As his stay in Paris continued, Mr. Stimson became more
puzzled. It was true that his arrival coincided with the
furious debate over President Hoover's moratorium and
that the United States then had reached the rock bottom
of its unpopularity. Nevertheless, Mr. Stimson felt piqued
that he was so ignored. In Rome, his wife had been lavishly entertained by the Cabinet ladies; in Paris, no one
even left a card. In fact, when Mrs. Stimson accompanied
Camilla Edge, wife of the American ambassador, to the
Colonial Exposition, the doorman even refused to admit
Mrs. Stimson on Ambassador Edge's ticket. Finally, Mr.
Stimson became so indignant that he decided to leave for
London, and took particular joy in departing on the eve
of M. Briand's state dinner, given chiefly in honour of the
American Secretary of State. As a subtle dig at French hos-
pitality, however, Mrs. Stimson conceived the idea of send-
ing flowers to the ladies who should have called upon her.
Selecting large bunches of roses, she sent them to every
wife in the Cabinet, then took the boat train for London.

Next day Premier Laval followed Mr. Stimson. He was
most apologetic. Apparently the flowers had struck home.
Calling upon Mr. Stimson immediately, he urged that the
Secretary of State return to France en route to America
so that he could be received with the proper *politesse
française*. Mr. Stimson, however, was much too busy.
Also, he was anxious to go on to Germany.

His reception in Berlin was that of a conquering hero. Here was the Secretary of State of the most powerful nation in the world. Here was the representative of the government which had launched a moratorium for Germany's reparation payments. Here was the man who proposed that the world disarm to Germany's level. Berlin opened its arms and agreed in principle with everything Stimson said. His proposals, however, were not hard to swallow, for Stimson had come to believe that one of the most dangerous trouble spots in Europe was the Polish Corridor and that Germany's claims in this area could not be ignored.

This and other things caused Mr. Stimson to strike up a special friendship with Foreign Minister Curtius. The latter had served as a captain in the Kaiser's army, commanding a machine-gun company in a sector opposite Stimson's 305th Field Artillery. The two men swapped war stories and enjoyed each other immensely. And when Curtius told Stimson that the French were difficult to deal with, the American Secretary of State, still smarting from his snub in Paris and French sabotage of the Hoover moratorium, was definitely inclined to agree. When they parted, Mr. Stimson gave his new friend a twenty-foot toy sailboat with instructions to keep it for his first grandson, whose birth during the moratorium discussions had made the German Foreign Minister more nervous than the expectant mother.

Mr. Stimson ended his European pilgrimage with a two weeks' rest in a cottage in northern Scotland. Far from debts and disarmament, he shot grouse and viewed the turmoil of the world with philosophical perspective. To him the problems of Europe were not insoluble. His talks in London, Berlin, and Rome encouraged him. Under the influence of his earnest optimism, Europe's leaders—with the exception of the French—had assured him that their troubles would yield to the pressure of public opinion, that disarmament was just over the horizon.

What they did not tell Mr. Stimson, but what they firmly believed, was that in the pilgrimage of this kindly naïve individual, their fondest hopes for American political coöperation soon would be fulfilled.

When the Secretary of State returned to Washington in the late summer of 1931, he told his chief at the White House that the Disarmament Conference could be held.

Three months later, Mr. Stimson completely changed his mind. The bilateral conferences which the statesmen of Europe had faithfully promised to hold had not materialized. The Polish Corridor was as full of dynamite as ever. Relations between France and Germany had not improved. France still eyed with suspicion Italian encroachment upon her territory in Northern Africa. Yugoslav troops still were massed along the Italian border. Even the optimistic Mr. Stimson could not close his eyes to the fact that the chances of success at Geneva were almost *nil*. Not even Mr. Stimson, however, dared suggest this to Mr. Hoover, who, on January 1, 1932, began the second year of the depression with his chief hope for reëlection pinned upon some major achievement in the realm of foreign affairs.

The World Disarmament Conference at that time was only one month and two days off.

Mr. Stimson, therefore, made a personal move which he hoped might postpone the Conference, or at least arouse Europe to the dangers ahead. He wrote a letter to Sir Ronald Lindsay, suggesting that Europe settle its political problems before the Conference convened. Mr. Stimson did not dare send this as the official position of the United States. He knew his chief in the White House never would approve it. Caught between the ambition of Mr. Hoover and the dread specter of disaster at Geneva, Mr. Stimson labelled his views "purely personal." In reply, the British attempted to put him in a corner. Count-

ing upon the reluctance of the Secretary of State to cite
openly the tender political subjects which the United
States, according to tradition, must shun, Sir Ronald replied that he did not know what Mr. Stimson had in
mind and asked him to indicate more clearly what specific
problems on the European horizon caused him such worry.
Still hiding behind the fiction that he was expressing his
own personal views, Mr. Stimson enumerated to the British Ambassador the all too obvious political pitfalls in the
path of disarmament.

The British reply was brief and to the point. It welcomed Mr. Stimson's ideas. It proposed that a committee
be appointed to solve these problems of the Conference.
It suggested that an American be named chairman of that
committee.

Mr. Stimson said no more. An American at the head of
such a committee brought the United States into the
European mess with both feet. Furthermore, it placed responsibility for failure chiefly upon the United States.
There is nothing in the world which scares any Secretary
of State, or, for that matter, any Foreign Minister, more
than the specter of responsibility. Mr. Stimson turned
down the so-called personal suggestion of Sir Ronald and
headed bravely into the disaster of Geneva.

The delegation representing the United States at the
Conference for which the world had spent six years of
preparation had the word "futility" tagged to every name.
Technically, it was headed by a Secretary of State who had
admitted in advance that the Conference could not succeed. But since Mr. Stimson planned to go to Geneva only
if he saw an opportunity to pull a diplomatic master
stroke, the actual head of the delegation was Hugh Gibson, jack-of-all-trades for the State Department and the
most disarmament-discouraged member in the American
diplomatic game. Gibson's chief assistant was Hugh Wil-

son, American Minister to Switzerland, who also had been watching disarmament from so close a vantage-point that its details had clouded his perspective. As watch-dog for the Senate, Mr. Hoover selected Claude Augustus Swanson, a Virginian who for thirty years had faithfully played the game of the admirals as a member of the Senate Naval Affairs Committee and who was sent to Geneva chiefly to increase the slender Republican majority in the Senate. Norman Davis, another Democrat, had been Under Secretary of State during the Wilson Administration and was grooming himself as Mr. Stimson's successor. And at the last moment, Mr. Hoover yielded to the pressure of Miss Dorothy Detzer and other feminists by including in the delegation Miss Mary Woolley, a kindly soul, president of Mount Holyoke College and devoutly desirous of peace.

This conglomeration, together with the representatives of sixty nations, met in Geneva February 2, 1932, to make the first attempt in the history of the world to reduce every phase of its top-heavy burden of armament. It was a solemn occasion. It should have been as momentous as it was solemn. But it was not. There is no audience in the world so disillusioned, so discouraged, so superficial as the carefully dressed gathering which gathers periodically at the League of Nations to discuss the ills of Europe. Its members are polite, suave, and indifferent. They applaud modestly at the right time, and adjourn to the cloakrooms to say what they really think of one another.

The long-heralded General Conference for the Limitation of Armament was no different. Despite the long years of preparation, despite the hopes of the world, scarcely a delegate arrived who did not know what Hugh Gibson knew, what Henry L. Stimson knew, what Herbert Hoover should have known—that the Conference was doomed before it started.

Only the Afghan Delegation was frank. "We have heard," its spokesman said, "that there was to be a general discarding of armaments, and we believed that if we had a delegation present we could acquire some of these arms at greatly reduced prices."

The Agenda was bogged down with such Utopian questions as the internationalization of armament, a League of Nations army, and the highly controversial question of when is a reserve a soldier and when is he a reserve. Underneath this gloss was the stark and inescapable fact that Germany was going to demand arms equality with France and France was not going to grant equality; that Italy was feverishly building warships to attain parity with France, and that France was building to prevent that attainment; that Poland's crack cavalry troops were concentrated in the Corridor; that finally and most important, the Kellogg Pact upon which the foundation of peace was supposed to rest had just been given a deathblow by Japan.

Only two high-lights gave relief to this gloomy picture, and they flickered feebly. One was the avalanche of disarmament petitions which deluged the Conference. The other was the arms holiday negotiated by Dino Grandi. The former were estimated by newspapermen as equivalent in size to two cords of wood. One petition, signed by women of almost every country, bore 8,000,000 names. Another bore 2,500,000, another 2,000,000. They were sincere testimonials of the world's desire for peace and were handled tenderly by League functionaries.

"They are not destroyed," Sir Eric Drummond explained to the press. "They are in storage with other documents."

"You must require considerable storage space."

"Yes," replied Sir Eric, "most of the cellars of Geneva already are full of our documents."

Grandi's arms holiday, inspired by Mr. Stimson during his week-end at San Gallo, had been proposed to the Council of the League of Nations September 8th. It applied to

increases in all classes of armament—land, sea, and air—
and was to serve as an arms moratorium until the Disarmament Conference could do its permanent work. Delegates to the League applauded vigorously and pretended
to be surprised. Actually they were not. Signor Grandi's
gesture had been discussed in the Foreign Offices of Europe
ever since Mr. Stimson put it up to him in July. This
advance warning, plus a reservation by the real author of
the holiday, gave the world all the loopholes it required.

Mr. Stimson's reservation read: "The proposed truce
shall not apply to construction which had begun or for
which contracts had been let, prior to its entry into effect."

This quieted the big-navy outcry in the United States,
the admirals having just laid down the keels for four
cruisers, two submarines, and let bids for ten destroyers.
The Italians also had just laid the keels of the cruiser *At-
tendolo* and four destroyers; and before the holiday proposed by their Foreign Minister actually went into effect
they contracted for twenty-two new submarines. The
French, in turn, slapped down the keels of three 7,000 ton
cruisers, five 2,200 destroyers, and eight submarines. Finally the Japanese, realizing the Grandi proposal was to be
taken seriously, laid the keels of the cruisers *Mogami* and
Mikuma, and on the final day of the truce ordered three
large submarines.

The shipyards of the world now had enough orders to
last for several years.

Meanwhile the delegates at Geneva chanted a parrot-
like refrain, "The failure of this Conference means the
beginning of the next war," but showed not the slightest
disposition to compromise their divergent viewpoints.
Russia, Germany, and Italy proposed the reduction of all
warships to a size suited to their pocketbooks—10,000 tons.
Great Britain, France, and Japan, possessing larger vessels,
stood out for a limit of 25,000 tons. And the United States,

always worried about her long trade routes across the Pacific, stood pat for 35,000.

The abolition of submarines was advocated by the United States, Italy, Great Britain, and Germany. France and Japan, with a big fleet of under-sea boats, opposed. Russia, Italy, Germany, and Japan, with few or no airplane carriers, wanted to abolish them completely. The United States and Great Britain refused.

The abolition of heavy artillery was preached fervently by Great Britain, Italy, Germany, and Russia, but blocked by Japan and France. Italy, Russia, and Germany banded together to rid the world of bombing-planes. The United States and Great Britain found themselves in the same camp for the purpose of preserving them. The same three countries also endeavored to outlaw tanks. Japan and the United States declined.

Equality in armaments was advocated by Germany and Italy. Reduction based upon special needs was the plea of France, Britain, and Japan. Progressive reduction based upon the *status quo* was urged by the United States. Complete and total disarmament was proposed by Russia.

In disgust, Salvador Madariaga of Spain finally told the conference:

"The animals met to disarm. The lion looked the bull straight in the eye and said, 'Let us abolish horns.' The bull looked at the eagle and suggested that they abolish talons. The eagle, eyeing the lion, recommended the abolition of claws. 'No', said the bear, 'let us abolish everything and then have just one universal hug.' "

Litvinoff, who had advocated complete disarmament, laughed the loudest.

To prevent complete frustration, Hugh Gibson finally found four things on which the Conference would agree— the outlawing of poison gas, bacteriological warfare, incendiary weapons, and the bombing of civilian populations. After accepting this in principle, the delegates decided that their real stumbling-block was the pending elections in France and Germany, and adjourned until after Easter.

Just before they were scheduled to return to Geneva, the Disarmament delegates read in their morning papers the announcement that the American Secretary of State himself had determined to come to Europe and goad them into accomplishment.

This was something of a surprise. Nominally, of course, Mr. Stimson was head of the American delegation, but no one had expected him to make the trip unless he saw an opportunity to throw the weight of the United States into a crisis from which might emerge real disarmament. In fact, Mr. Stimson had been confined to his bed for two weeks just before the announcement came.

To the public, word was passed out that Mr. Stimson had been ordered by his doctors to take a sea voyage. On the inside it was known that two important factors were behind his trip. The first and most immediate was the conviction upon the part of Norman Davis that the Secretary of State might persuade the leaders of Europe to patch up their political difficulties. The second, and much more important, in the mind of Mr. Stimson, was the crisis facing the cause of peace as a result of the Japanese invasion of Manchuria.

Davis, the one member of the American delegation able to rise above the pettifogging details of career diplomats, had returned to the United States during the Easter interim, convinced that disarmament could get nowhere without a prelude of political agreement. This was not a new refrain. Hugh Gibson and Henry L. Stimson had sung it before. But Davis, a product of the business world which had nurtured Herbert Hoover, carried more weight with the White House. The statesmen of Europe, he told Hoover, were moribund and floundering. Fully aware of their drift toward catastrophe, they seemed powerless to head it off. But they would respond to outside leadership, and if Mr. Stimson could be induced to go abroad, Geneva was all set for the United States to resume its position at the helm of world affairs. Here was an opportunity, Davis convinced Mr. Hoover, for his administration to make a ten strike.

Mr. Stimson got out of bed, hobbled to the White House, and listened skeptically. The Davis story had a familiar ring. Mr. Stimson had heard it before. And although he told himself that he didn't believe it, still it touched a cord of naïve idealism in his soul, which Mr. Stimson, no matter how hard-boiled he pretended to be, never could suppress. Also it touched an ambition he had been cherishing for some weeks—to go to Europe and present to MacDonald, Tardieu, Grandi, and Bruening first hand his own fears for the peace of the world unless they coöperated with the United States in blocking the rampant march of Japanese militarism.

A vague inner voice deep down in Mr. Stimson's subconscious self whispered that he was making a mistake, that Norman Davis was a super-optimist who had oversold the President on the chances of disarmament. To this, however, he closed his ears. Cabling Geneva to rent the most commodious villa on the shores of Lake Leman, he gathered up his code clerk, his special assistant, his special assistant's wife, and his inseparable military aide, and set sail for Europe.

April 18th was a red letter on the calendar of the League of Nations. For on that day the Secretary of State of the United States, after twelve years of official aloofness, took his seat at the council table of the League. Old Leaguers beamed and exchanged significant glances. "It won't be long now," they said. Mr. Stimson, they knew, had definite leanings toward greater American coöperation in world

affairs. But that Mr. Stimson's efforts toward coöperation
were to be snagged on Europe's own recalcitrance they
neither could foresee nor would have admitted.

After his official debut, Mr. Stimson's appearances in
the council hall were brief. Rhetoric and forensic he left
to Miss Woolley and Senator Swanson. The real work of
reconciling the political differences of Europe was transferred to the fireside of Villa Besinge.

Immediately upon his arrival, Mr. Stimson announced
that he came to offer Geneva no cut-and-dried plan of
disarmament. He only sought to be helpful. His detached
view, he thought, might help to smooth over disarmament
differences. Mr. Stimson was sincere in this, but nobody
took him at his word. Welcomed as a magician who would
wave a magic wand, the American Secretary of State produced nothing but conversation. Geneva frankly was disappointed.

Of conversation there was a surfeit. Ramsay MacDonald,
Chancellor Bruening, Dino Grandi, all visited Villa
Besinge, all talked together before the Stimson fireplace.

But their interest was divided. While Mr. Stimson's
guests talked disarmament, he insisted upon talking Manchuria. The aggression of Japan in that far-away corner
of the world, he argued, was a far greater threat to peace
than the menace of big guns in Europe. Unless the mad
rush of Japanese militarism could be checked, the League
of Nations, the Kellogg Pact, all the carefully nurtured
peace machinery of the world, was doomed.

Mr. Stimson recently had come to realize what almost
everyone else around him long before had realized, that
British and French diplomacy was sabotaging every effort
he had made in the Far East. So now he pleaded for a
united front—a united front to preserve the peace machinery of the world, a united front against Japan.

The premiers of Europe listened politely. They were
practical men. Manchuria was a long way off. They were

more interested in things near home. What could they get from Mr. Stimson in return for this far-away coöperation which he so ardently desired?

André Tardieu, the most practical, the most skeptical, and the bluntest of them all, put the question.

"Will the United States," he asked, "be willing to relinquish its traditional policy of neutrality in case of armed action by the League against an aggressor?"

Mr. Stimson's reply was no.

Many other proposals were placed before Mr. Stimson. He was asked if the United States would make concessions on war debts. He was asked if the United States would consider a consultative pact. In each case his answer was no.

Mr. Stimson had come to Geneva empty-handed. He had nothing to offer—nothing except peace. Peace was all right as a principle, but there was no American coöperation to back it up. To the statesmen of Europe this was not enough.

Mr. Stimson was branded the most naïve diplomat ever to grace the shores of Lake Leman.

There came a time some months later when France was to reverse the position of André Tardieu—when Édouard Herriot was to conclude that France would not condone aggression on the part of Japan and expect simultaneously to condemn it on the part of Germany.

But that came later. Now, Premier Tardieu contracted a convenient case of laryngitis and remained in Paris. Whether the laryngitis was feigned or real Mr. Stimson never knew. He did know, however, that André Tardieu did not want to talk; and with the head of the nation commanding the largest army, the greatest air force, and the strongest navy of the Continent absent, discussion either of disarmament or Manchuria became futile.

So Mr. Stimson went home.

His villa was rented for an entire month, and only one-half of that period had elapsed. But he packed his things and left for Cannes. Camping there for two days was far preferable to the defeatist atmosphere of Geneva. Five hundred dollars in prepaid rent had been sacrificed to the cause of peace.

Back in Washington, the Secretary of State gave an unvarnished report to his chief in the White House. The leaders of Europe, he said, were fully aware that they were drifting toward disaster but seemed incapable either of lifting themselves out of the quagmire or of accepting the leadership of outside nations. Results from Geneva would be almost *nil*. Europe was not exactly content to stew in its own juice, but as far as he, Stimson, was concerned, it was going to stew.

Claude Swanson expressed it in different language a few weeks later. He came back to tell the President that Europe would "disarm when hell freezes over."

None of this pleased Mr. Hoover. He had been chafing both inwardly and audibly at the waste and wordage of Geneva. Not merely his passion for peace was aroused, but also his propensity for playing politics. By this time achievement at Geneva had become for him a political necessity. At home he was surrounded by an ever deepening depression. Achievement abroad was his only avenue of accomplishment. Some of his advisers tried to dissuade him from this, pointed out that the American public had no pulsating interest in a problem chiefly affecting Europe, that platform haranguers acclaiming disarmament to torchlight mass meetings would receive only the raspberry. But Hoover was adamant. With the same inability to sense defeat that blinded him to the fact that he could not be re-elected, he groped stubbornly for a disarmament solution.

One of those who encouraged him in this was Stanley Baldwin. During the Easter recess at Geneva, Hugh Gibson had talked with Baldwin, and reported to Hoover the Tory leader's great concern over the prospect of disarmament. A genuine idealist, Baldwin said that Great Britain would even scrap battleships in order to hasten an agreement. Here at last was one ray of hope and Mr. Hoover grasped at it eagerly. He talked to Baldwin by transatlantic telephone, consulted him several times; and on the basis of this encouragement, plus poorly concealed disgust at the failure of his own delegates, Mr. Hoover decided to arrange for disarmament himself.

Two things may be said of the product which resulted. First, it was essentially Hooverian, and, second, it came closer to real disarmament than any other of the 101 plans which saw the light of day at Geneva.

Hoover had worked it out himself during midnight hours in the Lincoln study. With the exception of James Grafton Rogers, Assistant Secretary of State, no one helped him. Fortified with sheaves of statistics on the armies and navies of the world, he tackled disarmament as if he were applying a slide rule to an engineering problem.

The result was a double-edged program for the elimination of offensive weapons and the decrease of Mr. Hoover's pet aversion—waste. It scrapped tanks, chemical warfare, large mobile guns, bombing-planes, the bombardment of civilians, and in general tried to humanize the inhuman practice of war. On the side of economy it reduced all land armament by one-third, battleships by one-third, submarines by one-third, and airplane-carriers, cruisers, and destroyers by one-fourth. It was a carefully planned, closely-knit proposal calculated to take Geneva by storm.

For one day it did. For one day Geneva exuded praise and enthusiasm. Nothing too extravagant could be said of the great and unselfish work of the President of the United States. Reports cabled back to the State Department fairly burnt up the wires with their optimism. Geneva was electrified. The Italians pronounced the plan "admirable." The Germans gave their unequivocal support. The small neutrals—Holland, Sweden, Denmark, Norway—did like-wise.

But there was one distinct quality about the Hoover plan. For nations which did not want to disarm it made evasion impossible.

And in a day or two Geneva began to cool perceptibly. The British, French, and Japanese showed no real enthusiasm from the start; and now they quietly began applying cold water.

"An agreement on the reduction-of-arms question was not to be obtained by unilateral statements," intoned the pious Sir John Simon, "but by consultation and coöperation, by give and take, and by adjustments of points of view; and there seems to be little of that in the proposals of the President of the United States."

The French echoed Sir John. Altruistic as usual, they complained that the reduction proposed by Mr. Hoover would be unfair to the small countries, insomuch as it would cut their armaments to the vanishing-point. This was the official French reaction. Unofficial, but government-inspired reaction, was more pointed. *Le Petit Parisien* voiced it as follows: "America certainly relishes theatrical stunts. The Hoover proposals, undoubtedly a part of the coming presidential campaign, have upset the work accomplished at Geneva in the last five months." *Le Matin* added the warning: "President Hoover cannot be excused for forgetting that international conferences are held for the purpose of conferring, not receiving ultimatums."

Mr. Hoover, however, persevered. He swallowed his pride and cabled to Hugh Gibson that his plan was not a take-it-or-leave-it proposition. In no sense was it an ultimatum. He was merely trying to put new life in what appeared to be a dying Conference. He was willing to accept changes and amendments to suit anyone and everyone.

This was explained by Mr. Gibson to his colleagues at

the Conference. It got nowhere. No matter how much Mr. Hoover might have trimmed the terms of his proposal, it would have been spurned. Geneva had read too many reports of a belligerent Congress challenging Mr. Hoover's power, of angry veterans demonstrating before the White House, of revolt in the farm belt, of an impending political upheaval when the nation balloted in November. Why accept a plan which his own country may repudiate, the delegates argued. Probably no proposal, even though it granted every delegation exactly what it wanted, could have overcome the handicap of Herbert Hoover's name.

The British, completely oblivious to the fact that Stanley Baldwin had helped inspire the Hoover plan, now prepared one of their own. They fell back on the time-worn proposal to limit not the total tonnage of battleships and cruisers, but the size of individual ships. This meant a saving in the distant future when the next cruisers and battleships were built, but no immediate economy. Also it meant that the massive American battleships considered so essential for long-range cruising to the Philippines, would be outlawed. No American President could have accepted such a proposal, and the British knew it. However, with characteristic thoroughness, they lined up the French and Japanese in advance. Once more the Conference was deadlocked.

The demise of Mr. Hoover's disarmament attempt came quickly after that. The Conference was getting nowhere. The longer it remained in the spotlight as a living example of Europe's frustration, the faster dwindled its chances of success. Its leaders decided to go home until some ray of hope could brighten the disarmament horizon. They ordered indefinite adjournment.

Eduard Beneš, Czechoslovakia's Foreign Minister and Europe's outstanding man of peace, was selected to officiate at the concluding ceremonies.

Beneš is a gloomy man. Years of persecution by the political police of the Hapsburgs made him so. He has the perpetual air of a professional mourner.

And when on the morning of July 23, 1932, he rose to read the motion of adjournment, his sombre tie, his black frock-coat, the cadences of voice lent all the atmosphere of a funeral. The delegates sighed, shook hands, and promised to meet again under more auspicious circumstances.

The Hoover disarmament plan—and with it the Conference upon which hung the peace of the world—was buried.

Chapter III

THE WORLD DECLINES TO PAY FOR WAR

1. THE HOOVER MORATORIUM

UNTIL he became President of the United States everything which Herbert Hoover touched turned to gold. In Australia, China, Siberia, and Africa the wave of his hand, the mere incorporation of his companies, brought millions pouring into his coffers. Even his feeding of Europe's war-starved population was accomplished with a profit which benefited other charitable projects for years afterward.

But almost the day after he entered the White House, Herbert Hoover's financial fairy turned her back. The tremendous thud of the falling stock market was followed by a slow and sickening evaporation of the foreign trade upon which he had built his reputation as Secretary of Commerce. This, in turn, gave impetus to the default of the five billions which the United States had pumped into none too stable governments in Latin America. And no matter how many bullish statements he issued predicting prosperity just around the corner, it almost seemed as if the god of averages had decreed that everything Mr. Hoover now touched should turn to stone.

Finally he approached the last straw. In 1931, with his re-election campaign only one year distant, Mr. Hoover faced the prospect of watching the vast wealth which American bankers had poured into Germany run down the world's financial waste-pipe.

In all fairness to Herbert Hoover it must be noted that he had not approved of placing this tremendous investment in Germany. He did not like the idea of foreign factories being financed by American capital to compete against American factories; and as Secretary of Commerce he protested somewhat irritably, though ineffectively, both against the terms of the war-debt settlement and the enthusiasm of the international bankers for floating loans for Germany.

In his opposition to the latter Mr. Hoover was not alone. Frank B. Kellogg and S. Parker Gilbert also remonstrated vigorously—though always secretly—against the complete disregard of the bankers for the welfare of their customers. On November 3, 1926, Gilbert, then Agent General for Reparations, wrote to his former partner, Paul Cravath, that he was "constantly amazed at the recklessness of American bankers in offering to the public the securities of the German States. . . ."

At about the same time, Secretary Kellogg wrote Harris, Forbes & Company and other bankers contemplating a $30,000,000 loan to the State of Prussia, informing them that "the German federal authorities themselves are not disposed to view with favor the indiscriminate placing of German loans in the American market, particularly when the borrowers are German municipalities and the purposes are not productive.

"Moreover," Mr. Kellogg continued, "it cannot be said at this time that serious complications in connection with interest and amortization payments may not arise. . . . These risks which obviously concern the investing public should, in the opinion of the Department, be cleared up by you before any action is taken. If they cannot be definitely eliminated, the Department believes that you should consider whether you do not owe a duty to your prospective clients fully to advise them of the circumstances."

This warning, however, fell on deaf ears. Not only did the bankers fail to advise their clients of the risks involved, but they deliberately boomed the German market. So that Parker Gilbert, again writing to his former law partner, attorney for Kuhn, Loeb, said: "I have just noticed in the *New York Times* the American prospectus for the recent loan of the State of Hamburg. I don't know whether this is a prospectus which the Office [Cravath, Henderson and de Gersdorff] had to pass on, but it does seem to me open to much the same criticism"—that of leaving the American investor uninformed regarding the obvious risks involved in Germany.

This opposition, of course, was voiced not publicly, but within the privacy of that peculiar and intimate relationship which existed between Wall Street and the Coolidge-Hoover Administration, a relationship which did not prevent the bankers from taking the bit in their teeth whenever and however they wished. In fact, all that was required during October, 1927, when Mr. Kellogg really put his foot down against the second $30,000,000 Harris, Forbes loan to Prussia, was for Allen W. Dulles to come to Washington and play a few holes of golf with the Secretary of State. Mr. Dulles, of course, was the grandson of a former Secretary of State, the nephew of another, and for many years had worked for Mr. Kellogg. But he was also the attorney for the bankers. And the bankers, despite all the platitudes and protests of Messrs. Kellogg and Gilbert, in the end always had their way.

It was not until Herbert Hoover was safely elected, and Calvin Coolidge ready to step out of the White House, that he, Calvin, dared deliver a very mild slap at the bankers. In his Armistice Day speech, 1928, he glumly announced that we had loaned to Germany almost exactly as much as the Allies had paid to us.

Not even then, however, did the American public realize that it had been paying reparations to the Allies on behalf of Germany and that the regular curtailment of the national debt so proudly and so regularly proclaimed by Andrew W. Mellon came, not from Europe's semiannual war debt installments to us, but from the pockets of those in

Keokuk, Kalamazoo, and Kansas City who had invested their hard-earned cash in German bonds. It was a circle which ended nowhere, which served only to preserve the myth of prosperity, and which the bankers either could not see or did not want to.

In fact, it was not until April and May, 1931, that all too obvious storm warnings began to tell the bankers that Europe was in for heavy financial weather.

To many, these signs had been obvious ever since the ephemeral financial empires built by Wall Street during the days of the Coolidge bull market had come crashing around its ears. With that crash, the stream of American bond issues to Europe dried up overnight. Not merely Germany, but other European governments, suddenly found themselves as hard-pinched as the American bond houses which hitherto made life so rosy. To protect their stake already invested in Germany, some banks, notably the Chase National and Lee, Higginson and Company, pumped additional money across the Atlantic chiefly in the form of short-term credits which, although actually the funds of their depositors, did not have to be sold as bonds to an investment-soured public.

Despite these shots in the arm, however, Germany gasped that she could not continue reparations payments.

The first gasps took the form of subrosa appeals to the British for a readjustment of the entire debt question. The British should take the initiative, Germany argued, because any public proposal by Germany would mean a severe shock to German credit. The British, however, did not relish the idea. And although they were most energetic in pulling wires behind the scenes, it was not until early June, 1931, that Ramsay MacDonald was willing to come out in the open with an admission that he had discussed debts and reparations with Chancellor Bruening and Foreign Minister Curtius during a week-end at Chequers.

By this time the financial crisis had become most acute. Although the factors which led up to it were largely economic, the incident which brought on the climax was entirely political.

It was the same incident which brought to an abrupt end the Anglo-American attempt to bring France and Italy into the London Naval Treaty.

On March 20, 1931, an astonished Europe woke up to read blazing headlines announcing a customs union between Austria and Germany. It was Vienna's answer to the Treaty of St. Germain-en-laye, to her insoluble economic situation, to her ever-increasing burden of debt. Also it was Berlin's answer to the Treaty of Versailles.

But the French had an answer to both. Not only were naval negotiations stopped with a suddenness which baffled even the optimistic Dwight Morrow, but France also began using her most powerful peace-time weapon—gold reserves.

The Bank of France began to withdraw its credits from the Kredit Anstaldt, of Vienna, most important bank in southeast Europe. On May 11th the Kredit Anstaldt closed its doors. Runs immediately started on other banks in Austria, were rumored in Hungary, had a disquieting effect in Germany. Baron Rothschild, president of the Kredit Anstaldt, had appealed to the capitals of western Europe to save his bank—in vain. Now, however, the reverberations from its fall reached not only London and Paris, but even New York and Washington.

Wall Street got the jitters. Not only had it advanced tremendous amounts to Germany, but it knew also that much of the money it lent to British bankers had been passed on at higher interest rates to both Germany and Austria. American bankers stood ready to lose their shirts.

They did not, however, intend to lose without a struggle.

So they turned for help to those who had warned them to stay out of Central Europe.

Mobilizing all the big guns along Wall Street, including Owen D. Young, Parker Gilbert, and George Harrison, the bankers poured a devastating barrage on the Hoover administration. During late May and early June they almost swamped the State Department and the White House. Their long-distance telephone calls from New York, Chicago, London, and Berlin would have made a tidy contribution to the annual expenses of American diplomacy.

Bankers' conferences at Woodley, the residence of Henry L. Stimson, were almost a daily occurrence, and it was not difficult to convince the Secretary of State that his department should reverse its original position that German loans were a bad risk, and now go to the support of the American bankers. Early in the game Mr. Stimson was won over to the idea of an all-round moratorium. Mr. Hoover, however, was more difficult. It was not that he was opposed to the theory of helping the bankers. The question was, how to help them. On this he remained completely indecisive.

Meanwhile no public hint was given that debt postponement was even under discussion. On May 1st, Mr. Hoover solemnly informed his press conference that the idea was unthinkable. On May 5th, his Secretary of the Treasury carefully reminded the International Chamber of Commerce that the United States had "confidence in the willingness of Europe to honor its obligations".

But it was only a few days later that the continued crumbling of Austrian finances caused Mr. Hoover to consider the unprecedented plan of authorizing the Federal Reserve Bank of New York to coöperate with the Bank of England and the Bank of France in advancing $7,000,000 each to bolster the banks of Austria, then in imminent danger of collapse. Mr. Hoover might have given his O. K. to this plan had he not suddenly discovered a French catch.

Before the Bank of France would coöperate, it demanded that Austria give a definite pledge that she would make no future political or economic agreements without first informing France. In other words, France was not going to nullify its own efforts to thwart the proposed Austro-German Customs Union until she had some guarantee there would be no Union.

Informed of the French reservation, Mr. Hoover withdrew Federal Reserve coöperation; but the British, with vast amounts invested in Central Europe, went ahead. They put up the entire $21,000,000—much of it borrowed from the United States.

This made only a ripple in the tide of financial collapse which now swept in all directions from Vienna.

That tide now centered on Germany.

There Bruening and Curtius struggled desperately to keep a battered middle-course government from going down before the onslaught of a violent Communistic Left and an even more violent Nationalistic Right. Ambassador Sackett, on leave from his post in Berlin, advised Mr. Hoover that this might be the last stand of the German Moderates, that the crash of Bruening would throw Germany into the hands of a Fascist dictatorship.

Mr. Hoover groped frantically for a course of action.

Pressure upon him increased from all sides. Not only were the bankers camping continually on his doorstep, but he was also besieged by such financially potent members of his administration as Eugene Meyer, Ogden Mills, Henry L. Stimson, and Charles G. Dawes. As the days passed their efforts concentrated upon the idea of a moratorium on all debts during the next two or three years. But they could not carry their chief with them. The most he was willing to do was send his Secretary of the Treasury, Mr. Mellon, to Europe; and he was not even willing to admit that Mr. Mellon was going to report on the financial chaos. According to official announcements, Mr. Mellon made the trip to see his son Paul graduate from Cambridge.

Simultaneously—June 6th—Bruening and Curtius, having made their last appeal to Ramsay MacDonald during the weed-end at Chequers, announced that Germany could pay no more.

"In addition to the general crisis in which we live," read Chancellor Bruening's manifesto, "we have to carry the special burden of having to make payments as the vanquished in the World War. . . .

"The Reich's Government is compelled to ask the German nation to shoulder most heavy burdens and sacrifices in order to maintain the Reich's solvency. . . . It is better, even though it hurts, in orderly fashion to reduce outlays and demand contributions from those who still possess incomes, than to run the risk that payments upon which the subsistence of the broad masses rests can no longer be effected.

"The putting forth of the last power and reserves of the nation entitles the German Government, and makes it its duty toward the German people, to tell the world: 'The limits of the privations we have imposed on our people have been reached.'"

Bruening was making a desperate bid for two things.

By the sincerity of his appeal he hoped to win over Germany's creditors to a moratorium. In case this failed, he hoped to keep his government in the saddle by shifting responsibility for Germany's predicament to the Allies. For simultaneously with this appeal he had been forced to make public the new program of taxation and economy necessary to balance the German budget, and it brought forth gasps of resentment throughout the Reich. Especially did it bring protests from the German middle classes, already groaning under a terrific tax burden.

There were immediate demands for the convening of the Reichstag, and it was significant that they came not only from Nazis, Communists, and Nationalists, but also from Bruening's and Curtius' own middle-class parties. Unquestionably their tax program caused disastrous diversions of German Moderates to the Right and Left.

With these storm warnings ringing in his ears, Herbert Hoover departed for the Middle West.

It was a trip which he dreaded almost more than he dreaded making a decision regarding the dilemma facing him in Europe. For he was to dedicate the Memorial to Warren G. Harding in Marion, Ohio.

This was a ceremony postponed so long that it had become a genuine embarrassment to the Republican National Committee. Mr. Hoover did not want to dedicate it, nor did any other prominent member of the party. And yet party outcasts like Harry Dougherty kept making speeches proclaiming it an open shame that a memorial to the man who once had served as President of the United States remained unhonored, unadorned, and unrecognized by the man who once served in his Cabinet. Finally it was arranged that Mr. Hoover should make a trip to Springfield, Illinois, speak at the tomb of another Republican President—Abraham Lincoln; speak also at Indianapolis, and en route stop to pay his respects to the tomb of Harding.

Mr. Hoover embarked on that trip with the feeling that he was going to be booed from one end of it to the other. Months of sitting in the White House watching the economic toboggan touch lower and lower depths, months of scanning editorial comment which heaped bitter denunciation upon his head, had given the President an inferiority complex which materially handicapped his effectiveness. Everyone, he sometimes felt, must be against him.

His trip west, therefore, was a revelation. At Martinsburg, West Virginia, his first stop, friendly crowds were at the railroad station. They smiled and cheered. This continued. Mr. Hoover's confidence began to surge back. In Indianapolis, Springfield, even Marion, his welcome was enthusiastic and genuine. He began to feel like a new man. En route also, Mr. Hoover received a message from his Secretary of the Treasury, who by this time had arrived in London and reported first hand on the economic situation in Central Europe. The picture he painted was black. Unless the United States moved, the financial structure of most of Europe would come crashing around its ears.

Mr. Hoover came back from his trip refreshed and ready for action. Mr. Stimson was at the White House almost the moment he arrived. He had received a telegram direct from President von Hindenburg.

"Relief must come at once if we are to avoid serious misfortune for ourselves and others," the telegram read. "You, Mr. President, as the representative of the great American people, are in a position to take the steps by which an immediate change in the situation threatening Germany and the rest of the world may be brought about."

Mr. Hoover decided to move for a two-year moratorium on all war debts and reparations.

He acted just in time. This was Thursday, June 18th. By the following Monday, every bank in Germany would have been closed.

During his entire four years in the White House, Herbert Hoover never was able to conquer a deep-rooted antipathy for the French. There were several reasons for this, some of them going back to French recalcitrance during his food-relief days, some going back to French tariff reprisals during his term as Secretary of Commerce. The French, Mr. Hoover felt, were a most inefficient race— which to his efficient soul was the acme of condemnation. In addition to this they were not to be trusted. This feeling was heightened during the London Naval Conference when French refusal to coöperate upset the great gesture he had planned for world peace. And it reached its climax just before the moratorium proposal, when France, at the last minute, backed out of the Franco-Italian naval agreement just after Mr. Hoover had applauded it as one of the great achievements of recent diplomacy.

Mr. Hoover's antipathy toward the French showed itself in many ways, including among other things his relations with the French Ambassador. Paul Claudel, later Dean of the Diplomatic Corps, probably was as sincere a friend of the United States as his famed predecessor, Jules Jusserand—in addition to which he was ardently devoted to the pacific ideals of Henry L. Stimson.

Being a poet and a visionary, however, Claudel at times was definitely impractical. And on one well-remembered occasion he was impractical to the extent of allowing his girth to increase during the summer without taking the precaution to make corresponding alterations to his diplomatic uniform. On the occasion of the season's first White House reception—that to the Diplomatic Corps—the French Ambassador found himself in the uncomfortable predicament of being forced to don a tunic which was much too small. Being a man who at all times enjoyed comfort, Claudel decided that he would slip on his cape over his shirt, and carry his tunic carefully concealed under one arm until he got to the privacy of the White House cloakroom, where he could slip the tunic on again.

This would save at least twenty minutes of abdominal agony.

So the Ambassador of France stepped into his limousine and placed his tunic, carefully folded, on the seat beside him. Fortunately, Madame Claudel had not returned from her summer in Paris and there was no danger of his getting a scolding.

Being the second ranking member of the Diplomatic Corps, Claudel was one of the first to arrive and was ushered into the gentlemen's dressing-room without delay. He was about to take his place near the head of the glittering line which would file past the President, when one of his fellow ambassadors stopped him.

"My dear colleague, a thousand pardons," he said, "but you are not dressed. Where is your tunic?"

Claudel felt his bosom. His face registered horror and dismay. The tunic still reposed, carefully folded, on the rear seat of his car.

White House aides, immediately summoned, managed to keep straight faces while they sought the ambassador's chauffeur. He was not at the Embassy, nor outside the White House. Claudel remembered with increasing dismay that he had ordered the car to return at ten o'clock and that, on given that much time off, William undoubtedly would go to see his best girl.

District of Columbia police were summoned. They were instructed to find the address of William's best girl and send a motorcycle escort to procure him and the missing tunic.

Meanwhile, as the hour for the start of the reception approached, the Ambassador of France stood in the men's room, tunicless, frantic. At last a White House aide approached the President of the United States, explaining the predicament.

"Do you think we should wait for about ten minutes?" he suggested.

"Not one minute for the frog," snapped Mr. Hoover, and the reception began.

Glittering representatives of fifty nations filed into the Blue Room, from Sir Ronald Lindsay, towering above everyone in a marine uniform with a military belt, to the Japanese Embassy staff, all nineteen of them, dressed in plain evening clothes, bowing very low and saying: "Good evening, Mr. President. Very pleased. Very much honor."

In the men's washroom sat the Ambassador of France, dejected and alone.

Not until William returned the Embassy limousine,

more than an hour later, was he released from solitary confinement and allowed to go home.

It was Mr. Hoover's general antipathy for France which prompted his specific instruction to Secretary Stimson that no word of his moratorium proposal was to be given Ambassador Claudel before it was given to other diplomatic representatives.

Probably it was this failure to consult with the nation most concerned with German reparations which caused the failure of what the world at first hailed as the master stroke of Mr. Hoover.

Although the British had been in on the moratorium discussions for a month, although some twenty leaders of Congress were consulted, either in person or by long-distance telephone, and although Ambassador Claudel had been a frequent caller upon Secretary Stimson, no word of the momentous decision was communicated to him. And it was not until news of the decision leaked out through a long-distance telephone conversation between Mr. Hoover and Senator Vandenburg, who talked from a hotel telephone in Canada, that the French were taken into the moratorium secret.

This was on the morning of June 19th. On the afternoon of that day Mr. Stimson was given the job of breaking the momentous news to the other envoys. He did so in typical Stimsonian manner. Calling the diplomatic representatives of Great Britain, Italy, Germany, and Belgium, one by one, out to his colonial manor, he gave each a little pad of paper and pencil—an unheard-of reflection upon the mental caliber of a diplomat. Then he dictated the terms by which the United States was willing to suspend all war-debt payments to it from European creditors. These were:

That all German debt payments to the Allies be suspended.

That this include not only conditional payments, postponable under the Young Plan, but also unconditional payments which it was not contemplated Germany should postpone.

That the only exceptions to this rule were to be: (a) German payments of interest on the Young Plan and Dawes Plan bonds which had been sold to the public, and which, therefore, no government could hold up; (b) German payments to the United States on behalf of American citizens who suffered during Germany's submarine campaign, and for other damages awarded by the German-American Mixed Claims Commission.

Finally, that the Hoover moratorium must be accepted *in toto* by the Allies, or not at all.

Mr. Stimson was a little vague regarding other details, such as how long the moratorium was to last and how soon Germany was to pay the money back. There was good reason for this vagueness. First, few of the details had been worked out, and, second, there was considerable difference of opinion among Hoover's advisers regarding some of them.

Owen D. Young, Ogden Mills, and Eugene Meyer, for instance, urged that the moratorium extend for at least two years, preferably three. Anything less than that, they argued, would be futile, perhaps damaging, since it was impossible in only twelve months for Central Europe to put its house in order.

Mr. Hoover concurred. But confronted by such skeptics as Borah, Swanson, Carter Glass, Pat Harrison, Tom Walsh, and a score of other Congressional leaders summoned to the White House to approve the moratorium, he lost his nerve. The two-year debt suspension dwindled to only one. Some Congressional leaders opposed even that; and it took all the gloom that Mr. Hoover could inject into the international picture plus definite assurances that the moratorium in no way implied the reduction of debts, to get a reasonably unanimous Congressional O. K. stamped upon his proposal.

With this O. K. secured and with news of his move leaking fast, Mr. Hoover summoned a special press conference at five o'clock, Saturday, June 20th. To it, with careful emphasis on the fact that he did not approve "in any remote sense the cancellation of debts to us," the President announced his proposal of a one-year moratorium on Allied debts to the United States, contingent upon the Allies' sacrificing their payments from Germany. Later it was learned he had also discussed Federal Reserve coöperation with the Bank of England, the Bank of France, and the Bank of International Settlements at Basle, to advance $100,000,000 of short-term credits to the Reichsbank.

No other move during Herbert Hoover's four years in the White House received such enthusiastic acclaim as his moratorium announcement of June 20th. It lifted a discouraged Europe to unknown heights of optimism. It caused frantic bull trading on the stock market. And it heaped upon his shoulders more editorial praise than he received during all the rest of his administration.

But there were no pæans of praise from France.

In Paris the proposal burst like a bombshell. No hint of its advent had been conveyed to the French public. Only a few hours' warning had been given to the Quai d'Orsay. The result was a prodigious hue and cry that Mr. Hoover had completely upset the Young Plan, had no regard for the balancing of the French budget, was robbing the French peasant of his hard-earned savings, was making a martyr out of Germany, and under the cloak of altruism was safeguarding American investors at the expense of Germany's prior creditors.

Mr. Hoover's idealism was going to cost France at least $80,000,000!

"Uncle Shylock!" screamed the headlines.

"Not one centime for the gangsters!"

Mr. Hoover winced. He had expected a welcome in Europe as enthusiastic as in the United States. But he remained adamant. He had offered the world this child of his own brain, and France would have to take it or leave it.

This information, a little more subtly worded, was conveyed to Ambassador Claudel by Secretary Stimson on June 22nd, even before the French had recovered from their first bitter jolt.

The Quai d'Orsay countered with a note handed by Claudel to Stimson on June 24th, stating that, while France accepted the great humanitarian proposal of the President of the United States, it must, however, insist upon certain reservations. These reservations, from Herbert Hoover's point of view, meant rejection.

They included:

> Insistence that the Young Plan remain intact.
>
> A demand that the non-postponable payments under the Young Plan be paid by Germany into the Bank of International Settlements and then loaned back to various semi-insolvent French Allies—Jugoslavia, Rumania, Belgium, and Greece.
>
> Repayment by Germany of the postponed reparations within the next year.

This was rejection not only of the specific points of Mr. Hoover's plan; but even more disastrous, it was rejection of his thesis that only a decisive, clean-cut, generous gesture, accepted without diplomatic haggling, could restore confidence in the shattered finances of Central Europe.

Mr. Hoover had considered his plan most carefully. He had offered what he thought was an open-and-shut proposition, one which Europe could accept in its entirety or reject. It was based upon the ABC thesis that payment of all intergovernment debts be postponed for one year. The proposition was so simple that the man in the street could easily grasp it; so simple that political leaders of both parties and of both houses of Congress had given their consent. But they had given it to this specific plan, to no other.

And now France, that *bête noire* of all Herbert Hoover's foreign relations, had come along with proposals and counter-proposals, with complicated suggestions and detailed demands which left the American public in a maze of heterogeneous befuddlement, and which completely upset Mr. Hoover's apple-cart.

If the French had rejected the Hoover plan *in toto*, he would have been saved. He could have shoved the responsibility for Europe's financial collapse on French shoulders, and at least received the plaudits of the world for his noble attempt. But the French were much too clever for that. They accepted in principle, but rejected in fact. And Herbert Hoover saw before him a vista of diplomatic dickering, during which his plan would be picked to pieces to suit the chief vanquisher of Germany.

No wonder that he was vexed. No wonder also that he issued private diatribes, holding up France as the one nation blocking his moratorium. No wonder also that negotiations from that point on evolved into a digging-in contest between Paris and Washington.

"Mr. Hoover can intrench himself behind his Congress. I can intrench myself behind the Chamber," remarked Premier Laval. "I remain cordial but firm."

The battle was taken up by Mr. Hoover's subordinates, even percolated to the press.

Ogden Mills, Acting Secretary of the Treasury, warned M. Monick, financial counselor of France, that if the United States wanted to it could debase the French franc almost overnight.

"*Mais oui,*" replied Monick, with a smile, "France has nearly one billion dollars on deposit in New York. We can withdraw it tomorrow. We should not want to do so."

Mills changed the conversation.

Another attempted threat was planted with the unsuspecting correspondent of the Chicago *Daily News,* LeRoy
Vernon. Called by Mr. Hoover to the White House, Vernon was given a story intimating that, if the French insisted upon their recalcitrant attitude, they ran the risk
of world isolation.

"Italy's action yesterday in putting into effect a provisional moratorium," Vernon wrote after his White House
conference, "patently suggests that even a refusal by France
by no means ends the incident. It is admittedly possible for
the powers which agree with the Hoover Plan to join the
United States in a new plan to proceed without France.

"That situation is not desirable, but it is apparently the
only recourse left if France is not willing to help save Germany. President Hoover is known to have more than one
string to his bow."

But since publication of the story in Chicago might not
reach the French, Vernon was asked to see that a copy—
corrected, incidentally, in the President's own handwrit-
ing—got to French newspaper men. Subsequently, Pierre
Denoyer, correspondent of *Le Petit Parisien,* and Henry
Sweinhart, of the Havas News Agency, were approached.
Not sufficiently impressed by the story, however, they consulted the French Embassy, where it was dubbed a piece
of "clumsy propaganda." A strong sense of humor, however, got the best of Denoyer. Taking his copy to the
White House, he consulted Theodore Joslin, presidential
secretary, as to whether it represented Mr. Hoover's point
of view, and in Joslin's presence threw the story into the
waste-basket.

Meanwhile, the more irked Mr. Hoover became, the
more recalcitrant became the French. The more Mr.
Hoover demanded immediate action, the more the
French bid for delay. Immediate action, Mr. Hoover argued, was necessary to restore confidence, was essential to
save Germany. But Germany, in the opinion of France,

was not particularly worth saving. What was worth saving was the Versailles Treaty, French security, the system of French alliances.

It was the old, old question which had disrupted disarmament meetings, stymied the League of Nations, and kept Europe an armed camp ever since the Armistice—security.

And in her fight, France had able allies. Simultaneous with her first counter-proposals to Mr. Hoover, the diplomatic representatives of the Little Entente trouped down to the State Department ensemble and registered their emphatic and individual protests against the Hoover moratorium. For most of them suspension of debt payments meant a serious readjustment of the budget. For Jugoslavia it meant that she was relieved of paying $3,000,000 on war debts, but relinquished $19,000,000 from Germany, a net loss to her of $16,000,000, and no insignificant sum for a country of her resources.

So Dr. Leonide Pitamic, her Minister, protested violently.

So also did Charles Davila, Minister of Rumania. He embarrassed Mr. Stimson on several points.

"I note, Mr. Secretary, in the statement you gave me," he said—"which, by the way, you said was confidential but which I read in the press the same day—certain omissions as compared with the statement which I read in the press. Which of them am I to take as correct?"

"I think you will find the one in the press to be correct."

"I also was much interested to note the way President Hoover apparently linked Allied war debts and German reparations, which hitherto the United States has claimed had no connection."

Mr. Stimson replied that he did not care to discuss the question at the moment.

"Finally," persisted the Minister of Rumania, "I must call your attention to the fact that, since Rumania receives

more money from Germany than she pays to her former
Allies, she will lose by the moratorium $1,400,000—not a
large amount from the American point of view, but to us
very considerable indeed."

"Let us not go into that now," replied the impatient
Mr. Stimson. "Let us get this thing accepted first and
straighten out those details later."

These were grim, turbulent days for Herbert Hoover.
Closeted from all except the little group which ran back
and forth with bulletins from the moratorium front, he
watched the studied recalcitrance of France slowly under-
mine the plan which was to have been his and Europe's
salvation. He was being slowly submerged in the quicksand
of French inertia, but, refusing to admit it, struggled desperately, at times valiantly, against his engulfing adversary.
In a cubby-hole adjacent to the Cabinet Room he had in-
stalled one terminal of a transatlantic telephone. Other
terminals were in the offices of the Secretary of State and
the Acting Secretary of the Treasury, while two others were
headpiece phones used by State Department stenographers
who took down each word exchanged in the Hoover system of transatlantic diplomacy. With this battery functioning on one end of the telephone, Mr. Hoover got reports on the latest conversations between Mellon, Edge,
Laval, and Briand, growling petulantly but sometimes
making valuable suggestions regarding their next move.

More than at any other time, Mr. Hoover was his own
Secretary of State. Mr. Stimson, who worked at a much
more leisurely pace, sometimes gasped for breath in his
efforts to keep abreast. The only other individual who
really enjoyed the pace was the pink-cheeked Mr. Mills,
who tilted his Corona-Corona cigars at an even cockier
angle and wilted his monogrammed silk shirts to the point
of immodesty in scurrying back and forth between the
Treasury and the White House. The moratorium began
the gradual eclipse of Mr. Mellon and the gradual rise of

Mr. Mills. On one occasion, when the irrepressible Mills telephoned Mr. Stimson, that gentleman replied that he was busy writing a radio speech and could not talk debts, reparations, or anything else, not even to the Secretary of the Treasury.

Whereupon Mr. Mills called up Mr. Hoover and said: "I have some reparations information that I have to tell some one, and since your Secretary of State is too busy to talk, I thought I would tell it to the President of the United States."

Mr. Stimson's radio speech never was delivered. Like several others of his ill-fated attempts, it reached the stage of being completely mimeographed and ready for the press before French recalcitrance made it apparent that Hooverian optimism regarding an early agreement was most disastrously unfounded.

And before very long Mr. Stimson sailed for Europe to push his pet hobby, disarmament, leaving the moratorium discussions in the hands of his chief, Mr. Mills, and his all too willing under secretary, Mr. Castle.

The hectic period between Mr. Hoover's first public proposal of the moratorium—June 20th—and the first indication that a compromise was in prospect with France, lasted exactly ten days. On July 2nd word was passed out from the Quai d'Orsay that an agreement was near. That M. Laval was willing to have this word reach the press was due primarily to the fact that Mr. Hoover had surrendered far more to France than had France to Mr. Hoover. His position that the moratorium was a "take-it-or-leave-it" proposition had been cast completely to the winds. He had compromised all along the line. But so to a certain extent, also, had the French.

Their chief surrender had been on the question of security.

Almost on the first day of the moratorium proposal, the

French had made it all too obvious that they were not going to aid the financial rescue of a country which cherished ambitions toward the annexation of Austria, the construction of a modern navy, and the scrapping of the Versailles Treaty. The moratorium, therefore, took on some aspects of a political lever; and Aristide Briand, summoning Ambassador Hoesch, told him that France would be unable to make any financial sacrifices in favor of Germany, unless his Government abandoned the campaign of treaty revision and antagonism to France inaugurated with the death of Gustav Stresemann. In order to discuss these things, it was reported that Chancellor Bruening and Foreign Minister Curtius would come to Paris. This word was passed on to the State Department and the British Foreign Office, and reverberated joyously throughout the United States and Europe.

The meeting, however, never materialized.

The reasons for its non-fruition were most significant. Although carefully suppressed at the time, it remained an inescapable fact that Germany was unwilling to make important political concessions. Not only was she unwilling to make them to France, but she was unwilling to make them to the United States at that moment her financial savior.

Mr. Hoover had sent a suggestion to Chancellor Bruening by Ambassador Sackett on June 30th that, in view of Germany's economic straits, and in view of American interest in naval disarmament, the abandonment of the German pocket-battleship program would be a most gracious gesture of goodwill. There was little doubt in the mind of Mr. Hoover and his State Department advisers that Germany would gracefully acquiesce. In fact, the State Department predicted acceptance in advance and intimated to the press that Germany also would pledge her abandonment of the Anschluss.

But they were wrong. On July 3rd Ambassador Sackett

was informed that under no circumstances could Germany abandon her pocket-battleship program.

The answer to France was similar. The answer included the additional intimation that no Moderate government in Germany could publicly abandon revision of the Versailles Treaty and still remain in power.

Laval and Briand recognized the force of this argument. They had recognized it many times before. An extreme Nationalist government in Germany was the last thing they wanted. Bruening was vastly preferable to Hitler. Besides, they had two trump cards in reserve, which could, if necessary, bring the financial collapse of Germany almost overnight. And so, having got most of the concessions they wanted from Mr. Hoover, having been somewhat pacified by personal diplomacy from the alabaster hands of Mr. Mellon, and being all too conscious of the odium accruing to any one nation which blocked the moratorium, France intimated that she was ready to accept.

This was on July 2nd. Next day a French Cabinet meeting confirmed this decision, and the day following, July 4th, Herbert Hoover left for his Rapidan fishing-camp for what he considered a well-earned rest.

Sunday, July 5th, broke hot, sultry, and typical of the weather in which the nation likes to celebrate its natal day. Save for the occasional sputtering of a left-over firecracker, nothing disturbed the somnolent peace of the Virginia countryside. Newspaper men lounged over a bridge game in the lobby of the James Madison Hotel at the foot of the mountain. It was too hot even for gin. Up the mountainside, life was even more peaceful. Secret Service men dozed in their bunks or read the Sunday newspaper. Not even the trout in the pool where Ramsay MacDonald and Mr. Hoover held their historic conversation could be tempted out of the shadows.

Suddenly from the main cabin came evidence of brusque, inconsiderate activity. A servant scuttled over to the dining-

cabin, gave the order for immediate luncheon. Another ran
to wake a comatose chauffeur. Mr. Hoover came out of his
cabin, looked around for his car. He said he wanted to leave
at once, and when he said "at once" that meant "at once,"
not after luncheon. The car drove up. Secret Service men,
buttoning shirts and carrying coats, streamed from their
cabin. Climbing into another car, they raced after Mr.
Hoover down the mountain-side.

A few minutes later, a box of sandwiches, hastily thrown
together, was put in a third car, which finally overtook the
President at Sperryville, thirty miles distant.

Through Orange, past the James Madison Hotel, sped
the Presidential caravan. Perspiring newspaper men continued their bridge. Not until several hours later did they
learn that the President had received a telephone call that
his precious moratorium was in danger.

In Washington that same sultry afternoon, Under Secretary Castle had been conferring with the ambassadors of
France, Italy and Great Britain. The moratorium agreement scheduled for signature the next day had struck a
snag. France had brought forward some last-minute reservations regarding payments in kind.

Mills and Castle were waiting when Mr. Hoover arrived
from his fifty-miles-an-hour dash through the Virginia
countryside. And finally, after working both the cables and
transatlantic telephone overtime, a face-saving formula
was agreed upon. Payments in kind were to be settled by a
future conference of experts.

The Hoover moratorium was signed in Paris the next
day.

Half an hour afterwards its author stood behind his
broad mahogany desk, facing half a hundred newspaper
men. He was not his usually dour self. He wore a blue coat,
white flannels, white canvas shoes, blue necktie with white
polka dots, and he beamed as he said:

"I am glad to announce that the American proposal for

one year's postponement of all intergovernmental debts and reparations has now been accepted in principle by all the important creditor governments."

Simultaneously another celebration of the signing of the moratorium took place at the French Embassy. Ogden Mills, Mr. Castle, and Herbert Feis, economic adviser of the State Department, called to congratulate Ambassador Claudel on the success of their common effort. Claudel ordered a bottle of champagne and, lifting his glass, drank this toast:

"To the crisis which we have just avoided and to the catastrophe which will follow."

Paul Claudel was more poet than prophet, but in this case he was right. It required no profound understanding of politics to know that nothing could save the German economic situation except a direct understanding between Germany and France. Claudel also knew that Germany was in no mood to mortgage her political independence for economic recovery. Probably what he did not know, but guessed, was that his government had kept two trump cards up its sleeve.

What Herbert Hoover had been playing for throughout his moratorium negotiations was a return of confidence. Now with his agreement signed, he turned loose all his big berthas of official optimism—Castle, Mills, Harrison, and last but not least Julius Klein, who declared that the recent business upturn was due entirely to the Hoover moratorium.

Franklin D. Roosevelt, then Governor of New York, declined to comment.

Optimism prevailed for two days. Then on July 8th one of the French trumps became apparent. Hoover's return of confidence depended upon speed. French sabotage of German finance depended upon delay. The French still insisted upon delay.

They raised the question of whether the moratorium actually was in effect. They cast doubts as to whether the German payment of July 15th under the Young Plan was not due, despite the moratorium. They started a whispering campaign regarding the stability of Hungarian finance. And most important of all, they proclaimed the absolute impossibility of attending the conference of experts in London before July 17th.

Meanwhile the wabbly condition of German finances became daily more apparent.

The world and Herbert Hoover had supposed that once Germany was relieved of her tremendous reparations burden, financial confidence would bounce back overnight. Imagine, therefore, the surprise, later translated into consternation, with which the world saw Germany in need of more and more funds. Central banks in London, New York, Paris, and Basle had advanced $100,000,000. A group of 100 German business men had put up $119,000,000 more. But now Dr. Hans Luther, president of the Reichsbank, suddenly let it be known that Germany must raise the stupendous sum of $400,000,000.

Then became apparent for the first time France's second trump.

It was her short-term credits, invested chiefly in London and New York. She was withdrawing them almost as fast as boat and airplane could carry gold back to Paris. The result was even greater withdrawals from Germany. For the gold which France had placed in London and New York had been relayed by British and American bankers, greedy for higher interest rates, to Central Europe.

Three days after the signing of the Hoover moratorium, therefore, one of the greatest bank runs in history got into full swing. The French had merely touched off the fuse. With British and American withdrawals from Germany came Swiss, Dutch, and Scandinavian withdrawals. Most important of all was the "flight from the mark" by Germans themselves. The memory of 1924 and the millions of paper marks required for a plate of soup caused a German stampede to buy dollars, guilders, and pounds.

Hans Luther flew to London. At Victoria Station he met Montagu Norman, traveled with him on a boat train to Dover, and was refused a loan. In Paris he met Clement Moret of the Bank of France. Again he was turned down. He took an airplane to Basle to put his case before the Bank of International Settlements.

Meanwhile runs on German banks accelerated with horrifying speed. On July 6th, the day the Hoover moratorium was signed, a total of $20,000,000 left Germany's vaults for safer deposits in neighboring countries. A slight recovery of confidence next day diminished the runs to $5,000,000. But the day following, they jumped back to $10,000,000, and so on, until during the half-day of Saturday, July 10th, $25,000,000 in gold was withdrawn from Germany. A total of $95,000,000 had left German vaults during the week.

With the close of business on Saturday noon, July 10th, it was apparent to all Europe that drastic steps would have to be taken before nine o'clock the following Monday. The great Darmstaedter Bank in Hamburg had closed its doors. The banks of Hungary were on the verge of collapse. The Mercurbank in Vienna could stay open but a few days— possibly hours—longer. And runs were beginning to develop on the banks of Czechoslovakia.

Ambassador Sackett cabled Hoover that unless Germany received help before Monday all of her banks would close.

Once again this message reached Mr. Hoover at his Rapidan fishing-camp. But this time he did not rush back to Washington. Gradually it had percolated to his reluctant brain that unless Germany and France got together the United States could pour all of its vast gold reserve into the Reichsbank and it would only provide more funds for the Germans themselves to export to France, Holland, England, and Switzerland.

So while the German Cabinet sat all of Sunday and until three o'clock Monday morning, Herbert Hoover fished for trout in the peaceful waters of the Rapidan.

He had decided to let Europe help itself.

One who did not spend so peaceful a week-end was Pierre Laval, Premier of France. He was summoned from his country estate by Ambassador von Hoesch, who asked, almost with tears in his voice, if France was going to abandon Germany to her fate.

Laval was unmoved. Once before he had talked to Herr Hoesch about the Anschluss and the Versailles Treaty. He had made it clear that Germany could yield to France politically or go to the wall financially. Now, he had nothing more to say.

The next day—Monday, July 13th—opened with all German banks closed, the Bourse locked, the banks of Hungary barred, and the chief banks of Vienna inoperative.

Paul Claudel's prophecy had been fulfilled.

That day 15,000 troopers of the old Imperial Cavalry gathered on a German parade-ground for review by Field-Marshal von Mackensen, who, in command of the famous Black Hussars, had smashed the Russian front in 1915. Blessing the review, the Imperial Chaplain preached from the text: "The land trembleth, but I hold its pillars firm."

Next day was Bastille Day in France.

It witnessed the reconstructed armies of France file past cheering thousands up the Champs Élysées. There was the Royal Roussillon Unit, which served under Montcalm in 1758, the Santo Domingo Regiment of 1775 resplendent in uniforms of white and green, the Royal Artillery of 1769 in blue and red, the Volontaires of Debussy, who fought with Dupex in the Indian War of 1753, the Swiss Karrere in red and blue, and so on, until the crucial years 1914-18, when all the races of the Republic which fought under the tricolor, from Indo-China to Martinique and from Senegal to Madagascar, marched through the Arc de Triomphe in rhythm with the heartbeats of their countrymen.

France had not forgot. France was taking no chances. Unless Germany foreswore revenge, France would see her neighbor's financial structure in ruins and not lift a finger.

The end of Mr. Hoover's moratorium negotiations came quickly after that.

They were featured by three things. One was the ability of Germany, once she realized that no further help was forthcoming from the outside world, to put her own house in order. If Germany had moved three weeks before to check the flight of the mark instead of begging for outside aid, part of her agonies would have been avoided.

The second was the continued sabotage of France. Up until the last detail was decided at the conference in London, France pursued a policy of retaliation against the Anglo-Saxon-Germanic alliance for giving birth to the Hoover moratorium.

The third was Mr. Hoover's political ineptness in trying to salvage out of the moratorium mess some shreds of glory for himself.

French sabotage began immediately after Ramsay MacDonald issued his invitation for a Conference of Experts in London. The French asked for delay, then for a preliminary conference in Paris, finally agreed to meet in London July 17th—by which time Germany's banks already had been closed.

Mr. Stimson rushed to London twenty-four hours ahead of the French delegates, in order to have a heart-to-heart talk with his old friend, Ramsay MacDonald. He took with him a new plan concocted in Washington by Mr. Hoover. Its most essential feature was a "standstill" agreement for all German short-term credits, by which the bankers holding these credits agreed not to withdraw them during the present emergency. Before cabling the plan to his Secretary of State, Mr. Hoover had secured pledges, through the Herculean efforts to Senator Dwight Morrow, that the New York bankers would not withdraw their $600,000,000 of short-term credits.

The plan was flawless, except for one thing:

It had been devised by Herbert Hoover. And that gentleman's name was so unpopular with the French that, had he been the author of an American guarantee of French security, the French would have rejected it. Also, the French had a plan of their own, a long-term loan to Germany coupled with the inevitable political concessions.

So to circumvent the French, Stimson and MacDonald decided to dress the plan in British clothes. They had to push it to an immediate decision, for a few days' absence on the part of Bruening meant the end of his government.

Meanwhile Mr. Hoover, fretting in Washington at the long delays which undermined the effectiveness of his moratorium, and anxious that the world realize who was the guiding genius of the entire negotiations, ordered Mr. Castle to give the plan to the press properly labeled regarding its real authorship. This news, telephoned to the Secretary of State by the Acting Secretary, almost made that harassed gentleman drop the receiver. He told Castle that, if it leaked out that the plan under discussion emanated from Mr. Hoover, the conversations would come to an abrupt finish.

Mr. Castle replied that the President was most anxious to have the world know of his constructive proposal, and that the story must be given out in Washington at once. However, in view of Mr. Stimson's demurrer, he would agree to a brief delay. Mr. Stimson replied that conversations were proceeding so satisfactorily, they probably would not be upset if the plan was made public twenty-four hours later.

The next day, therefore, Mr. Castle distributed to Washington newspaper correspondents copies of Mr. Hoover's

238 THE AMERICAN DIPLOMATIC GAME

latest plan for saving his earlier plan. Its authorship was
carefully designated and it was cabled in complete detail
to London.

The havoc which it created there almost caused the
resignation of Mr. Hoover's Secretary of State.

Mr. Stimson was at the Ritz Hotel when newspaper men
rushed in to ask him about the new plan he had received
from Washington. Whatever surprise he may have experienced inwardly, he showed no trace outwardly. He described the report as a "gross fabrication." Whatever he
had been discussing with the other delegates was "more
British than American in conception."

"I don't know where that story came from," he concluded. "I shall have to establish a bureau of denials."

Washington was flabbergasted. So also was London. German delegates in London frantically tried to find copies of
the new plan which was to bring their resurrection. Newspaper men in Washington rushed to the Acting Secretary
of State to find out why he and his chief did not pull together.

Mr. Castle shrugged his shoulders. He said he "did not
know what Mr. Stimson had said in London."

Confronted, however, with an official statement by Mr.
Stimson that the plan was first advanced by Ramsay Mac-
Donald, Castle finally volunteered the information that the
plan "first advanced by MacDonald" represented textually
the instructions sent to the Secretary of State on July 17th.

"The proposal which was given out in Washington," declared Mr. Castle, "was worked out here in Washington
without any consultation with the British. It was the President's idea as to the best way to meet the situation, and if
the British reached the same conclusion that is all to the
good. But they did not consult us and we did not consult
them in working it out."

Europe was laughing. Hoover was furious. Stimson
looked the goat, and rumor was rife that he would resign.

In Washington, therefore, considerable political attention focused upon his return. He had had some differences with his chief in the White House before. Also with his Under Secretary. He did not know during those days that the latter had been chiefly responsible for his own appointment as Secretary of State. It happened that shortly after Hoover's election he submitted to his friend Castle a list of names he was considering for the chief Cabinet post.

"Whom would you choose, were you in my place?" he asked.

"Stimson, by all means."

"Why?" asked Hoover, "do you know him?"

"No, but I do know the others."

It was Mr. Hoover's idea that Castle should simultaneously become Under Secretary of State, but the newly appointed Secretary had different ideas. He chose as his chief aide Joseph P. Cotton, one of the most outstanding members of the New York bar, and during the two years until Mr. Cotton's death there existed ill-concealed antagonism between Stimson and Castle, who at that time remained an assistant secretary. Reading in the Baltimore *Sun* one day that he was handling the Dolly Gann-Alice Longworth social war "as gingerly as if trying to smuggle an army of Mexican revolutionists into the State Department courtyard," Mr. Stimson exploded:

"I'll bet Bill Castle was responsible for that damn story!"

It was not surprising, therefore, that all the State Department looked forward to Mr. Stimson's homecoming with the same tingling anticipation felt by inveterate fight fans gathered to settle a world's heavyweight championship.

The Secretary of State sent for his Under Secretary immediately. He accused him of not obeying orders. Castle looked astonished. He replied that he had released the American proposals in accordance with his telephone conversation, whereby it was agreed the plan should be made public twenty-four hours later.

Stimson, angry, proclaimed that he had consented to no such thing.

But Castle had been careful to take from the files the report of his conversation, transcribed, as was done with all transatlantic calls, by two stenographers who listened in.

"You are right," admitted Stimson, shaking his head. "I must have forgotten what I told you."

For the rest of their term of office the two men were the best of friends.

In Europe, however, nobody cared whether the final moratorium plan was made in America. The standstill agreement was signed, withdrawals from the Reichsbank had stopped, Germany was relieved of a large burden of debt, and the German government could enjoy a breathing space in which to work out its own salvation.

On the whole, Mr. Hoover's work was considered good. By many he was even hailed as the financial savior of Europe.

Man's vision, fortunately, is short.

At that time Mr. Hoover knew, and Mr. Stimson knew, and Mr. Mills knew, that Europe would default either on war debts or private debts, and that either the American taxpayer or the American investor must foot the bill. But neither Hoover nor Stimson nor Mills wanted the American public to know this; and they had their wish.

It was not until three years later that the American public woke up. By that time both war debts and private investments had run down the waste-pipe of Europe's financial sink, and it began to be apparent that Germany had no intention of honoring either the short-term credits which Mr. Stimson had struggled so valiantly to protect, or the long-term bond issues which Mr. Hoover considered so sacred.

It took a lot of pummeling before the United States woke up. It was not until Hitler had thrown his country

into a political maelstrom, and the mild-mannered Cordell
Hull had sent him a scathing note pointing out Germany's
ability to pay for the next war while defaulting on the
cost of the last, that the American public began to realize
that, no matter what the President or the Congress may do,
say, or feel about debts, the American taxpayer, in the end,
is going to pay Europe's war bills.

The Hoover moratorium was forgotten.

2. M. LAVAL SEES AMERICA FIRST

Not long before Pierre Laval, Premier of France, arrived
in the United States, Herbert Hoover, his host, remarked
to the Secretary of State:

"What is this Frenchman coming over here to talk
about?"

This represented a frame of mind which Mr. Hoover,
try as hard as he would, could not shake, and which, at
times, reacted poignantly upon his conduct of foreign
affairs. Since his moratorium negotiation, his attitude toward the French had turned to undisguised and vitriolic
antipathy. So that when Henry L. Stimson, returning from
his European pilgrimage in the summer of 1931, mentioned casually that he had suggested something to Premier
Laval about a trip to the United States, Mr. Hoover grunted
in disgust, thought his Secretary of State too oversold by
European hospitality, and promptly forgot about the whole
thing.

Mr. Stimson, however, did not forget. He had come to
be a great believer in personal diplomacy; so much so that
his series of "cross-conferences" with Mussolini, Briand,
Bruening, and MacDonald had made him the walking
peace delegate of Europe. It was his firm conviction that if
the world's chief statesmen sat down before an open fire

with whisky and soda, pipe and tobacco, plus a certain amount of goodwill, the ills of their governments would vanish as easily as their pipe smoke. And he practiced this diplomacy on every conceivable occasion.

In addition to this, Mr. Stimson was much concerned about relations between the United States and France. Ever since the days of the Anglo-American naval negotiations and the conversations at the Rapidan, popular suspicion between those two traditional friends had increased. Sometimes Mr. Stimson was inclined to think that if France were represented by a more outstanding ambassador— another Jusserand, for instance—the American public would better understand its great sister republic. Sometimes he felt the same way about the American ambassador to France. Again he blamed the press. But whatever the cause, he was convinced in his idealism that a heart-to-heart talk between the heads of these two great states would have a salutary effect.

With Pierre Laval, other considerations weighed more heavily. More important to him was the fact that the Washington pilgrimage enhanced his own political prestige. It gave him a spectacular opportunity to even the score with the British for the pilgrimage of Ramsay MacDonald and it gave him a chance to offset the forthcoming visit of the Italian Foreign Minister, Dino Grandi. Finally it gave him an opportunity to divide some of the glory which Aristide Briand had wrapped around his name as the peacemaker of Europe—a move which pleased the Old Fox not at all and caused him to withhold from Laval's entourage the experts of the Quai d'Orsay who otherwise would have been among the foremost members of the party.

Laval had other vague motives for making the trip, and so did Stimson. The former nursed a general notion that he might induce the United States to give some sort of security pledges to France, as well as open the question of debt reduction; while the latter had equally hazy ideas about persuading France to revise the Versailles Treaty as a prelude to disarmament.

Mr. Hoover, however, cherished no such illusions. He remained aloof and uninspired. And it was only after his Secretary of State, with the greatest difficulty, persuaded him that a talk with Laval might lead to concrete results for the Geneva Disarmament Conference—on the success of which he had set his heart—that Mr. Hoover entered the Laval conversations with the remotest semblance of a smile.

Thus with the diplomats of Europe wondering what Laval could want badly enough to repay him for the fatigues of American hospitality, and with the American public looking forward to a spectacular celebration of Franco-American friendship, the Premier of France embarked for New York.

Pierre Laval came from Auvergne, which once had sent another Frenchman, the Marquis de Lafayette, to America. Between that day and 1931, however, few of its citizens had ventured far from home, and even Laval, most celebrated of its recent sons, never left the shores of France until Mr. Stimson persuaded him to cross the English Channel, to participate in the moratorium conference at London.

In more ways than one, therefore, this was an historic pilgrimage for M. Laval, and in the story radioed daily from a score of avid newsmen on shipboard, nothing was lost in the telling.

Laval sprang from the soil of France. As a youngster he drove a one-horse omnibus between his father's café and the railway station; and since the horse knew every inch of the way, Pierre spent most of his time studying. One day one of his passengers, a priest, discovered him struggling with Greek grammar and encouraged him not only to study but to become a teacher. Thus Laval worked his way through schools at Saint-Etienne, Lyons, and law school in Paris, studying by night and teaching by day, until finally he found himself a full-fledged barrister—without a brief. Politics, law, and journalism are pretty well intertwined in France, and through the medium of all three Laval managed to be elected to the Chamber of Deputies in 1914. He was a devout Socialist in those days, and his experience as an ordinary poilu in the World War which interrupted his parliamentary career, deepened convictions which never deserted him, despite the future kaleidoscope of party labels. He came back to politics after the war, left Socialism for the Republican party, and after election to the Chamber in 1924 began a long career as a member of the Painlevé, Briand, and Tardieu Cabinets.

It was not so much Laval's official career, however, which newspaper correspondents radioed to the American public, as the fact that Laval smoked two packages of Old Golds per day and never was without a white string necktie. The tie probably was a heritage from impecunious student days when the chief requirement in neckwear was washability. At any rate, it contrasted vividly with the Laval complexion, for the Premier was an aboriginal Frenchman, a descendant of the race of Vercingetorix before the Frankish invasion.

His daughter, Josette, a vivacious eighteen-year-old brunette, probably received as much newspaper linage as her father. No detail, from the leopard cuffs worn at departure to the orchids received every day from an unknown admirer, was missed by an avid American public.

"I had no intention of bringing her," explained M. Laval, "until she read in the newspapers that she was going. Then she insisted; and what was I to do? But she is going to work to make up for it. We have 200 telegrams already today, and she must answer them."

Laval's reception, though not hilarious, was as hearty as the average. It did not, however, please the young army of

French newspaper men intent upon gauging the Premier's future at home by his success in America.

There were the usual ceremonies in New York: Secretary Stimson in person at the dock despite the fact that Laval had not welcomed him in Paris; the freedom of the city; the introduction by Hector Fuller of "His Excellency the Prime Minister of France, M. Paul Claudel." And in Washington there was the usual red carpet rolled across the station platform, the line of saluting marines, the cavalry escort from Fort Myer, the courtesy calls at the White House. But the tricolor was not in evidence, there were no cheering crowds along the way. Pedestrians scarcely looked up even when Laval's *chef de baggage*, clad in cutaway and silk hat, came riding down Pennsylvania Avenue atop twelve trunks, twenty-three suitcases and half a dozen hat-boxes.

There was no question, however, that the American public liked Laval. They liked him because of his quiet charm. He was not the Adolphe Menjou or Maurice Chevalier type of Frenchman. He was completely unassuming. His modesty was disarming. His speeches were not florid. When he talked, he did not gesticulate. Facing a battery of cameras, Klieg lights and a hundred newspaper men in the lower hall of Ambassador Edge's house, M. Laval talked with as much composure as if he were before his own fireside.

Personally, nothing bothered him. Politically, one point did. Obviously his host, Mr. Hoover, did not expect vast results to spring from their joint conversations. Obviously, also, Pierre Laval could not risk returning to a critical public in France admitting that he had come to the United States on nothing more than a goodwill joy ride when such important problems as debts, disarmament, and security continually vexed relations between the two republics.

Obviously, also, the two viewpoints did not, could not, agree.

Questioned, therefore, by newspaper men as to whether he expected definite agreements with Mr. Hoover or whether he hoped merely to improve general relations, Pierre Laval for once hesitated. Then, standing upon the lower step of the Edge stairway, and choosing his words with the utmost care, he replied:

"If the sole purpose of the President of the Council of Ministers in coming to Washington was to improve relations between the United States and France and create a warmer spirit between the two sister republics, the trip would have been unnecessary and superfluous. It is necessary for us to arrive at a definite and concrete . . ."

Here the Premier of France paused. He was treading delicate ground.

"Don't bother to translate that," he commanded in an aside to his interpreter. Then thinking primarily of the American press, he continued:

"Let me give you a résumé of the entire situation. President Hoover and I expect to discuss all problems and as far as possible seek a solution in regard to some of them. Coming after the conversations in Paris, London, and Berlin, this meeting in Washington marks an epoch in the direction of closer international coöperation."

How delicate was the ground on which M. Laval trod he did not fully realize until he discovered that both the White House and the State Department had issued blunt reminders that the Laval pilgrimage was expected to bring no new millennium in Franco-American relations.

In fact, so strongly did Mr. Hoover feel on this subject that next day he put the French Premier in the position of eating his own words.

"The sole purpose of these conversations," read a communiqué issued by the two men, "is the earnest, frank exchange of views with a view to finding common ground for helpful action in the promotion of constructive progress in the world."

Certainly no one could find fault with that.

Laval dined in state at the White House the first night of his arrival, sharing honors with Marshall Pétain, who had come to celebrate that memorable occasion when the Marquis de Lafayette stood beside General Washington at Yorktown in receiving the sword of General Cornwallis. The White House dinner, one hundred and fifty years later, was a most appropriate Franco-American celebration, and was marred only by the fact that Warren Delano Robbins, Chief of Protocol, had forgotten to invite Senator Borah, chairman of the Foreign Relations Committee, an oversight remedied at the last minute only by Mr. Hoover himself, who telephoned the Senator and persuaded him to ignore the slight.

Mr. Hoover did not know it at the time, but the Senator from Idaho was to play an important part in the visit of the French Premier. For next day, while Mlle. Josette was shopping with Reine Claudel, and while her father went through the formalities of laying a wreath on the Tomb of the Unknown Soldier, shaking hands with the dignitaries of the Capital, and paying his respects to the Supreme Court, French newspaper men who accompanied Laval called upon the chairman of the Senate Foreign Relations Committee.

That gentleman had come to have a more fearsome reputation in France than almost any other official of the United States. Presidents had come and gone. Secretaries of State had risen to fame and been forgotten. But still stood that ancient advocate of American isolation, that critic of the Versailles Treaty, that apostle of disarmament, William Edgar Borah.

An interview with Borah, therefore, meant more to French journalism than an interview with the President. And Borah, flattered at the compliment, believing this to be an opportunity for real missionary work with France, determined to be frank.

Very early in the interview he found the opportunity. Questioned as to what he thought of the prospects for disarmament, Borah switched the subject to his favorite theme.

"There must be changes in the Versailles Treaty," he said, "before disarmament can come about."

"Would you allow the German army to be restored to its pre-war strength?"

"My ideas about the Versailles Treaty have nothing to do with the German army. Do you want me to speak frankly?"

The assembled journalists nodded, a trifle breathless.

"All right, there can be no disarmament in Europe as long as certain conditions arising out of the Versailles Treaty exist."

"Can you be specific, Senator?"

"Yes," replied Borah, only too anxious to oblige. "I refer to the Polish Corridor. I refer to Austria and Hungary. You cannot expect Czechoslovakia, Rumania, and Jugoslavia and Poland to disarm as long as a part of the territory once belonging to Austria and Hungary is in their hands and remains in dispute."

Borah had his heel on the thing France cherished most —the carefully built, carefully nurtured system of alliances between those countries which had most to lose by revision of the Versailles Treaty. French journalists were accustomed to hearing this system condemned in Germany and Italy, or even in the liberal press of Great Britain. But to hear a great, a distinguished statesman, representative of one of the traditional friends of France, fling this in their faces with such complete sang-froid, made some of them wince.

Still this was news—first page, seven-column banner news—and they asked for more.

"Is it not possible," asked the representative of the *Petit Parisien*, "to modify the Versailles Treaty gradually, meanwhile working out some form of security agreement for Europe?"

"A structure of that kind," replied the unrelenting Borah, "means nailing down the Versailles Treaty permanently. The more security is pledged, the more tightly the Versailles Treaty is nailed down. It means the continuation of the *status quo*.

"As far as modifying the treaty," he continued, "the League of Nations itself can make changes in it without the consent of the respective nations, but are the nations in power willing to make such changes?"

"But," Borah was reminded, "the Versailles Treaty will maintain peace without armies if we put teeth in the Kellogg Pact."

"What do you mean by teeth?" shot back the Senator. "You have plenty of teeth in the Covenant of the League of Nations to handle the Manchurian situation. But you have been afraid to show your teeth against Japan!"

For nearly an hour Senator Borah talked. And there was almost no phase of Europe's economic or political ills which he neglected. He discussed the Polish Corridor, the danger of economic boycotts, the lip-service paid to disarmament, the cancellation of war debts and reparations, and he did it with the same complete frankness, the sincerity, the powerful logic that he would have used on the Senate floor. French journalists were being treated to William E. Borah at his best, and Senate galleries would have emptied to hear him.

At the end, he was asked whether the revision of the Versailles Treaty would not make for even greater unrest in Europe.

"Not at all," flung back Borah. "If Germany had restored Alsace-Lorraine to France without the use of force, the problem would have been settled and much ill-will would have been avoided."

And then, as the interview ended:

250 THE AMERICAN DIPLOMATIC GAME

"The Treaty of Versailles is going to be changed, whether that change comes by negotiation or whether it comes by force."

Meanwhile other conversations also pertinent to the Treaty of Versailles were taking place in another part of the Capital.

Premier Laval had concluded his routine of doing the things which every distinguished visitor to Washington has to do, and almost simultaneously with the Borah interview, had settled down to his first serious conversation with Herbert Hoover. Ogden Mills interpreted for the latter. M. Jacques Bizot, despite a scanty knowledge of English, interpreted for Laval; while Henry L. Stimson, who had picked up a little wartime French, listened in.

He was the most eager participant of all. For months he had been working toward disarmament, for months he had dickered with diplomats, for months he had explored every conceivable security solution, and every path he took led to that same immobile obstacle—France. Now he hoped that in this heart-to-heart talk between the heads of the two nations, important misunderstandings might be cleared away. And as a step in this direction he had prompted his chief to sound out Laval regarding the Polish Corridor, which he, Stimson, had discussed with the Frenchman during the summer. At that time Laval had agreed in theory that as long as the Corridor cut Prussia into two parts, there could be no permanent peace in Europe.

Mr. Hoover was primed and ready. Taking advantage of what he thought was a favorable moment in the conversation, he emphasized the great interest of the United States in peace, the fact that the Germans never would permanently permit the Corridor to remain in the hands of the Poles, then asked Laval what he thought about revision of the Versailles Treaty.

Laval congealed like Lot's wife. He replied that he had not come to Washington to discuss a revision of a treaty considered by the people of France to be the cornerstone of their security.

And shortly after that he veered the conversation to his own pet problem. Under what conditions, Laval asked the President of the United States, would his government be prepared to take a more definite part in European affairs, especially in regard to the question of security for France?

It was now Mr. Hoover's turn to freeze. And he did so with characteristic gusto. He fell back upon the traditional policy of the United States, its firm desire to help preserve the peace of the world, its proven pacifism through the initiation of the Kellogg Pact, but the necessity, in fact the value to the world through that necessity, of remaining aloof from the petty partisanship of European politics.

M. Laval shrugged his shoulders and lapsed into a long polemic on the desire of France to coöperate in disarmament, but the simultaneous determination of France not to reduce her army until she had some compensating form of security.

And so on, far into the night.

Far into the night also French newspaper correspondents pondered the Borah interview. What was its significance? Why had the Senator spoken so frankly? Some were convinced that he was merely the mouthpiece of Mr. Hoover, that he was saying what the President of the United States would not dare say to the press or to the premier of a former ally-in-arms. Had not the two men dined alone together just two nights before the Laval visit?

The more French newspaper men pondered the situation, the more convinced they were that Borah was Hoover's mouthpiece. Particularly convinced were members of the Nationalist press. To them, Pierre Laval was not a strong man. Although he had the support of that arch-

Nationalist, André Tardieu, he had been reluctant to break with his old colleagues of the Left. Furthermore, his pacifism was suspect. He had seen too much of the war.

The Nationalist press long before had predicted that when Laval got to Washington he would be stood in a corner of the White House and would lose his shirt. Now they were sure their prediction had come true.

Other journalistic friends of Laval were not. The problem, however, was to get concrete evidence of that fact. Laval was inaccessible. Having spent one night in the bed of Ambassador Edge, he had been shunted to a guest-room in the White House. The problem of getting a message to him behind those sacred portals seemed like sending a message to the dead. Finally, however, M. Bassée, of Agence Havas, managed it.

Among those who know him well, Pierre Laval has one great quality. Seldom does he lose his temper. He is considerate of others' views, compassionate of their follies. Standing beside his desk in a rowdy, tumultuous Chamber, he could answer questions, subdue his hecklers, make himself heard without lifting his voice.

But on this occasion Pierre Laval blew up. First the President of the United States privately had proposed the necessity of revising the Treaty of Versailles, and now he was informed that the chairman of the Senate Foreign Relations Committee publicly had urged the same thing.

So the Premier of France dictated the following statement to M. Bassée.

"I have not come to Washington to engage in polemics with Senator Borah or to discuss the revision of the Versailles Treaty. Tell the journalists not to be disturbed by the words of a Senator which represent only his personal opinion."

Representatives of the Nationalist press slept peacefully that night. They knew that their Premier, even though almost lost in the giant bed of Abraham Lincoln, still clutched the problem of French security firmly to his breast.

The remainder of the Laval visit seemed uneventful after that.

For Josette, probably, it was not. Clad in ravishing blue, "because it is papa's favorite color," she expressed regret at meeting so few American men, but made up for it by being the most photographed and sought-after young lady in Washington. She drove through Rock Creek Park with Madame Patenotre, attended a movie, learned to drink clam juice out of the shell with lemon, and, to please an Italian waiter, ate ravioli at the Mayflower. Her one real disappointment was not attending a football game at Princeton, and it was being a dutiful daughter that caused her to miss that. When the train pulled out for Princeton, she was still standing before the movietone machines repeating to her father what Mr. Hoover told him and repeating back to Mr. Hoover her father's replies. That evening, however, she attended a cavalry drill and dance at Fort Myer, and the next day had a tête-à-tête with a handsome Navy football player at Annapolis. No matter what happened to the Polish Corridor, for Josette Laval the trip to America was a success.

Her father, meanwhile, had recovered from Senator Borah's attack on the Versailles Treaty. After debating two hours with Ambassador Claudel as to whether his statement of the preceding night should be officially denied, he finally sent an emissary to Borah, explained that although there were many things in the Senator's statement which he, Laval, appreciated, he could not let the interview go unanswered without risk of losing his Nationalist support —which meant, of course, the defeat of his government.

And that night Laval and Borah sat down in the privacy of the Stimson mansion and got to know each other. Laval had cooled off and Borah never had been angry. Completely unabashed by the furore he had caused, the Senator from Idaho reiterated his belief that the peace treaties must be revised if there was to be stability in Europe. Laval listened carefully. At the bottom of his heart he agreed with Borah. But he had come to Washington not to air his own views. He was Premier of France.

"Senator," he replied, "if we revised the frontiers of Europe, there would be immediate war. And that is a responsibility which France does not want on her shoulders.

"Therefore, I leave it to you, our good friend, to persuade the Poles, the Rumanians, the Czechs and the Serbs that you are stabilizing the peace of Europe by tearing up their boundaries and readjusting their territory. As far as France is concerned, we consider the primary condition of peace is to create no new disorder and tear up no signed contracts."

This ended the political phase of the Laval visit. He and Mr. Hoover made a few more desultory stabs at an agreement, but Laval would yield not one inch from the historic position of his country for security first and disarmament afterward; while Hoover would not budge from his refusal to satisfy French demands for security.

France is already protected, argued Mr. Hoover, by various security pacts—the League of Nations, Locarno, and the Kellogg-Briand Pact.

To which Laval shrugged his shoulders and replied:

"Yes, witness the effect of the Kellogg Pact and the Covenant upon the Japanese in Manchuria."

Hoover would not even listen to Laval's desire for a consultative pact, and Laval, in turn, would not satisfy Hoover's hopes for early Franco-Italian entrance into the London Naval Treaty—a problem which frequent hints from the British that they might apply the "escalator clause" really made serious. Pressed on this point, Laval replied:

"We must take this up at some future date."

So there remained only the task of summarizing for the press the results of their historic conversations.

This was difficult because there was so little to summarize. One point only had been definitely decided, and this was worked out in New York, not Washington. Experts of the Bank of France and the Federal Reserve agreed that France would abandon raids on the dollar and that both countries would support the gold standard.

So the joint communiqué finally issued by Laval and Hoover established a record as one of the most nebulous doctrines in the archives of diplomacy.

"It is our joint purpose that the conference for limitation of armaments will not fail to take advantage of the great opportunity which presents itself," proclaimed the two statesmen ". . . the duty of statesmen is not to overlook any means of practical coöperation for the common good . . . the traditional friendship between the United States and France . . . the absence of all controversy between the two governments . . . informal and cordial discussion has served to outline with greater precision the nature of the problems . . ." and other diplomatic drivel which international negotiators find useful for camouflaging their disagreements.

Pierre Laval signed the communiqué and took the train for New York. There he climbed the Empire State Building, took one last look at the sprawling conglomeration of skyscrapers called Manhattan, nearly lost his hat in the wind, and boarded the *Île de France*.

He had seen America and he had had enough.

Chapter IV

THE LABORATORY OF WAR

WHEN the next War to End War is over and statesmen once again begin their drive to perfect the machinery of everlasting peace, they can take as their perfect laboratory test the struggle between Paraguay and Bolivia for that vast and worthless wilderness, the Gran Chaco.

Here is a war which, although not always officially called by that name, has dragged out longer than the European catastrophe of 1914-18. Here is a war which, in arousing bitterness and national passion, has been unsurpassed, possibly unequaled, by any that historians have recorded from the Crusades down to the invasion of Belgium. Here is a war which has been subjected to every possible peace test conceived by men, during a period when peace was the passion of the hour—and which resisted them all. Here, finally, is a war unique in the fact that, although men fought, bled, and died by the thousands, they dragged in no one but themselves. No civilian populations were wantonly punished. No women and children suffered. No neighboring countries were invaded. It was fought in a wasteland where winter rains lie for weeks in pools among the palm trees, where orchids among the mahogany clash in color with goldenrod among the savannas; only an occasional drove of peccaries or a lone jaguar witnessed the perfidy of man.

No scientist in his laboratory ever isolated a dread germ more completely and under circumstances more favorable for observation than the disease of war was isolated in the Chaco.

And if future generations are to profit by the clinic of

the wastelands, it should be from this one conclusion: War against war must be marshalled with as much scientific care and concentration as the greatest military campaign; it is not a battleground for prima donnas of peace.

Had it not been for the rivalry of individuals wanting credit for bringing peace to the Chaco, had it not been for the jockeying of the world's peace organizations, jealous of their prestige, the agony of the green jungle, the massacre of hundreds of Indians conscripted to serve a cause they did not understand, long ago would have terminated.

There was a time when wars were waged for honor, for righteousness, or for the possession of a beautiful lady. More recently wars have degenerated into struggles for markets, raw materials, trade routes. But it remained for Paraguay and Bolivia to go to war over a water-soaked jungle whose meandering rivers lose themselves in its wilderness. Two Spaniards, the first Europeans to cross the Chaco in 1536, reported its vast area to be valueless. Tex Rickard tried to turn its pasture land into cattle ranches before developing the more profitable business of promoting prize fights. Even Alfalfa Bill Murray gave up his attempt to found an American colony in the Chaco, in favor of the Oklahoma prairies.

In fact, no one save a few Paraguayan settlers had attached more than passing importance to the Chaco until landlocked Bolivia's attempt to get an outlet on the Pacific was thwarted by Chile in the War of 1879. From that moment on, a port on the River Paraguay bordering the eastern side of the Chaco became one of the great goals of Bolivian national life. This goal was intensified when Frank B. Kellogg's settlement of the Tacna-Arica dispute between Peru and Chile closed forever Bolivia's still lingering hope of an outlet on the Pacific. In fact, it was in 1928—just a few months after the Tacna-Arica settlement—that Bolivia got State Department approval

of the Dillon, Read loan by which $5,000,000 of muni-
tions were purchased for the pursuit of the war with
Paraguay.

Actual hostilities started December 5th, were checked
by the Pan-American Arbitration Conference, and the
present story begins on March 13, 1929, when the Neutral
Commission created by that Conference started to function. It was a commission of five—Colombia, Cuba,
Mexico, Uruguay, and the United States—all, with the
exception of Uruguay, countries located at the farthest
possible distance from the scene of hostilities, but all represented by capable commissioners charged with the sole
and specific duty of ironing out the difficulties between
Paraguay and Bolivia.

Heading the Commission was Brigadier-General Frank
R. McCoy, a man who, in the opinion of some of his
West Point colleagues, won promotion by playing the
social side of the army game. He had served as aide to
Theodore Roosevelt during three colorful years in the
White House, as aide to William Howard Taft when the
latter was Secretary of War, and in the same capacity to
General Leonard Wood in the Philippines. But with all
this, McCoy's service in Cuba, in Mexico, and in super-
vising presidential elections in Nicaragua had injected into
his character a combination of iron and tact which
achieved results even with the representatives of Bolivia
and Paraguay.

The Neutral Commission, under General McCoy,
achieved what it was instructed to do—but its instructions
were limited. Its task was to fix responsibility for the
razing of Fort Vanguardia, and, if possible, conciliate the
two disputants. Only six months were given in which to
accomplish this.

There were times during this six months when it seemed
to General McCoy as if Latin-American diplomacy were
one long and continuous nightmare. What plagued him

most was the problem of locating Fort Vanguardia. The demolishment of this thatched-roof shack in the jungle had started all the trouble. Built by Bolivian forces on what Paraguay alleged was her territory, it had been burned by a Paraguayan patrol on the morning of December 5th, and the two countries now agreed to run an imaginary line through the site of the fort, withdrawing their armies to either side.

But when the Neutral Commission attempted to fix the exact spot on the map where the fort had been, a heated debate started.

Bolivia claimed that Vanguardia lay north of the Otuquis River. Paraguay claimed it lay south. And when Paraguay, in order to settle the dispute, sent a technical mission to find Vanguardia's ashes, Bolivian troops fired upon it with a reverberation which echoed through every corner of Latin America and promised, for a time, to disrupt the Washington negotiations altogether.

Conciliation already had progressed too far, however, to be completely upset. Repatriation of prisoners had been arranged. Further troop movements had been condemned. The pressure of Latin-American opinion still was strong against war. And so when General McCoy patted the Bolivian and Paraguayan commissioners on the back and told them to forget their foolishness, they did so—at least temporarily.

But all the persuasiveness of General McCoy plus all the pressure of Latin-American opinion could not force the two countries into the arbitration of the fundamental question of partitioning the Chaco. Bolivia was adamant that the area awarded to Paraguay by President Rutherford B. Hayes in 1878 should be arbitrated all over again, and no government of Paraguay which accepted this could have survived twenty-four hours. In fact, not even the Neutral Commission was willing to make such a request of Paraguay.

And having failed to budge Bolivia, and having ex-hausted most of its allotted six months, the Commission prepared to put the two countries on as friendly a basis as possible. Obviously the fixing of responsibility for the destruction of Fort Vanguardia was impossible. Paraguay admitted capturing the fort, but merely as an act of "law-ful ownership and possession." Bolivia frankly explained that "when we convinced ourselves that we should not be able to secure from Paraguay the peaceful cession of what we wanted of the Chaco, we decided to abandon lawful methods and began to advance our positions."

Faced with two such admissions, the Neutral Commis-sion sidestepped the question of guilt and did the only thing possible. On September 12th, the last day of its existence, it held a glamorous plenary session. Good will exuded from the lips of everyone present. Dr. Rowe wore his rosiest smile. Henry L. Stimson paid tribute to one of the most important epochs in Pan-American conciliation. The Commission announced that Paraguay would rebuild Fort Vanguardia which it had demolished, that Bolivia would rebuild Fort Boqueron which it had demolished. Then as a parting shot at the settlement of the funda-mental question, the Commission urged both countries to renew diplomatic relations and submit the partition of the Chaco to an international court.

And since the State Department had paid the entire conciliation costs, including the hotel bills of the commis-sioners, Benjamin Cohen, the Commission's Chilean secre-tary, introduced a resolution asking Bolivia and Paraguay to pay at least the cost of publishing the record. Where-upon the meeting adjourned.

This ended Chapter One of the Chaco. Chapter Two was an exasperating period of haggling which dragged out for almost two years.

It began the next day. Bolivia sent a note to General

McCoy stating that it appreciated the plea of the Neutral Commission to submit the Chaco dispute to arbitration, but since the Neutral Commission had ceased to exist, obviously it was impossible for Bolivia to answer the Commission's note. So the grand climax so carefully planned by General McCoy achieved nothing.

The truth of the matter was that powerful forces in Bolivia were making for war. The $5,000,000 of munitions financed through Dillon, Read & Company was stored and ready for use. A militant war party was itching to lay hands on it. During the six months of conciliation General Hans Kundt, German military adviser, had been strengthening Bolivian forces. For a long time he had been waiting *der Tag*. He was being paid $10,000 a month, the largest salary received by any military man. He was anxious to prove his worth.

So despite the encomiums of Henry L. Stimson and his prediction that the two hostile countries shortly would resume diplomatic relations, the five Neutral Commissioners called upon him October 1st and laid before him the grave situation resulting from the fact that there were some fifty forts facing one another in the Gran Chaco, supported by two good-sized armies, both anxious to smell blood. Mr. Stimson, worried, dispatched another volley of notes to the disputants. The result was exactly the same as that of the olive branches of General McCoy.

Peace was preserved, however, by another factor not at that time fully appreciated by Mr. Stimson. The stock-market crash of 1929 later was to wreak irreparable damage to the administration to which Mr. Stimson belonged; but also it had a decidedly calming effect upon the military aspirations of Bolivia.

The price of tin began to fall.

And with the end of the Coolidge Bull Market and the crash which ushered in the days of the Hoover Depression, the price of tin dropped lower and lower. With it dropped the political future not merely of Herbert Hoover, but of Hernando Siles, President of Bolivia. Almost while Secretary Stimson was sending his first note asking for arbitration in the Chaco, President Siles was busy exiling his political opponents.

The ensuing months, in fact the next two years, were not happy ones for either Bolivia or President Siles. There continued moves for peace by the Neutrals—particularly the United States and Uruguay. There continued bickering, side-stepping and threats on the part of both Bolivia and Paraguay not to rebuild the two razed *fortinas*. But more important than any of these, there continued the steady decline in the price of tin and the simultaneous decline in the prestige of President Siles.

Finally, on March 8, 1930, his Cabinet resigned. One month later the continual downward thud of tin did all that the Neutrals and Neighbors of the Western Hemisphere had failed to do. Bolivia and Paraguay renewed diplomatic relations. And one month after that, with the price of tin still skidding toward unprecedented depths, revolt broke out in southern Bolivia, Siles left the Presidential palace and a military junta took over the shattered finances of the Bolivian Government.

Simultaneously General Hans Kundt took refuge in the German Legation, then fled for the Peruvian border and Berlin.

General Kundt sat in his modest home in the suburbs of Berlin for nearly two years. His pretentious residence in La Paz was looted by students. In Bolivia he had become a naturalized citizen, but back in Germany he resumed the nationality of the Fatherland. Save for the four years of the World War he had lived in Bolivia since 1910. He had built up the Bolivian army to the formidable total of 5,000. And now through the impetuosity of some university students, plus a fall in the price of tin, his work was ended.

But on the morning of December 6, 1932—nearly two years later—the train which puffs up the steep face of the Andes from Arica was met by a crowd of shouting people who threw flowers at a gray-haired gentleman of military bearing as he alighted on the station platform. Enthusiastically they escorted him to his hotel, where, from a balcony, he stilled their cheers long enough to say:

"I have returned with the desire to be useful to Bolivia. This is a difficult moment. The military crisis in the Chaco is serious. But if the situation can be saved we will save it, and if justice, human or divine, exists, Bolivia should emerge triumphant from this war."

General Kundt had exacted $300,000 for the destruction of his home, after which he had consented to come back.

During the two years that General Kundt remained away from his adopted fatherland many things had happened. It was one of the most hectic and unhappy periods of peace in all the hectic and unhappy days which have followed the negotiation of the Kellogg Pact. It came to be called the Non-Aggression Chapter of the Chaco, made memorable by the failure of all the peace forces of the Western Hemisphere to force a non-aggression pact upon Paraguay and Bolivia.

Failure can be set down to two factors. There was the personal rivalry of those who wanted credit for achieving peace in the Western Hemisphere; and there was the international rivalry of nations and peace organizations for the same credit. Without this bickering, war might have been avoided.

Trouble started again in the summer of 1931—just one year after the ousting of General Kundt. During that year Bolivia enjoyed a period of external peace but internal hardship. The price of tin remained so low that it was hardly worth mining. Indian tin-miners, employed under conditions of virtual slavery, were deprived even of starvation wages. There were revolts and Cabinet turnovers. Bolivia defaulted on the Dillon, Read loan which had made war in the Chaco possible. She defaulted on other loans held by American bondholders. Perhaps this lightened her burden, made war finances easier. Perhaps, also, depressed economic conditions made war in the jungles of the Chaco no worse than slow starvation at home. Finally, there was the inescapable fact that patriotic emotion, aroused by the threat of war with Paraguay, made it easier for Bolivian Cabinets to sit more comfortably in La Paz.

What started hostilities again, no one ever knew. Bolivia claimed that it was Paraguay, and Paraguay claimed it was Bolivia. In general, it was probably the fact that Paraguay was weathering the depression much better than Bolivia and saw a chance to score against her rival. A secondary factor was an exchange of compliments between the Bolivian and Paraguayan Legations in Washington which they aired in the press.

The bomb burst on a sultry day in June. Every diplomat who could afford it was basking on the sands of Newport. For Diez de Medina, Minister of Bolivia, the summer was particularly dull. He alternated between riding with a blonde in Rock Creek Park, dancing at the Villa Roma and scanning the news for an opportunity to crash the headlines. Finally he found it. Paraguay had purchased two Italian gunboats and was employing an Argentine military mission. Summoning the press, Diez de Medina issued a scathing statement.

This was enough to make the headlines throughout Latin America. But Louis J. Heath, most indefatigable reporter of the United Press, called up Pablo Ynsfran, charge d'affaires of the Paraguayan Legation. That gentleman promptly dashed to United Press headquarters, where on

Mr. Heath's typewriter he laboriously punched out a reply. Mr. Heath cabled this reply to South America. This, in part, is what it said:

> The Bolivian Legation has made reference to the reduction in military expenditures by its government. But this reduction is not attributable by any means to pacifism on the part of the Bolivian government, but to some financial difficulties, well known in American financial centres, and derived from previous enormous contracts for armaments in Europe. If Bolivia reduces her military expenditures it is merely because she can no longer make them. On the other hand if Paraguay modernizes her armaments, she is doing so without committing herself to any burdensome indebtedness and without borrowing a single penny abroad and without defaulting her financial obligations.

Two days after this statement had sizzled across the front pages of La Paz newspapers, the Bolivian Government sent a formal note to Asunción asking for the recall of Pablo Ynsfran and a formal apology for his statement criticizing Bolivia. The rest was a foregone conclusion. Paraguay refused the apology. Bolivia severed diplomatic relations. The armies of both countries mobilized. And despite a bombardment of pleas for peace on the part of the Neutrals, the two countries found themselves back in the identical positions they had occupied before the efforts of the McCoy Commission.

This was in June and July, 1931. And so incensed was Bolivia at the impugnation of her finances by Pablo Ynsfran, that not until November could she be persuaded to send delegates to Washington.

The strategy of the Neutrals by this time was to get Bolivia and Paraguay to negotiate a non-aggression pact, leaving the fundamental question of partitioning the Chaco to be settled after the two countries had definitely pledged not to attack each other.

Negotiations dragged interminably. Both delegations

communicated with their capitals chiefly by mail. While they waited for answers, their troops in the swamplands sat in *fortinas* only a few miles apart. While they waited also, interest in Paraguay and Bolivia became keener, populations more aroused, and the dilemma of the two governments in accepting unpopular compromises more difficult.

The chief *bête noire* of the Neutral Commission during these negotiations was the press. Francis White, Assistant Secretary of State and chairman of the Commission, favored secret diplomacy. He argued that any peace proposal must mean concessions from both sides. He pointed out that local populations, not realizing this, must inevitably consider every proposal unfair; that with public opinion aroused, no government could accept the Neutral Commission's proposals and remain in office. None of the Commission's work, therefore, was to be made public.

Mr. White argued, however, without taking into consideration some of the frailties of human nature. He did not realize, apparently, that Paraguayans always will publish anything inimical to Bolivians and that Bolivians will return the compliment. Also he argued without proper appreciation of the cut-throat competition between two great Argentine newspapers and the two great press associations which feed them. Between *La Nacion* and *La Prensa* of Buenos Aires is a bitter, undying feud. Between the Associated Press, which feeds the first, and the United Press, which feeds the second, there is equal rivalry. The Chaco dispute, involving armed forces on the Argentine border, is of tremendous interest in Buenos Aires, and despite the secrecy of Mr. White, thousands of words daily were cabled to South America.

In fact, on the night of December 10th, when the entire Diplomatic Corps made its annual trek to the White House to pay its respects to the President, a great many additional words were put on the wire. For on that night

Señor Eduardo Diez de Medina and Señor Enrique Finot, delegates of Bolivia but not diplomats, stepped over the silken cord which separates the diplomats from the *hoi polloi* and shook hands with the President of the United States and Mrs. Hoover long before other non-diplomats. Waiting patiently in the long line of non-diplomats, meanwhile, were Señor Juan José Soler and Señor Cesar A. Vasconsellos, delegates of Paraguay. Slowly, six inches at a time, they moved toward the Mecca of their pilgrimage. Their Bolivian colleagues were nowhere to be seen. The room was hot, their knees were tired, but a great honor lay ahead of them.

Suddenly, as they were about to attain that honor, they were nonplused to see standing among the diplomats who already had shaken hands with the President, Señors Finot and Diez de Medina. Finot flaunted the great green Order of the Condor de Los Andes. Medina exhibited the blue, red, and yellow sash of the Venezuelan Order of Busto de Los Andes. Both looked as if they had just swallowed a canary.

Señors Soler and Vasconsellos took one look and stepped out of line. They called for their wraps and went home.

The next morning a formal protest arrived at the State Department. Paraguay was sorry that its delegates had had to forego the pleasure and privilege of greeting the President of the United States, the note said, but to have done so after the act already had been performed by the Bolivian delegates, would have been a slight to Paraguayan national honor never to be tolerated. Was it not a fact, the Legation of Paraguay asked the State Department, that lots had been drawn at the start of the non-aggression negotiations by which Paraguay, not Bolivia, was given precedence in all social matters?

For most of the Diplomatic Corps the incident was the outstanding joke of the year. For Francis White and his Commission of Neutrals, however, it was not. The people of Bolivia chortled with glee. The people of Paraguay demanded redress. It looked for a time as if the chances of war in the Chaco, instead of being removed by American conciliation, had been materially enhanced. In the end Francis White sent Paraguay a formal note of apology, in which Lieutenant Raymond R. Waller, a naval aide at the White House, was made the goat. It was explained that in an effort to be courteous, he had moved the Bolivians over the sacred silken cord into the Diplomatic guest line.

Six months dragged by. The chief stumbling-block was Bolivia's claim that the Non-Aggression Pact must be based on the present position of both armies, thus taking advantage of her recent military advances. Paraguay, on the other hand, proposed that both sides withdraw to a line agreed upon in 1907 and long since violated. Finally, in May, 1932, the Neutral Commission submitted a take-it-or-leave-it proposition whereby the two governments were to establish a neutral zone of five kilometers between their armies, resume diplomatic relations, and do the rest of the dickering afterward.

The proposal came too late. Even while it was being formulated, rumblings of new troop movements were heard in the Chaco. And on June 15th, while the Non-Aggression Pact was under consideration at both capitals, a mud-walled, thatch-roofed stockade belonging to Paraguay and bearing the imposing name of Fort Carlos Antonio Lopez was captured by a Bolivian patrol.

This was what the militarist party in Paraguay was looking for. A hue and cry went up from Asunción that national honor be avenged. The Paraguayan delegates were withdrawn from the non-aggression conversations in Washington. Paraguayan troops were given orders to atone for the Bolivian attack.

The Neutral Commission entreated the Paraguayan delegates to return to the deliberations. Telegrams to

this end were sent to Asunción. Foreign Minister Zalles of
Bolivia, genuinely anxious to avoid hostilities, issued an
explanation that the attack on Fort Carlos Antonio Lopez
occurred only because it was newly built and Bolivian
pickets had not known it was there.

All of which carried little weight. Señors Soler and
Vasconsellos purchased tickets on the S.S. *Southern Cross*
bound for Buenos Aires and went to New York preparatory to embarkation. Two automobiles they had acquired
in Washington were loaded aboard the ship. Both delegates obviously were anxious that no last-minute peace
move interfere with the prospect of driving their new
models through the streets of Asunción.

Their sailing date was July 21st. On July 20th, Paraguayan troops recaptured Fort Carlos Antonio Lopez.
Asunción suspended all business. The crowds went wild.
National honor was appeased. The Paraguayan delegates,
about to step on their ship, were ordered to return to
Washington. Dr. Juan José Soler unloaded his car and
obeyed the instruction. For Dr. Cesar Vasconsellos, however, the itch of his new automobile was too much. He
went home.

It was now Bolivia's turn to be aroused. Her government sent a circular telegram to all Bolivian legations
abroad detailing instances of recent Paraguayan aggression in the Chaco. The Bolivian military party demanded
withdrawal from the Washington conversation. *La Re-
publica* proclaimed: "War is the only dignified step for
Bolivia as a reply to constant bloody aggressions by Paraguay." Foreign Minister Zalles was in a difficult spot. He
refrained, however, from actually withdrawing his delegates from Washington. Perhaps this was a political blunder as far as he was concerned, for the Bolivian military
demanded his removal and eventually got it. Zalles was
replaced by War Minister Guiterez, a rabid jingo. There
were more skirmishes, more demands on both sides for

war. Part of the Bolivian army entrained for the front. Women offered their services as nurses. On the other side of the Chaco, youths swarmed around Paraguayan army headquarters, clamoring to be the first to enlist. A notice posted on the bulletin board of the National Military Academy notified cadets that classes were suspended in order to form an infantry battalion for service at the front.

Meanwhile the Commission of Neutrals continued its deliberations in Washington. On this particular chapter of the Chaco alone it had been deliberating nine months —earnestly, altruistically, conscientiously—and got nowhere. Its chairman, Francis White, was a man of fanatic devotion to the cause of Latin American friendship, but with an unfortunate inability to lift himself above the immediate ruts in his path. It was perhaps poetic justice that he who had approved the loan which touched the match to the conflagration should now be charged with its settlement.

Mr. White had built up a reputation among Nordic friends as a great glad-hander of Latin Americans. Actually he was too austere, too dictatorial, too cognizant of the aristocratic Maryland forbears from which he sprang. His colleagues—diplomatic representatives of Colombia, Cuba, Mexico, and Uruguay—also were sincere and conscientious strivers for Latin American peace. But unlike the members of the McCoy Neutral Commission which had struggled with the 1928 conflict, they had other important duties. Their ordinary work as chiefs of embassy or legation was absorbing enough, and the task of bringing peace to the Chaco became only a stepchild. An additional handicap was the fact that some of the ablest members of the Commission frequently were away. At the height of the crisis in the summer of 1931, Ambassador Orestes Ferrara of Cuba, most distinguished representative among the Neutrals, was engaged in chasing a concession for the International Telephone and Telegraph Company in Japan;

while Ambassador José Manuel Puig Casauranc spent much of his time commuting between Washington, where he was supposed to steer the course of American-Mexican friendship, and Mexico City, where he was much more absorbed in steering the course of his own political future. As a result the destinies of the Chaco were left largely in the hands of their *chargés d'affaires*, together with the Minister of Colombia, Dr. Fabio Lozano, the Minister of Uruguay, Dr. J. Varela, in addition, of course, to the ever-present Francis White.

Aside from Mr. White, the man who took the greatest interest in the work of the Neutral Commission was the Minister of Uruguay. There were several reasons for Dr. Varela's interest. In the first place, he was dean of Latin American Diplomats. He also ranked next to Viscount d'Alte of Portugal, now deceased, as the dean of all Ministers. He had, therefore, considerable prestige at stake. Finally, however, and much more important, the chief personal rival of Dr. Varela was Señor Guani, Uruguayan representative at the League of Nations. Señor Guani once had been President of the Assembly of the League, in fact, the first Latin American President. This was an honor not to be taken lightly, and Dr. Varela was the last one to make such a mistake. To counterbalance it, he strove valiantly to make the Commission of Neutrals an instrument of peace, power, and a vehicle for his own personal prestige.

Despite his efforts, however, and despite the ambitious zeal of Francis White, two powerful groups in different parts of the world rose up from time to time to challenge the efficacy of the Neutral Commission. One of these was the ABCP group—Argentina, Brazil, Chile, and Peru—known as the "Neighbors" of the two disputants. The other was the League of Nations.

The League, at times, had stuck its head inquiringly into the Chaco dispute, only to have it soundly smacked, first by the State Department, which objected to European meddling with Pan-American troubles, and second by Dr. Varela, who objected vigorously to any move which might increase the prestige of his ancient enemy, Guani. Despite these rebuffs, there were many who felt that the League of Nations, to which both Paraguay and Bolivia belonged, was the only organization which could hale them into court and force good behavior—especially since Bolivia is not a party to the Kellogg Pact. There were those, on the other hand, who believed that only the Neighbors of the two countries actually had enough at stake to compel peace in the Chaco.

In deference to this view, the Neutral Commission had suggested to the ABCP group on April 13, 1931, that they join the Neutrals in proposing the Non-Aggression Pact to the two belligerents. Argentina, most active in conciliation attempts prior to 1928, declined. She gave no reasons for unwillingness to coöperate, but the interpretation placed upon her negation was that the Neutrals, having lifted conciliation from Argentine hands, now deserved the unmitigated pleasure of bringing about peace. Brazil followed the Argentine lead; and Chile and Peru, seeing that their coöperation without Argentina and Brazil was valueless, said nothing.

So the Chaco continued in the lap of the Neutrals.

But three months later—midsummer, 1932—with reports of mobilization from La Paz and Asunción, with women and children clamoring to enlist, and with every prospect of a war bursting in her own back yard, Argentina was in a much more coöperative mood. At this point Francis White called in the Argentine Ambassador, Dr. Felipe Espil, and proposed that his government take the initiative in uniting all the countries of Latin America against the recognition of territory seized by armed force. Espil was skeptical. He knew that this non-recognition policy—or Stimson Doctrine—was what the United States was trying to put across in Manchuria, and he saw Argentina in the none-too-popular rôle of playing the Yankee game. But what was much more important, he saw real difficulties in getting Chilean acceptance of a non-recognition doctrine if that doctrine were proposed by Argentina. The military schools of Chile, he told White, still toasted the day when Chilean armies might conquer Patagonia, once awarded to Argentina by the arbitration of Edward VII; in view of which, Chile certainly would oppose the non-recognition of territory gained by armed force. However, Ambassador Espil telegraphed his Foreign Minister in Buenos Aires, Saavedra Lamas.

Saavedra Lamas was enthusiastic. He had been endeavoring to jolt Argentina out of its isolation under President Irigoyen and to establish it as the leading peace force in South America. Particularly, he saw himself at the head of that force. President Justo, however, was more cautious. He felt that Argentine initiative in a move of this kind would arouse opposition from both Brazil and Chile. So in the end Francis White was informed that, while Argentina could not take the lead against the recognition of conquered territory, she would heartily support any initiative by the United States.

This was something which Mr. White was not at all anxious for. It looked too much as if the United States were lining up its dominions to the south in support of Stimsonian policy in Manchuria. A spontaneous move on the part of the Latin Americans themselves would have looked much better. However, passionately devoted to the cause of peace and zealously anxious to please his chief, Mr. White called a meeting of the ABCP countries plus his five Neutrals, and proposed broadening the Stimson doctrine to include all Latin America.

True to his word, Ambassador Espil heartily seconded the proposal. He also proposed that Mr. White be delegated to draw up the Non-Recognition formula. True, also, to Espil's prediction, Chile objected. All of the other consulted countries—Brazil, Peru, Cuba, Mexico, Colombia, and Uruguay—gave enthusiastic support. But it was not until Miguel Cruchaga—a powerful factor in Chilean politics—threatened his resignation as Ambassador to Washington that the Chilean Government telegraphed reluctant coöperation. After this, approval by other Latin American governments was easy.

The resultant communication dispatched to Paraguay and Bolivia on August 3rd was a real triumph for the cause of peace and Pan-American harmony. It invited the two belligerents to stop the movement of troops, to settle their dispute by peaceful means. It warned that none of the signatory governments would recognize any territorial arrangement not obtained through peace. Every member of the Pan-American Union signed it. Never before had the republics of the Western Hemisphere been so united in the cause of peace.

But there was one blemish. After the document had been signed, the envoys of the nineteen republics were asked to pose for the news reel. And here occurred one of Francis White's most fatal blunders. Afraid to make the suggestion openly, he tipped off the photographers to place his beloved Neutral Commission in the center of the picture. So while the Neutrals—some of them mere Ministers— were given seats of honor, the ABCP Ambassadors, representatives of the most powerful states in South America, men who had made this unified move successful, were forced to stand in the background. What made it worse, Francis White planked himself down in the very center.

Precedence is very dear to the Latin American heart. And some of those who were forced to stand in the rear never again gave Mr. White their fullest degree of coöperation.

There was one other blunder with which Mr. White had no connection, but which contributed materially to the definite divorce between the Neutral Commission and the Neighbors.

Newspaper reports attributed the united Pan-American front against war to the canny diplomacy of Argentina. And Foreign Minister Saavedra Lamas, always enthusiastically for the idea, took the credit. The powerful *La Prensa*, however, claimed otherwise. So did Lissandro de la Torre, a member of the Argentine Senate. He interrogated Saavedra Lamas, tried to pin him down regarding the exact part he had played. Mr. White, in Washington, was anxious to have Saavedra Lamas get full credit and maintained discreet silence. Other members of the Neutral Commission, however, did not. Peeved at the Argentine Foreign Minister for assuming responsibility for something he did not do, they told the real story.

Carlos Saavedra Lamas was a man of pride and ambition. Grandson of Cornelio Saavedra, first President of Argentina, he married the daughter of Rocque Saenz Pena, another President. And he had gone a long way toward equaling their distinguished careers. At the age of twenty-eight he was elected to the Chamber of Deputies. At thirty-five he became Minister of Justice and Public Instruction, and at the age of fifty achieved the distinction of being Minister of Foreign Affairs. He founded the University of La Plata, held a professorship of political economy at the University of Buenos Aires, established a record as an authority on international law, and had the vanity of a child.

In view of this it was not surprising that after the Neutral Commission exposed Saavedra Lamas, he was as bitter against it as some of those in Washington who had to be photographed behind Francis White. It was not surprising also that from this point on, coöperation between the Neutrals and the Neighbors was cast to the winds. More than ever the Chaco became the football of personal jealousy and international rivalry. It was pulled this way by the Neutrals, that way by the Neighbors, the other way by the League of Nations. Saavedra Lamas developed a violent dislike for Francis White, and Francis White for Saavedra Lamas. Dr. Varela of Uruguay was more anxious than ever that his rival, Dr. Guani, should not gain more glory at Geneva. The United States watched resentfully the intrusion of the League, while, among the Neighbors, Chile was suspicious of Peru, and Brazil of Argentina.

Of all these hates, however, that between Francis White and Saavedra Lamas was the most intense and the most prejudicial to the peace of South America. It is not often that the State Department official charged with promoting friendship with Latin America speaks disparagingly of the maternity of the Foreign Minister of a friendly country, but in such language did Mr. White refer to his colleague of the Pampas.

Saavedra Lamas, of course, was not in a juxtaposition to appreciate properly the expletive, but it is a safe assumption that even at a distance of 5,000 miles he was speaking with equal candour and ruggedness regarding the personality and paternity of Mr. White. Certainly his subsequent efforts to thwart Mr. White's diplomacy in the Chaco indicated this.

From that point on Mr. White with his Neutrals and Señor Saavedra Lamas with his Neighbors played a game of tic-tac-toe, with the Gran Chaco as the stake and the question of peace or war in South America hanging in the balance.

Mr. White and his Neutrals followed up the united Pan-American plea for peace by urging that both belligerents withdraw their forces to the positions they had occupied on June 1st. This meant that Bolivia would relinquish four forts captured from Paraguay, while Paraguay would relinquish nothing. Bolivia promptly objected; Paraguay unconditionally accepted.

Whereupon Señor Saavedra Lamas and his Neighbors came forward with a proposal that the two belligerents cease hostilities, holding the positions they then occupied. This meant that Bolivia would keep four of Paraguay's forts. Bolivia promptly accepted; Paraguay objected.

Señor Saavedra Lamas next proposed informally an immediate conference of all Pan-American countries to be held at some South American capital near the scene of hostilities, which would throw the united weight of the Western Hemisphere against war and which would continue in session until war ceased. Such unity of action was what Francis White had proposed in the preceding April. It would have eliminated the bickering between the Neighbors and Neutrals. But now White rejected the proposal. The State Department, he informed Ambassador Espil, had no funds at its disposal for such a conference. Almost simultaneously the State Department was sending delegates to the Fifth International Congress on Electricity at Paris, the Forty-third Congress of the Royal Sanitary Institute at Brighton, the Fourteenth International Congress on Secondary Education at London, the Fifth International Congress for Scientific Management at Amsterdam, the Fifth Triennial Congress for Commercial Education at London, the Tenth International Congress of Psychology at Copenhagen, the Congress of Prehistoric and Protohistoric Societies at London, the International Congress of Mathematicians at Zurich, the International Cacao Conference at Brussels, the International Congress on Biliary Lithiasis at Vichy, the Second International Congress of Otorhinolaryngology at Madrid, the International Conference of Migration Statistics, the Third International Congress on Rheumatism, the Fourteenth International Congress of Ophthalmology at Madrid and the Paris Conference on Fruit as a Food.

Mr. White and his Neutrals made up for lack of ingenuity by unflagging energy. They now countered with another proposal. They urged both parties to cease hostilities immediately and submit their dispute to arbitration without reservation. Should either country subsequently violate the truce, the violator should be declared an aggressor and American diplomatic and consular representatives be withdrawn.

This was a situation made to order for Señor Saavedra Lamas. In a note delivered to the State Department October 18th, he protested that Mr. White and his Neutrals had adopted "coercive measures" toward the two belligerents. He said that Argentina had coöperated with the Neutrals in the united Pan-American plea upon the understanding that "only moral pressure would be involved." If the Neutrals were now going to get rough, Señor Saavedra Lamas warned, Argentina could not play ball.

Mr. White and his Neutrals took more than two weeks to reply, and then remarked pointedly: "If there is one thing patent in all these negotiations, it is the patience, loyalty, and personal disinterestedness with which the Neutral Commission has dealt with this complex and trying problem."

Meanwhile the armies of Bolivia and Paraguay continued to fight it out for possession of the Chaco. Meanwhile, also, the League of Nations, alarmed at the smell of blood and distressed at the inability of the Western Hemisphere to settle its own feud, addressed two polite but pointed inquiries to Mr. White and his Neutrals, asking if it could be of any assistance. The first of these was answered with a reasonable degree of courtesy, the second with a curtness which amounted to a snub. Mr. White, always an ardent opponent of League meddling in Pan-American affairs, replied that the "question must be handled with patience" and that negotiations "were proceeding satisfactorily."

Here again was a situation made to order for Señor Saavedra Lamas. His composure by this time was comparable to that of a militant porcupine. In a barbed reply to Mr. White, November 19th, he suggested the urgent advisability of the Neutrals' abdicating the throne of conciliation and passing their work onto the League of Nations.

And in a wholly gratuitous and uncalled-for peroration, he slapped the policy nearest the heart of Francis White—the Monroe Doctrine.

"If the League is to act, within the purpose which inspires us all," said Saavedra Lamas, ". . . it can and must develop its action without finding an obstacle in *regional or continental doctrines* which . . . have neither the adhesion of Argentina nor a sanction created by the unanimous will of the countries of the continent."

This was a slap difficult even for the patient Mr. White to bear; but despite it, he continued to plod toward the goal of peace. He now occupied a most unfortunate position. In the first place, he was unwilling to let the League enter into the conciliation negotiations, although simultaneously urging the League to settle the Leticia dispute between Peru and Colombia. Meanwhile he opposed the transfer of the negotiations to South America, although his own Neutrals had not succeeded in preventing open war between Bolivia and Paraguay.

Finally, in the early days of December, Mr. White and his Neutral Commission prepared what they hoped would be the *pièce de résistance* for at least a cessation of hostilities. They laid their plans most carefully. Paraguay, hitherto, had consistently opposed an armistice with both armies occupying the *status quo*. She contended that this left Bolivia much nearer the Paraguayan frontier and offered an excellent opportunity for Bolivian forces to consolidate their position preparatory to a fresh attack when peace parleys failed. Bolivia, on the other hand, claimed that if both armies withdrew from the Chaco altogether, her forces had a much greater distance to travel back in case hostilities were resumed. In order to meet both objections, the Neutral Commission compromised. It stipulated that Paraguayan forces retire to the Paraguayan River, and the Bolivian army to about Meridian 62—only half as far as the Paraguayans—but at the same time a position farther from the fighting than Paraguay once before had demanded. After withdrawal by both armies, the American Geographical Society, the Royal Geographical Society of London, and the Geographical Society of Madrid were to decide the limits of the Chaco.

To the outside world it was a most equitable proposal.

Conditions, however, had changed since Paraguay clamored for an armistice. Paraguay was now winning. She had recaptured the four forts previously lost to Bolivia and her armies were on what they thought was a triumphal march through the very heart of the Chaco. It was at this moment that Bolivia, with defeat grasping at her heart, had cabled General Hans Kundt to come back and rescue his adopted fatherland.

Under these circumstances Paraguay could see no object in accepting the Neutrals' proposal. With a considerable show of wounded dignity, she refused. Moreover, she threatened to withdraw from the Conference her one surviving delegate, Juan José Soler.

The Neutrals mobilized all possible weapons to force acceptance. They appealed to the League of Nations, which promptly and energetically supported the proposal. They appealed to the nineteen other members of the Pan-American Union, which also urged the disputants to accept.

Despite this, Paraguay stood pat. Crowds of people in Asunción milled through the streets, demanded the reason why Paraguay should yield to such injustice. Her armies were winning. Juan José Soler, in Washington, heard the crowds shouting. He had Presidential ambitions. He admitted privately to Francis White that the proposal was just and equitable, added that if White quoted him to this effect he would deny it. Finally, at 12:20 on December 31st, spurning the entreaties of two continents, Dr. Soler walked across the gangplank of the S.S. *Northern Prince* and returned to Asunción.

He helped to thwart the best chance peace ever had in the Chaco. But in his own country he was a hero.

Meanwhile war in everything but name raged back and forth among the fever-infested swamps, the flamboyant trees, the mucky hell of the Chaco. The rainy season had come. The meandering rivers lost themselves more completely than ever in the swampland. Trenches filled with water. The foundations of artillery pieces oozed away in a slimy, slippery, endless sea of mud. Still the armies fought on.

In England, 5,000 miles away, agents for both sides recruited British war veterans—a shadow army of sad-faced men, disillusioned by years of barren peace, snatching at a bonus of $100 plus $15 a week, knowing nothing of the jungle warfare that awaited them, caring less.

In Washington, *blasé* tea parties got a new thrill. Learning for the first time of the existence of the Chaco, they listened to the wife of the Bolivian Minister, Crystal Hyland Abelli, and the wife of the Paraguayan *chargé d'affaires*, Señora Pablo Ynsfran, argue over their respective right to use the National Woman's Party as a forum for winning war funds and sympathy.

In Asunción, a thousand school children read in their history books how a children's battalion fought for Paraguay against Brazil, Argentina, and Uruguay in 1867; so they came trooping down to general-staff headquarters to ask permission to form a regiment.

On the battle front, General Kundt employed all the strategy of a lifetime in the Kaiser's army to take Fort Nanawa. For four days Bolivian artillery pounded the Paraguayan stronghold, mired itself deeper in the mud with each shot. Attacking Bolivians waded waist deep through the swamps in the face of Paraguayan machine-gun fire. Again and again they deployed, charged in waves across the marshland. Again and again they were repulsed. In the end neither side could claim victory. Casualties totalled 2,500.

"More thousands have been killed than anybody cares

to tell," wrote Dr. Arthur E. Elliott, an American missionary in Paraguay. "Asunción is a city of hospitals."

Almost in the center of these hostilities had settled 5,000
people who, with their ancestors, had spent a century and
a half fleeing from war. Conscientious objectors against
military service, these Mennonites had been buffeted from
Germany to Russia, to Mexico, Canada, the United States,
Manchuria; finally, after they had sent agents over half the
earth's surface looking for a land where they could live
in peace, Paraguay promised them a haven in the Chaco.
To the savannas of the Chaco, therefore, they came, their
expenses paid in part by the League of Nations, in part
by the sale of Canadian farmlands, in part by contributions from their wealthier members. And on the drier up-
lands of that vast area lying between Paraguay and
Bolivia they had set up their own schools, promulgated
their own laws, established their own model villages.

But the very fact of their arrival helped disrupt the
peace which they sought. Paraguay had encouraged their
migration, knowing that the more settlers she put in the
Chaco, the greater her claim to its territory. Bolivia knew
this also. And in June, 1932, just after the League transported the last Mennonite colony from Manchuria, Foreign Minister Zalles decreed: "No more Mennonites will
be permitted to enter the Chaco except with the express
permission of Bolivia."

And shortly after this the weary seekers of peace found
themselves in the middle of the worst maelstrom to disturb the peace of the world since the Armistice.

It was a maelstrom, which after the withdrawal of Juan
José Soler from the Neutral Commission in Washington,
did to Paraguay exactly what was done to Bolivia when,
flush with victory, it rejected the peace proposals of the
previous summer. When Dr. Soler boarded the S.S. *Northern Prince* on December 31st, the population of Asunción
was confident that a few more weeks would see the Boliv-

ians chased out of the Chaco *in toto*. But they reckoned without General Kundt. That veteran of von Mackensen's campaigns set up headquarters in a thatch-roofed shack at Fort Munoz; and a few weeks after Asunción refused the Neutrals' truce proposal, Paraguayan troops were forced back just as far as the Neutrals originally proposed they should retire.

With the intensification of hostilities, the neighboring countries bestirred themselves. Saavedra Lamas, who had been watching from the side lines, decided it was time to expose the Francis White brand of diplomacy. Simultaneously Miguel Cruchaga, now Foreign Minister of Chile, did the same. And in order not to work at cross purposes, Cruchaga proposed a meeting with Saavedra Lamas at the little town of Mendoza in northern Argentina, February 1 and 2, 1933. Out of this came the Pact of Mendoza and the definite substitution of the Neighbors for the Neutrals as crusaders of peace. Brazil and Peru joined forces with Chile and Argentina, and all four held forth to the two belligerents an olive branch essentially similar to the Neutrals' proposal of December 15th.

Both countries accepted in principle, but threw up so many reservations that their acceptance amounted to rejection. Finally, after considerable pressure, Paraguay withdrew her reservations. She was losing. Also she had confidence in Chile and Argentina. The former had moved twice to block the transportation of Bolivian supplies over the Arica-La Paz Railway. Citizens of the latter had heavily invested in the Paraguayan sector of the Chaco. Argentine arms had been captured in the hands of Paraguayan troops. Finally Argentina had sent to Asunción as military *attaché* the officer who once trained the Paraguayan army.

But the more confidence Paraguay showed in Chile and Argentina, the more suspicious became Bolivia toward the good faith of the two Neighbors. The grandfather of Saavedra Lamas was born in the Bolivian City of Potosi, oldest mining town in South America; but despite this Bolivia distrusted his grandson. Finally, she flatly refused to remove her reservations; whereupon Saavedra Lamas swallowed his pride and appealed to his chief rival for the Nobel Peace Prize—Mr. Francis White.

The situation was now reversed. A few months before, Francis White had appealed to Saavedra Lamas in vain. But now, Mr. White came to the rescue of Saavedra Lamas. He made informal representations at La Paz supporting the Neighbors and urging Bolivia to withdraw her reservations.

In no uncertain terms, Bolivia refused.

The Neighbors then prepared new notes, and through their Legations in La Paz exerted the strongest possible diplomatic pressure upon Bolivia. A few months before this, Saavedra Lamas had protested bitterly when the Neutrals used similar tactics. Now the Bolivian Foreign Office used almost his identical language in charging Argentina and Chile with seeking to "impose" peace by diplomatic ultimatum.

Having been rebuffed, the Neighbors once again asked Francis White to come to their support. This time he refused. Their cause already was hopelessly lost, he said. Besides, he could not desert his Neutrals. Tomas LeBreton, Argentine Ambassador to France, even went over White's head to President Roosevelt during the Washington conversations preceding the London Economic Conference, but it had no effect. Mr. White remained adamant.

It was now May, 1933. Mr. Hoover had left the White House. Mr. Stimson had left the State Department. Mr. White lingered on.

At this point the simultaneous development of three wholly unrelated incidents conspired to bring the first formal declaration of war since 1914.

For several months, relations between Argentina and Chile, on the one hand, and Bolivia on the other, had been anything but cordial. Now they became even worse. On April 27th a squadron of Bolivian planes traversed the entire Chaco, penetrating as far as Puerto Casada and Puerto Pinasco, where they bombed an Argentine quebracho plant, together with ranch property owned by an American named George Lohman and the International Products Company of New York.

Puerto Casada is owned by Alberto Casada, brother-in-law of the President of Argentina. The Argentine protest, therefore, was loud and vigorous. Saavedra Lamas intimated to Francis White that he also should protest. Mr. White, however, was in no mood to pull Argentine chestnuts out of the fire and the inquiries he made of La Paz regarding the damage to American property were very discreet indeed.

Argentine resentment against Bolivia was now at the whitest heat conceivable without an actual break in diplomatic relations. But it was fanned to fiercer flame by Enrique Finot, who had succeeded the tin magnate, Abelli, as Bolivian Minister in Washington. Finot had ambitions for bigger and better things. And one point which did not escape him was the fact that Washington made an excellent sounding-board from which to broadcast the story of his heroic efforts for Bolivia. To this end he wrote a note to the Neutrals denouncing Argentina and Chile for exerting pressure on his government. To this end also, he gave a copy of his note to one of the great press services feeding Latin America, and next morning it was splashed all over Buenos Aires newspapers for the startled and indignant Saavedra Lamas to read at his breakfast table.

With this incident, the Paraguayan Government could be absolutely certain of one thing. It could be certain that if it declared war, the highly incensed Argentine Government and the even more highly incensed Saavedra Lamas would lose no time in declaring neutrality, thereby shutting its borders to all military supplies to both belligerents.

Paraguay, having access to the sea, could laugh at such an embargo. Even if Brazil, Chile, and Peru failed to follow the Argentine example, landlocked Bolivia would be virtually isolated. For it was through the Argentine port of Embarcacion that Bolivia transported nearly all its war supplies for the Chaco.

So the Paraguayan Minister, Enrique Bordenave, came to the State Department to explain to Francis White that if no further conciliation efforts were forthcoming, his government must declare war.

Here occurred the third wholly unrelated event which conspired to bring the first violation of the Kellogg Pact.

Francis White was not in his office. He was in a Johns Hopkins hospital having a fish bone removed from his throat. Mr. Bordenave looked round the State Department for some one else with whom to talk. The Secretary of State was absorbed with European delegations in preparation for the Economic Conference in London. The Under Secretary, Mr. Phillips, was busy with something else.

The chief of the Latin-American Division, Mr. Edwin Wilson, was ill. The Acting Chief was busy conferring with the Argentine Economic Delegation to London. So Mr. Bordenave went home. The next day he came again. Finally he told his troubles to Dr. Leo Rowe, Director-General of the Pan-American Union. Dr. Rowe was sympathetic but without a solution.

Finally, at the end of the week, Francis White came back to his office. The fish bone had been extracted. He was feeling much better. But the five-day period during which he had been absent helped to bring a declaration of war in South America.

Dr. Bordenave called on the same day that Mr. White returned, and told him of Paraguay's predicament. Either there must be immediate peace negotiations or else declaration of war, he said.

On occasion, Mr. White could work rapidly. Now he did. He called a meeting of the Neutrals for the following Monday—May 8th. The Neutrals, in turn, were to invite the four Neighbors to participate. At last there was to be complete unity between the Neighbors and the Neutrals —or so Francis White hoped. The bickering was to cease. Pan-America was to pull together. Mr. White even expressed willingness to hold future negotiations in any capital of South America—a concession he had never before been willing to make.

The Neutrals convened, cabled the necessary invitations to Argentina, Brazil, Chile, and Peru. They proposed that the diplomatic representatives of these countries in Washington meet with them two days later to arrange the details for future negotiations.

This later meeting took place at nine o'clock on May 10th. The Neutrals arrived punctually. So also did Ambassador Lima e Silva of Brazil and Ambassador Freyre y Santander of Peru. They sat and waited. Their Argentine and Chilean colleagues did not come. They never came.

The Chilean *chargé*, Benjamin Cohen, received instructions to ignore the meeting. The Argentine Ambassador telephoned that he had not had time to decode his instructions.

The fact was that both Argentina and Chile were irked that Francis White would not support their last drive for diplomatic pressure on Bolivia. They were giving the Neutrals a dose of their own medicine.

The next afternoon Dr. Bordenave called at the State Department. He served formal notification that Paraguay had declared war.

"Paraguay is a signatory of the Kellogg Pact," Bordenave announced to the press, "but there is a principle of international law which is higher than any pact, and that is the right of self-defense."

"That," remarked a reporter, "is the same excuse Germany gave in 1914."

During the early days of the New Deal, Francis White was absorbed with the problem of finding a good political bed on which to land. After ten years of molding Pan-American policy under Harding, Coolidge, and Hoover, he had become stamped with an indelible brand of Republicanism which did not easily wash off under a Democratic administration. He had made a notable record in Latin America. He had played an influential part in settling the Tacna-Arica dispute. He had pushed Honduras and Guatemala into a settlement of their boundary question. He had worked toward the withdrawal of American marines from Nicaragua. At the same time he had helped to pull Andy Mellon's Barco oil concession out of the fire in Colombia. He had said nothing when the National City Bank with J. and W. Seligman bribed the son of President Leguia while negotiating a $100,000,000 loan to Peru. He had approved the Dillon, Read loan by which Bolivia financed $5,000,000 of munitions to prosecute a war with Paraguay. And he had put the Coolidge-Hoover stamp of approval on Gerardo Machado, puppet President of Cuba for the Chase National Bank and Electric Bond and Share.

Despite all this, Francis White, for reasons known to himself, considered himself anointed to be Ambassador to Cuba under the New Deal. To achieve that honor, White pulled many wires. He marshalled some of the most powerful friends of the New Deal. Felix Frankfurter, Professor Moley, George Rublee all went to bat for him. But Democracy was adamant. As a gesture in recognition of his service, Roosevelt offered him the post of Minister to Czechoslovakia.

"You'll love Prague," said Harry Payer, who succeeded him as Assistant Secretary.

"Yes," replied White, skeptically.

"You'll love its charming society, the gay uniforms, the ancient castles, the beer concerts in the evening," persisted Payer, who was the son of a Czech officer.

White made a sour face and accepted the job.

He accepted just as Paraguay declared formal war upon Bolivia.

From that moment the State Department adopted a new policy toward the Chaco. During the past two years of intermittent turmoil it was apparent to almost everyone that the chief difficulty in the Bolivian-Paraguayan dispute was lack of cohesion between the conciliators.

Now, for the first time, Francis White proposed to end this. In June he called a meeting of the Neutrals and moved that they cease to exist. He pointed out that Bolivia proposed forsaking the Neutrals for the League of Nations. He did not mention the fact that he also planned to forsake the Neutrals for Czechoslovakia. But other members of the Commission did not overlook it, and two of them bitterly opposed his plan to disband. They were Minister Varela of Uruguay, who had his personal prestige and his rivalry with Señor Guani to consider; and Fabio Lozano, Minister of Colombia, who once had been Foreign Minister of his country, and believed in carving out a solemn and commanding rôle for himself in Washington. Oscar Cintas, the Cuban Ambassador, who lacked strong convictions on any subject other than sugar and Machado, voted with his two colleagues. Mexico voted with Francis White.

By a vote of three to two, therefore, the Neutrals, despite Mr. White's imminent departure, voted to continue to follow the football of peace in the Chaco.

Mr. White, by this time, had become just as ardent an advocate of disbanding the Neutral Commission as he had once been a defender of its inalienable right to conciliate. And he had one trump in reserve which Señors Varela and Lozano did not know about. The President of Cuba,

Gerardo Machado, at that time was anxious to do almost anything short of resigning in order to curry favor with the United States. So a few days later, for a reason never publicly explained, Ambassador Cintas got instructions to change his vote.

The vote now stood three to two for ending the checkered career of the Neutral Commission. Minister Varela, however, did not yield without a fight. In fact, he fought every inch of the way. He fought first against any kind of dissolution. He argued that the eager desire of Saavedra Lamas to have the Commission disbanded was the very reason why it should continue to function. When finally overruled, Varela pleaded that the Neutral Commission die in aloof and "elegant" silence. No official word of its disbandment should be sent to the two belligerents, not even a message of good will to the League of Nations. The League, and the Neighbors should be snubbed, Varela argued. He also maintained that the Neutrals should leave open the door to further conciliation in case either Paraguay or Bolivia wanted to bring back their dispute.

On the first of these, the Uruguayan won his point. The Commission voted to send no notice of its death either to the League or the two disputants. On the second point he lost. The doors of the Neutral Commission were slammed shut, never to be opened without the individual consent of all five of its member countries.

Varela, White, and the Neutrals now have passed completely out of the Washington picture, and the Latin American Diplomatic Corps is free to devote all its time to *yerbe mate*, increasing its wine quota, and gossip regarding the sleeping-mask of Ambassador Lima e Silva. Francis White deserted diplomacy four months after the end of the Neutral Commission. He got tired of the gay uniforms, the ancient castles, the beer concerts of Prague, yearned for his thankless hours at ironing out Latin American disputes. Also the garden of the American Legation in Prague would not drain. He resigned. Varela got a reprimand from his government the day after the details of the Neutrals' last debate were cabled to South America. His remark that the Neutral Commission should continue because Saavedra Lamas wanted it to disband brought a yowl of protest from across the River Plate. The yowl was heard all the way to Washington and caused the Uruguayan Government to remove Varela as chairman of the Seventh Pan-American Conference, where he would have to rule on motions made by the Argentine Foreign Minister. This was too much for the venerable diplomat and he resigned.

As for the Chaco dispute, it passed on to the League, where the same thing happened which always had happened. Both sides deadlocked over a truce, and one side thought it could get a better bargain elsewhere. The ambitious Mello Franco, then Foreign Minister of Brazil, saw an opportunity to rival the pacific reputation of Saavedra Lamas, and undertook to transfer the dispute back to the Neighbors. The League was horrified. Saavedra Lamas, a little dubious, coöperated temporarily, but was not one to let a Brazilian tarnish his escutcheon of peace. As the first formal arbitration proposal was made by Brazil, Argentina withdrew; after which the dispute went back to Geneva.

The League now insured the lives of five commissioners for 200,000 Swiss francs each and sent them to the mosquito-infested swamps of the Chaco.

It was at exactly this time that the statesmen of the Western Hemisphere gathered at Montevideo to congratulate themselves on the everlasting glory of Pan-American peace. There was some worry, it is true, as they arrived at the Uruguayan capital as to what they should do about the war raging just across the border. Some argued that discretion was the better part of valor; that Pan-America's reputation for peace should not be jeopardized by intruding in so thorny a dispute, especially one already under the protecting wing of the League of Nations.

Others claimed that if the elaborately developed peace machinery of the Pan-American Union could not combine with the League to prevent war between the two weakest countries in South America, there was never any use in trying to prevent war anywhere.

In the end the latter won.

"Let us constitute ourselves a friendly assembly of conciliation to see if we cannot end this awful war in the Chaco," pleaded Felipe Barreda Laos of Peru.

"Peace is the ardent desire of my government," shouted David Alvestegui of Bolivia.

"Paraguay will be grateful for the solution of a war already protracted too long," proclaimed Justo Pastor Benitez, Foreign Minister of Paraguay.

Again public opinion was mobilized. Again the head of every American government sent urgent cables pleading for peace.

At last factors for conciliation were favorable. At last, this was the big moment for peace. All the governments of the Pan-American Union were represented. The commission of the League of Nations was present. The jealousy, the bickering between the League, the Neighbors, the Neutrals, for the time being, was eliminated. Cordell Hull, Secretary of State, had gone out of his way to win the personal friendship and coöperation of Saavedra Lamas. He had dangled before him the Nobel Peace Prize.

"Señor Savanna," Mr. Hull insisted on calling him, despite the whispered promptings of Jimmy Dunn. But the sincerity in Mr. Hull's voice, the deference which he showed, completely won the Argentine Foreign Minister. In the end Saavedra Lamas accepted the high honor of serving on the Conciliation Commission between the United States and Estonia, thereby sealing the new-found friendship between the one-time rivals of North and South America.

One other factor, however, was not so favorable. The Bolivian army was in complete rout. Paraguay's formal declaration of war and the consequent closing of the Argentine border had their effect. Forced to import their supplies from the Pacific, carry them laboriously across the Andes, across the plateau of Bolivia, across the savannas of the Chaco, the Bolivians diffused all their strength on transport. They had been fighting for two years 2,000 miles from their base in a swamp 15,000 feet below the high altitudes of their homeland. Suddenly their morale collapsed. Throwing their arms to the jungle, they retreated toward their mountains. Even the personal airplane of General Kundt, purchased in Buffalo and equipped with three motors, was abandoned to the enemy. The General himself was removed from his command and recalled to La Paz where he was almost mobbed. The Paraguayan army, once armed with little more than machetes, overnight became one of the best equipped in South America. It was superbly victorious.

Just before Christmas the further rout of Bolivia was saved by a truce. Both sides agreed to suspend hostilities until the League Commission, with the friendly help of the Pan-American Conference, could propose a permanent settlement.

That settlement, as first drafted in Montevideo, provided that if either belligerent violated its terms, the Neutrals and Neighbors who sponsored it would sever diplomatic relations with the violator; if necessary, invoke sanctions.

Fifteen months before, Francis White had proposed almost exactly the same terms to Argentina and other Neighbors. The United States had been willing to go the limit, was willing to set a new precedent for international cooperation, even accepted the League principle of sanctions. But Argentina refused. In fact, the reply of Saavedra

Lamas to Mr. White was one of the most scathing documents in Pan-American peace-time history.

Now, however, Saavedra Lamas accepted, and the proposition was put up to his friend, Cordell Hull. Mr. Hull had established a life reputation as a Jeffersonian Democrat. He had championed the League of Nations. He had fought for Woodrow Wilson when Republican irreconcilables gutted his Versailles Treaty. He was a "world cooperation" man.

But now he balked at the basic principle which his dead chief promised Europe.

"I lay awake all night considering this," he told newspapermen next morning. "And I finally decided that I could not be responsible for a decision by which the United States might be obligated to send warships up the Parana River."

So the peace proposal was emasculated. Without teeth, it was sent to Paraguay and Bolivia.

"The Secretary of State of the United States is responsible for killing the chances of peace in the Chaco," announced President Terra of Uruguay.

Mr. Hull, then en route to Buenos Aires, was awakened by Jimmy Dunn at 3:45 A.M. He issued an aggrieved denial.

Whether it was Mr. Hull's fault or not, peace did not come to the Chaco after that. The truce terminated. Paraguay resumed its advance. Old rivalries between the prima donnas of peace cropped out again. Enrique Buero, secretary-general of the Pan-American Conference, had been a member of the League of Nations secretariat. Also his brother, Juan, was secretary of the League Commission for the Chaco. Ardent pro-Leaguers, they claimed that the Pan-American Conference was dwarfing the work of the League, therefore moved the League Commission from Montevideo to Buenos Aires.

President Terra of Uruguay was furious. Señor Saavedra Lamas was pleased.

From Montevideo the League Commission rallied its forces and put forward a new peace proposal. But by that time Paraguayan troops had pushed far into Bolivian territory. Crowds in Asuncion were triumphant and cocksure. They demanded the rewards of the victor. In the face of this, the League brought forward only the old formulas of arbitration.

Even so, its proposal would have had some chance of success had not its members completely neglected the chief key to peace in the Chaco. That key remained Argentina and Saavedra Lamas, its temperamental Foreign Minister. Argentina had helped train the Paraguayan army, supplied it with munitions, supported it with credits. The brother-in-law of President Justo was the largest property-owner in the Chaco. And if Argentina gave the word to Paraguay, almost any peace terms would be accepted.

But the League commissioners woefully neglected Saavedra Lamas. Instead of taking him into their confidence, instead of letting him play a part in making new overtures, they left him in the background. First word of their work came to him through the morning newspapers.

Saavedra Lamas immediately made an announcement. The League proposal, he said, did not have the support of Argentina.

Many other proposals to end the war in the Chaco have been made since then by many other prima donnas of peace. And more will be made in the future. But probably long after this is written, men of Paraguay and men of Bolivia will be splashing through the pools under the palm trees, wading knee-deep in the goldenrod of the savannas for the sake of uninhabited areas of jungle, the honor of their countries, and the petty prejudices that make men go to war.

Chapter V

THE WORLD PREPARES FOR WAR

1. THE INVASION OF MANCHURIA

SEPTEMBER, 1931, found the Western World very much absorbed with its own pain. Europe and the United States were in the throes of a depression which gripped men's stomachs and sent creeping paralysis into their post-war vision of a warless world. Henry L. Stimson, returning from a tour of Europe, was significantly silent regarding his cherished hopes for disarmament. Premier Laval, hoping to settle war debts, was preparing a goodwill pilgrimage to America. Dino Grandi, not to be outdone, was angling for a date on which to follow him. Germany, having partially got back on her financial feet after the débâcle of the Hoover moratorium, was proceeding with her pocket-battleship program. An apathetic Assembly of the League of Nations went about the important work of inviting Mexico to return to Geneva. A French-dominated World Court handed down a decision finding the Austro-German customs union in violation of the Versailles Treaty—Frank B. Kellogg and six other judges dissenting. British sailors, tired of being fed on patriotism and women's smiles, paralyzed the British fleet—backbone of the Empire—during the annual maneuvers off the coast of Scotland. Simultaneously, runs on the Bank of England developed greater momentum than those which closed the doors of the Reichsbank. A hypodermic of $400,000,000— then $200,000,000,—was advanced by the Bank of France and the Federal Reserve, until the greatest credit in financial history was pumped into British vaults.

"England yet shall stand," shouted Chancellor of the Exchequer Snowden as he hunched his crippled body before the House of Commons.

There was indeed sufficient to absorb the statesmen of the United States and Europe.

An age was dying. It was the age of international optimism—the age of Kellogg Pacts, disarmament drives and goodwill pilgrimages—the aftermath of the war to end war. But it did not know that it was dying.

It was September, the drag-end of a hot and hectic summer. Jimmy Walker was in Paris, having just been made a Commander in the Legion of Honor. The body of Benjamin P. Collings, missing from his yacht for seven days, was cast ashore on Long Island, hands and feet tied. The Catholic Bishop of Mainz refused burial rites to one of the first Nazi members of the Reichstag. Jack Dempsey divorced Estelle Taylor at Reno. The chief of police and the ex-mayor of Hartford, Alabama, shot themselves to death in a duel over a road-scraping machine. A hurricane demolished the capital of British Honduras. Episcopalian bishops meeting at Denver debated the liberalization of divorce laws. The Reverend Myron Taylor, African missionary, died after having both hands and one foot chewed off by a lion. President Hoover, speaking at Detroit, tried to convince the American Legion to forego the bonus. Stock Exchanges in London, Paris, Berlin, Vienna, Amsterdam, and Athens closed as a result of runs on the Bank of England. Police at Malm, outside Helsingfors, pumping a spring dry, discovered a woman's head, nine human feet, seven hands, seven fingers, and a woman's scalp. The United States Steel Corporation announced a wage cut of ten per cent for a quarter of a million employees. Bethlehem Steel, General Motors, and the United States Rubber Company prepared to follow.

An age was dying. And the world, too absorbed in its own woes, did not sense impending tragedy.

It did not even sense anything more than customary skirmishes with Chinese brigands when eight trainloads of Japanese troops, loaded and waiting on Korean sidings on the night of September 18th, were rushed across the border to seize the five most important cities of South Manchuria.

Mukden, capital of Manchuria, awoke on the morning of September 19th to find its historic walls in the vise-like grip of the Japanese army. The troops of Governor Chang Hsueh-liang had been dispersed over the wild Manchurian plain. According to Tokyo, a stretch of track on the South Manchurian Railway, south of Mukden, had been bombed by Chinese. Although the incident took place at 10 P.M., and although the 10:30 train, traversing the same track, arrived in Mukden on time, the Japanese had brought in an entire army corps to avenge the incident.

Next day every town along 693 miles of railway was occupied by the Japanese army.

With such precision moved the military machine of Nippon that it created scarcely a ripple on the surface of the Western World. Great pains were taken to see that it did not. Foreign Minister Shidehara himself did not know of the incident until he read about it in the newspapers. He expressed "deep chagrin" that "a clash between small forces, under junior officers," should have interfered with his efforts to inject a more rational spirit into Sino-Japanese relations. The Japanese military commander in Manchuria, he said, acted entirely on his own initiative. Instructions had been telegraphed for him to withdraw from Mukden "as soon as the panic in that city had subsided." General Honjo's "military measures were intended to protect the local interests of Japanese citizens and were merely a police measure."

Unquestionably Baron Shidehara was sincere in what he said. Unquestionably also he knew little more about the Mukden incident than did Mr. Stimson, himself. Nor was he soon to know. His Consul-General in Mukden, instructed to get a report from the military authorities as to what they were doing, was kept waiting two days before General Honjo would see him.

Ambassador Debuchi, meanwhile, repeated Shidehara's assurances with an accompaniment of smiles and gestures to Henry L. Stimson; and, on the whole, Mr. Stimson believed. Somewhat worried, however, he sent identical notes to China and Japan urging them to confine their military operations to "the requirements of international law," but tactfully refused to invoke the Kellogg Pact. It was evident to all, especially the Japanese, that he was leaning over backward to give them a break.

Kenkichi Yoshizawa, Japanese delegate to the League of Nations, repeated the same soothing promises to the Council, and the Council also believed. Spanish Foreign Minister Lerroux, presiding over the Council, devoted ten minutes to hearing the Chinese and Japanese sides and then expressed satisfaction that Japan would correct the situation.

"Mr. Yoshizawa assures us that Japan is now withdrawing her troops," reassured Viscount Cecil of Chelwood.

"President Lerroux's expression of hope that the incident will soon be settled is the sentiment always arrived at by a pacifist meeting," scoffed the more skeptical *Journal des Débats*. "That is all the Council of the League has been able to do so far. What a fine peace organization!"

Pacifist assurances, however, continued to be believed. After all, did not Mr. Stimson know Premier Wakatsuki as an old friend at the London Naval Conference? Had they not worked together side by side for peace? And was not Baron Shidehara one of Japan's most renowned disciples of friendship with China? Give him the confidence of the United States and he will be able to calm the militarists of Japan. Such was the refrain which diminutive Ambassador Debuchi continually poured in the ear of the Secretary of

State; and such was the refrain which Mr. Stimson at first believed.

Katsuji Debuchi, although no bigger than Mr. Stimson's aged negro messenger, was a convincing individual. He had, what is so rare with Orientals, a smile. In the Samurai school, where Katsuji studied, he was taught that no one smiled unless he considered the person at whom he was looking to be ludicrous. Therefore, it was most discourteous to smile. Long years of association with the world of Western diplomacy, however, had taught Katsuji that his smile was a valuable asset, and with Henry L. Stimson he used it with notable success.

Mr. Stimson had other reasons for relying upon the good faith of the Japanese Government. He had inherited from his predecessors, Mr. Hughes and Mr. Kellogg, a secret understanding with Japan, which, although never reduced to writing and never called by any name, deserved the title of "Japanese-American Alliance." Supplanting the Anglo-Japanese Alliance, which died at the Washington Arms Conference, there had developed a tacit understanding based on the fact that the United States bought one-third of all Japan's exports, and Japan in turn bought the same proportion from the United States. It was an understanding between merchant princes. In Japan, Baron Shidehara, Minister of Foreign Affairs, spoke for the great House of Mitsubishi, whose daughter he had married, for the equally powerful Mitsuis, and for all the rest of Japan's ruling merchant class; while in the United States the Harding, Coolidge, and Hoover administrations spoke for General Electric, United States Steel, Standard Oil, General Motors, and for all the others which found Japanese markets profitable. Especially they spoke for J. P. Morgan, who even sought to loan $30,000,000 of American investors' money for Japanese exploitation of Manchuria.

At Mr. Stimson's right hand during these crucial days sat

an Under Secretary of State who had been suckled on the same diplomatic dogma.

William R. Castle, Jr., sprang from a family of Hawaiian missionaries which had amassed great wealth from cheap Japanese labor. He, himself, had served as American ambassador to Japan, and despite the fact that Admiral Kato publicly refused to attend a dinner at the American Embassy because the ambassador had induced Japan to accept the London Naval Treaty, Castle had built up a healthy admiration for the Japanese. Certainly, he informed his chief, Japanese rule in Manchuria was vastly preferable to that of the mercurial son of that old brigand, Chang Tso-lin.

Unquestionably this view carried weight with Mr. Stimson.

At Mr. Stimson's left hand, however, sat another adviser whose views were diametrically different. Stanley K. Hornbeck, chief of the Far Eastern Division, had taught American political economy in Chinese Government colleges, Chinese political economy at Wisconsin and Harvard, and in one way or another had devoted almost a lifetime to the study of China.

And Dr. Hornbeck knew what Stimson and Castle only vaguely knew, that for Japan the situation in Manchuria had become one where it had to fish or cut bait.

Past Japanese policy in Manchuria had been one of subsidizing a Chinese leader who could maintain order and would bow with reasonable regularity to the ·wishes of Japan. That leader for years had been the famous Chang Tso-lin, a village brigand, who had amassed both army and fortune and become the most powerful individual in China. As long as old Chang stuck to his knitting in Manchuria, the Japanese sent him a regular monthly installment for his army and all went well. But when Chang got ambitions to become dictator of China, took his number-six wife to Tientsin and began to mix unruliness toward the Japanese with frequent military expeditions to the capital, he found himself one day in the pretty predicament of being bombed just as his private railroad car passed through a Japanese-guarded underpass.

That was the end of Chang Tso-lin. The Japanese, who wanted law, order, and obedience in Manchuria, turned to his son as their next figurehead.

But Chang Hsueh-liang proved even more difficult than his father. Young Chang had acquired Western ideas. He had studied English. He could play a fair hand of bridge at the Mukden Club. He had not learned how to hold more than three Martinis, and he was addicted to his father's keen appreciation of concubines. But what was all-important from the Japanese viewpoint, Young Chang was contaminated with that new and wholly unreasonable Chinese attribute—patriotism. He had been contaminated by the students who dominated the capital in Nanking, and they moved him to coöperate in forming a unified government for all China.

This—and other things—made young Chang even less amenable to Japanese reason than his fierce and aged father. The other things, however, were not unimportant. They included, first, the fact that Chinese capitalists were becoming so strong in Manchuria that they threatened Japan's economic grip; and, second, the fact that the Chinese were building a system of rail lines which in many cases paralleled and competed directly with the Japanese-owned South Manchurian.

Finally and most unsusceptible of settlement, was the growing conflict between Korean settlers and the Chinese, on whose land they settled. In one instance just before the invasion of Manchuria, an attempt by Korean farmers to divert irrigated water from Chinese farms near the village of Wanpaoshan led to such serious rioting and to such subsequent resentment that 127 Chinese were massacred and 393 wounded during demonstrations in Korea.

It was this which touched off the Chinese boycotts against Japan, destined to play such an important part in the subsequent bombardment of Shanghai.

Simultaneously and just before the storm broke, Captain Shintaro Nakamura, a Japanese General Staff officer disguised as an agricultural expert in Inner Mongolia, was shot by Chinese troops.

The incident caused terrific reverberations in Tokyo. In fact, it was the very excuse which leaders of the Japanese military were seeking. Several of the younger leaders, especially Colonel Doihara and Colonel Yoshihara, claimed that the army must act immediately. And in a session with General Honjo, commander of the Manchurian forces, they demanded that troops advance or else the officers commit hara-kari.

So openly was the invasion of Manchuria discussed during early September that Ambassador Cameron Forbes went to the Foreign Office to inquire about it. The ambassador was troubled because he intended to sail September 17th for a vacation in the United States. Baron Shidehara, however, was most reassuring. The economic and political situation in Japan, he said, was much too serious to permit any military adventure. The American ambassador could enjoy his vacation in perfect peace.

The demands of the military, however, became insistent. And despite Chinese assurances for redress in the Nakamura incident, the army invaded Manchuria.

Forbes read a radio dispatch to that effect on September 19th, two days at sea.

All of this, of course, was the basis of an intimate day-to-day study on the part of Dr. Hornbeck. Dr. Hornbeck also knew what Secretary Stimson and Mr. Castle did not at all know, that the old regime with which the United States had maintained its American-Japanese Alliance was slipping.

Mr. Stimson, in fact, unwittingly had helped to put it

on the skids. His close friendship with Premier Wakatsuki at the London Naval Conference aroused the suspicion of the Japanese admirals, and their backstage maneuvering to defeat the Naval Treaty constituted the first definite indication that Japan's merchant-prince rule was near its end. Later the frank testimony of American admirals before the Senate Foreign Relations Committee, that their cherished big-gunned cruisers were aimed chiefly at Japan, further strengthened the hands of the Japanese naval-military. Finally there was the bombshell released by Major Herbert Yardley, after the scrupulously honest Mr. Stimson ousted him from the work of decoding the cabled dispatches of foreign embassies in Washington. Faced with the necessity of making a living, Major Yardley published a book, *The American Black Chamber*. In it he told how, under sanction from Charles Evans Hughes, he had intercepted cables between Tokyo and the Japanese delegation to the Washington Arms Conference which showed, among other things, that Baron Shidehara, then Ambassador in Washington, favored acceptance of the American naval proposals. The book sold 40,000 copies in Japan. It left no doubt in the minds of Nipponese jingoes that the United States cherished military designs against Japan and that Baron Shidehara had sold out to the enemy.

What was considered conclusive evidence of this came a few months later when three American naval aviators, straying from their base at Tientsin, flew over Dairen, a Japanese fortified area. Shortly afterward two American civilians flying round the world were arrested for taking photographs of Japanese fortifications in the north island of Hokkaido. The naval aviators were released upon representations of the American Embassy, but the two civilians, Clyde Pangborn and Hugh Herndon, were caught with the undeveloped films in their possession. The State Department was most embarrassed. The Japanese saw red. American spy stories blazed across Tokyo newspapers.

Shidehara and Wakatsuki, who finally released the two fliers, were attacked almost as bitterly as the United States.

This point Dr. Hornbeck continually hammered into the head of his chief, Mr. Stimson. He believed that the Mukden incident was the beginning of a carefully laid Japanese plan to take all of north China. He maintained that the United States must be prepared to act with firmness or else withdraw completely from the Far East.

But Mr. Stimson, just returned from his pilgrimage to Europe, intent upon the problem of inter-government debts, and worried about the success of his coming Disarmament Conference, grasped these things only vaguely. He still had faith in Wakatsuki.

Besides, his Under Secretary of State was continually telling him the opposite.

So there developed a bitter personal feud between two of Mr. Stimson's chief advisers. The feud began even before the Mukden incident, when Castle, then ambassador to Japan, was about to address the annual dinner of the American-Japanese Society. The address was approved by the President and by the late Joseph P. Cotton, then Acting Secretary of State, but for some reason it was not shown to the Chief of the Far Eastern Division. Dr. Hornbeck read it in the press the day following, and immediately sent an emphatic cable to Castle protesting certain passages. Castle expressed extreme irritation. To appease him, Cotton, not a career diplomat, cabled as follows:

"Don't worry. We are all pleased with your speech and happy, except Hornbeck, who is having kittens in the corridors."

Faced with diametrically opposite advice, Mr. Stimson veered toward his suave Under Secretary of State. Much as he had distrusted Castle at one time, he preferred him to the doctrinaire Stanley Hornbeck. The latter was addicted to tediously long reports, never could be convinced that his views were not one hundred per cent right, lectured his chief as if he were a delinquent Harvard freshman, and generally reeked of the classroom. There was no question but that the pedantic personality of Dr. Hornbeck had much to do with Mr. Stimson's delay in adopting a firm hand in Manchuria.

During this period Mr. Stimson continued to pin his faith upon conciliation and Wakatsuki. In fact, he almost held his breath during the early stages of the Manchurian invasion, for fear the League of Nations would act too vigorously toward Japan. A statesman of Mr. Stimson's experience should have known better.

"The Council of the League of Nations," M. Briand, its President, informed him, "has no preconceived method for solving the difficulties which have arisen."

Unfortunately, this was all too true. Even more unfortunate, however, was the fact that Mr. Stimson, while professing constant anxiety for complete coöperation with the League, simultaneously was soft-pedaling any action which might arouse the Japanese military against the Prime Minister of Japan. He even went to the extent of frowning upon a League proposal to send an investigation commission to the scene of action.

Mr. Stimson still regarded the affair as a local incident caused by Chinese brigandry.

Meanwhile the Council of the League of Nations, after exchanging desultory and unfruitful notes with Japan and China, came to the conclusion that it was getting nowhere and decided to await further developments. It adjourned until October 14th.

Japan's first swift military moves around Mukden in mid-September were followed by a lull. General Honjo needed time to bring up reinforcements. Equally important, military leaders in Tokyo needed time to gauge the reaction of the Western World. Much as they scorned the League of Nations, much as they hated the United States, they still retained some respect for world opinion—especially the opinion of the French and British Governments.

So while the Council of the League of Nations "noted this" and "noted that" in Geneva, Tokyo announced that "it had caused the Japanese military forces in Manchuria to refrain from any further acts of hostility."

Ambassador Debuchi rubbed his hands and beamed.

"You see," he said, "it is as I predicted. The Government has taken the matter in hand. Provided the Chinese do not play the fool again, there will be no further military action."

But behind this smoke screen, the Japanese military worked unobtrusively to consolidate its gains. Puppet Chinese Governments, functioning under Japanese advisers, were established in every city. Chinese bank reserves were impounded. Bank deposits were seized. Corporation records, military and individual supplies, telegraph lines, power plants, radio stations, telephone systems, post-offices, all were taken over by troops from Nippon. Not even the occupation of Belgium in 1914 was more efficient than the Japanese occupation of Manchuria in 1931.

South of the Great Wall of China the effect of all this was similar to the repercussion of a series of time bombs. One after the other the cities of China exploded. Anti-Japanese resentment had begun during the Korean riots. Now it flared forth in an ironclad boycott against everything pertaining to Japan. Japanese ships arriving at Shanghai could get no dockhands to help them berth, no coolies to unload cargoes, no Chinese middleman to sell goods, and no customers to buy those goods already landed.

Committees of frenzied Chinese students policed the great trading cities of the China coast, smashing in Japanese shop windows, burning Japanese goods, mobbing such Japanese nationals as dared to venture out, flaunting posters condemning Japanese conquest. One of these committees, invading the Chinese Foreign Office in Nanking, threw inkwells, chairs, clubs, at C. T. Wang, who had failed to secure League action against Japan.

"Traitor," yelled irate students, beating the Foreign Minister black and blue. "You have betrayed China! Death to Wang!"

A student army, 3,000 strong, massed in Nanking, declared they would starve until the Government avenged China's honor. Another army threatened to wreck Shanghai station when refused transportation to Nanking. Finally President Chiang Kai-shek ordered them taken halfway to Nanking and left on a siding while the engine and train crew retreated to Shanghai.

The Council of the League of Nations adjourned September 30th. Its members had been home scarcely a week when the Japanese military, quiescent during the League debate, burst into the open with their most flagrant outrage.

At Chinchow, a town midway between Mukden and the Great Wall of China, young Chang Hsueh-liang had gathered the remnants of his scattered army. Here he had set up a provisional government and prepared to fulfill Japan's demand that China demonstrate an ability to maintain law and order as a prerequisite to the withdrawal of Japanese troops.

No Japanese citizens or property were in Chinchow.

But over that city on October 8th flew eleven Japanese planes. They dropped eighty bombs, chiefly on the university buildings and the hospital, then returned to Mukden. The Chinese did not return the fire.

Mr. Stimson's patience had been tried severely in the past. He had received repeated assurances from Ambassador Debuchi that Japanese troops would not move south of their original positions. He had received similar assurances from the Foreign Office in Tokyo. And he had heard the same identical pledge from Ambassador Yoshizawa in

Geneva. And while he heard these pledges, he also received word that twenty Japanese warships were stationed along the Yangtze River; read the statement of Count Uchida, president of the South Manchurian Railway, "I do not think that Chang Hsueh-liang will return to Mukden"; knew how Senator Borah arched his eyebrows over State Department inaction; and heard the acid inquiry of Senator Johnson: "Where now is the bugle call of Mr. Stimson trumpeted so loudly and prematurely but a short time ago, when Russia and China were making faces at each other? Where is the League of Nations? Where is the sacrosanct Kellogg Pact?"

All this and more Mr. Stimson suffered in silence. But the bombing of Chinchow was too much.

All the next day he closeted himself with Far Eastern advisers. The old feud between Castle and Hornbeck gave way before the demands of an emergency.

"I cannot give out what I have done or what we are doing," Mr. Stimson told the press, "but the State Department is working hard."

Actually he was drafting instructions to Prentiss Gilbert, Consul-General at Geneva, to sit with the Council when it convened a few days hence.

This was an historic step. It was historic from the point of view of the United States, it was perhaps even more historic from the point of view of Europe, and finally it was the most historic event ever to enter the phlegmatic life of Prentiss Gilbert.

Irreconcilable isolationists in the Senate shook their heads in all too visible distress. Fortunately for Mr. Stimson, Johnson and Borah, their most vocal leaders, had been most vociferous in demanding action; now Mr. Stimson had them at his mercy.

Their distress, however, was mild compared with that of the career diplomats. For Prentiss Gilbert was not of their kind. He had been appointed to the key post in Geneva over their heads and despite their protests. And ever since he had been in Geneva there had been covert, at times ruthless, rivalry between him and the career group headed by Hugh R. Wilson, American minister to Switzerland. Despite a background of wealth and ease, Wilson was a slave-driver. He drove himself as hard as he drove others. He was ruthless but efficient. He hailed from the old school that believed the Government of the United States should be dominated by those in whom the wealth of the nation was vested, and he let this color his conduct of foreign relations. Gilbert came from more proletarian background. He had managed the state fair in Rochester, New York, fought Moros in the Philippines, browsed through most of the countries of the Orient, had a sense of humor, a broad streak of liberalism, did not look upon all Russians as anathema, and once shocked his State Department colleagues by admitting that he had lunched with Senator La Follette.

But Gilbert suffered from an inferiority complex which sometimes proved his undoing. It did in Geneva. Not only did he become self-conscious of the fact that he was pushed into the background of such minor League problems as opium, trade barriers, and counterfeiting by the relentless Wilson, but also Gilbert's inferiority complex ran afoul of Sir Eric Drummond. As Secretary-General of the League, Sir Eric at that time was the League. Everything in Geneva revolved around him. A person of extreme social intolerance, either he liked people a lot or not at all. With him, newcomers in Geneva went through a period of trial— sometimes hell. Gilbert resented this. And when, after a prolonged period of waiting, Sir Eric finally invited him to dinner, Gilbert declined.

This finished him as far as the Secretary-General was concerned. After that Sir Eric went round Geneva, saying: "That terrible American! Why do you keep him here? He goes to dinner only with these funny Latin-Americans."

Career men, of course, ate this up, relayed it to Washington, broadcast it throughout Europe. Particularly did they broadcast it when Gilbert—due to Wilson's absence in the United States—took his place at the Council table of the League of Nations.

This handicap, however, was insignificant compared with the obstacles thrown up by some of the League's staunchest supporters. At the signing of the Pact of Paris in the Salle de l'Horloge only three brief years before, the statesmen of Europe—especially France—had hailed it as the bridge by which the United States came back once more to coöperate with the world. And when the London Conference was in the throes of hammering out a Naval Treaty it was France which insisted upon a consultative pact, or some such understanding, with the United States, before it would agree to abandon its naval building program.

Now, however, it was the French press, and its satellites in Poland, which screamed the loudest in support of the Japanese contention that the United States had no place at the Council table. Without the United States France dominated the Council. With the United States, that domination disappeared. Manchuria might prove a dangerous precedent.

Meanwhile Japanese public opinion, whipped up to a boiling-point by the War Office, added its protest.

"The League has exposed its weakness by inviting America, and America has provoked the Japanese people by attending the League," roared General Minami. And at the dictation of the War Office a note was sent to Ambassador Debuchi for delivery to Secretary Stimson. It pointed to the traditional policy of the United States to shun the League as it would the plague, and it made this protest in language not conducive to amity among nations.

Ambassador Debuchi had spent his entire life in diplomacy. It was his only means of livelihood. He knew that one of the duties of a diplomat was to obey orders, and also he knew that he needed his job. Nevertheless, he did not deliver this note to Secretary Stimson. To do so, he cabled his Government, would have caused disastrous repercussions in the United States. Secretary Stimson, he said, was sincerely endeavoring to play the part of the neutral. He advised that the note be withdrawn.

Several days passed. Finally Ambassador Debuchi appeared at the State Department, again his face beaming. Emerging from a conference with Mr. Stimson, he announced the withdrawal of Japanese objection to Prentiss Gilbert's presence at the Council table.

This objection, of course, already had been circumvented by the skill of Aristide Briand, who ruled that the entrance of the United States was a mere matter of procedure, not of principle, and therefore did not require a unanimous vote. Briand did not know it at the time, but this was to be his last great battle for peace. What he did know, however, was that the peace machinery of the world was on trial. For years he had labored to perfect and strengthen the League of Nations. For years he had endeavored to soften the bitterness between Germany and France. More recently he had conceived a United States of Europe and helped to negotiate a Pact to outlaw war. It had been tedious work. There had been many failures. But on each occasion that the League had coped with a dispute, it had lacked the coöperation of the United States, and this had been given as the reason for indifferent success. And on each occasion that the United States had endeavored to settle a dispute in the Chaco or between Russia and China it had lacked the coöperation of the League, which in turn was given as the reason for its indifferent success.

Now for the first time in history these two powerful factors for peace—the United States and the League of Nations—were in harmony. M. Briand knew, and Mr. Stimson knew, that if they failed now there could be no hope for disarmament, no hope for security, no hope for peace in Europe.

Yet that harmony even now did not reach complete perfection. There were one or two rifts in the lute. There was first of all French resentment against the intrusion of the United States, expressed behind Briand's back. Then there was Mr. Stimson's own timidity about arousing the ire of the Japanese military. For even at that late date he still cherished a faint hope that the forces for peace within the Japanese Cabinet might triumph over the forces for war; and for the time being at least he preferred that the League lead the attack.

This fact the Japanese twisted skillfully to their advantage. Mr. Stimson's notes were sent in secret. They were emphatic and to the point, but no one outside a limited circle of diplomats realized it. And despite the repeated urging of Stanley Hornbeck, and despite frequent criticism from the press, he declined to make them public. The Japanese made the most of this. Both in the Orient and Europe they spread the impression that the United States actually favored the occupation of Manchuria. Chinese students, believing this propaganda, started demonstrations against the United States. Geneva diplomats, hearing these reports, became discouraged. The impression grew that Washington had patched up an agreement with Tokyo, was letting the League fritter away valuable time in Geneva. It was at this point that Lord Reading, knowing Mr. Stimson's fondness for "telephone diplomacy," called up the Secretary of State from London. What actually was said during that conversation is not known. Transmission may have been bad; his Lordship is slightly deaf or he may have deliberately misunderstood. At any rate, the impression which the British Foreign Minister conveyed to his colleagues in Geneva was that Stimson had left the League sitting high and dry. He was ready, it was reported, to let China and Japan settle their dispute without even the evacuation of Japanese troops.

Next day it looked as if all the carefully nurtured cooperation between the United States and the League of Nations had burst like a toy balloon. Smaller nations were indignant. Manchuria to them was a precedent of flagrant aggression by a powerful nation against a helpless neighbor, a precedent they could not condone, a precedent which meant that the prestige, the power, almost the life of the League was at stake.

France and Great Britain, on the other hand, were indifferent; secretly, in fact, delighted. Behind the lone idealism of Aristide Briand and Viscount Cecil, the Foreign Offices of both nations had sabotaged in favor of Japan. Now the United States had given them an excuse.

"The Council," they said, "was not willing to be more pro-Chinese than the United States."

Working on this thesis, pro-Japanese members of the Council cut the ground from under M. Briand and forced adoption of a resolution completely straddling the issue. But the Japanese, cocksure of their position, made the fatal error of not accepting it at once. Ambassador Yoshizawa telegraphed to Tokyo for instructions.

While the Council waited for a reply, reports of Lord Reading's telephone call reached the astounded ears of Prentiss Gilbert. Mr. Gilbert was not so surprised that his chief in Washington had changed his mind—he had been in diplomacy too long for that—but he could not understand why he had not been told about it. So he resorted to telephone diplomacy himself. The result was a strong statement to M. Briand that the United States hoped for a firm policy on the part of the League and would continue to support it as far as possible.

Briand was delighted. He had become almost a pathetic figure. Old, tired, dozing occasionally at the Council table, he had been pushed by forces he could not control into a position which was about to wreck all his cherished hopes for world peace.

Repeatedly he had been made ridiculous by the Japanese. Ambassador Yoshizawa had taken particular delight one night in routing him out of bed at 1 A.M. to deliver his first ultimatum that the United States could not participate in Council meetings. Again, Yoshizawa stalled for days while the Council endeavored to get an explanation of the Japanese bombing of Chinchow. His perennial reply was, "I am awaiting instructions from my Government."

On one occasion he kept the Council waiting a full hour before he appeared. Aristide Briand jerked nervously at his watch. Prentiss Gilbert gazed raptly at the ceiling. Newspaper men waited hopefully, ready to startle the world with the news flash that Japan had withdrawn from the Council. Not a member of the Japanese delegation was in the room. It was an act of Oriental effrontery calculated to show Japan's disdain for the Western World.

Finally appeared little Mr. Yoshizawa. He was puffing at his stogie quite unconcernedly and he bowed with more than his usual politeness to Lord Reading in the seat beside him. The British delegate did not even turn his head.

No wonder, therefore, that M. Briand almost embraced Prentiss Gilbert when the latter assured him of complete and continued American support. No wonder, also, that M. Briand proceeded to push through the Council the most categorical warning ever sent to a major power in the entire history of the League of Nations.

Technically the resolution did not pass; for a unanimous vote was necessary and Ambassador Yoshizawa dissented. Nevertheless, Japan was notified that it must withdraw its troops from Chinese territory, that this withdrawal must be overseen by neutral observers, and that the withdrawal must be completed by November 16th.

Whereupon the Council looked toward the United States to fulfill its pledge of unqualified support and adjourned until the date upon which its ultimatum was to be carried out.

But Mr. Stimson did not carry out his pledge. He sent a note to Japan, and it was identical with that of the League —except in one important particular. He carefully omitted the date on which Japan was to evacuate.

This was the nubbin of the League note. Mr. Stimson's omission was to have dire consequences.

Far north of the fighting in South Manchuria, where the Chinese Eastern Railway cuts through dreary wastes of millet, soya beans and brown prairie, is a little mud-walled, thatch-roofed town named Tsitsihar. Trains on the Chinese Eastern stop regularly at Tsitsihar while the engine takes water, and the Chinese guard, suddenly galvanized into action, paces up and down the platform as in a scene from "The Chocolate Soldier." But aside from the guard, a few fur-clad natives who watch the train, a branch rail line running south, and a pack of half-starved dogs in the street, there is nothing about Tsitsihar to make a Transcontinental passenger look up from his book.

It is probable, therefore, that only a few hundred people outside of China ever had heard of this placid Manchurian village until the autumn of 1931, when its name suddenly became first-page news throughout Europe and the United States.

For at the very moment Ambassador Yoshizawa was sparring for time in Geneva, Japanese troops were sparring for position against the army of General Ma Chan-shan, with the broad steppes of North Manchuria as their battlefield and the village of Tsitsihar as their objective.

It was the unobtrusive rail line running south which made Tsitsihar important. Crossing the Russian-controlled Chinese Eastern at right angles, it traversed the rich soya bean area of North Manchuria, connected with other Chinese lines, and after a circuitous route through wealthy

South Manchuria finally reached the Gulf of Liaotung and the sea. Tapping the Chinese Eastern and running parallel to the South Manchurian, it served as an important competitor to Japanese investments, one which the military leaders in Tokyo could not permit to remain in hostile hands.

On the upper part of this vital rail line, General Ma suddenly blew up the Nonni River bridge. Immediately this half-frozen marshland became the focal point of the Far East. On one side of the bridge was a Japanese army of 2,000 men, perfectly equipped, efficiently trained, commanded by officers raised on the doctrine that all Asia must bow to the Rising Sun. On the other side of the bridge was the army of General Ma, ten times as strong, indifferently equipped, poorly trained, but fighting to defend Chinese soil. To the outside world the Nonni bridge became a test, not only of Japanese military efficiency, but of Chinese patriotism.

Even more important, however, it became a test of the rôle Russia was to play in the Far Eastern conflict. Tsitsihar was in the zone of Russian influence. Her guards patrolled the Chinese Eastern. Would they try to stem the advance of the Japanese army? Would Japan push her conquest up to the Siberian border? As if in answer to that question, long trainloads of Red troops began steaming along the Trans-Siberian.

To the Western World the situation looked precarious.

To bland Ambassador Debuchi, however, it did not. Appearing at the office of the Secretary of State he announced:

"Japan is acting from entirely altruistic motives in this case. The bridge over the Nonni River has been destroyed by brigands. The peaceful farmers of China have just finished harvesting their crop of soya beans. And in order to prevent any hardship to the Chinese farmers, the Japanese commander has sent engineers to repair the bridge. Of course, it was also necessary to send troops to protect the engineers, but I have the assurance of my Government that as soon as the bridge is repaired every Japanese soldier will be withdrawn."

It had become axiomatic of Japanese policy by this time that, so long as the Western World was watching, Japanese militarism trod softly in Manchuria. But the minute the world was absorbed with other things, Japanese militarism went berserk.

As long, therefore, as the October meeting of the Council parried questions with Ambassador Yoshizawa, Japan stood by Debuchi's pledge. Japanese troops at the Nonni River bridge contented themselves with pot-shots at the enemy. But, almost the moment the Council adjourned, Japanese troops served an ultimatum of advance. And although General Ma offered to comply with all Japanese terms, the advance continued. It continued, moreover, until the fur-coated, ear-muffed men of General Honjo methodically penetrated to the Chinese Eastern Railway.

It was on November 17th that Japanese troops reached the outskirts of Tsitsihar. On that day and the day previous two important things happened.

First, the dead line set by the League of Nations for the withdrawal of Japanese troops expired. Simultaneously the Council of the League met in Paris to consider how to deal with Japan's rebuff.

Second, Soviet Russia, celebrating the fourteenth anniversary of the Revolution, watched 1,000,000 of its citizens march seventy-five abreast, like a great human river, past the Kremlin, past the red-granite tomb of Lenin, past the stern visage of Josef Stalin, in a grim testimonial of Russia's ability to defend itself.

The world watched a little breathlessly next day when Japanese troops reached Tsitsihar. But General Honjo's men carefully refrained from interference with Russia's railroad. China, at that moment, was enough for Japan to handle.

Ambassador Debuchi came down to the State Department to describe this northward trek as "self-defense." The Council convening in Paris did not know what to call it. In the end it chose to ignore it. Most of its members had been far too absorbed in the British elections, an impending political crisis in France, the audience of Mahatma Gandhi with King George, and the elopement of Prince Nicholas of Rumania, to pay more than passing attention to confused reports regarding events in the Far East. Even Mr. Stimson, busy with the visit of Dino Grandi, gave only routine attention to what had become the chief worry on his international horizon. Mr. Stimson by this time had passed through two distinct phases of policy in regard to the Far East, and was about to enter a third. He had, first of all, acted as a brake upon the League, fearful that too vigorous action by it would unseat his friends Wakatsuki and Shidehara. Later, he had come forward to a position just short of complete support for the League. Now at last he was prepared to go just as far as the League.

The only difficulty was that the League, by this time, was not prepared to go very far. The more the members of the Council looked at the Manchurian dispute, the more inclined they were to think that it was something which could only burn their fingers. And it was so far away, they argued, that it did not concern them, anyway. This was true especially of France and Great Britain, whose rapidly cooling enthusiasm over the prospect of curbing Japanese militarism was carefully concealed behind the dunce-cap diplomacy of the new American observer at the Council.

That observer was none other than the ex-Vice-President of the United States, at that time ambassador to Great Britain, Charles G. Dawes.

For Charlie Dawes this was the fag end of a none too salubrious diplomatic career. For him diplomacy had not been what it was cracked up to be, and Charlie was fed up. He was fed up with the London weather, with the perpetual parade of umbrellas along Piccadilly, with the thick ankles of British beauties, with the Court levees at Buckingham Palace, especially with the ladies-in-waiting who tittered audibly at the one ambassador who scorned silk stockings and breeches. Charlie even was fed up with making a spectacle of his lunches at Ye Cheshire Cheese, with lighting his pipe at formal dinners before the cigarettes were passed, and with prompting Leon Errol to spill cold lobster in the lap of the Duke of Norfolk. Charlie had spent his entire life just behind the public footlights. Now he had been shoved over toward the wings. Diplomacy began to pall.

The invitation to act as American observer at the Council, therefore, came as a welcome fillip to a waning diplomatic career.

Charlie had been picked for the job chiefly because of the protest of career diplomats against the continued functioning of Prentiss Gilbert. Like the career men, Charlie felt that Gilbert had bungled. And so strongly did he feel, that he even refused to let Gilbert come from Geneva to Paris, where the Council now convened, in order to give him the history of the case.

"I already know all about it," Dawes exploded.

Since Gilbert had worn out the headlines by sitting at the Council table, Dawes' instincts for good showmanship told him to do just the opposite. And since his chief in the White House had become a bit jittery over the new alliance with Geneva, he decided to boycott the Council, remain a shadowy figure in the background. For the first few days it worked. Dawes, and the vacant chair which stood awaiting him at the Council table, became the talk of Paris.

Long experience had taught Charlie how to gauge public psychology. He had learned first as a young lawyer competing with William Jennings Bryan in Nebraska. He had

learned also as a sporting young National Guardsman with
Frank O. Lowden in Illinois. He brought it to a high
climax as Director of the Budget when he shook his fist
under the furry chin of Charles Evans Hughes and proclaimed that the buying of brooms must be coördinated.
And now he tried it out on the most delicate diplomatic
crisis Europe had experienced since the World War.

What the League of Nations needed, in the opinion of
the American observer, was more punch. And he groomed
himself to be the savior who at the appropriate time would
deliver that punch. Until then he busied himself with
secret conversations in his suite at the Ritz. He called in
his old friend and London colleague, Tsuneo Matsudaira,
with whom he was sure he could talk business. Another
caller was Dr. Alfred Sze, the Chinese Minister.

"Sit down, Dr. Sze," bellowed Dawes. "I know absolutely
nothing about this business, or about diplomacy, either. So
sit down and tell me all about it."

"Really?" replied Sze. "When a man tells me he knows
nothing about a card game, then I am always on the alert."

Though he did not realize it himself, Dawes told Dr.
Sze the truth, as Sir John Simon discovered when he tried
to give the American observer a brief background of what
had happened since the League took over the Manchurian
dispute. Explaining a complicated diplomatic problem to
Dawes was like teaching discipline to a pup. Nothing fazed
him except the opinion of his own importance.

"I'll have a dead secretary if anything leaks out," he
shrilled at newspaper men.

"But suppose, Mr. Ambassador, that news of what you
are doing leaks out from other diplomats with whom you
talk?"

"They are not telling anything about what I have been
doing," he bellowed back, "because nobody knows that
except myself."

Which, unfortunately, was all too true. No one, not even

the State Department, knew what Dawes was doing. And there is grave doubt whether he did, himself.

Gradually League delegates left him in his hotel suite in a state of splendid isolation, forcing Dawes to fall back on the servants of the Ritz as an audience for his theatricals. These he performed at breakfast by singling out a particular waiter and staring at him with rapt attention. Finally, he would call the waiter to his table.

"Garçon," he would rasp, "didn't I use to see you here during the war?"

The waiter would reply in the affirmative.

"I thought so. Here," and he would hand the man a ten-franc note.

This ceremony was repeated every morning until all the waiters in the dining-room, much to their delight and secret amusement, had benefited by the Ambassador's largess.

Meanwhile Dawes' absence from the Council-room, coupled with the secret diplomacy of Henry L. Stimson and the deliberate propaganda of the French, Japanese, and British, gave credence to the old rumor that the United States had walked out on the League and made a separate deal with Japan. Ambassador Dawes, it was whispered, was strongly pro-Japanese. So also was reputed to be his chief adviser, Eugene Dooman, who had served for many years in Tokyo before becoming secretary of the American Embassy in London. Actually this was by no means the case. But the Quai d'Orsay, now more active than ever in sabotaging the idealism of Aristide Briand, gave subtle encouragement to the rumors. The French press, its ear always attuned to the voice of official wisdom, gave them wider circulation. British imperialists, their position reinforced by the overwhelming electoral victory of two weeks previous, chimed in the chorus. Every nation, it was discreetly pointed out, must consider the protection of the life and property of its citizens abroad. The Chinese, it must be remembered, are disorderly, impossible people.

"If the United States condemns Japan too strongly," suggested the conservative *Journal des Débats,* "it realizes that it may interfere with its own actions in Central America, where it has intervened with no more scruples than have the Japanese in Manchuria."

The dismemberment of China, once the definite objective of the Powers, was discussed again in many chanceries. The French long had had their eyes on Yunnan, southernmost of the eighteen provinces and just across the border from French Indo-China. The British had quietly slipped Kashmir and Tibet from the Chinese map. The Germans talked about the absolute necessity of colonial possessions, while the Italians were already at work expanding their domain across the Mediterranean.

Delegates of the smaller nations were dismayed. With the simple transfer of proceedings from Geneva to Paris, the sentiment of the Council had changed over-night. Delegates once boiling with condemnation of Japan, who once had discussed the withdrawal of diplomatic representatives from Tokyo, who even sounded out the United States regarding sanctions, now sat vacillating and ineffectual. Even Aristide Briand, champion of peace, suggested to China that she withdraw her troops from Chinchow in order to avoid conflict. The British went so far as to give a secret promise to the Japanese that the British fleet never would be used to enforce sanctions.

The Japanese smiled and waited. All that their military leaders had predicted regarding League of Nations bungling had come true. At one time secrecy so surpassed itself that the League Secretariat officially announced the conclusion of a truce between China and Japan—an announcement later denied with equal vigor by both Dr. Sze and Ambassador Yoshizawa.

At the height of the Council's confusion came a blast from the author of the Pact of Paris. Sitting at his home in St. Paul, Frank B. Kellogg had watched with increasing nervousness the futile gesturing of European diplomats and the secret diplomacy of Henry L. Stimson. Under Marquis of Queensbury rules for diplomacy, an ex-Secretary of State does not criticize his successor. But to Kellogg peace was more important than precedent; finally he could stand it no longer.

"The time for secret diplomacy in grave instances of this kind is past!" he announced to the world. "Private conversations are apt to be misunderstood and misinterpreted. War is no longer the private affair of belligerent nations!"

There was a day when Mr. Kellogg had used open diplomacy to roll up such irresistible public opinion as to force an outlawry of war treaty upon an apathetic world. There was a day also when he had used the forces of public opinion to check a war between Bolivia and Paraguay. There was a day, furthermore, when Mr. Stimson himself had used open diplomacy to bring China and Soviet Russia to their senses. And probably there was a time when the same force, backed by the unanimous opinion of the world, might have repeated this achievement in Manchuria.

But now it was too late.

Mr. Stimson, however, did not then realize that it was too late. Later he tried desperately to secure a unanimous mobilization of world opinion. But now, still pinning his hopes upon the League of Nations and on Wakatsuki, he resorted to this matter-of-fact announcement:

"I want to correct certain erroneous statements which have appeared lately in the press. It is not true that this Government has changed in any way the attitude on the Manchurian situation which it has held from the first. . . ."

Simultaneously he ordered Dawes to inform Briand that the Council had the unalterable support of the United States. There was a distinct feeling in Washington that Charlie Dawes had bungled.

Traffic along the Peiping-Mukden Railway during November, 1932, was as uncertain as life along the wind-swept Manchurian plain. On those rare occasions when trains managed to creep up from Pieping they were forced to stop at Chinchow, where young Chang Hsueh-liang had established his concubines and still was trying to rally the remnants of his once prosperous Mukden Government. Beyond Chinchow the rail line led through a snow-swept no-man's-land into which, it was rumored in late November, Japanese troops had begun to advance.

This was in direct contradiction to the pledges given at Geneva; and Lieutenant Harry Aldrich, American military observer in Chinchow, was ordered to proceed north in a wild-cat locomotive for investigation.

It was not a pleasure trip. The thermometer hovered around forty degrees below zero. The night was inky black. The chances of hitting a bombed bridge were excellent. There was no signal system. But seated in the cab behind a Chinese engineer, Lieutenant Aldrich plowed into the night.

Suddenly his locomotive ground to a sudden stop. It had almost run down the approaching vanguard of the Japanese army.

Lieutenant Aldrich jumped out of the cab. He knew that his one chance for life lay in acting as if he owned the railway.

"What you mean get in my way," he shouted. "You makee no noise, makee no lights, nearly wreck my engine. Now! Get out my way! Beat it! Bou-jow!"

The bluff worked. Instead of shooting him in his tracks they sent this strange creature back to their superior officers in Mukden.

Henry L. Stimson read of the Japanese advance one morning at breakfast. At Geneva the Japanese had just agreed to discuss the idea of a commission of inquiry. In Washington, Ambassador Debuchi had just given assurances that there would be no more Japanese aggression.

And in Tokyo, Baron Shidehara had repeated similar solemn promises to Ambassador Forbes. In fact, Ambassador Forbes, realizing that the Foreign Office had no control whatsoever over the military, had gone one step farther and received assurances from both the Minister of War and his Chief of Staff that there was to be no advance on Chinchow.

Now American army observers cabled the opposite.

Probably for the first time in the entire length and breadth of the Manchurian dispute all of the Puritan indignation latent in Mr. Stimson's soul came boiling to the surface. Japanese militarism in all its stark madness lay revealed before him. He realized that he had been made ridiculous.

Going to the State Department, he cabled this communication to Ambassador Forbes for delivery to Baron Shidehara:

"Your Excellency will remember that on November 24th, you assured me that, with the concurrence of the Minister of War and the Chief of Staff, there would be no movement of Japanese troops in the direction of Chinchow and informed me that orders to that effect had been given to Japanese troops. In reliance upon this assurance, I have urged conciliatory steps upon the Chinese Government and an acceptance of the proposal of the League of Nations, which proposal was in part based upon a proposition of the Japanese Government. Insomuch as, according to Mr. Yoshizawa's statement to M. Briand, there are only some twenty thousand Chinese troops in the Chinchow area and north of the Great Wall, and insomuch as Chinchow is substantially 120 miles by rail from the South Manchurian Railway at Mukden, I am quite unable to see how there can be any serious danger to that railway or any serious danger of a clash between the Chinese and the Japanese troops, unless the latter troops should fail to observe the orders which your Excellency assured me had been given."

Indignant as was Henry L. Stimson, Cameron Forbes was more so. He, too, came from Puritan lineage as distinguished, if not quite as old, as that of his chief in the State Department. And although it was true that Mr. Forbes was so unfamiliar with that lineage as once to ask who had written a well-known quotation from his grandfather, Ralph Waldo Emerson, and although it was a fact that as Governor-General of the Philippines Forbes had distinguished himself chiefly as the founder of Philippine polo, nevertheless he had moments when his sense of justice rose to heights unsurpassed even by his New England ancestors.

The delivery of Mr. Stimson's note to Baron Shidehara was such a moment.

Ambassador Forbes delivered the note personally. And with it he added some remarks of his own. Lexicographers might have called them expletives. In effect, he said that the Japanese had lied.

Ambassador Forbes had delivered several other protests to Baron Shidehara during the Manchurian turmoil, and most of them had been accompanied by simultaneous protests by the ambassadors of France, Great Britain, Italy and Germany. What Ambassador Forbes did not then realize, however, was that no sooner had his colleagues returned to their respective embassies than they went back to the Foreign Office to give the wink to their earlier representations.

In deference to the United States, they explained to Baron Shidehara, they had been forced to go through the motions of a formal protest. However, His Imperial Majesty could be assured that their respective governments fully appreciated the rectitude of Japanese policy in Manchuria.

Cameron Forbes became *persona non grata* after that. Reports to this effect were denied by Secretary Stimson at the time, but they were true. Tokyo indicated that relations with the United States would be more harmonious if

the ambassador returned to Washington, and after a dignified lapse of time he did. He remained long enough, however, to receive another protest against Japanese attacks on
Chinchow. This time the city was captured. This time,
also, his instructions were to call at the Foreign Office in
company with the British ambassador. An agreement for a
joint protest presumably had been worked out between
Washington and London.

Forbes called Sir Francis Lindley on the telephone,
asked when it would be convenient to make the call.

"I haven't received my instructions as yet," replied Sir
Francis. "But don't wait on me, my dear fellow, don't wait
on me."

Sir Francis never did receive instructions. And Cameron
Forbes never called at the Foreign Office. He was beginning to understand Old World diplomacy.

Henry L. Stimson at that time had as his military aide
and closest adviser a young cavalry officer named Eugene
Regnier. Captain Regnier was a likable youngster. But
aside from society and horses, with both of which he was
equally at home, his horizon was distinctly limited. This
did not prevent him, however, from preparing profound
memoranda on Manchuria and poking his nose into every
situation the Far East developed.

And one situation regarding which Captain Regnier
considered himself particularly expert was the press. Secretary Stimson's press relations, he concluded, were anything
but salubrious, and he, Regnier, determined to remedy
them. To this end he conceived the idea of holding newspaper salons in the spacious living-room of the Stimson
mansion, to which were invited only those correspondents
friendly to Mr. Stimson.

At one of these conferences, Mr. Stimson explained in
meticulous detail the domestic situation in Japan, the irresponsible advance against Chinchow, the fact that the Gov-

ernment was completely dominated by a little band of military officers.

"The Japanese military," he concluded, "is running amuck."

This statement was made for the guidance of the hand-picked group of newspaper men considered friendly to Mr. Stimson, and was not to be attributed to him.

Imagine Mr. Stimson's surprise, therefore, when in flaming headlines, the Tokyo press quoted him as saying that the "Japanese military party simply had run amuck."

This surprise, however, was as nothing compared with his chagrin and humiliation at the castigation meted out to him by Toshio Shiratori, spokesman of the Japanese Foreign Office.

"If a man in Mr. Stimson's official position loses his head at such a critical moment in the affairs of Japan," barked Mr. Shiratori, "very grave results may develop. Mr. Stimson said that the Japanese army in Manchuria has run amuck. This is considered a very bald statement indeed and it is to be wondered if he considered the definition of the word before using it. . . . Mr. Stimson says Japan expressed regret and gave assurances that such a thing would not happen again each time there was a fresh military advance in Manchuria. Japan never expressed regret to anyone for her action in Manchuria."

Nations have been known to go to war for less than this, and the capitals of Europe waited a trifle breathlessly. Mr. Stimson's feelings lurked just beneath a notoriously thin skin. There had been occasions when relatively gentle pin-pricks had caused him to see red. Fulminating in press conference was one of his pet pastimes. This time, however, the situation was too serious. Mr. Stimson swallowed his pride and turned the other cheek.

What had happened, he discovered, was that Byron Price, of the Associated Press, had reported the official reaction that the Japanese military was "running amuck" without attribution to Mr. Stimson. But the Rengo News Agency, buying the Associated Press service, had lifted this sentence and neatly embroidered it with quotes.

The incident was important in that it proved conclusively the truth of Mr. Stimson's words. The Japanese military had run amuck. It had turned its back on a generation of Japanese development noted for the progress of parliamentary reforms, and had established a military rule more powerful than the Government. It had run amuck in Manchuria. It had run amuck along the China coast. Even in the United States, the arrest of Japanese spies in San Pedro harbor, at Coronado and adjacent to Boulder Dam, indicated that Nippon's military clique had run amuck.

In Japan itself, Fascist organizations, secretly encouraged by the military, instituted a reign of terrorism. One by one they mowed down the men who stood in their path, the men who had guided Japan toward liberalism—until Premier Hamaguchi, Baron Takuma Dan, and Premier Inukai all fell before the assassins' bullets.

The murderers of the latter brazenly boasted of their achievement. Any man who had urged Japan's ratification of the London Naval Conference, they proclaimed, deserved the death of a traitor.

Admiral Kato issued a statement congratulating the Japanese people on rearing young men so devoutly imbued with patriotism. When brought to trial, they were virtually acquitted.

With such as these did Henry L. Stimson struggle to preserve the freedom and integrity of China.

Early in the Council's deliberations, some of Japan's friends in the Quai d'Orsay had given Yoshizawa a discreet tip that the best way out of the deadlock was to appoint a Commission to visit Manchuria and make an investigation. This, they pointed out, was a good face-saving device for both sides. It meant nothing to Japan, since the Commis-

sion would consume months in fact-finding, and then—
they predicted—bring in a noncommittal report. But, at
the same time, it meant an escape for the League of Nations, which faced the alternative either of doing something
or else shutting shop altogether.

The Japanese at first shied away from this proposal.
Cocksure and over-confident, they resented any suggestion
—even from a traditional ally—which detracted from their
omnipotence in Manchuria.

Also they seemed to take a diabolic pleasure in slowly
breaking down the peace machinery of the world. This
was especially true of Ambassador Yoshizawa. During the
march on Chinchow all of the Council called upon him for
explanations, demanded assurances that General Honjo's
troops advance no farther. Yoshizawa smiled benignly,
puffed his stogie, replied always that he awaited instructions from Tokyo.

After several days of waiting, a special meeting finally
was called at Yoshizawa's request. Rising with the air of
one about to make an important announcement, he asked
for permission to address the Council in Japanese. French
and English, Yoshizawa spoke fluently; but the Council,
sensing the importance of the occasion, gladly assented.

Yoshizawa spoke. He spoke at length and with what appeared great feeling. Council members leaned forward
with expectation. Finally he paused, waited for the trans-
lation.

"Mr. Yoshizawa," announced the interpreter, briefly,
"desires to thank the Council for permitting him to use his
native language."

Council members leaned back again.

Again the Japanese delegate took the floor. Again he
barked in staccato monosyllables. Again his speech continued for at least ten minutes. Again members of the
Council leaned forward, sure that at last they were to get
the long-expected message from Tokyo.

"Mr. Yoshizawa," announced the interpreter, "says that he regrets that he has received no instructions from his Government."

It was a deliberate and carefully studied affront to the League, and M. Briand was so upset that he could not eat what for him was the most relished meal of the day—luncheon.

Finally, as the Council sessions dragged on and as Tokyo received repeated assurances of secret French and British support, the Japanese themselves took the initiative in proposing a Commission of Inquiry—provided that the inquiry include the whole of China, and provided also that Japan be under no definite obligation to remove its troops.

A loosely worded resolution along these lines finally was drafted on November 25th, but suited nobody. The Chinese raised a hue and cry against the fact that it did not end Japanese military occupation; Japan denounced the resolution as placing too much emphasis on the importance of troop withdrawal; while the smaller nations complained that the League, by thus straddling the issue, was signing its own death warrant.

As a matter of fact it was.

Mr. Stimson knew this, Sir John Simon knew it, and most tragic of all Aristide Briand knew it.

Briand was dying. He was dying before men's eyes. He was dying at the Conference table which he had dominated during most of his latter years. He was dying, yet he refused to give up. He refused to surrender his dream of a new and warless Europe.

Those were days when Briand seldom returned to his farm at Cocherel. Once he had roamed among its willow trees every week-end, fished in the placid Eure, sat before a huge fire in his three-room cottage, and made plans for the new peace between France and Germany.

But now he remained in the Quai d'Orsay every night. His office looked out on an old garden sheltered by high

trees in which roosted flocks of birds. And sometimes, when
he could not sleep and work dragged endlessly, Briand
stood in his great open window looking out upon the trees
and the moon and the shadows they cast upon the garden,
and remembered the days of Verdun when he was Premier of France. Out among the poplars he saw again that
line of men from the fields, the factories, the sea, going
forward, and the line of women, wounded men, exhausted
troops, going back. A panorama of his life lay before him
on those nights—from his youth in Brittany to the days
when he argued with Clemenceau that no peace could live
in Europe unless built upon equity and understanding.
Most of his years since then had been given to rebuilding
that equity and understanding between France and Germany.

And he had failed.

Those were long and sleepless nights at the Quai
d'Orsay.

"How heavy," wrote Briand to his old friend, Sir Austen
Chamberlain, "a simple dove, bearing an olive branch,
can weigh upon a man's wrist."

The resolution providing for an investigation of Manchuria was adopted December 10th with more than the
usual display of oratory. Every nation, fully cognizant that
the peace machinery of the world was crumbling, made
pronouncements which sometime in the future might suit
their own special needs.

The delegate of Peru rose to point out that the weaker
states looked to the League of Nations to protect them
against the coercion of the strong. Therefore, the Council's
resolution regarding Manchuria must not be interpreted
as meaning that one state can invade another to protect
the life and property of its nationals.

Panama and Guatemala evinced enthusiastic support.
Nor should this resolution, the Peruvian continued, be

interpreted as validating the right of one state to occupy another in order to compel the execution of treaties.

The delegate of Haiti frantically applauded.

Every other nation, with the exception of the United States, proclaimed publicly that the Manchurian case was exceptional, that Japan's lease of the South Manchurian Railway, the presence of her troops in the railway zone, created conditions which could not be dealt with by ordinary League procedure. The mild rebuff now meted out to Japan, therefore, did not prejudice future action by the League in other parts of the world.

The closing ceremony was held in the Salle de l'Horloge.

The lingering rays of the December sun penetrated its deep-curtained windows and danced among the great crystal candelabra much as it had on that historic day just three years before, when the statesmen of the world had placed their signatures on a solemn treaty outlawing war for all time to come. Many of the same statesmen were there. Aristide Briand again presided, and his great drooping mustache seemed to droop even lower as the League of Nations washed its hands of further direct action in Manchuria.

The Kellogg Pact was dead.

2. Roosevelt Abandons Disarmament

At few times in history has the advent of a new President of the United States been awaited with such world hope as was the inauguration of Franklin D. Roosevelt.

For one year the Powers had been deadlocked. On no major policy had they made progress. For months they had struggled with the depressing burden of armament. For months they had side-stepped taking a stand in Manchuria. And whenever they attempted to move on any one of these problems, they ran head-on into the fact that the most powerful country in the world had at its helm a President who at no time was sure of carrying his people with him. When, for instance, Europe considered setting a definite date for the Economic Conference, it always came back to the fact that no dicussion of the world's economic ills could escape consideration of the tremendous burden of war debt owed the United States, and that Herbert Hoover—even though he favored drastic reduction of those debts—was politically powerless to discuss them. Or when Europe struggled with disarmament, its statesmen reasoned that even before the proposals of the American President could be signed, he would be swept out of office. Even regarding Manchuria, where the Hoover administration had taken a most militant stand against Japanese aggression, Europe expressed doubt whether succeeding administrations would carry on.

So for a period of nine months during and after the presidential campaign the world marked time and waited for the new leader to enter the White House.

Few Presidents-elect have been subjected to such microscopic scrutiny as was Roosevelt during this period. Every chancery in Europe and Asia studied the character of the man who was to mold the foreign policy of the United States. Libraries were combed for his past utterances. Friends were cross-examined regarding his opinions. A volume of *Asia Magazine* in the Library of Congress, containing an article on Japan written by Roosevelt when Assistant Secretary of the Navy, became dog-eared and dirty.

Despite the intensity of this search, the net gleanings regarding Roosevelt's foreign policies could have been written on a postage stamp. The President-elect had been much too busy to bother about the distant and intangible problems of Europe. During his early years he had been busy leading the life of an intelligent rich man's son. He

spent his boyhood winters at Groton or Harvard, his vaca-
tions at the family home on the Hudson, his summers in
Europe or New Brunswick. At Harvard he made Hasty
Pudding and the Fly Club, wrote editorials for the *Crimson*, and was a highly dogmatic, big-voiced, typical Harvard
undergraduate.

As Assistant Secretary of the Navy under Woodrow Wilson he had been an enthusiastic promoter of bigger and
better battleships, took credit for writing the constitution
which General Smedley D. Butler rammed down the throat
of the Haitian Government, dived in a submarine off
Hawaii in a spectacular attempt to rescue the sunken F4,
and was about to resign his Cabinet post in favor of a
uniform when the war ended in 1918. He was a somewhat
superficial, rather efficient, buoyantly enthusiastic rooter
for the navy and all that went with it.

Beyond this, there was not much in Roosevelt's life for
the chanceries of Europe to discover. They knew he was a
Wilsonian Democrat, had favored the League of Nations.
But whether he still stuck by that creed, Roosevelt gave
them no inkling whatsoever. Recent years had been entirely absorbed with the agony of recuperating from a long
illness and with the wholly domestic problems facing him
as Governor of New York, so that Europe woke up on the
morning of November 9th, after the greatest electoral landslide in American history, facing the prospect of doing
business with a complete enigma.

Only one man was more anxious about the foreign policies of Franklin Roosevelt than the chanceries of Europe,
and he was Henry L. Stimson. Mr. Stimson had known the
President-elect ever since 1910, the fatal year which swept
young Roosevelt into the New York Senate and Mr. Stimson into the political discard as aspiring Governor of New
York. The acquaintanceship, Mr. Stimson told his friends,
had not been inspiring. Roosevelt, he was convinced, was
a poor imitation of his cousin Teddy, charming, but with-

out stamina. Stimson came to know more of him during the negotiation of the St. Lawrence Waterway Treaty, in which the Governor of New York wanted to take part, and the experience—as far as Stimson was concerned—had not increased his estimate.

But Mr. Stimson's most outstanding characteristic is that of a good soldier. He believes in obeying orders. Furthermore, he had come to have almost a fanatical reverence for the office which he held and the policies he had formulated. During the long period between the elections in November and the inauguration in March, those policies faced severe crises. The next war debt installment was due December 15th. Japan was concentrating troops for another drive south of the Great Wall. The League of Nations faced the severest test in its history—the Lytton report. The question of whether to convene or abandon the World Economic Conference was suspended in midair. And finally, the Disarmament Conference for the success of which the United States had so consistently striven was marking time in Geneva, awaiting the change of administrations in Washington.

Mr. Stimson, therefore, sent word to the President-elect that the entire State Department was at his service. Problems of tremendous import awaited decision, he said, and no one but Roosevelt himself could decide them. To this end he suggested that Roosevelt select his Secretary of State at the earliest possible moment and send him to the State Department before March 4th. Except for the mere formality of signing mail, he, Stimson, would abdicate to the new designate.

To this Mr. Roosevelt turned a deaf ear. Politics at that time were more important to him than world peace. Engrossed in the problem of selecting a Cabinet, harassed by thousands of deserving Democrats, and with no real conception of the vacuum into which his advent had thrown the world, the President-elect did not even reply to Stimson's invitation.

He was jogged out of this rather abruptly, however, when Herbert Hoover, en route from voting at Palo Alto, made public a telegram inviting Mr. Roosevelt to confer with him regarding the pressing problem of war debts.

For urgent political reasons a genuine discussion of war debts had been postponed a half dozen times before. It was postponed first by the Hoover moratorium. It was postponed second when that moratorium terminated simultaneously with the Republican National Convention to renominate Mr. Hoover, at which time a renewed discussion of war debts would have been political suicide. It was postponed again during the campaign; and now with the election over and the next debt installment only five weeks off, another postponement was the last thing Europe wanted. But with neither political party in power it looked as if this was exactly what Europe would get. Talking to Herbert Hoover about war debts was as futile as negotiating with last year's leaves; yet Europe could not talk to Franklin Roosevelt.

Mr. Hoover's telegram from his train was calculated to find a way out of the dilemma. Also it was calculated to put his successor on the spot. The victorious candidate could now put up or shut up. Mr. Hoover, furthermore, had come to have an exalted opinion of himself as an authority on international affairs, especially debts and disarmament, and he felt that he should lend this maturer experience to the man who was to succeed him. In fact, he shuddered a little at the thought of this novice from New York State putting his bungling hands upon the delicate machinery of international relations even after a period of Hooverian tutelage.

No meeting born of such antecedents could have been anything more than the Hoover-Roosevelt conference turned out to be—a complete dud. Mr. Hoover did most of the talking. Mr. Roosevelt listened attentively. But each proposition put to him by the President was answered by Raymond Moley, before the President-elect had time to answer.

Mr. Hoover was infuriated. On only one point did he get from Professor Moley anything but a negative answer. Apropos of Mr. Hoover's remark that he thought the expenses of the American delegation at Geneva were too high, Moley said:

"You might have Mary Woolley and Senator Swanson bunk together."

After it was all over and Mr. Roosevelt had boarded his train for Warm Springs, he issued a statement in which he rather clumsily tried to camouflage the fact that he had refused point blank to take any responsibility whatsoever regarding debts, disarmament, or any other chapter of international relations.

This shying away from the international horizon did not at all please two Wilsonian Democrats who had envisaged for themselves important rôles in the foreign-affairs picture. One was Colonel E. M. House, the other Norman Davis. The latter returned from Geneva shortly after the Roosevelt-Hoover meeting, and at the instance of Colonel House immediately urged the President-elect to confer with Mr. Stimson. This he did early in January, with results rather better than either Mr. Roosevelt or the Secretary of State expected. Instead of the young Harvard graduate in riding-breeches who had campaigned against him in 1910, Stimson found a man keenly aware of the responsibilities which faced him, but not anxious to be pushed into support of his predecessor's policies prior to March 4th. On one point, however, Mr. Roosevelt made an exception. Because the question of Japanese aggression in Manchuria faced an early test before the League of Nations, Mr. Roosevelt agreed to give unqualified support to the Stimson policy of non-recognition of territory gained through force of arms.

This delighted Mr. Stimson and brought a much greater degree of coöperation between the incoming and outgoing administrations. In fact, the two Presidents, at the urging of Norman Davis and Stimson, held one more conference at which at least one thing was agreed—that Mr. Roosevelt should receive a British representative to talk over war debts immediately after March 4th.

A few days later Sir Ronald Lindsay, in search of political sentiment on war debts, dropped in on Joe Robinson of Arkansas, Democratic leader of the Senate. What Sir Ronald specifically wanted to know was how the Democrats felt about drastic debt reduction and how far they would support their new President in taking such a step. Flattered at this attention, Robinson paraded his distinguished visitor on the floor of the Senate, thereby causing his Republican colleague from Indiana, Arthur Robinson, to scream treason and vituperation and demand by what right an ambassador of a foreign nation invaded the sacred precincts of the Senate. Aside from this, Sir Ronald's pilgrimage netted him no debt knowledge. Joe Robinson advised that he see Roosevelt in Warm Springs, and called up the President-elect to arrange the appointment.

The British Ambassador's trip to Warm Springs a few days later marked the beginning of Roosevelt's career as a crusading international reformer. He had known Sir Ronald a long time and could speak frankly with him. He had known him first as counselor of the British Embassy during the closing days of the World War, later as the husband of Elizabeth Hoyt, schoolgirl friend of Eleanor Roosevelt. Together with Isabella Greenway, Mrs. Roosevelt and Lady Lindsay called themselves the "Roaring Forties"—a tribute to their complete disdain for age—and during one skylarking summer in Paris, not long before Mrs. Roosevelt was to enter the White House, they celebrated that disdain by chasing everyone off a Montmartre merry-go-round and monopolizing it until long after those under forty had gone to bed.

Simultaneous with Sir Ronald's visit, William C. Bullitt, another old friend of the President-elect, was on a pilgrimage to sound out Paris and London on debts, disarmament, and the World Economic Conference. Bullitt's peregrinations were shrouded in mystery and aroused tremendous speculation. He denied he was on an unofficial mission for the President-elect. So also did Mr. Roosevelt. But on the very day Roosevelt's denial was issued Bullitt telephoned his chief in Warm Springs to say that Ramsay MacDonald was ready to come to Washington on March 5th. Bullitt was phoning from MacDonald's bedroom.

The culmination of all this caused Roosevelt to unburden himself freely to Sir Ronald Lindsay. Viewed from the distance of Warm Springs, debts and disarmament melted before the buoyancy of the President-elect. He painted an ambitious picture of American participation in world affairs. War debts, he felt, were a relatively unimportant item which should be relegated to the side lines. The reestablishment of trade, reciprocity between nations, the breaking down of tariff walls, were much more important. Disarmament was essential, and the United States was anxious to coöperate. In fact, the United States was coming back to assume much of the world responsibility it once shared under Woodrow Wilson. The Harding-Coolidge-Hoover era of power without responsibility was over.

Interviewed by the press after the conference, Sir Ronald Lindsay commented on the cloudless sky and the informal way the President-elect did things. But even his placid Scots soul was bubbling over with the vision he had seen of American coöperation with the Old World.

While Franklin Roosevelt was being elected President of the United States two important things were happening in Europe. One was the gradual elevation of an Austrian house-painter to a position rivaling Roosevelt's as a power for war or peace. The other was the slow stagnation of the Disarmament Conference into a complete stalemate.

The chief question beyond which the Conference could not pass was that which the Austrian house-painter used in order to push himself to power. Ever since 1926 Germany had made it clear that she intended to demand arms equality as her price for adherence to any disarmament treaty; but ever since that date France and her allies had made it equally clear that they would ignore the German plea. And when Eduard Beneš, in his solemn valediction to the Disarmament Conference in July, 1932, continued to ignore Germany, Chancellor Bruening issued an equally solemn warning that his goverment could not "undertake to continue its collaboration if a satisfactory solution of this decisive point was not reached by the time the Conference resumed its work."

This, of course, was chiefly window-dressing for the German people. Bruening, meanwhile, had received advice from MacDonald and Stimson to approach the French confidentially. The French were ready to be reasonable, they said, if handled the right way.

On August 19, 1932, Foreign Minister von Neurath handed the French ambassador at Berlin an *aide-mémoire* proposing that both countries "enter into a confidential discussion" regarding the best means of solving the contentious question of arms equality. As a basis for discussion, the memorandum outlined certain ideas for the reorganization and increase of German forces.

The note found the French in anything but a reasonable mood. Whether Stimson and MacDonald, in advising confidential conversations, actually spoke for the French or only for themselves, may never be known and no longer is material. But the result is important. A "leak" to the press, so frequent from the Quai d'Orsay, spread a summary of

Baron von Neurath's highly confidential document on the front pages of the Paris papers. With it was published a scathing criticism of Germany for jeopardizing success at Geneva by confidential approaches to an individual power. The Disarmament Conference was for all countries, read the rebukes, not France and Germany alone. And much to the surprise of Wilhelmstrasse, London joined in the chorus.

The very idea of secret diplomacy made MacDonald and Herriot shudder.

From this point on Germany was as good as out of the Disarmament Conference. There were times when her delegates boycotted Geneva altogether, and when Ramsay MacDonald and Édouard Herriot held frantic meetings in order to induce them to return. There were other occasions when Norman Davis was selected as the man who could bring Germany back. All of which only helped to elevate to a higher position of power the Austrian house-painter who had used Germany's treatment at the hands of the Allies as a battle-cry with which to revitalize the German people.

Some queer quirk of fate had decreed that Adolf Hitler, a poor Viennese, and Franklin Roosevelt, a son of the rich, should simultaneously emerge as leaders of the two most vibrant but leaderless peoples of the New World and the Old. The hold which they had on their people was equal, but not the methods by which they attained it. Both master showmen, Roosevelt had staged an appeal to men's hopes for economic salvation, for a new order of things, for a New Deal, Hitler included this appeal, but went farther. Using salutes, shirts, flags, all the arts of mass-suggestion, all the tricks of American advertising, he had dug up the ghosts of long-laid religious passions, the ever-present distrust of the traditional enemy to the south, the bogey of class warfare. Combining the showmanship of Barnum and Bailey with an Ethel Barrymore dramatization of Germany's misfortune, he sent truckloads of Brown Shirts into the villages of Holstein and Saxony, pulled sobs and cheers from vast audiences as if sitting at a pipe organ, and whipped into a passionate awakening the great middle classes of Germany.

And while Franklin Roosevelt was in Warm Springs building up his Cabinet and conferring with Sir Ronald Lindsay regarding the ills of the world, his dynamic rival for the world's spotlight achieved his long-cherished dream of becoming Chancellor of Germany. One month later— at the very moment Roosevelt was asking for sweeping powers looking toward a firm centralization of government in the United States—the new Chancellor staged a general election making him the complete dictator of the Reich.

On that same day Hitler gave momentum to two moves which were to add more complications to the already complicated life of Franklin Roosevelt. One was the beginning of the official Nazi attack on the Jews. The other was a loud and vociferous hammering for armament equality with France.

Neither of these was new, but with Hitler's advent as supreme dictator of Germany, they assumed devastating proportions.

On March 4th, when the anti-Jewish campaign first broke, the United States and its new President were far too absorbed in their bank crisis to give it more than passing notice. But on March 14th, by which time various American Jews had been attacked, Secretary of State Hull sent a timid cable to the American Embassy in Berlin suggesting a report on the situation. In reply the Embassy telegraphed suave assurances on the part of the German Foreign Office that American Jews would be protected. The police, they said, had been overwhelmed with other duties. This satisfied Cordell Hull's career diplomats, but it did not satisfy the large Jewish contingent which had labored to elect the New Deal. Samuel Untermyer, who had signed his name to handsome cheques on several occasions when Jim Farley lacked rent for Democratic Headquarters, protested vigorously. So also did Felix Frankfurter, one of the powers behind the Brain Trust. Professor Moley listened absentmindedly and referred Frankfurter to Justice Brandeis. Secretary Hull, however, lent a more attentive ear. His latent liberalism, frequently capable of genuine outbursts for the under dog, was stirred. Finally he sent another discreet inquiry to the American Embassy in Berlin and received in reply a cable that all Nazi attacks had ceased, that reports of anti-Jewish demonstrations were vastly exaggerated, and that the German Government had assured the Embassy that Chancellor Hitler did not condone the Jewish attacks, but found it difficult to restrain the lust of his Brown Shirts.

Mr. Hull accepted this, announced in press conference that anti-Jewish trouble in Germany was ended.

This was on March 27th. Next day Hitler himself supported a formal order for a complete business, professional, and educational boycott against the Jews.

"I was convinced that I had the entire matter settled," remarked Mr. Hull, a little ruefully, next day.

For the next few weeks Nazi attacks intensified. Hitler, with two radio broadcasts, one of them announcing that the United States had no right to object, led the attack. Nazis even demanded that government officials married to Jewesses divorce their wives or leave their jobs. Only once did the German Government hold out a restraining hand —to warn Brown Shirts that breaking the glass of Jewish shops did not injure the Jews nearly so much as it did insurance companies.

Old Henry Morgenthau, contributor of $7,000 to Mr. Roosevelt's political aspirations long before anyone else took them seriously, made an indignant trip to Washington. Three Congressional resolutions authorized the State

Department to make representations to Berlin. Mass meetings in Madison Square Garden were as bitter as those held during the World War.

But Roosevelt refused to act. And as the effect of retaliatory embargoes and incensed world opinion began to be felt in Germany, Adolf Hitler gradually turned to other things.

Chiefly he turned to the demand for arms equality with France. This was just as popular as Jew-baiting and lacked disastrous economic repercussions.

By this time the full fury of the banking crisis was spent, the American public was beginning to disgorge its hoardings, and Europe was again getting restless about debts and disarmament. Mr. Roosevelt therefore dumped his remaining monetary details into the lap of the dazed Mr. Woodin, and turned his still insatiable enthusiasm toward the international situation.

First on the Presidential calendar was the visit of Ramsay MacDonald, scheduled for March 5th but postponed by the banking emergency. MacDonald had been invited chiefly for the purpose of discussing war debts, but as time passed and the new President became more familiar with the international problems confronting him, it became more and more apparent that a discussion of war debts alone would bring no relief to the world and that there were other important countries besides Great Britain in the international picture. Transcending the urgency of war debts, Mr. Roosevelt came to realize, was the World Economic Conference rapidly approaching its convention date; and also the Disarmament Conference, so long marking time in anticipation of his inauguration. In both of these the French played just as important a part as the British. In fact, Norman Davis argued that if Roosevelt repeated the Hoover mistake of ignoring them, their nuisance value was beyond belief.

However, the French could not be invited without the Italians, nor either of them without the Germans. Japan was extremely sensitive regarding her position as a world power and equally jealous of her sprawling Asiatic rival, China. Finally there were the chief Latin American neighbors, the importance of which Sumner Welles had pounded home upon the President for months. So in the end all of these, including Argentina, Brazil, Chile, Mexico, and Canada, found themselves invited to Washington to discuss the problems facing the world in general, and the London Economic Conference in particular.

Out of an insignificant talk between Ramsay MacDonald and William C. Bullitt had sprung an international gathering of major proportions. In fact, so momentous had become the Washington conversations in the eyes of the public that they almost dwarfed the London Conference for which they were to prepare, and some of the President's advisers warned him of disaster on two fronts. One was the disaster of shifting responsibility for success at London away from Europe, which called the Conference, to the shoulders of the United States, which was merely a participant. Another was the disaster of creating the impression on the part of the American public that the Roosevelt administration, after only one month in office, had simulated the last days of the ill-fated Wilson administration by throwing the United States into the treacherous whirlpool of European machinations.

For the newly inaugurated President, however, it was a grand show. Unquestionably, also, it was in the hands of a grand showman. Washington was to become the Mecca of world affairs. All the stars on the international stage were to pass in review. Mr. Roosevelt had only one regret. The chief showman of Europe declined to enter the ring. Despite the cabled entreaties of Ambassador Rosso, Benito Mussolini knew that the cardinal principle of good showmanship is never to compete with a past master at the game.

Mussolini stayed at home.

Although the purpose of the Roosevelt conversations was threefold—debts, disarmament, and the London Conference—disarmament played an important part only in the discussions with Ramsay MacDonald and Édouard Herriot. But with these two it was all-important and led to the culminating gesture which the President made on May 16th to pull the world off the rocks of rearmament.

Between January and March the Disarmament Conference had continued to mark time at Geneva. A few tourists, the professional pacifists, and a handful of newspaper men under the necessity of cabling news whether it existed or not, remained faithful to the cause of peace. Actually there was little to cable. The warmth of MacDonald's sentimentalism, the tremolo in Herriot's voice, long before had ceased to bring thrills from blasé Geneva. Confining itself to routine questions, the Disarmament Conference droned on. Only once did it emerge hopefully from its doldrums.

On March 16th Ramsay MacDonald brought forth a new disarmament plan. Outlined in eight sections, nine chapters, three subchapters, and ninety-six articles, his proposal boiled down to this:

On paper, France, Germany, Italy, and Poland each should have the same number of armed effectives—200,000 men. But for the protection of overseas colonies, France could maintain an additional 200,000 men, while Italy could arm an additional 50,000.

On paper the plan seemed feasible. But not to Germany and Italy. Why should Poland, with only 30,000,000 population, have the same army as Germany with 60,000,000, sneered the Germans. Why should France, with only 40,-000,000 population, have 200,000 additional colonials capable of being transported across the Mediterranean in less than a week. Italy's reaction was equally negative. Mussolini pointed to Czechoslovakia with a population of 15,-000,000 and asked why she should have the same army as Italy with over 40,000,000 people. In fact, so negative was Mussolini's reaction that for purposes of pacification Mac-Donald and Sir John Simon left for Rome the next day.

In Geneva, the MacDonald proposal was referred to commissions and subcommissions to be "studied" while the Conference adjourned until April 25th. By this time MacDonald himself could appeal to the new President of the United States to resuscitate the Conference before its dying gasp.

Ramsay MacDonald embarked on the same vessel on which he had made his historic pilgrimage to the Rapidan nearly four years before. His daughter Ishbel once again was with him; also Sir Robert Vansittart, permanent Under Secretary of the Foreign Office. They occupied the same suite on the *Berengaria*, received the same culinary masterpieces from the same chef.

But it was not the triumphal voyage of four years before. MacDonald was an older man and both years and experience had left their mark. The Tory upheaval in Great Britain which made him nominal head of the Nationalist government, actually left him weaker than at any time since he was ostracized as a pacifist during the war. He was lonely, weary, sadly in need of some spectacular achievement to recoup his prestige.

The Anglo-American rapprochement which he had cemented during his other famous visit, had suffered the same fate. The naval agreement worked out with Herbert Hoover, which they had hoped would be the corner stone for world disarmament, stood feebly and alone. The Kellogg Pact, on which they built their hopes for peace, had been punctured by Japanese militarism. Dissension over trade, shipping, tariffs, Far Eastern policy, and debts had left scarcely a skeleton of the understanding once so heralded in England and America.

This time also the Prime Minister of Great Britain did not go alone. Other nations, notably France, were competitors for the favor of the United States. His old friend Édouard Herriot was scheduled to sail on the *Île de France* on April 19th for the same Mecca in the New World. But the Quai d'Orsay, always suspicious of MacDonald, particularly suspicious of what his eloquent imagination might conceive when the heads of the two English-speaking nations got together, decided that MacDonald must not be left in Washington alone. The Compagnie Transatlantique was asked to speed the departure of the *Île de France*, with the result that Herriot and his six experts sailed from Le Havre only two days behind the *Berengaria*.

This time also the voyage of the *Berengaria* was not so placid. Its star passengers were made worse than seasick by news which the wireless operator gave them of the White House press conference on April 19th.

The President, on that day, had a cold. The newspaper men were invited to come to his study. Despite his cold, Mr. Roosevelt seemed in high spirits. He wore a purple dressing-gown and tilted his ivory cigarette holder at a cockier angle than ever. He complained that even his Old Golds had no taste, and that there was practically no news to feed a hungry press.

"If I had to write a story today," he continued, "and had nothing else to write, I should say that on this day the United States went off the gold standard and that the dollar will be allowed to find its own level."

There was a rush for the telephones. In less than half an hour the world knew the momentous news. Ramsay MacDonald received it with stoic Scotch silence. But a few hours later there appeared a trail of white specks in the wake of the *Berengaria*.

They were not sea gulls. The British experts had thrown

overboard all their carefully prepared data for a universal return to the gold standard.

On the *Île de France*, reception of the news was typically Latin.

"We should return to Paris at once," expostulated Édouard Herriot with both hands. "If we were not in mid-ocean we would."

And for a few hours he even considered returning on the *Île de France* without disembarking in New York. But Finance Minister Bonnet, whom he consulted by telephone, advised him to make the best of a bad situation.

"It is a typical Yankee trick," said M. Bonnet, equally upset. "But since you are already halfway there, you can at least find out whether Monsieur Roosevelt is abandoning gold permanently or only for the moment. And since economic problems are now out of the question, perhaps you can obtain some satisfaction on political matters."

MacDonald's arrival in New York April 22nd was not the triumphal march he had made from the Battery four years before. This was not due solely to the absence of Jimmy Walker or Captain Eugene Regnier. History seldom repeats, and to blasé Broadway, accustomed to one-season sensations, Ramsay MacDonald had come to be an old story. Not even Secretary of State Hull came to New York to meet him.

New York newspaper men were there, however. And their first question was whether he was disappointed at the United States' going off the gold standard.

"Gracious no!" he replied. "As a matter of fact, I am without information on the subject."

Arriving in Washington the same day, MacDonald was met on the White House portico by Mrs. Roosevelt, Mrs. Dall, and Meggie, the pet Scottie. They led him to the Lincoln study, converted into a temporary bedroom in his honor. That night the MacDonald and Roosevelt families enjoyed an informal dinner, after which the two men talked late into the night, MacDonald—for sentiment's sake—smoking the underslung pipe which Charley Dawes had given him during the hectic days of the pre-London Naval Conference negotiations.

This was the first time the two men had met. When Roosevelt visited England in 1918 he was a bustling young Assistant Secretary of the Navy, too busy to see an outcast pacifist member of Parliament even if he had thought of it. So the first evening was devoted chiefly to getting acquainted. The next day also was politically uneventful. MacDonald had one conference with his host, addressed the Press Club, and attended a reception at the British Embassy; while his daughter Ishbel told a group of eager girl reporters about her work as a member of the London County Council, said Bernard Shaw should not be taken seriously, and that Englishwomen factory workers were underpaid compared with men. That night MacDonald sat through a state dinner at the White House, listened patiently to a recital by Princess Te Ate and politely applauded an exhibit of drawing-room dancing by Myrtle Chaney and Edward Fox.

The golden October week-end he had spent with Herbert Hoover on a Virginia hillside seemed very remote, very beautiful, and never to return.

His old friend Herriot, meanwhile, was steaming anxiously into New York, with visions of a complete Anglo-American alliance consummated before his arrival. He had little need to worry. It was not until Sunday that Roosevelt and MacDonald really got down to a discussion of the thing which vitally absorbed France—disarmament.

Early that morning the two men, accompanied by Sir Robert Vansittart, Ishbel, Mrs. Roosevelt, and Meggie—described by one French correspondent as Mrs. Roosevelt's daughter—boarded the presidential yacht Sequoia for a cruise down the Potomac. Soon after the ship cast off, Roosevelt and MacDonald sat down to a conference which,

with the exception of a few brief intervals for dinner and a
turn on deck, lasted until the yacht pulled into dock again
late in the afternoon. During this time they talked, not
economics or war debts, but disarmament.

Ramsay MacDonald can paint as vivid a word picture as
any man in Britain, and on this April afternoon he left
nothing to the imagination. Europe, he said, faced war—
stark, certain, unprecedented war—if the Geneva Disarmament Conference failed. The statesmen of Europe, he said,
were impotent. They stood frozen in their tracks, staring
at the disaster which swept down upon them. Prejudice
and politics paralyzed every attempt to escape.

The United States, MacDonald pleaded, was the one
nation with the power, the prestige, the perspective to
lead. Given this leadership, Europe would follow. Europe
was eager, anxious, groping for a leader.

Roosevelt was moved. He was won over not only to the
idea that he must lead, but to the idea that the disarmament plan offered by MacDonald at Geneva had the best
chances of success. He saw himself in the same rôle hewn
out by his former chief, Woodrow Wilson—the rôle of
world savior which has allured every recent President,
even at times the taciturn and aloof Mr. Coolidge.

In the end, Roosevelt gave assurances to Ramsay Mac-
Donald which caused the British Embassy that night to
issue a carefully worded but, for it, significant statement:

> Today was occupied in a thorough survey of the dis-
> armament conference at Geneva which contains a multi-
> tude of sidelines. It was felt by both the President and the
> Prime Minister that the results of today's conversations
> would considerably advance the prospects of the success
> of both the Disarmament Conference and the London
> Economic Conference.

While the President and the Prime Minister still were
busily engaged with planning this advance, Édouard Her-

riot with his newspaper retinue was greeted by Cordell Hull in top-hat and cut-away at the Union Station. The French emissary wore a blue worsted suit, a cream shirt, a blue tie, sturdy shoes, and a generously formed black hat, and was permeated with a pungent atmosphere of suspicion. This grew more acrid as Herriot was driven down Pennsylvania Avenue to the Mayflower Hotel. The Capital, on that Sunday, basked sleepily in the April sunshine. The Avenue was listless and empty. Roosevelt and MacDonald, the Secretary of State informed him, had left on a tête-à-tête cruise down the Potomac.

When were they coming back? Some time tonight, but nobody knew exactly. Herriot frowned. The gloomy news of the gold standard had been dispelled by the natural buoyancy of his character and by his reception in New York; but now it all came back again.

Especially did gloom settle down on the watch-dogs of France, that group of newshounds which preys upon the slightest slip of every French statesman, and which had raised dire predictions regarding the fate in store for the portly Deputy from Lyons even before he sailed. Now they reported how their predictions were coming true and played the dismal dirge of the Anglo-American alliance.

M. Herriot chafed outwardly. He decided immediately to see his old friend Ramsay and find out from him what was going on. But Ramsay was enjoying his day in the bosom of the Roosevelt family and was in no hurry to return. Coming back from the *Sequoia*, the party went for a leisurely drive along the Potomac Parkway, even stopped at the Folger Library.

Secretary Hull hastened to inform the emissary of France that an invitation awaited him to see the President the next day at 5:10—a long time to wait when one considered the many hours MacDonald was having alone with Roosevelt. Herriot again determined that he would at least see MacDonald, but this time ran up against the fact that his friend was a guest at the White House and nobody, not even an ex-Premier of France, could intrude upon its sanctity. Finally Herriot sent a card to MacDonald at the White House. He hoped that this would draw an invitation from his friend to meet him somewhere that evening. All he got in return was an official statement issued by the British Embassy to the press that "the Prime Minister is looking forward to meeting again his old friend, M. Herriot. He feels that M. Herriot's presence in Washington is a happy augury for the world Economic Conference."

And that was all. Macdonald, at that moment, was enjoying eggs cooked in a chafing-dish by Mrs. Roosevelt herself.

Herriot was gloomy. Laboulaye was gloomy, the French experts were gloomy, and the French newspaper men enjoyed a gala of gloom cabling their Parisian public how France, as usual, was being slighted and ignored. Again there was talk of Herriot's curtailing his visit and leaving by the *Île de France*.

Next morning it was worse. Blatant headlines featured the disarmament discussions of MacDonald and Roosevelt aboard the *Sequoia*. There was wild speculation regarding a new working agreement between the two English-speaking governments. What, exclaimed the French, were these two men talking about during an all-day voyage? It must have been important. What right had they to come to an agreement without even consulting France? Was France of so little consequence to disarmament that her position could be ignored? It was preposterous!

Not even André de Laboulaye, the new ambassador, could do anything about it; and he had been especially selected to supplant Paul Claudel because of his old friendship with the new President. Laboulaye had been secretary of the Embassy when Roosevelt was Assistant Secretary of the Navy. His family had been bosom friends of the Roosevelt family. He had even come to the Gare du Nord to meet Roosevelt one summer when he was a mere Governor of New York. And so he was made Ambassador to the United States.

But on this particular occasion the old friend of the Roosevelts found his friendship in about the same category of usefulness as that of another old friend—Al Smith.

M. Herriot bit his tongue and said nothing. While MacDonald was breakfasting with Senator Borah next morning, conferring once again at the White House, calling upon Senator Reed and having tea with ex-Secretary of State Stimson, Herriot went through the important routine of breakfasting at the French Embassy, laying a wreath on the Tomb of the Unknown Soldier, making a pilgrimage to the Tomb of the Father of the Country, lunching with his own experts at the Mayflower, and receiving a National Life Saving Medal for his work during the landslide of Lyons.

Only one person outside the circle of M. Herriot's own friends raised his voice against the White House monopoly of Mr. MacDonald, and this protestant did not do so on behalf of the French.

"Why," asked the irrepressible Representative Ham Fish, "was only one Republican—Senator McNary—invited to meet the British Prime Minister? He did not come to Washington to be the guest of the Democratic party."

Finally M. Herriot's big moment arrived. Promptly at 5:10 he was at the White House. Roosevelt was ready, awaiting him on the south veranda. He greeted his visitor in his best French. Mrs. Roosevelt was in the drawing-room. Despite his girth, the gentleman from Lyons bowed low and kissed her hand. Tea was served. It was a charming affair. No politics; just a pleasant family chat.

"Come back tonight," Roosevelt said, as his guest departed. "Come at about nine and we will have a good talk together. And no interpreters. Between my French and your English we can get along admirably."

The evening was even more pleasant. Roosevelt talked without the studied care of the average diplomat. He was sincere, frank, and made his visitor feel like an old friend. Also he knew France, understood her plea for security, was completely sympathetic when Herriot told him of Germany's secret arms stores. Roosevelt showed genuine alarm over this, and Herriot made the most of his opportunity. He detailed the French General Staff's report on German arms factories abroad, the twenty-four hour shifts operating in Switzerland, Holland, and Russia. He told of the tremendous strides taken by German electrical and chemical laboratories to develop new means of destruction. He told all the blood-curdling tales he could think of about Germany; and he left nothing to the imagination.

The President was impressed. Despite Herriot's suspicion of his British colleague, MacDonald actually had paved the way for him. Roosevelt was in a mood to help preserve the peace of the world; and the program he outlined to Herriot, contrasted with the international waverings of Herbert Hoover, was not a milk-and-water one. Roosevelt was willing first of all to accept the consultative pact which had been such a bone of contention at London. He was also willing, under certain circumstances, to abandon the traditional American policy of the freedom of the seas. Finally, and probably most important from the French point of view, he favored an American embargo on arms shipments to any nation declared to be an aggressor.

This, more than almost anything short of an alliance, was what France wanted, and Herriot was delighted. At last he had found an American with a really broad-gauge point of view.

Roosevelt, however, expected some degree of French reciprocity. He made it clear that he was not going to yield traditional American isolation without some *quid pro*

quo; and while he was rather discreet about it, he intimated that the area in which France could reciprocate most
was the Far East. He asked Herriot many detailed questions regarding French naval strength in that area, questions which indicated a much greater knowledge than the
Deputy from Lyons ever thought of having. Roosevelt
wanted to know, for instance, how the development of
Saigon harbor was progressing, how many large warships
it could accommodate.

"How many ships," he asked, "could you get out there
in case of emergency, and how quickly?"

Late that night Herriot returned to the hotel, hot but
happy. A small army of newspaper correspondents from
many countries awaited him in the lobby.

"My conversation with Monsieur Roosevelt was most
cordial," he announced, with a wave of his plump arms.
"Charming man! Charming! You can't help liking him. We
had a delightful visit.

"I also had a separate conversation with the Prime Minister of Great Britain," he continued.

"Which talk did you like the best?"

"Oh, I enjoyed very much meeting my old friend Monsieur MacDonald, but I cannot comment."

And walking almost on air, he went to his apartment.
There a select group of French newspaper men waited to
get the real lowdown. With these men Herriot could afford
to let himself go. And he did. Mopping his brow, a hand-
kerchief stuck between neck and wilted collar, he became
lyric.

"What a man! What a man!" he sighed. "Imagine, *mes
amis,* that before leaving he slapped me on the back—you
know the American habit—and reminded me that he was
expecting me to dinner tomorrow night. 'Just a little family dinner, you know,' he said.

"What a charming, gracious informality!

"And on his table there were flowers—blue, white, and

red flowers—the colours of France. What delicate attention! How can one help loving such a man?"

As if exhausted by this outburst, he mopped his brow
again and asked to be excused. He had to cable details of
the interview to Paris.

And over the cable to Paris that night went the glad
tidings that the United States was ready to go a long way,
farther than ever before, to assure disarmament success in
Europe by coöperating with France. Henceforth, France
could count on Roosevelt.

Next morning Herriot had time for discreet talks with
two or three close newspaper friends, and the cables which
they sent back to Paris that day substantiated all that he
had sent the night before. Particularly was it emphasized
that the United States would put itself in a position to
embargo arms shipments to an aggressor nation. Upon this
depended the entire French scheme of security under the
League of Nations.

But Roosevelt's pledge to France depended upon his getting the power of embargo from both houses of Congress;
and some of Herriot's advisers, skeptical Frenchmen,
warned him that the American Senate had proved a disappointment to one other Democratic President and to
France.

Herriot, therefore, made a pilgrimage to Capitol Hill,
where he called upon the man who, in the eyes of Europe,
epitomized the stubborn reluctance of the Middle West to
be drawn into the vortex of European politics. Borah was
cordial but noncommittal. He was, however, no longer
chairman of the powerful Foreign Relations Committee.
This time the Democrats were important, and Herriot was
given an opportunity to meet them at a luncheon given in
a private room of the Senate restaurant by Majority Leader
Robinson. The Democratic Senators were proud and
pleased that their advice was being sought. Flushed with
the first taste of power, they were confident that Congress

would give the President authority to declare an arms embargo against any foreign country—always provided he
retained the right to decide when such an embargo should
be declared.

M. Herriot's work was now done. Politically he had accomplished more than his fondest dream, and with Ramsay MacDonald's departure leaving him the center of the
stage, Herriot remained to enjoy Washington for a day or
two.

MacDonald had been a disappointment. When Roosevelt first invited him no one had realized how weak he was,
that his political convictions had vanished, that he remained a mere figurehead for an arch-Tory government;
except for his passionate plea for disarmament, MacDonald
had no program and few convictions. He could speak for
the National Government in Great Britain with no more
authority than Borah for the Roosevelt administration.

When he departed, Mrs. Roosevelt walked with him to
his car, accompanied by the younger Mrs. James Roosevelt
and her baby. Aside from this, MacDonald's passing was
unnoticed. There were no crowds at the Union Station or
in New York. Even the newspaper men who, during the
Prime Minister's first visit four years ago, were almost converted to Socialism by his eloquence, now were restless
and inattentive during their luncheon in his honor.

Herriot enjoyed many pleasant ceremonies during the
remainder of his stay, but nothing pleased him so much
as that first delightful tête-à-tête with the President. He
talked with Mr. Roosevelt once or twice again, was entertained by the French ambassador, and presented to Mr.
Woodin—the musical Secretary of the Treasury—a copy
of his own lengthy and somewhat labored *opus, The Life
of Beethoven*. At his departure, Roosevelt gave him his
photograph inscribed: *"À mon ami, Édouard Herriot. Vive
l'amitié Franco-Américaine,"* and told the Frenchman that
he was the man whom he had wished to meet most in the

entire world. Beaming, M. Herriot replied that the Sons of the Declaration of Independence and of the Rights of Man always would be able to understand each other, and left for the Union Station. There the Ministers of Czechoslovakia, Rumania and Yugoslavia—faithful satellites of France—waited to see him off. M. Herriot stopped for a moment to tell them of his great triumph.

How great a triumph it was Geneva began to find out almost immediately. While Roosevelt was conferring with MacDonald and Herriot, in fact one day after the latter's famous tête-à-tête with Roosevelt, the Disarmament delegates had come wearily back to their work. For most of them this was mere routine. Few had any more hope of achieving success than the Afghan delegates who came to buy cast-off armament.

But even before they had time to conclude their opening pyrotechnics, the delegates were electrified by an announcement from Norman Davis indicating that the United States had taken one important step in accepting the thesis of Édouard Herriot. Davis announced that his government favored the international supervision of armament.

This, for the United States, was an important step. As far back as 1927, when the State Department first began sending delegates to preparatory disarmament discussions, Frank B. Kellogg had proclaimed that the idea of having an international commission invade the sovereign soil of the United States, poke its nose into our forts, our arsenals, and our munitions factories, was unthinkable anathema to a free country. This, although expressed less pungently in subsequent years, had continued consistently to be the policy of the United States. The sudden revision by Franklin Roosevelt, therefore, was important, and behind it Geneva saw the plump hand of M. Herriot.

The British, French, and their allies were delighted. The Italians and Germans were not. The latter considered

international supervision of arms just another French trick
to suppress the Fatherland. The plan, they suspected, would
work chiefly against the Reich. The Italians were more
practical. What was the good of international arms control,
they asked, when it could not possibly yield results? If the
Allies with their powerful military commissions in Germany after the war were not able to detect the manufacture of German munitions under their very noses, how
could they detect them now?

Geneva was still arguing learnedly about these hypo-
theses when word began to filter into the chanceries of
Europe that the realistic Herr Hitler was tired of talking
theories and was preparing to talk facts. For the first time
in years, Germany had at her helm a man who could talk.
Adolf Hitler by that time had been granted the powers of
complete dictator by a subservient Reichstag, had relegated to the background the Nationalists who helped elect
him, and with the coöperation of Baron Gustav Krupp,
head of the famous Krupp works, had dissolved all German trade unions and reorganized them under the complete dictatorship of the Nazis and the Ruhr industrialists.
Obviously Germany was getting back to her old pre-war
footing.

At the height of all this, Count Nadolny, German disarmament delegate at Geneva, demanded that the half million Storm Troopers of the Nazis should not be reckoned
in the total strength of Germany's armed forces, following
which Hitler issued a sudden call for the reconvening of
the Reichstag and announced that he would address it on
Germany's right to rearm.

Scare headlines blazed throughout Europe.

"There is no death more beautiful than to be killed by
the enemy," Vice-Chancellor von Papen told a cheering
crowd at Münster. "Mothers must give themselves to bearing children and fathers must fall on the battlefield to
assure the future of their sons."

"Mothers to Provide Cannon Fodder," was the head-lined reply of the London *News Chronicle.*

"War or Peace?" asked the *Daily Express,* and itself answered that "not one British soldier should cross the Channel."

Hitler's address was scheduled for May 17th.

On May 13th Senator Hiram Johnson, calling at the White House to discuss the Securities Act and the protection of American bondholders from the chicanery of defaulting foreign governments, found the President so absorbed with Europe that he was unable to concentrate on anything else.

On May 15th Herr Hitler went to one of his old hide-aways near Munich to prepare his momentous address.

"From now on he will be secluded and commune with himself," announced a Nazi spokesman, with all the reverence of one speaking of Christ. "He will marshal his thoughts, array his arguments as he intends to present them to the world on Wednesday."

The thoughts which Hitler marshaled never were delivered to the world in their original form.

For at about the time Senator Johnson found the President so engrossed in Europe, another marshaling of thoughts got under way in Washington. Those who planned the campaign were Secretary Hull, his Under Secretary, Mr. Phillips, Professor Moley, and the President himself. Roosevelt already had spoken in the bluntest possible language to Dr. Hjalmar Schacht, emissary for the pre-London discussions. He said that Germany's financial situation did not permit heavy expenditures for rearmament. He described as preposterous the German contention that Hitler's private army of Storm Troopers should not be reckoned in disarmament. He said that the United States definitely had thrown its weight on the side of those nations desiring actual arms reduction, and in this case he considered those nations to be France and Britain.

The impervious Dr. Schacht blinked behind his thick lenses and said nothing.

So Roosevelt and his Brain Trust group worked feverishly. They were planning a diplomatic bombshell which they hoped would ward off the steel gauntlet which Hitler planned to throw in the face of the world. All Sunday they worked, and by Monday at midnight cabled to the heads of fifty-four governments the text of a Roosevelt plan for disarmament and world peace.

The plan was in five parts:

In order to achieve definite reduction of armament, Roosevelt urged acceptance of the MacDonald Plan.

In order to satisfy the French fetish for the preservation of the Versailles Treaty, he proposed that "no nation should increase its existing armaments over and above the limitation of treaty obligations."

In order to appease the French demand for security, he proposed that the entire world enter into a solemn pact of non-aggression.

In order to clarify the controversial word "non-aggression," he proposed that nations agree not to send their troops beyond their own borders.

In support of this non-aggression thesis and also in order to achieve some degree of immediate disarmament, he proposed that offensive weapons be abolished.

The message was a direct rebuff to Herr Hitler and took immediate effect. The solitary confinement of the Nazi leader was interrupted by the cabled text of the Roosevelt statement handed him by his followers. And the ultimatum which Europe had awaited so breathlessly on May 17th turned out to be a milk-and-water acceptance of Mr. Roosevelt's general propositions. Hitler agreed that economic reconstruction was impossible without a solution of the disarmament problem and magnanimously pledged Germany "to go as far as any nation in disarming, even to the extent of scrapping the whole military equipment," provided that . . . "other powers do the same."

It was a safe pledge at a time when arsenals were working overtime, but not even the French newspapers of the Nationalist Right could find any great fault with it.

Meanwhile French reaction to the Roosevelt message was joyful in the extreme. Herriot was exuberant. He saw himself—the man who had delivered America into the arms of France—once more Premier of the Republic.

Roosevelt had backed the French thesis almost one hundred per cent. He had laid down as fundamental the doctrine that no nation must increase its arms above treaty limits. He had placed special emphasis on ridding the world of aggressive armament. "Modern weapons of offense," he said, "are vastly stronger than modern weapons of defense. Frontier forts, trenches, wire entanglements, coast defenses—in a word, fixed fortifications—are no longer impregnable to the attack of war planes, heavy mobile artillery, land battleships called tanks, and poison gas."

Once before the Germans had been told this in the homely words of Norman Davis.

"Those forts can't be moved," he told the German disarmament delegates when they protested the vast network of concealed French fortifications extending from the Netherlands to Switzerland. "And if you people don't go up and shoot at them they'll never bother you."

Norman Davis was in Paris when the Roosevelt message burst upon the world, and went immediately to the Quai d'Orsay. For fifty minutes he was closeted with Paul-Boncour, at the end of which time the French Foreign Minister beamingly announced that "the French anxiety over German rearmament is allayed." The French press was even more optimistic. It announced that preparations were under way for a common front against Germany by France, Great Britain, and the United States.

President LeBrun was deeply moved, praised the "high

sentiments which have inspired this initiative of the President of the United States." The late King of the Belgians expressed his "admiration" for the President's courage. Mussolini announced that "Italy subscribes most cordially to the proposals of the President of the United States." Even the venerable von Hindenburg, always a power with the German people, declared that Mr. Roosevelt's message had "awakened a profound echo in the Reich."

On the crest of this enthusiasm Norman Davis hurried back to Geneva to translate words into action and to bask in the admiration of his colleagues.

He found Geneva in one of its rare moments of genuine optimism. The delegates were elated and relieved. They felt that the destiny of their Conference henceforth was safe in the arms of President Roosevelt. Any man who could induce the belligerent Chancellor of Germany to hammer upon the rostrum of the Reichstag and proclaim that "there is but one great task before us, to secure the peace of the world," certainly was capable of breaking the long-drawn disarmament deadlock. But Geneva wanted more facts, definite, concrete facts. And so the Commission asked Mr. Davis if he would induce the new disciple of disarmament to come down from the realm of generalities and express himself clearly on the following points:

1. Did the United States favor the rigid control of arms?

2. Would the United States participate in a world pact embodying the pledge not to resort to force?

3. Would the United States assist the League in defining an aggressor nation?

4. Would the United States refrain from helping an aggressor, once such a nation had been singled out by the League?

5. Would the United States participate in an arms embargo?

6. Would the United States abandon its traditional right

of neutrality and the freedom of the seas in the case of war?

These were hard questions for any President of the United States to answer even when he had a country as whole-heartedly behind him as Roosevelt at that time did. They were questions which penetrated to the roots of principles which had been instilled into the American people ever since the early days of the Founding Fathers. They were questions which had been answered so emphatically in the negative during the Presidential campaign of 1920 that even the party of Woodrow Wilson had shied away from them in subsequent political platforms.

The questions were not asked in Geneva publicly. Only a handful of delegates knew that they had been submitted to Norman Davis for transmission to Washington. Roosevelt could have dodged them. He could have claimed that he had made the first move to cut the disarmament knot and that the next move was now up to Europe.

But Mr. Roosevelt was in the first full flush of his power. He had heard of the friendly reaction in France. He had been encouraged by the conciliatory broadcast of Herr Hitler. He had received enthusiastic reports from Norman Davis. Probably he knew that action was not Geneva's forte, but whatever his motives—whether a genuine desire to sweep aside the impediments to peace, or the strategy of giving Geneva no excuse for placing the blame on the shoulders of the United States—the President decided to answer the Conference questions.

The exposition of American foreign policy which he cabled to Norman Davis a few days later put the United States in a more intimate relationship to Europe than at any time since Mr. Roosevelt's former chief, Woodrow Wilson, had consented to a definite alliance with France and Britain.

The new creed of international coöperation was outlined on May 22nd in a speech by Mr. Davis. It contained the following major points:

> American willingness "to consult with other States in case of a threat to peace with a view to averting conflict."
>
> American willingness to abandon its traditional policy of neutrality and not insist upon the right of trading with the enemy in case the League of Nations takes action against an aggressor.
>
> American willingness to participate with other powers in designating an aggressor nation; and withdrawal of the protection of the American flag from any national tending to defeat the collective effort of the other nations to restore peace.
>
> American willingness to participate in a commission to carry out the terms of any armament treaty.

Overnight Roosevelt granted to Europe more than Messrs. Hoover and Stimson were willing to offer after three fretful months, hundreds of cablegrams, and after jeopardizing the success of the London Naval Conference. Roosevelt put the United States definitely on record as willing to consult in case the peace of the world was threatened.

But in granting such sweeping concessions Roosevelt made it clear, through his ambassador in Geneva, that the compensatory price asked by the United States was immediate and appreciable reduction of armament.

Having carried out, with two masterful strokes, all of the pledges he had given to M. Herriot during their intimate talks in Washington, Roosevelt thrust a warning finger at the French and their fetish of security.

"We are firmly convinced," he said through Mr. Davis, "that in the long run security can best be achieved through a controlled disarmament by which the military strength of the most heavily armed nations is progressively reduced to a level such as that provided for in the peace treaties."

"As far as the United States is concerned," Mr. Roosevelt concluded, "our abilities and our incentive to collaborate whole-heartedly in the continuing task of helping to maintain world peace depend in large measure upon the results achieved in disarmament."

It was now up to Europe.

During the ebbing days of the Hoover administration Henry L. Stimson urged his chief to send a message to Congress asking for the power to embargo arms shipments to any nation. This, Mr. Stimson hoped, might be the crowning achievement of his career. That career had been one disappointment after another. The Kellogg Pact, which he had tried so hard to make a vital document, had flattened like a punctured football. The Hoover moratorium, which he helped inspire, proved the stepping-stone to debt default. Thanks to the tacit approval of France and Great Britain, Japan had perforated Stimson's policy of not recognizing territory gained by force of arms. Bolivia and Paraguay, where Stimson sought to prevent war, were at each other's throats. So also were Peru and Colombia.

Now Stimson cherished one last ambition. It was to prevent the shipment of arms to belligerent countries. This power he considered not only essential for the President to have in preventing disputes in Latin America, but also essential if the United States were ever to coöperate with the League of Nations in checking an aggressor nation.

Only recently had Mr. Stimson awakened to the real importance of the arms embargo. In fact, there was a time just a year before when he pulled frantic wires to prevent consideration of such a resolution in Congress.

During the early part of Japan's invasion of Manchuria in 1931, Dorothy Detzer, executive secretary of the Women's International League, had sold Ham Fish the idea of a resolution prohibiting the shipment of arms to nations in conflict. Fish had introduced the resolution, February

10th had been set as the date for public hearings, and a large number of witnesses were assembled in the hearing-room of the House Foreign Affairs Committee, when Representative Linthicum, Democratic chairman of the committee, suddenly became panicky. Clearing out all witnesses and the press, he called an executive session. That session lasted for two hours. During it Linthicum, always putty in the hands of authority, telephoned the State Department. The State Department telephoned the White House. And after two hours of heated discussion, Representative Fish emerged from the committee-room red-faced, irate, and sputtering to announce that the committee had refused to give him the hearing which it had promised.

"We were afraid the Japanese would be offended by the idea that we didn't want to sell them munitions," explained the docile Mr. Linthicum. Emphatically he denied that he had telephoned the State Department.

"But you couldn't have voted against the hearing?" newspaper men asked Representative Ruth Bryan Owen, daughter of the outstanding peace apostle in the Democratic party.

"Yes," she explained, "I was afraid it might irritate the State Department."

Later James Grafton Rogers, Assistant Secretary of State, gave the State Department's explanation:

"All last Sunday afternoon the President, Secretary Stimson, and I debated the resolution. We were afraid of it for fear the Japanese would interpret it as directly aimed against them. Almost anything could upset the apple-cart in the Pacific right now. Finally we decided the investigation would attract no public attention, so we let it go. Later when Linthicum phoned me that the hearing room was packed, we said thumbs down. Besides," added Rogers, "American firms aren't selling munitions to Japan, anyway."

This took place February 10th. The next day a news dispatch from Hopewell, Virginia, reported five vessels cleared from the docks of the Atmospheric Nitrogen Company loaded with nitrate for Japan.

It was about one year after that—December, 1932—that Henry L. Stimson finally became convinced that the right to declare an arms embargo was a vital instrument of peace. Many things had helped to form this conviction. One was the increasing number of vessels which sailed from Hopewell for Japan. Another was a discussion with the British regarding the practicability of an arms boycott against the Japanese. And finally there was the sudden awakening of Francis White to what almost everyone else around him had realized long before, that it was impossible for him to bring peace to the Chaco as long as the two countries were able to import ample arms from outside.

So during the very first days of the Seventy-second Congress, Stimson laid his case before Mr. Hoover, and afterward held a special press conference to explain the importance of an arms embargo. To obtain such powers, he said, the President would soon send a special message to Congress.

But the message was not sent. Several weeks passed, and still the message lay in a drawer of Mr. Hoover's desk. Apparently that gentleman's convictions on the matter were not nearly so strong as Mr. Stimson had thought them to be. Apparently also they blew hot and cold, according to who saw him last.

And there were a lot of people seeing him on the subject. One of the most effective was James H. Rand, Jr., famous during the Roosevelt administration as instigator of Dr. William H. Wirt's attack against the Brain Trust. Mr. Rand manufactures typewriters, office machines, and rifles. He is a devout Republican, a consistent contributor to the G. O. P. campaign fund. As such he had entrée at the White House.

On leaving it one day, he was questioned by Henry Misselwitz of the United Press.

"You seem to be coming down a good many times to see the President about that war in South America?" Misselwitz suggested.

"Oh, the President and I are old friends. I just came down to see him personally."

"But no one spends whole afternoons on personal business. It must be pretty important to spend all afternoon at it."

"Well, I had some business matters to discuss also."

"These rifles you are selling to South America?"

"Oh, we make a lot of other things—typewriters, for instance. We have just put out a swell new typewriter. I'll send you one tomorrow."

And he did.

There were others besides Mr. Rand with influence at the White House. Among these were the du Ponts, executives of the biggest munitions firm in the United States. The list of contributions from the du Pont family to the Republican National Committee looked like a betting sheet on the favourite at the Kentucky Derby. From 1919 through the 1932 elections, the twenty-five officers and directors of the du Pont firm had contributed $432,000 in political campaign funds, chiefly to the Republican party.

But perhaps the most active of all lobbyists was Mr. Stimson's colleague, the Secretary of War and his generals. Patrick J. Hurley lobbied not only directly with the President, but also through the munitions companies. His army officers staged lobbying classes for the munitions representatives, told them which Congressmen were most susceptible to big-business pressure.

During all this period Mr. Hoover fingered the pages of his special arms-embargo message to Congress and tried to make up his mind whether to send it or not. Finally, the peace lobby, plus Mr. Stimson, won out. After the landslide of November 8th he had nothing to lose politically, anyway. So he sent the message.

The resultant resolution was reported out of the Senate Foreign Relations Committee rather suddenly one day and, much to everyone's surprise, passed.

Next day the miracle was dispelled. Senator Hiram Bingham of Connecticut asked for reconsideration. He explained that he had been out of the Chamber when the vote was taken. Senator Burton K. Wheeler of Montana supported him.

Probably there are no two members of the United States Senate between whom there is less in common than Hiram Bingham and Burton Wheeler. The former, born in Hawaii of missionary parents, once taught Latin American history at Yale, has explored most of South America, is an expert on the lost Inca race, is an arch-Tory Republican, and based his campaign on boosting beer and big business. Wheeler, on the other hand, is a rough-and-tumble lawyer who settled in Butte, Montana, because a last-minute poker game took his railroad fare out of town. He is a radical Democrat, a champion of the American Indian, believes in soaking the rich, and based his campaign on attacking big business.

But as far as the arms-embargo resolution was concerned, both had one thing in common. Senator Bingham was backed by the Colt, Remington, and other small-arms munitions manufacturers in Connecticut. Senator Wheeler numbered among his constituents the world's greatest copper interests, heavy suppliers of raw material to the munitions industry.

The arms-embargo resolution, therefore, went back to committee.

Meanwhile the resolution had come up for hearing before the Foreign Affairs Committee of the House. This time its fate looked more favorable. Representative Linthicum having passed on to another world, Sam McReynolds, a rather intelligent Congressman from Tennessee, had become chairman of the Committee. He was coöperating with the peace organizations which, although heartily supporting the resolution, were carefully refraining from offering testimony. To make a public appearance, they feared, would be like waving a red flag at the Daughters of the American Revolution.

But they miscalculated two things.

One was Ham Fish. That mercurial gentleman, having fought so hard for an arms-embargo resolution the year before, was considered a sure supporter this year. But he was not. In fact, he was a vigorous opponent, fought the resolution to the end. Pride of authorship is an important thing in Congress, and this time Ham was not the author of the bill.

The other factor took the form of a rather mouse-like lady who attended the first committee hearing and suddenly demanded an opportunity to be heard. She introduced herself as Mrs. Helen Hoy Greely of the Women's International League for Peace and Freedom. Members of the committee scowled. The Women's International League had been coöperating closely with them and was one of the organizations which had decided to remain quietly in the background. But Mrs. Greely had just come from Geneva, said she had been commissioned by the Council of International Relations there to "do something for peace," and being both devout and insistent she did it then and there.

She spoke at length and with determination. Some members of the committee, already favorable to her cause, became restless—some a little sour. Publication of her testimony attracted attention. The patriotic societies began to unlimber. Particularly Melvin J. Maas, Republican Representative from Minnesota, got into action. Maas prided himself on his knowledge and use of firearms. Just a few days before, when an unbalanced youth from Pennsylvania stepped into the House gallery, brandishing a revolver, and demanding to be heard, Maas had stepped over and taken the gun away from him. Maas had served as a Marine Corps aviator during the war and still kept up his contacts with the aviation companies. With his support they brought all their guns to bear against the resolution.

It was in this condition of stalemate when the Seventy-third Congress, with Franklin Roosevelt's overwhelming majorities, came into power on March 4th. It was also in this condition when Roosevelt's midnight pledges to M. Herriot suddenly revitalized the arms-embargo resolution and made it, not a matter of mere dividends to munitions companies, but an issue on which hung the century-old question of American neutrality in war.

The President's pledges to M. Herriot were not, of course, immediately made public. Democratic Senate leaders who lunched with the Frenchman next day knew something of them and were prepared to give them unqualified support. The British had been informed regarding them and were enthusiastically anxious that they be given formal effect. But the general public, including the majority of Congress, was kept in complete ignorance and would have remained so had it not been for a private conference which Herriot had with French newspaper men the morning after consummating his new alliance with Roosevelt. The news he gave at this conference immediately leaked to the American press and made the arms embargo stand out as the pivot on which hung the traditional isolation of the United States. Dormant passions of irreconcilable Senators awoke. They remembered the League of Nations fight, the World Court debates, the resolves to keep the United States out of European entanglements.

After the smoke of the oratory finally cleared, President

Roosevelt and France found their resolution saddled with the Johnson Amendment by which the President of the United States, if he imposed an arms embargo at all, must impose it against both belligerents. The French plan of boycotting an aggressor nation was out.

Roosevelt went to some lengths to save his resolution. He forced it through the House by an overwhelming majority and made it clear that the United States would not be committed against an aggressor nation through the action of Europe.

Asked who would decide when a nation became an aggressor, Roosevelt replied:

"Papa, sitting right here in Washington, will do the deciding."

But Senate suspicion of entangling alliances could not be allayed. The arms-embargo resolution was mangled beyond all use to Europe.

The action of the Senate had immediate and disastrous repercussions in Geneva; but even had the resolution passed, it is doubtful if the fate of disarmament would have been different. Despite Roosevelt's pledges of coöperation, despite Hitler's protestations of peace, France had fallen back upon her traditional stand. The most powerful army in Europe, she reasoned, was a far more dependable guarantee of security than intangible promises which might vanish with the fall of a British Cabinet or a Presidential election in the United States.

On May 28th, only twelve days after Roosevelt's peace appeal to the world, Paul Scott Mowrer cabled from Geneva:

"The better feeling consequent to clarification of the American position proved to be short-lived. Today it is difficult to find any delegate who, in private conversations, will admit that he believes even the broad outlines of a disarmament agreement are possible."

Roosevelt was disgusted. His first sally at assuming

world leadership had resulted in exactly the same fate which befell Herbert Hoover.

He wired Davis to make it clear that Europe could not count on American action against an aggressor, and turned toward the London Conference and the economic situation at home.

Sunday, October 15th, was a busy one for the President of the United States. After a brief motor trip through the red and gold of the Maryland countryside, he settled down to an afternoon at his desk. General Johnson was having trouble with the bituminous-coal operators. There were strikes and shootings in Pennsylvania. Discussion over inflation churned the nation. His Brain Trust was hatching almost daily ideas for the devaluation of the dollar. American warships formed a circle around the revolution-ridden island of Cuba. The air was rent with pleas for intervention and warnings against it.

Europe and the perpetual problem of disarmament seemed very distant indeed.

Yet on that day hopes for disarmament reached their lowest ebb, and Roosevelt, for the moment, turned from domestic problems to the question whose settlement had once been his fondest dream. It had scarcely entered his mind since he threw it aside in disgust four months before.

During that interim Europe had toyed hopefully but a little skeptically with Mussolini's ambitious plan of a Four Power Peace Club, watched her statesmen go through their perpetual merry-go-round of goodwill visits, and listened politely to the optimistic statements emanating from Geneva.

Meanwhile the French Socialists, hitherto opposed to a large military budget, saw the specter of a rearmed Germany and suddenly voted all the money requested by the General Staff. Meanwhile, also, Marshal Pilsudski reviewed

the massed Polish army, first at Vilna, then at Cracow—
with the entire Diplomatic Corps and the Papal Nuncio
present. Meanwhile, also, Eduard Beneš of Czechoslovakia
proclaimed that Mussolini's plan of revising the frontiers
fixed at Versailles could be accomplished only by war, a
sentiment immediately echoed by his colleague, Nicholas
Titulesco of Rumania.

In reply, the Germans unveiled near the Polish border
a statue, on the pedestal of which was inscribed a list of
German towns within Poland which "await liberation."

"Germans! Bide the hours which will expiate these
bleeding frontiers!" the statue challenged.

Finally Sir John Simon had left London, grim and determined, to force a showdown with Germany. Like Henry
L. Stimson, Sir John is a trial lawyer. He has spent a lifetime convincing juries of the guilt or innocence of his
clients, and he has done it so successfully that never in
recent years has he touched a fee of less than £1,000. Now
he was convinced that he had the jury of world opinion
with him, and he determined to handle Germany as he
would a criminal in the dock at Old Bailey.

He proposed that Germany be permitted no rearmament; that the Arms Treaty extend for eight years; that
during the first four years the *status quo* in armament be
strictly maintained; and that an international commission
be empowered to maintain it. Only after four years were
the Allies to begin arms reduction, and then only provided
proper confidence was instilled in the hearts of the French.

Not even Sir Austen Chamberlain, who loved France as a
mistress, could have brought forward a plan more acceptable to the French General Staff.

What Paul-Boncour and Simon were banking on was
that Germany would not dare flaunt a united front. But
the question never came to a head. The take-it-or-leave-it
resolution with which Sir John had intended to confront
Germany leaked to the press. The Germans read it in the

afternoon papers. Probably their reaction to Sir John's spanking would have been the same in any case, but they allowed no time for a formal presentation. Count Nadolny, self-confessed plotter to blow up American bridges during the World War and now head of the German Disarmament Delegation, appeared at Sir John Simon's hotel just before dinner. Sir John was talking with Norman Davis.

The "conditions" put to Germany, he said, were unacceptable; and he left for Berlin by airplane. A special session of the Cabinet awaited him.

Friday, October 13th, was the blackest in the history of Disarmament. On that day it became evident that Germany would withdraw not only from the Geneva disarmament discussions, but also from the League of Nations. The news, flashed around the world, started political reverberations surpassed only by those of nineteen years before at the word that Archduke Franz Ferdinand had been assassinated at Sarajevo.

In Paris a Foreign Office spokesman said: "It is the gravest news in twenty years. We are surprised, but not upset. Confident that might and right are hers, France feels safe."

In London, Ramsay MacDonald ordered the Foreign Office to be silent in order to "keep hotheads from rocking the boat."

In Rome, Mussolini saw in the disaster a chance to revive his Four Power Pact.

In Tokyo, a War Office spokesman remarked: "It is easy for Japan to sympathize with Germany's demand for arms equality." Simultaneously, more troops of Nippon were concentrated on the Siberian border.

In Geneva, the Council of the League of Nations gave calm consideration to a plan for eradicating slavery in Liberia, passed on to the question of Assyrian massacre in Iraq, referred it to a commission. No one looked at the chair of Germany, third on the right, and that of Japan, third on the left. Significantly empty, they faced each other.

In Washington, Cordell Hull lost some of his characteristic gentleness.

"The action of Germany," he said, "naturally slows down, impedes and halts the disarmament movement. The United States is seriously disappointed and regrets the development."

In Washington, also, President Roosevelt sat at his desk on Sunday, October 15th, and surveyed the wreck of disarmament which he once sought so theatrically to save. Also he surveyed the reverberations caused by Secretary Hull's displeasure at Germany. Hull's critical statement had had far-reaching effects. One effect was upon his friend Norman Davis, who went one step farther than his nominal chief in Washington.

"I am glad," Mr. Davis told the Bureau of the Disarmament Conference, "to be able to endorse and support the position Sir John Simon has taken on the important questions of substance before us. . . ."

Another effect was loud applause from the French and British. They were jubilant. At last America had come back into the wartime alignment against Germany. All of the pledges given by Mr. Roosevelt to M. Herriot during that famous spring evening in Washington were being more than carried out.

Mr. Roosevelt did not relish this jubilation. He did not relish the interpretation being placed upon it by the Hearst press. He did not relish the obvious restlessness of some of his isolationist friends in the Senate. More than anything else, he did not relish the implication that in bargaining with Europe he had given everything, received nothing.

Having finished a brief discussion of the Cuban crisis with Assistant Secretary of State Caffery, Roosevelt asked what he thought of the reaction to the Hull-Davis statements.

Caffery had served as counsclor of the American Embassy in Berlin and knew Europe. In a nervous sort of way he could be amazingly frank. On this occasion he was. He told the President that the Hull-Davis statements were being interpreted as unequivocal support for Great Britain and France, and that the foreign policy of the New Deal was headed for trouble.

Mr. Hull was immediately called to the White House. A telegram was drafted and sent to Norman Davis. Next morning Mr. Roosevelt's ambassador for disarmament summoned the press. Slowly and with obvious embarrassment he took back all that he and his friend, the Secretary of State, had said regarding American displeasure at Germany's withdrawal from Geneva.

"We are in Geneva," said Mr. Davis, "solely for disarmament purposes. We are not interested in the political element, or any purely European aspect of the picture. We again make it clear that we are in no way politically aligned with any European power. . . .

"Whether or not conditions are favorable to continuing the present disarmament effort is now a question for Europe, not the United States, to decide."

And with this statement, all disarmament interest on the part of Franklin Roosevelt came to an end.

3. THE NEXT WAR

Franklin Roosevelt sat in his cabin on the U.S.S. *Indianapolis*. He had visited his mother's old summer place at Campobello. He had spent three weeks away from the turbulency of starting the New Deal. He had enjoyed a good rest, put on a little weight, experienced reasonably good luck fishing, and now he was going home.

Only one thing bothered him as the *Indianapolis* steamed south.

On the desk before him lay a pile of radiograms from

the London Economic Conference. That Conference, obviously, was on the rocks. It had started in a blaze of glory
—the same refulgent blaze which played upon war debts,
disarmament, non-aggression, and Mr. Roosevelt's other
short-lived attempts in the international field.

The world's most resplendent statesmen had come to
Washington. They had dined at the White House. They
had listened patiently to Cordell Hull's utopian harangue
on tariff reduction. They had drowsed a bit during Senator Pittman's forty-five-minute lecture on silver. But—with
the exception of brusque Hjlmar Schacht, president of
the Reichsbank, who declared: "We accept the American
position on silver. Now what can you do for us regarding
the Jewish boycott"—the currency discussions had got nowhere.

And as the delegates convened in London the deadlock
continued. In fact, currency stabilization became the one
absorbing obsession of the Conference. Mr. Hull kept his
economic adviser, Herbert Feis, busy every night writing
and rewriting statements on tariff reduction. The British
and French intimated that the one great factor depressing
international business was war debts. All agreed that exchange restrictions must be lifted if world trade was to
revive.

Yet none of these could be settled unless that most uncertain of all economic factors—the value of currency—
was established in advance.

In the radiograms piled before him Franklin Roosevelt
had a diffuse and disturbing set of opinions. He had private messages from William C. Bullitt, supposedly special
assistant to Cordell Hull. He had a report that Professor
Moley had ordered an airplane to take him off his ship in
Ireland for a spectacular dash to London—a plan which
the President promptly sat upon. And he had a private
cable from Moley giving his personal and confidential
views of each member of the American Delegation.

Aside from tapping on the walls of Claridge's in order to locate British dictaphones, the American Delegation apparently had accomplished nothing. Apparently also it would accomplish nothing.

While Franklin Roosevelt cruised on the *Indianapolis*, Professor Moley was at No. 10 Downing Street, closeted with Ramsay MacDonald and other delegates. They had drawn up a deftly worded compromise formula—one which they thought would prevent currency fluctuation, at the same time giving each nation a certain amount of stabilization freedom.

"Will you come over and initial this agreement, Mr. Secretary?" Moley telephoned his chief, the Secretary of State.

"What agreement?" replied Mr. Hull. "I have no authority to approve a stabilization agreement."

Mr. Hull was right. The Conference waited two days for that approval. The French Finance Minister postponed his return to France. The delegates sat up one night until three in the morning. Still no word from the President of the United States. Even Professor Moley got nervous.

It was at this particular moment—June 30, 1933—that Franklin Roosevelt, looking over the sheaf of radio reports from London, picked up his pencil and scribbled the following for immediate dispatch to Mr. Hull:

> I would regard it as a catastrophe amounting to a world tragedy if the great conference of nations called to bring about a more real and permanent financial stability and a greater prosperity to the masses of all nations, should, in advance of any serious effort to consider these broader problems, allow itself to be diverted by the proposal of a purely artificial and temporary experiment affecting the monetary exchange of a few nations only.
>
> Such action, such diversion, shows a singular lack of proportion and a failure to remember the large purposes

for which the economic conference originally was called together. . . .

This is not the time to dissipate gold reserves. . . . The conference was called to better and perhaps cure fundamental economic ills. It must not be diverted from that effort.

Having written this message to Mr. Hull, the President put it aside for the evening. Next morning he got it out and read it again.

"The more I looked at it, the better I liked it," he told a friend later. "And I knew that if I took it back to Washington those timorous souls in the Cabinet would want to take out a word here and soften a word there until there wouldn't be anything left of it. So I sent it immediately."

At No. 10 Downing Street, Ramsay MacDonald read the message. His face was white, his hands clenched. He said:

"When a man says something you disagree with and says it in a disagreeable way, you can at least answer him. But when a man says nothing in a disagreeable way, there is no answer."

Ramsay MacDonald did not realize it at the time, but he had just received Roosevelt's last important pronouncement in the field of international affairs.

Perhaps Franklin Roosevelt himself did not realize that he had launched on a new policy of isolation.

When Henry L. Stimson surrendered his roomy office in the State Department to his Democratic successor from Tennessee, he did not relinquish his baronial estate in Washington. Woodley remained for him a haven where he could rest, play deck tennis, and entertain his old friends, away from the legal routine in New York.

It was not for the purpose of resting at Woodley, however, that Mr. Stimson returned to the Capitol in May, 1933. Another visitor arriving simultaneously was Viscount Ishii, veteran Japanese diplomat, and Mr. Stimson was

worried about the reception he might have at the White
House.

Mr. Stimson, in fact, continued to be just as worried
about the situation in Manchuria and the Far East generally as he was while Secretary of State. Many things had
happened in the closing months of Mr. Stimson's term in
the State Department. Most important of all, of course,
was the brutal and wholly unwarranted Japanese attack on
Shanghai, interpreted by many in the State and Navy Departments—Mr. Stimson among them—as a deliberate
attempt to draw the American fleet beyond its depth across
the Pacific and provoke a brush with Japan. And it almost
succeeded. For at one time when the entire Japanese fleet
sailed under sealed orders, Secretary Stimson and the admirals experienced a bad case of the jitters. The Philippines, they suspected, were the Japanese destination. And
they had visions of American forces bottled up at Corregi-
dor, just outside Manila, while the American public demanded their rescue.

Rescue, Mr. Stimson and the admirals knew, would be
a matter of five years and construction of the most powerful fleet ever assembled by one country. And in order to
head off the dreaded Japanese move on the Philippines,
the Navy actually considered the immediate transfer of its
forces from Hawaii to Manila.

Japanese forces turned up at the Caroline and Marshall
Islands a week later, however, and the admirals breathed
easier.

Mr. Stimson, however, did not.

He was so worried about the danger of war in the Pacific
that his diplomatic envoys discussed the question with the
governments of Canada, Chile, and Mexico. In case of
war, these three controlled the Pacific coastline. And to
prevent the establishment of Japanese naval bases, they
pledged Mr. Stimson their coöperation with the United
States.

Simultaneously Mr. Stimson arranged with the Commerce and Navy Departments to send an expedition to the Aleutian Islands on the pretext of making a scientific study for the Coast and Geodetic Survey. Actually it was to examine sites for Aleutian air bases in case of a war in the Pacific.

Another thing which perturbed Mr. Stimson somewhat was the continual number of Japanese spies being apprehended in this country. Most of the information they collected was ludicrous, but their activity showed how assiduously the Japanese High Command seemed to be preparing for war. There was the Japanese naval captain arrested for taking soundings in San Diego Harbor. There was the disguised Japanese naval officer who traveled back and forth on the buses between San Pedro and Los Angeles, checking with enlisted men on Navy morale. There was the Japanese major arrested in Detroit for organizing a colored league against white imperialism. And there were the two young Japanese naval officers from Harvard who wrecked their car near San Pedro and in whose pockets were found sketches of the bay.

Then there was also the extreme frankness with which Ambassador Debuchi discussed the situation when he had more than four cocktails under his belt. The Japanese army and navy general staffs, he admitted frankly, favored settling the score with America as soon as possible. As youngsters most of them had been schooled on the inevitability of war with the great Power across the Pacific, had practiced war games with that in view, had toasted the day when they could put them into operation. Now they approached retirement age with that ambition unfulfilled.

Simultaneously, Japanese observers in the United States reported that the American people were less prepared for war than ever before in history. They were softened by too much prosperity, their morale had been shaken by the depression, and their antipathy to war had been inflamed by peace and church societies to a point where they would never fight to defend distant possessions in the Pacific. Japan could seize the Philippines, Japanese observers reported, and the United States would never embark upon a war to get them back.

Ambassador Debuchi disagreed emphatically with the reports of his naval and military *attachés*, but it was their word, not his, which carried weight in Tokyo.

Finally, what worried Mr. Stimson was the total blindness of France and Great Britain to the seriousness of the Far Eastern situation, or else their frank intention to thwart the United States by playing into Japanese hands. Mr. Stimson could scarcely believe at first the reports he got that the French and British were secretly informing the Japanese Foreign Office of tacit support. But after January 7, 1932, he knew that this was true. For he was then working on his famous policy of non-recognition of territory seized by force, and he had secured what he thought was advance approval from France, Great Britain, and Italy. In fact, he announced to the press with complete confidence that these nations would follow the lead of the United States in proclaiming a policy of non-recognition of Japan's seizure of Manchuria.

Days passed after that announcement. Mr. Stimson waited patiently. But Great Britain, France, and Italy never followed his lead.

So, finally, following the election of Franklin Roosevelt, Mr. Stimson went to New York and explained to the President-elect just how close the United States had been to war in the Pacific.

Mr. Stimson in the past had cherished no great regard for Mr. Roosevelt, but he came back to the State Department glowing with praise for the man who was to take the helm of the country.

Mr. Roosevelt had approved emphatically his policy in the Far East.

Four months had passed, however, between the meeting in New York and the visit of Viscount Ishii to Washington. During that time the new President had been engrossed with the most pressing problems of domestic policy, and Mr. Stimson feared that he might have forgotten the pledge made in January. So he dropped in at the White House to express the hope that Roosevelt would not be influenced by Viscount Ishii's attempts to secure the recognition of Manchukuo.

Leaving the White House, Mr. Stimson's face once again glowed fervently. A friend walking with him asked what the President had said.

"He said," replied Mr. Stimson: " 'I won't even discuss it!' "

From the viewpoint of the admirals, no more perfect Secretary of the Navy ever was appointed than Claude Augustus Swanson. During a third of a century in Congress he had forced through his own pet appropriation bills with as much success and more finesse than any other member on the Hill. And as a prominent member of the Senate Naval Affairs Committee he had used that finesse whole-heartedly and consistently in favor of a big navy.

Swanson came to the Navy Department, therefore, knowing nothing of battleships, but everything about legislation. This was exactly what the admirals wanted. They had some one who would get them ships and would not interfere with their running them.

Even the admirals, however, under-estimated Swanson's devotion to the cause of a big navy. With the enthusiastic approval and help of the President he had secured not only a regular naval appropriation from Congress of $286,-000,000, but also $444,700,000 from public works and emergency funds to be spent at the Navy's discretion. It was the greatest fund for ship-building since the World War.

However, the admirals wanted more. They wanted not only ships, but extra trimmings. And while Swanson was vacationing in Virginia, the admirals fixed up a plan by which the Navy Department was to build a grandiose new office-building as its headquarters in Washington.

Following Swanson's return, the plan was laid before him with eloquent ceremonies. Members of the Park and Planning Commission were present; also admirals, captains, chief clerks, all crowded into Swanson's gloomy office in the temporary war-time Navy Building.

They showed him the magnificent new walnut-paneled offices which were to be his, the immense open fireplace, the private elevator, the little anteroom where he could lie down for a nap after lunch. It would be the finest suite to be occupied by any Cabinet officer, they explained. What did he think about it?

Mr. Swanson listened without a word, chewed his black, pencil-like stogie, finally inquired:

"The Public Works Administration will give us the money?"

"Yes, that's all arranged."

"That's fine. We'll take the money—all they'll give us. But——"

"But what?"

"But we're not going to build a new Navy Building. I can run the Navy from an attic. We'll use the money for ships."

Gradually during the first year of Mr. Roosevelt's administration it began to dawn upon the chanceries of Europe that without any blare of trumpets he had adopted as his three chief foreign policies the building of a giant navy, an attitude of almost bitter coldness toward Japan, and—with the exception of Latin America—a position of complete isolation in regard to the rest of the world.

Probably the British were the first to realize this and

become concerned about it. They had reason to do so. For after subtly indicating to the Japanese that London and Tokyo would work together against Yankee domination of the Pacific, they began to discover that Japan's military-naval government had launched a determined campaign to drive British trade out of the Far East and the Union Jack eventually off the Pacific.

Trouble came to a head first in India. Cheap Japanese textiles began flooding the Indian market. Simultaneously Japanese agents started a crudely camouflaged campaign to convince India's 300,000,000 brown men that Japan was the protector of all colored races against the imperialism of the white. Lancashire cotton manufacturers emitted a howl of protest. Even pro-Japanese members of Britain's Tory Cabinet, were concerned, served notice of the abrogation of the Indian-Japanese Commercial Treaty.

The Japanese campaign spread to other parts of the Empire. In British East Africa, in Ceylon, in Britain's South Sea Islands tariff barriers were raised virtually barring Japanese goods. In Siam, a government long dominated by British advisers was shaken by Nippon's persistent propaganda that it was the protector of the yellow race. Eventually King Prajadhipok, "Descendant of Buddha, Supreme Arbiter of the Ebb and Flow of the Tide, Brother of the Moon, Half Brother of the Sun, Possessor of the Four and Twenty Umbrellas," and, above all, life-long friend of the British, left his tottering throne.

What the Japanese wanted in Siam was the Isthmus of Krim, a slender filament of land connecting Siam with the Malay States. Through this a canal would cut two days off the route to India. More important, as far as Japan was concerned, it would completely nullify Britain's powerful naval base at Singapore.

Farther east, the Japanese had violated the Four Power Pact of the Pacific by establishing secret naval bases on the Caroline and Marshall Islands. An American naval officer, visiting the islands in the guise of a Malay, reported the construction of concrete artillery foundations, oil-tanks, airdromes, and harbor facilities for submarines. The Mandates Commission of the League of Nations raised caustic questions.

"Why," it asked, "has Japan declined to permit foreign visitors in the islands?"

"We have been holding naval manœuvers there," replied Nobubumi Ito, "and naturally did not welcome foreigners at that time."

"And what is the purpose of improving four harbors at a cost of 200,000 yen each?"

"The sea is very rough," replied Mr. Ito.

"How does it happen that the sea has changed its habits after so many hundreds of years?"

The British Admiralty, fully awakened to Japanese intentions, now concentrated on the Far East. On a warship off Singapore, Field-Marshal Allenby conferred with the high officers of the fleet. Two new mine-laying cruisers were ordered to the China coast. Additional ships were transferred from the Mediterranean to Ceylon. Conversations took place between Sir John Simon and Mussolini regarding the use of the Italian fleet to protect British interests in the Mediterranean in case of trouble in the Far East. Night shifts were put to work to complete the base at Singapore. All night the tat-tat of automatic riveters rang through the Malay jungles; all night the flood lights played upon the bulwark with which the British were preparing to maintain their prestige in the fight against the yellow man.

What they were preparing to defend was a trade laboriously built through two centuries—a network of steamship lines traversing every navigable river in China; a system of railroads—the only lines functioning in the Eighteen Provinces; rich iron mines up the Yangtze; a piece-goods market at Shanghai which did a daily business of $1,000,000 gold in normal times; plus a lucrative trade in opium, a share in China's vast tobacco market, and control of the silk trade of Canton.

Four hundred million people constitute a market worth fighting for. And until the emergence of their energetic yellow competitors from Nippon, the British held undisputable sway as commercial middlemen of the Far East.

But now in the summer of 1934, Ambassador Matsudaira—urbane envoy to the Court of St. James's, dropped in at the Foreign Office for a talk about the Far East. And with his usual suavity he hinted that the day might come when resentment against the white race in China might make it expedient for the British to relinquish Hongkong, Gibraltar of the Orient and commercial clearing-house of South China. In such an emergency Japan would be glad to acquire it.

The hint was conveyed with all the finesse of Oriental diplomacy. But it was not lost upon the British.

Almost simultaneously the Japanese minister to the Netherlands dropped in at the Foreign Office in The Hague. And with the same delicate subtlety he hinted that the time might come when Japanese interests would require Sumatra and parts of the Dutch East Indies. No thought of conquest, he hastened to make clear; Japan would be delighted to pay the proper price.

No wonder, then, that as the American fleet prepared to desert the Pacific for review by President Roosevelt in New York, June, 1934, the British naval *attaché* in Washington called upon Admiral Stanley, Chief of Naval Operations, to suggest the expediency of leaving part of the American fleet in the Pacific.

"But where," asked Admiral Stanley, "was the British fleet when we needed it during the Manchurian troubles two years ago?"

Probably no keener student of naval strategy ever sat in

the White House than Franklin Roosevelt. The etchings of clipper ships, of early war vessels, which cover his walls are not mere hobby. His appointment as Assistant Secretary of the Navy was not pure chance. At the age of fourteen he was a devout student of Admiral Mahan, one of the driest but most profound writers on naval strategy. Reared on this reading, Roosevelt has become what is common in Great Britain but rare in this country—a genuine navalist. He believes that the United States exists through the strength of its fleet.

Motivated by this belief, he has not only kept every shipyard in the country working overtime, but shortly after he entered the White House adopted the identic policy toward the Japanese and British as the British in the past have adopted toward the United States and Japan.

British policy has been to play the two great powers of the Pacific off against each other. Just as she has endeavored to maintain the balance of power between Germany and France, so Britain has juggled the ambitions of the Japanese against the strength of the United States.

Mr. Roosevelt reversed this. Realizing all too well that the British stake in the Orient is infinitely greater than our own, remembering that whenever Japanese imperialism has gone on the rampage London has come running to the United States for help, recalling how many times the British have urged the United States not to withdraw from the Philippines, and knowing finally the dread fear of the British Dominions of Japanese conquest, Mr. Roosevelt decided to give the British a taste of their own policy. Henceforth they could act as the bulwark against yellow imperialism.

Simultaneously he turned toward Russia.

And the invitation to Maxim Litvinoff to visit Washington in November, 1933, was dictated almost entirely by conviction that Soviet Russia—then at odds with both

Britain and Japan—had exactly the same interests in the Far East as the United States.

But despite the reconciliation between Russia and the United States, despite the now all too obvious Roosevelt policy of aloofness in the Pacific, and despite the brazen effrontery of the Japanese in extending their grip upon China, the British continued their policy of silence.

The Dutch—always at the mercy of Japan in the Far East—had rushed into the British Foreign Office immediately after the hint of Japanese interest in the Dutch East Indies. And they had been given assurance of British support. Sumatra was a key factor in the defense of Australia and New Zealand, the British pointed out; under no circumstances could its rich oil resources fall into Japanese hands. But when a Japanese commercial mission accompanied by two warships arrived at Batavia in the summer of 1934 and proceeded to conduct negotiations for a new trade treaty with all the cocksureness of a conquering nation, the British did little or nothing about it.

The truth was that the British were too busy in Europe —and the Japanese knew it.

It is an axiom of Japanese policy that when Europe is absorbed with its own pain, Japan runs berserk in the Orient. It did so during the World War when it seized Shantung, invaded Siberia, and forced the Twenty-one Demands upon a prostrate China. It did so again during the war debt-disarmament dickering, when it seized Manchuria. And now with Europe tense over the fate of Austria, absorbed with the future of a leaderless Jugoslavia, harassed with the specter of a clash between France and Germany over the Saar, and fully cognizant of the bargain between Germany and Poland to annex the Ukraine, Japan knew that she was free to go berserk again.

Great Britain might issue diplomatic warnings until the cows came home, but Japanese admirals knew that she did not have enough ships to desert the precarious waters of the

Atlantic and Mediterranean to be half a match for Japan's modern, full-strength fleet in the Pacific.

War in Europe may come in any number of ways now. It may come almost immediately. It may not come for five years. But when it does come to Europe it will come also to the Far East.

It may come through the struggle over the Saar and its 8,400,000 annual tons of coal upon which French industry has become so dependent, but which Hitler has promised shall be returned to the people of Germany.

It may come through the invasion of the Russian Ukraine, where Germans and Poles claim many thousands of their countrymen await redemption from the Soviet.

It may come through the campaign of terrorism and assassination which already has taken the lives of Duca of Rumania, Dollfuss of Austria, Alexander of Jugoslavia, and Barthou of France—all, significantly, defenders of the Versailles Treaty and promoters of friendship with France.

It may come through the aftermaths of the assassination of King Alexander—through the bickering of Jugoslavia, Hungary and Italy.

It may come through Hitler's program of an economic Mittel Europa extending from the Baltic to the Black Sea —which, with Austria within his grasp, Jugoslavia more pro-German than French, and with Rumania strongly influenced by Belgrade, gives virtual realization to Bismarck's policy of *Drang nach Ostend* only sixteen years after the Allies thwarted it in 1918.

War will come.

In preparation for its coming Italy decreed military training for all youth over the age of eight. Poland declared women subject to conscription up to the age of forty-five. Switzerland erected new forts along the German border and increased her annual period of universal military service. Belgium ordered the modernization of her army and the erection of new bulwarks against Germany. The Netherlands multiplied their air forces. France authorized three new battleships and increased her army and air estimates. Italy ordered two new battleships and $100,-000,000 in new airplane construction. Britain voted forty-one new air squadrons, helped supply ten new squadrons to Egypt, and rushed work on air bases at Daiban, Colombo, Singapore and Port Darwin—the air route so vital to the defense of Australia. And finally the United States, casting off Stimsonian secrecy regarding the military importance of Alaska, publicly proclaimed the intention of establishing air bases in the Aleutian Islands, staged two spectacular flights of army and navy bombers to Nome, and began secret preparations for fortifying its islands in the Pacific.

During the height of these preparations winners of the Nobel Prizes gathered in New York to honor the hundredth anniversary of the birth of Alfred B. Nobel, founder of the awards. Frank B. Kellogg, speaking on that occasion, said:

"The nations' peoples have not forgotten nor will they forget the awful horror, misery, and beastliness of the last conflict."

Mr. Kellogg, unfortunately, was wrong.

Unfortunately, also, if the leaders of the nations' peoples had followed his psychology, he would have been right.

On the eve of June 28, 1914, there lurked in the hearts of the nations' peoples no desire for war. War was forced on them by the nations' rulers—proud of their war machines, ambitious for empire, thirsty for power. The assassination at Sarajevo was a signal which they seized.

This has now changed.

There followed the war to preserve democracy and after it the drive on the part of the leaders of the nations' peoples to convince them of the efficacy and necessity of war. Big armies and navies depended upon appropriations from democratic legislative bodies. Election to office sometimes depended upon stirring up the fear of an enemy. Hate and passion were more effective vote-getters than appeal to reason. Distrust and fear had powerful effect upon the alliances of Europe.

In France, the great munitions firm of Schneider sold machine-guns to the German Nazis through its subsidiary in Czechoslovakia; then used the plea of German rearmament to get larger armament appropriations from the Chambers of Deputies.

In Africa, France kept relatively insignificant difficulties with Italy constantly before the public eye, chiefly to strengthen her alliance with Jugoslavia.

In Germany, Hitler used the Versailles Treaty and France as a stepping-stone to power.

"Under my leadership," he proclaimed, "Germany will fight before she submits to the degradation suffered with such silence in the past."

In Italy, Mussolini rattled the saber against the eastern neighbor he had bottled up in the Adriatic and against the latter's powerful ally, France.

"Fascism," he declared not long after the Kellogg Pact was signed, "does not believe in the possibility of perpetual peace. Only war carries all humans to the height of tension and gives the seal of nobility to peoples that have the courage to enforce it."

And the nations' peoples believed. Fear, distrust, suspicion, hate, became seared into their minds—seared not only by the words of their leaders, the headlines of their government-inspired press, but by a depression which gave millions of unemployed time to ponder their own empty bellies and the reputed wealth of their neighbors.

They pondered and believed.

Even their leaders by now were powerless to change them.

In October, 1934, Benito Mussolini, Premier of Italy, having effected a new era of cordial relations with France, sought to apprise his people of the glad tidings. Standing before a crowd of 500,000 Fascists at Milan, he said:

"Relations with France have notably improved."

The vast throng roared with laughter.

It was too late. The seeds of war had been too deeply planted.

Supplementary

to

The American Diplomatic Game

by

Drew Pearson and Constantine Brown

PRINTED AT THE *Country Life Press*, GARDEN CITY, N. Y., U. S. A.

MUSSOLINI MOVES TO ABYSSINIA

A DESERT SUN shone down with midday fierceness on a body
of dust-covered Abyssinian troops in the late morning of
November 23, 1934. As an escort to the British-Abyssinian
Boundary Commission, headed by Lieutenant-Colonel E. H.
M. Clifford, Royal Engineers, they were assisting in a survey
of the border between Abyssinia and British Somaliland at
a point verging near Italian Somaliland.

Water is a precious thing in that part of Abyssinia, and the
700 soldiers of Emperor Haile Selassie felt new life surge into
their tired mules as they sniffed the waterholes of Walwal a
mile or so away. Arriving at the holes, they unslung their
red leather saddlebags and prepared to rest for several days.

Suddenly a detachment of native Italian troops appeared.
Captain Roberto Cimmaruta, in command, ordered the
Abyssinians to move on. The British, he said, could draw
water at Walwal, but not the Abyssinians. They were trespassing on Italian soil.

It happens that all standard maps place the Walwal wells
sixty miles on the Abyssinian side of the tentative boundary
between Abyssinia and Italian Somaliland. In fact, even
the 1933 map of the Italian Ministry of Colonies verifies
this, and caused untold Italian wrath when hung by League
of Nations officials in the press room at Geneva, where it was
almost immediately replaced by an Italian War Office map,
just off the press and showing Walwal within Italian territory.

Colonel Clifford, however, had only the British General
Staff map in his possession, and using this as his authority

3

he pointed out emphatically to Captain Cimmaruta not only that Italian troops were trespassing on Abyssinian soil, but that he, Cimmaruta, was "preventing by force" the execution of an international treaty. The Italian, however, remained obdurate. His 250 troops, he knew, were powerless against a force of 700 Abyssinians, so he withdrew them a few yards distant from the wells and waited for reinforcements. During the ensuing interval, however, Captain Cimmaruta conducted himself in a manner best described by Colonel Clifford, himself.

"The British Mission," Colonel Clifford reported, "made every effort to arrive at an equitable solution, but was constantly thwarted by the unconciliatory and disobliging attitude of the Italian officer, which may be judged by his remarks, several times repeated: 'Take it or leave it,' 'Just as you please,' and by the threat that in case of refusal he would send for 'several hundred soldiers.'"

Colonel Clifford also reported that two Italian planes flew "very low" over the British camp, training a machine gun on the British flag and members of the British commission. Immediately thereafter, Colonel Clifford "expressed to Captain Cimmaruta his great indignation at this provocative demonstration and announced that, in order not to complicate the situation for the Abyssinian Government, the British mission would retire to Ado."

This it did the next day, leaving the superior Abyssinian force free, if it desired, to clear Italian trespassers from Abyssinian soil.

The Abyssinian commander, however, did not take advantage of the British intimation. His men continued grazing their mules about the wells of Walwal, and about ten days later, at 3:30 on the afternoon of December 5th, were still "grazing their mules or in their tents" when Italian aircraft, supported by tanks, opened fire. At sundown, the Abyssinian forces withdrew, leaving behind 107 dead. Italian casualties totalled 130 wounded and thirty dead.

Two days later the news trickled across the desert down to Italian Somaliland and was flashed to Rome, where the Stefani official news agency issued the following communiqué:

A strong detachment of armed Ethiopians attacked on the afternoon of December 5 the isolated garrison at Walwal in the Italian Somaliland. The garrison resisted until reinforcements were brought up, when the attackers were heavily defeated.

In Addis Abeba, on the same day, the Italian Chargé d'Affaires presented a note to the Abyssinian Foreign Office, protesting against "this unexpected aggression" and stating that "on the 5th instant armed Abyssinians attacked our positions without warning and in force."

In the Palazzo Chiagi, Benito Mussolini pounded on his long desk.

"Italian honor must be avenged!" he bellowed. "We demand an immediate apology from Abyssinia and an adequate indemnity for the brave soldiers who gave their lives for the flag of Italy."

Long years of viewing news reels of Il Duce playing with his lion cubs, or at the wheel of his speedboat, or taking the salute of his Black Shirts, has left no doubt in the mind of the world that he is Europe's most consummate actor. But at no time in his spectacular career was Mussolini more the actor than when he berated Abyssinia for the alleged attack on Italian forces at Walwal.

That attack was as deliberately calculated as the historic skirmish of September 18, 1931, which gave Japan her excuse for seizing Manchuria.

There were, of course, certain differences between the start of Japan's rape of Manchuria and the start of Italy's conquest of Abyssinia. Japan did have, after all, a treaty right to station troops in Manchuria. She also had a treaty right to protect her nationals and property within certain areas in Manchuria. And she had a tremendous investment in mines, steel plants, hotels, banks, railroads, and warehouses throughout Manchuria.

But in the length and breadth of Abyssinia, Italy had nothing. Her treaty rights were nil. Her investments did not amount to a thin dime. Aside from her legation staff in Addis Abeba, there was not even a hurdy-gurdy grinder on Abyssinian soil whose protection could justify the dispatch of a Carabiniere.

Abyssinia represented just one thing—the only area in Africa which had not bowed before the white man. And an avaricious Italy, barren of raw materials, bursting with Mussolini's bonus-inspired babies, was determined to devour it.

All this Europe knew. All this was matter of semi-official record before the peacemakers at Geneva. Yet not one who had preached the righteousness of the League of Nations, who had hailed the triumph of the Kellogg Pact, who had advocated more and better Locarnos, lifted either voice or finger in defense of the one remaining independent government of Africa. Captain Anthony Eden, ardent British mendicant for the cause of peace, filled his pipe and declined to be worried by the Abyssinian delegate in Geneva. Édouard Beneš, Czechoslovakia's persistent pacifier, declared there were bigger interests at stake than the mere independence of Abyssinia. Even Maxim Litvinoff, who every year had piqued his Geneva colleagues by demanding complete and unequivocal disarmament, turned his back on Abyssinia.

Four years previously, Geneva had heard the representatives of at least some nations denounce the rape of Manchuria. It had watched the outraged idealism of Henry L. Stimson attempt an almost universal though futile mobilization of public opinion against Japan. It had seen the Council of the League of Nations at least go on record in opposition to Japanese invasion.

But now, faced with much more brazen evidence of armed encroachment, Geneva did not lift a finger.

Such was the transformation of the war mentality of Europe between 1932 and 1935. The hopes for peace, the reliance upon the machinery of the League of Nations, the idealism regarding the rights of lesser nations—all had vanished.

Whatever may have been the reaction of the rest of the world to Italian ambition for the conquest of his country, there was at least one individual who took the news with a reasonable degree of complacency. He was Haile Selassie, "Anointed of God, Emperor of Ethiopia, King of Kings, Conquering Lion of the Tribe of Judah, Light of the World, Descendant of Solomon, Protector of the Faith and Ruler of the Universe."

The Emperor was one who had been so busy most of his life keeping together a kingdom which was no more loyal than it had to be and not overly fond of paying taxes, that another war, more or less, did not at first greatly worry him. His wars began in 1916, shortly after German agents persuaded his cousin, Emperor Lij-Yasu, to embrace the Islamic faith, thereby qualifying himself to join the Turks in waging war against the British. Against this there were violent repercussions throughout the kingdom. The Abyssinian Church is the oldest unreformed Christian church in the world, and a deeply rooted desire on the part of its people to keep it so soon caused the Emperor to find himself without a throne. Whereupon that seat of power became the object of a long and acrimonious feud between Queen Zauditu, daughter of the great Emperor Menelik, and his cousin Ras Tafari, now Emperor Haile Selassie.

Purity of blood is an important thing in Abyssinia. Both Zauditu and Ras Tafari could claim an undiluted blood stream dating back to the night three thousand years before when Makeda, Queen of Sheba, inveigled King Solomon the

Wise to become the father of her son, Menelik I. That blood stream, Ras Tafari claimed, must not be diluted. So he decreed that Empress Zauditu must be separated from her last husband, Ras Gucksa, in order that there might be no issue. A son of Zauditu, of course, presented serious obstacles to Tafari's ascension to the throne.

The Empress Zauditu, however, was a lady both of passion and ambition. Ras Gucksa was her fourth husband, and she had not married him with the prospect of an enforced separation. Therefore she objected violently, and her objections became more vehement as she watched her cousin daily increase his grip over the empire. One day while he was paying a dutiful visit to her palace, Ras Tafari suddenly found himself a prisoner and was kept there until his wife ordered out a tank, gift of the Duke of Abruzzi during a visit to Abyssinia, with which the Empress's gates were battered down.

After this, Zauditu had to consent to Tafari's being crowned King of Shoa, most important province of Abyssinia. But as his power increased, jealousy smouldered stronger in the breast of her husband, Ras Gucksa, until finally he raised a rebel army and began a march on the capital.

This was in 1930. France and Italy at that time were scarcely bothering to conceal a bitter rivalry in the Mediterranean, along the shores of North Africa, and particularly for power and prestige in Abyssinia. Italy, anxious to have anyone on the throne save Ras Tafari and regretful that the tank donated by the Duke of Abruzzi once had rescued him, bet its money and a consignment of machine guns on Ras Gucksa.

France, on the other hand, sent three airplanes under the command of André Maillet to back the Prince Regent. Airplane-bombing had not reached the degree of efficiency it has today, but even so, it won the day. Perhaps because the Frenchmen were aided by the scarlet tunics and plumed headdresses of the enemy, they accomplished almost the impossible—a direct hit. Ras Gucksa, husband of the Empress, contender to the throne, dropped where he stood, the most ignominious of all Abyssinian deaths. He had no opportunity even to lift a spear. And, as if to give comic relief to the tragedy, his demise occurred on April Fool's Day. Surely the Lord God Jehovah was guiding the destinies of Ras Tafari.

And to bring further confusion to his enemies, Empress Zauditu died two days later. The alleged cause was pneumonia. Some Abyssinians saw behind this the hand of Jehovah. Europeans suspected Ras Tafari had pushed Jehovah's hand a little. At any rate, she was dead.

Ras Tafari was a devout believer in the philosophy that in the end right reigns triumphant. Nevertheless his early youth in a French mission school had made him susceptible also to the theory that Jehovah helps those who help themselves. This theory he expounded to Constantine Brown during a trip he took during the early days of his regency for the purpose of keeping his empire abreast of the world. With him on this tour he took eight Rases, most powerful of his provincial rulers, who suffered excruciating pain at the necessity of wearing shoes in the dining room of Shepheard's Hotel in Cairo. Only the occasional possibility of slipping their shoes off under the table deterred them from open rebellion against their chief, who dined in state in his suite upstairs, barefoot.

"These men are able, faithful souls," said Ras Tafari, explaining why he had brought such a retinue. "But their minds follow simple fundamentals. I am merely regent of my country now, and it is possible that during my absence one of them might conceive the idea of replacing me. I did not wish anyone to lose his head as a result of such a brainstorm, so I brought my Rases with me. It is safer for them and safer for me.

"Furthermore, if they see all the things that I shall see in

France and Great Britain, they will be less reluctant to adopt the reforms which I have in store for Abyssinia when I return."

Thus did Ras Tafari tour Europe.

It was a triumphal march. His royal colleague, George V of England, set forth his most sumptuous entertainment. President Doumergue of France did likewise. The latter did not mention the mineral wealth of Abyssinia. The former did not mention Lake Tsana, famous natural reservoir in the Abyssinian mountains which feeds the Blue Nile and the cotton fields of the British Sudan. Nor did either mention Italian ambitions in Eastern Abyssinia along the borders of Eritrea and Somaliland.

They did not need to. Ras Tafari had a Western sophistication far superior to his dusky-skinned colleagues from Siam, Arabia, and Afghanistan, who had been wined and dined by the crowned heads of Europe. He had, furthermore, the experience of his elder cousin Emperor Menelik to guide him.

Ras Tafari came into the world during the height of those turbulent years when Menelik was discovering what it meant to have avaricious Europe as a neighbor. Italy, arriving late in the scramble for Africa, had sent an expedition to the Turkish Sudan in 1885 and sliced off what is now Eritrea. Robbing the Turk at that time was one of Europe's most popular sports, and the British Agent in that area applauded. France and Russia, however, did not.

And, although the Italians had purchased peace with Menelik for the price of $800,000, he could not resist the tributes to his prowess whispered in his ear by French and Russian agents. And when they supported their praise with a consignment of old-fashioned rifles, Menelik looked the other way while Ras Makennen, his most powerful prince, and father of Ras Tafari, marched upon the Italians. The enemy—only 2,000 strong—was annihilated. In Rome, vast crowds surged around the Royal Palace demanding vengeance.

Most vociferous demander of vengeance was General Francisco Baratieri, Minister of War, who got as a reward for his enthusiasm command of the Italian expeditionary force to Abyssinia. General Baratieri had a color complex similar to that of Pat Harrison, senior Senator from Mississippi. To him Negro troops were fit only to clean stables. Landing at Massawa, where Italian Eritrea comes down to meet the Red Sea, Baratieri threw all his men into battle against an Abyssinian army which lay hidden in an unmapped chain of mountains.

Again Italy suffered a stinging defeat. Half of Baratieri's proud army was left lying on the battlefield. Almost a second half was marched over scorching deserts to Addis Abeba to be ransomed by the Italian Government eighteen months later.

It cost Italy a pretty penny, and was the most ignominious defeat she ever suffered. The crowds in Rome, which once had shouted for war on Abyssinia, now shook angry fists at the Crispi Government, forcibly prevented the departure of reinforcements, and demanded "Abbasso Africa!"

Six months later—October 26, 1896—Italy signed a peace treaty with Menelik recognizing him as sovereign of the independent state of Abyssinia.

Menelik's peace of mind, however, was not to last long. His empire was too rich, Europe's struggle for new territory too keen. By 1906, France, Great Britain, and Italy realized that in unity there is strength, and signed a tripartite agreement to help each other help themselves to the economic advantages of Menelik's rich domain. They agreed that:

1. France, Great Britain, and Italy shall coöperate to maintain the political and territorial *status quo* of Abyssinia;

2. In regard to demands for agricultural, commercial, and industrial concessions in Abyssinia, the three powers undertake to act in such way that concessions accorded to one of the three states shall not be injurious to the interests of the others.

3. France, Great Britain, and Italy shall make every effort
to preserve Abyssinia's independence against any nation
endeavoring to disturb the *status quo*.

The agreement was concluded without advance consultation with Menelik. After it was blotted, stamped, and
sealed, however, they sent him a copy. Six months of dignified
delay—then the grizzled monarch addressed the following to
the French, British, and Italian Governments:

We have received the agreement made by the three powers.
We thank them for their communication and their desire to
maintain the independence of our government. But let it be
understood that this arrangement in no way limits what we
consider our sovereign rights.

For thirteen years thereafter the people of Abyssinia were
free to pasture their flocks, till their fields, steal each other's
wives, and wage their own tribal wars for the most part
untrammeled by the ambitions of their more civilized neighbors. Those neighbors were then engaged in preparing for
and waging the most uncivilized war in the history of
civilization, and Abyssinia for the most part was forgotten.
Only for one brief moment in 1915, when France and Britain
were endeavoring to tempt Italy into the conflict, did her
long-coveted wealth enter the picture. In the Treaty of
London, it was agreed that, to balance the acquisition of
German colonial possessions by France and Britain, Italy
had a right to demand compensation at the expense of the
"colonial areas adjoining the British and French colonies."
This, Italy maintained at the Paris Peace Conference,
referred to Abyssinia. France argued to the contrary, with
the result that the tripartite agreement signed in 1906 went
aglimmering and with it evaporated Abyssinia's chance of
peace. From that moment, the mountain fastness of equa-
torial North Africa became a pawn in the poorly concealed
struggle between France and Italy. In this struggle, as far

as Abyssinia was concerned, the British sided with Rome. They had their eyes on one thing which they could get in no other part of North Africa—water for the cotton fields of Egypt and the Sudan. For the giant reservoir of Lake Tsana, feeding the turbulent Blue Nile, can be regulated so as to fill the irrigation ditches of the Sudan all the year round, thus giving Lancashire mills a steady British-grown supply of long staple cotton.

So, shrouded with the utmost secrecy, Sir Ronald Graham, His Britannic Majesty's Ambassador at Rome, requested of Mussolini "support and assistance at Addis Abeba, in order to obtain from the Abyssinian Government a concession for His Majesty's Government to construct a barrage at Lake Tsana . . ."

In return Sir Ronald promised equal support to the Italian Government in securing "an exclusive Italian influence in the west of Abyssinia," and the right to build a railway through Abyssinia joining the two adjacent colonies of Eritrea and Italian Somaliland. Since the railroad passed through barren desert, economically valueless, its purpose could be only strategic. It was interpreted as a step toward subsequent Italian encroachment upon the wealthier areas to the southeast.

This deal was consummated on December 20, 1925. But by June of the following year the French, always jealous of Italian expansion in North Africa, had smelled out the documents and advised their friend and ally, Prince Regent Ras Tafari, to appeal to the League of Nations.

By this time, Abyssinia had become a full-fledged member of the League and was proud of it. As a matter of fact, it was a considerable job for her to get in, chiefly because the Italians and British, recognizing the dampening effect which Geneva might have upon their Abyssinian ambitions, had raised heaven and earth to keep her out. Abyssinia, they claimed, was slave-ridden and unfit to be a member of the family of nations.

Once a member, however, Ras Tafari did exactly what the British and Italians had feared. He used the League as a sounding board with which to broadcast Anglo-Italian avariciousness to the world:

> On our admission to the League of Nations [he notified each of its members], we were told that all nations were to be on an equal footing, and that their independence was to be universally respected, since the purpose of the League is to establish and maintain peace among men in accordance with the Will of God.
>
> We were not told that certain members of the League might make a separate agreement to impose their views on another member, even if the latter considered those views incompatible with its national interests. . . .
>
> The people of Abyssinia are anxious to do right, but throughout their national history they have seldom met with foreigners who did not desire to possess themselves of Abyssinian territory, and to destroy their independence. With God's help and thanks to the courage of our soldiers, we have always, come what might, stood proud and free upon our native mountains.
>
> It must not be forgotten that we have only recently been introduced to modern civilization, and that our history, glorious though it be, had not yet prepared us for ready readjustment to conditions which are often quite beyond the range of our experience. Nature herself has never gone forward by sudden bounds, and no country has been metamorphosed in a night.
>
> With our well-known eagerness for progress—given time and the friendly advice of countries whose geographical position has enabled them to outdistance us in the race—we shall be able to secure gradual but continual improvements which will make Abyssinia great in the future, as she has been in the past. But if we try to go too fast, accidents may happen.
>
> We should like to hear from the members of the League whether they think it right that means of pressure should be exerted upon us which they themselves would doubtless never accept.

This note, together with some clever diplomatic footwork by Ras Tafari in playing the United States against Great Britain, and France against Italy, postponed the present attack on his homeland for exactly ten years.

The immediate effect of the note was to force Great Britain and Italy into the open.

Caught red-handed, Italy and Great Britain filed their notes with the League of Nations and naïvely expressed the hope that the "Abyssinian Government will find them acceptable." From that point, their immediate dreams of economic conquest on the plateaus of Abyssinia evaporated like the mists over Lake Tsana. The peace machinery of the League was too well oiled at that time, the wrath of outraged public opinion too potent. Furthermore Abyssinia at that time had the backing of France, and France was in the throes of an economic, naval, and colonial rivalry with Italy which was to cause such heartburn to Henry L. Stimson's ambitions for naval disarmament.

Italy, therefore, could do nothing except pigeonhole her secret agreement and wait—which she did. She did so, however, with scant good grace. Italy was still hungering for Abyssinia. It was the only spot in the world where her bulging population, increased by Mussolini's tax on bachelors and his bonus on babies, could expand into new territory.

When Ras Tafari made his pilgrimage to Europe shortly after the beginning of his regency, there was only one important country which did not send him an enthusiastic invitation. The Abyssinian ruler did not know then—perhaps does not even know now—that the apparent lack of hospitality on the part of President Coolidge was due entirely to the fact that public opinion below the Mason-Dixon Line would have rebelled at the idea of a gentleman of color being entertained in the White House. Not even had Ras Tafari occupied the bed built for that great emancipator, Abraham Lincoln, and then used by Mrs. Coolidge in the White House guest room, would Mrs. Coolidge's cautious husband have risked a call by Ras Tafari.

Ras Tafari, though he did not appreciate these political delicacies, did appreciate the fact that the United States was the only government in the world of white and avaricious nations lying beyond his mountains, which nursed absolutely no political or economic ambitions toward Abyssinia and at the same time was powerful enough to disregard the jealousies of Europe. To Washington, therefore, Ras Tafari dispatched Dr. Waldo Martin, a native Abyssinian educated in England and long a member of the Indian Civil Service.

Through this less hazardous channel Mr. Coolidge got to know something of his would-be guest and the key position he held in regard to the peace of Europe.

Dr. Martin's pilgrimage took place in 1927, just a few months after the Anglo-Italian plot had been unearthed, and in the very year that the British Empire was openly challenging the predominance of American trade in South America and the predominance of American politics in that most sacred of all areas—Central America and the Panama Canal. Dr. Martin's visit, therefore, was not unwelcome. It was not, of course, the triumphal procession which might have attended the arrival of his chief, the Prince Regent. In fact, it is probable that only an infinitesimal section of the United States, not even including the New York ship reporters, realized that an envoy of the future Emperor of Abyssinia was in the U. S. A. for the purpose of getting American support to combat the greed of Europe.

When Dr. Martin left, however, he had two trump cards in his hand. He had secured from the State Department the promise to send an American Minister to Addis Abeba, despite the fact that both the House and Senate Appropriations Committees had ruled that the $10,000 salary to be paid a Minister was an extravagance not compatible with Coolidge economy. And he had secured from the J. G. White engineering firm a tentative agreement to survey and construct the long-debated dam at the mouth of Lake Tsana.

Both of these were triumphs far greater than anyone outside the foreign offices of Europe realized.

An American Minister at the Court of the Emperor of Abyssinia hitherto was almost unheard of. Only twice, for very brief intervals, had the United States sent a representative there. Abyssinia was earmarked as within the British-African sphere of influence, and Americans who chose to do business there were referred by the State Department to the British Legation. Nearest American Consulate was at the desert port of Aden across the Red Sea. The establishment of an American Legation in Addis Abeba, therefore, was considered a direct move to counteract British influence in an area where British influence was supposed to be supreme.

Much more of a move against the British, however, was the J. G. White Company's contract for the dam at Lake Tsana. This was denounced as a blow aimed at the heart of Britain's African empire. The London press howled in protest. The Foreign Office called Ras Tafari's attention to the treaty of 1902, in which his cousin, Menelik, promised that no dam should be built at Lake Tsana without the consent and coöperation of the British. A spokesman for the Foreign Office emphasized this to the press:

"It is the intention of the British Government to have no nation except Great Britain herself build a dam across the Blue Nile," he said. "It is axiomatic that Egypt depends upon the waters of the Nile for her very existence. The Nile likewise is a vital factor in the prosperity of the Sudan. Great Britain is recognized the world over as having the preponderating interest in those countries both on account of the importance of Egyptian and Sudanese cotton to Lancashire mills and the indispensability of the Suez Canal highway to those parts of the British Empire in the Orient. Abyssinia agreed thirty years ago that the British Government shall build the canal and the British Government intends to build it."

Nevertheless Ras Tafari proceeded with his plans for closer American coöperation, and the State Department, overjoyed at British discomfiture, proceeded to meet him more than half way.

From the J. G. White Company offices came the statement that it intended to push the work and expected no diplomatic difficulties. From the State Department came word that Everett A. Colson, former Receiver General of Haiti, had been appointed financial adviser to Abyssinia. From the State Department also came news that E. F. Work, a cousin of Mr. Coolidge's Secretary of the Interior, had accepted appointment as Ras Tafari's adviser, to revise the educational system of Abyssinia. Finally, from the White House came the appointment of Herman Murray Jacoby, New York banker, as special ambassador of President Hoover to represent him at the coronation of Tafari as Emperor of Abyssinia.

This was an occasion at which the crowned heads of Europe vied with each other to court Abyssinian favor. King George, who so ardently cherished the dam at Lake Tsana, sent his royal son, the Duke of Gloucester, plus a Marine Band clad in bright red, plus a coronation cake weighing one ton, which was transported across the arid deserts and perilous highlands of Abyssinia without serious mishap, save for the mental anguish of the chef. King Victor Emmanuel of Italy, who so ardently cherished the lowlands of Abyssinia and the right to build a railroad through them, sent as his emissary the Prince of Udine plus 500 bottles of Chianti. President Doumergue, who so ardently desired that neither Italy nor Britain should get a foothold in Abyssinia, sent that illustrious soldier, Marshal Franchet d'Esperey, together with an airplane especially equipped for the Emperor's personal use.

President Hoover, in turn, sent only a German-American banker, who had become a naturalized citizen only in 1920, accompanied by Charles Lee Cooke, whose many years of State Department service in advising Washington dowagers who should sit where entitled him to a vacation. As the coronation gift of the President of the United States to Haile Selassie, King of Kings, Conquering Lion of the Tribe of Judah, Emperor of Ethiopia, this delegation carried an autographed photograph of Herbert Hoover. This present was guarded by Mr. Cooke to the exclusion of all else, with the result that his pocket was picked to the tune of $300. And when finally it arrived in Addis Abeba it was appreciated by its recipient perhaps more than the coronation cake and the wine and the specially bedecked airplane which His Majesty knew had certain definite motives behind them. He also appreciated the unofficial presents sent by American commercial houses—an electrical refrigerator, the rose bushes, and the films of *Ben Hur* and Byrd's Antarctic Expedition, even though no motion-picture machine existed in Addis Abeba with which to show them.

And His Majesty, being something of a salesman, and appreciating the friendship of the most powerful and politically platonic country in the world, went to some pains from that time on to keep his contacts warm. He sent back to the President of the United States by his son-in-law an autographed photograph of himself, and having heard that Bishop James E. Freeman, of the Protestant Episcopal Diocese of Washington, had offered a prayer in his behalf, Haile Selassie sent the Bishop a gold-encased Bible, done in the original Coptic script, depicting Christ and His disciples as Negroes, and bearing the inscription:

"HAILESELASSIE I EMPEROR
OF ETHIOPIA HAS PRES
ENTED TO WASHINGTO
N CATHEDRAL 1930."

Accompanying the Holy Book was a note which read:

May peace be unto your Beatitude.

Our heart was touched with joy and appreciation when His Excellency, the American Minister, told us of the prayer you had made for us on the day we were crowned with the imperial crown, by the Will of God.

Just as the Lord Jesus Christ gave His grace to all that believed in Him, both near and far, without distinction, likewise you, without distinction as to country and sovereign, made a prayer equally for a Christian king and country, thus proving that you are true followers of Christ.

We request you not to forget us and our country of Ethiopia in your spiritual prayers.

Emperor Haile Selassie did not realize it at the time, but he was going to need the Bishop's prayers.

From a juridical point of view, they should not have been at all necessary. His Majesty and his country were protected by almost every form of treaty devised by international jurists for the maintenance of harmony between nations. Shortly before he became Emperor he had signed with Italy a solemn pact, providing that under no circumstances should either country take action which might be harmful to the other's independence. Both governments, furthermore, pledged themselves to arbitrate all differences which might arise between them. In no case were they to resort to arms.

There were many other treaties also guaranteeing Abyssinian independence and sovereignty. There was the pact of 1896 between Great Britain, Italy, and France. There was the similar treaty signed in 1906. And, finally, there was the Kellogg Pact which outlawed war forever, to say nothing of the Covenant of the League of Nations, of which Abyssinia was now a full-fledged member.

Imagine the surprise of Haile Selassie, therefore, when, a few days after the skirmish at Walwal, the Italian Chargé d'Affaires at Addis Abeba presented him with a note not at all unlike the fatal document which Austria-Hungary handed to Serbia on the eve of the World War twenty years before.

It stated that there could be no doubt that Walwal belonged to Italy; that the conduct of the high-handed Captain Cimmaruta was beyond reproach; that the Abyssinians had taken the initiative in the attack; and, finally, that Abyssinia must tender the following apologies and retribution:

1. Abyssinian troops to render honors to the Italian flag.
2. A payment of 200,000 thalers ($45,500) as compensation for Italian casualties.
3. Punishment and dismissal of all officers "responsible" for the "attack" on Italian troops.

Haile Selassie, much as he had learned from his contacts with the outside world, still retained what now may appear to be a naïve belief in existing treaties. He replied that he would be glad to arbitrate the Italian request under Article 5 of the treaty of 1928.

There followed more exchanges of this kind, Mussolini categorically insisting that "responsibility for the attack rested exclusively with the Abyssinian forces," and refusing to arbitrate a question involving Italy's national honor.

Dogmatic and vituperative as his notes were, however, they did not put him too far out on a limb until he could be absolutely certain of the attitude of France. That country had been the traditional patron of Abyssinia ever since the days when Emperor Menelik marched nearly a thousand Italian prisoners through the streets of Addis Abeba. And, although a new rapprochement between Italy and France was at that very moment under discussion, Mussolini did not want to go too far until he had complete French consent.

He waited, therefore, until Pierre Laval, Foreign Minister of France, arrived in Rome to consummate the marriage of the Mediterranean.

This was an object which Henry L. Stimson had devoutly wished. For more than three months at the London Naval

Conference he had struggled to bring France and Italy together. For an even longer period after the Conference adjourned he had attempted, by long-distance telephone, by personal pilgrimage, and by the loan of his most trusted emissary, Dwight Morrow, to bring the two countries together.

But Stimson lacked the inducement which now existed in the winter of 1935—a powerful, potential enemy. Both France and Italy feared the overflow of a now fully armed and economically discontented Germany. And France, fearing Germany, was willing to give in order to gain Italian support.

The diplomacy of Pierre Laval, therefore, was crowned with success. Four years before, he had visited the United States and returned empty-handed. Beyond the charm of his vivacious daughter, Josette, and the quaint philosophy he exuded to the press, he had nothing to offer the parsimonious and hard-headed Herbert Hoover.

But in Rome four years later it was different. M. Laval was now in a position to give. What he gave was:

> 400,000 square miles of French Somaliland immediately opposite Aden, and from which Italy could command the bottle-neck of the Red Sea.
>
> Italian participation in the narrow-gauge railroad stretching from the French port of Djibuti to Addis Abeba—the only rail line penetrating Abyssinia.
>
> And, most important of all, he gave Mussolini the blessing and benediction of France in any move Italy might make against that proud and independent African Empire.

In return for this, M. Laval got the finest hospitality Rome could offer, the Grand Order of the Cross of Biano from the Pope, a papal rosary for Josette, a united stand against German annexation of Austria, and, last but not least, an Italian pledge of support in case of aggression by Germany.

Haile Selassie now had just cause to be nervous.

Not only was his one access to the sea in the partial control of an unfriendly power, but his chief supporter in Western Europe had gone over to the enemy. So the Emperor, fed up with the diplomatic dickerings of Mussolini and still believing in the prestige and power of kings, addressed a personal letter to his royal colleague, Victor Emmanuel of Italy.

Victor Emmanuel once had sent his royal son and 500 bottles of Chianti as a coronation present to the Emperor of Abyssinia. Whether or not he remembered this or, whether he still retained any notions about the divine right of kings, Victor was too well trained a monarch to say. He merely sent the letter to the real ruler of Italy with a penciled notation on the margin: "What do you think of it?"

There was already ample evidence as to what Mussolini thought of it. Shortly after M. Laval departed for France on January 8th, there was a shake-up in the Italian Cabinet. Emilio di Bono resigned as Minister of War and Il Duce added this portfolio to his others. Di Bono, however, was a sensitive individual and did not like to have it thought that he had left the Cabinet because of any inadequacy on his part, or any quarrel with the leader of Fascist Italy. So at the café tables before he departed, he passed out the word that he was leaving for an important mission in Africa and the world soon would hear important news.

It did. Even before Emperor Haile Selassie could formally lodge an appeal with the League of Nations, reserve officers in northern Italy received notice of mobilization, Italian aircraft factories received rush orders for new planes, and troops in Milan had orders to be prepared for an emergency.

Meanwhile, and as his last resort, Emperor Haile Selassie prepared to invoke the lofty idealism of the brotherhood of nations.

The steering committee of that brotherhood—formally known as the Council of the League of Nations—was scheduled to meet on January 18th, and one day before that date, Tecle-Hawariate, Abyssinian delegate at Geneva, filed formal notice that he would present the case of his country before the Council. In substantiation of that case, he presented a documentary review of the Walwal incident and its aftermath. Many countries have put their cases before the League of Nations in the past, but those who sit around the Council table never had known of a case more dispassionately prepared and obviously correct than that of Abyssinia. What made the case doubly convincing was the affidavit of the neutral British observer, Colonel Clifford.

There was no question in the minds of Italy's chief allies—France and Great Britain—that Abyssinia was in the right. But this made it all the more urgent to avoid a public airing of the dispute before 200 newspaper correspondents in the open forum of the Council. Such an airing would have meant not only a further weakening of Geneva's prestige, but also the public refusal of Premier Mussolini to discuss the question.

Both Geneva's prestige and Mussolini's face must at all costs be preserved, and to this end Hawariate was summoned to the hotel of Captain Anthony Eden. There he found awaiting him not only Britain's youthful Lord Privy Seal, but also M. Laval. The latter was all too frank in saying that there was nothing he could do about the Italo-Abyssinian conflict. His recent visit to Rome and the new agreement between France and Italy placed him in a prejudiced position. But, Laval added, there was no reason for anyone to question the impartiality of Captain Eden.

Eden accepted this suggestion and said he would be delighted to see Baron Pompeo Aloisi, Italian delegate, in order to arrange for immediate direct negotiations between the two countries. On the strength of this pledge, Hawariate agreed to postpone placing his case formally before the Council of the League of Nations.

Next day the Abyssinian once again was summoned to the hotel of Captain Eden. The Britisher was all smiles. Baron Aloisi, he said, had been extremely reasonable. He was quite prepared to meet the Abyssinians in every possible way in order to close the unfortunate incident. All he desired was

that Abyssinian troops should salute the Italian flag and pay
$45,500 for the families of the troops killed in action.

Tecle-Hawariate has had almost as much experience with
European diplomacy as his cynical chief in Addis Abeba,
but the proposition of the debonair Eden made him blanch
grey under his dark skin.

"That," he flung back, "is no compromise. That is merely
a reiteration of the Italian demands which already have
caused us to take this question to the League."

Then, recovering his poise and realizing that he had been
maneuvered into a difficult position, he proposed that both
sides declare the Walwal affair a mere border incident and
both pay an indemnity for those killed and wounded.

Italy, of course, emphatically vetoed this proposal.

Then Hawariate decided to play his trump card.

"Very well," he informed Eden, "the Italians are adamant.
Then tomorrow I submit our case to the Council."

"But you cannot," interposed the Lord Privy Seal with one
of his blandest smiles. "It is provided that no dispute can be
submitted to the Council when direct negotiations are in
progress."

"But they have broken down."

"That is a statement by you which I will not admit before
the Council," replied Eden, filling his pipe.

Hawariate had only one friend in Geneva. He was Dr.
Pitman Potter, an American professor at the Université des
Hautes Études Internationales in Geneva, who acted as
official Abyssinian adviser. He advised that Hawariate take
a private poll of members of the Council in order to see what
chance he had in case he decided to push his case regardless
of the British.

First he called upon Édouard Beneš of Czechoslovakia,
famous champion of the League of Nations and advocate of
justice for small nations. Scores of times during his long
career in Geneva, Benes had taken the floor to champion the
cause of downtrodden peoples. But now he was cool.

"It would be unwise," he said, "for Abyssinia to upset the present important work of the Council. There are larger European considerations involved."

M. Beneš did not specify what these "larger considerations" were, but he did not need to. Hawariate knew he meant the new Franco-Italian rapprochement against Germany.

Hawariate next approached Maxim Litvinoff. Even more ardently than Beneš, the Soviet Foreign Minister had fought the cause of equality among peoples. By the smaller nations he was considered their sincerest champion of peace and equity. To Hawariate's plea he listened carefully. Two days passed before he gave an answer. But when it came the answer, like all the others, was negative.

There remained chiefly Latin-American nations and Spain. To the Argentine, Chilean, and Mexican members Hawariate gave his most eloquent plea.

"You also are weaker countries," he said. "You also may suffer at the hands of a powerful neighbor. You have a vital interest in this dispute. For, if Italy gets away with this, it will be only a forerunner of what will happen to you."

But the South Americans replied that they were too busy attempting to conciliate war in the Chaco. The truth was that any meddling in the embroglio of Europe was the last thing they wanted to do.

Señor Madariaga of Spain was next in line. He would have liked nothing better than to champion the lost cause of Abyssinia, but only a few weeks before his government had warned him that he had been fighting too many lost causes. Sorrowfully Madariaga informed the Abyssinian delegate that Spain could do nothing.

One last member of the League Council remained from whom Hawariate thought he might get a favorable response. It was Denmark. Denmark, he knew, had consistently raised its voice in Council sessions for peace and the rights of small nations. If Abyssinia could only get one champion at Geneva, her cause was not lost.

So Hawariate approached the Danish delegate. He almost fainted with fright.

There was nothing much for Hawariate to do after that, except report back to his American friend, Professor Potter. But as a last resort Hawariate made a special plea to Prentiss Gilbert, American consul, that the United States exert its great prestige and power in behalf of his country.

"With eleven million Negroes in America," he said, "you cannot afford to ignore the one independent Negro government remaining in the world.

"What," he continued, "would the Negroes of Harlem say if you stood by and let Italy vanquish their brethren in Abyssinia?"

"What they would say," replied Mr. Gilbert, "could only be equaled by what the residents of Little Italy would say, should we follow your suggestion."

Many things have happened during the clash between Italy and Abyssinia since then—many things which have made France and Britain regret the carte blanche given to their new ally against Adolf Hitler.

But Mussolini has marched on.

Division after division was mobilized and sent to Africa. Even reserve regiments of Fascist Militia, the crack Division of March Twenty-third and the Division of October Twenty-eighth, commemorating famous days in Black Shirt history, have been called from peace-time tasks and placed on a war footing. Vessels loaded with war materials sent from Bari and Brindisi clutter the harbor of Massawa in the Red Sea. Native labor, working day and night, struggle to unload them. Even white labor, imported from Italy, has proved inadequate. One German freighter, tired of paying harbor dues, dumped her cargo of Italian purchased lumber in the water and departed to escape further payments.

Drilling on the hot sands of Eritrea and Somaliland, Italian troops grumbled, sometimes collapsed. Their water allowance, reduced to two bottles a day, was alive with insects. Imported mineral water purchased from native merchants cost one dollar a bottle.

Still the troop concentration continued. Monsoon winds off the almost harborless coast of Africa made that concentration necessary months before the rainy season, months before any campaign is possible.

In Rome, meanwhile, Mussolini addressed notes of protest to countries selling arms to Abyssinia. His Under-Secretary for Colonies, Alessandro Lesstna, publicly accused Abyssinia of the exploitation of subject races. Corrado Zoli, former Governor of Italian colonies in Africa, publicly explained the necessity for further troop concentration on the Abyssinian border.

"The Abyssinian state of mind," officially reported Mussolini's Ministry of Foreign Affairs, "has not changed. Their most irreconcilable and irresponsible circles continue to regard us as most undesirable neighbors."

Mussolini, meanwhile, continued to demonstrate his own policy of neighborliness. Two thousand Assai Imarras, nominally under the rule of Emperor Haile Selassie but actually as independent as any other African tribe, attacked a band of Nomads on the border of French Somaliland. This time, not the Italians but the French were involved. And Albert Julien Bernard, a French District Officer in command of 120 native troops armed with machine guns, went to the aid of his wards. Bernard and 96 of his men were killed.

The French Ministry of Colonies, accustomed to such incidents, made no representations at Addis Abeba. The incident was chalked up as just another border clash, to be regretted but difficult to be avoided. Bernard was given the Legion of Honor posthumously, received a citation from the Colonial Office, and Louis Rollin, Minister of Colonies, announced that the Abyssinian authorities could not be blamed for the incident.

But suddenly Italy objected. The Italian press flamed with

indignation. Mussolini's ambassador in Paris called at the Quai d'Orsay. France, he hinted, was not playing the game. It must not take such slight notice of aggression by Abyssinia.

Reluctantly the French Government reversed itself. An official demand was made of Emperor Haile Selassie that he pay an indemnity of $5,000 for the life of Albert Julien Bernard. And Haile Selassie, badgered from all sides, paid the bill.

Thus was played the great game of diplomacy in Africa.

This part of the game was played in the months of January, February, and March, 1935. By April and May, however, Franco-British worry had intensified to a point only equaled by the intensification of Il Duce's troops along the borders of Abyssinia. Captain Anthony Eden, who once played Italy's hand at Geneva, now had occasion to caution Mussolini's diplomats. Pierre Laval, who sat complacent while Italy first began pushing her demands against Abyssinia, did the same. What they both emphasized was that the line-up in Europe had changed. Overnight, Hitler had renounced the armament limitations in the Versailles Treaty, Germany had emerged with an army as large as the French, an air force larger than Britain's, and a fleet of submarines under construction which sent shivers down the back of the British Admiralty. Hitler, they pointed out, was aching for the opportunity to send his Nazi Brown Shirts into Austria, and there could be no better opportunity than while the Italian army was engrossed in Africa.

But Mussolini pushed on. He pushed on until the May meeting of the Council of the League of Nations, by which time it became apparent that at last Abyssinia could not be prevented from placing her dispute before her fellow members. To have shunned the Abyssinian plea would have made the League the laughing-stock of the world. Yet to censure Italy meant that country's immediate withdrawal.

So once again Captain Anthony and Pierre Laval got busy. All day before the convening of the Council they were closeted with Baron Pompeo Aloisi of Italy. Frequently during the day, Baron Aloisi was on the telephone to Rome. Once during the day, Laval and Eden paid a call on Hawariate, informed him that Abyssinia would have to grant Italy certain economic concessions—chiefly the long-proposed rail route uniting Italian Somaliland with Eritrea. This was to be the price of Italian mediation.

Finally, at 12.47 A. M. on May 25th, Maxim Litvinoff, chairman of the Council, rapped his gavel. Italy and Abyssinia had decided to arbitrate. Each were to appoint two mediators, and these four were to select a fifth. But if by July 25th the fifth mediator was not selected, the League of Nations was to make the selection. And again, if by August 25th, the dispute had not been settled, the League reserved the right to take it over completely.

It was a great day for peace.

The Abyssinian delegate hailed the fact that the agreement banned further troop movements from Italy. Baron Aloisi looked pale and nervous, as one who has told his chief some extremely unpleasant truths and was afraid to go back to Rome. Newspaper headlines blazed forth the momentous news. Members of the Council beamed with satisfaction.

Next day Mussolini spoke in Rome.

"The procedure of conciliation," he told the Chamber of Deputies, "is limited—as is well understood—to the incident at Walwal; but no one, especially in Italy, should nourish too many illusions on this subject.

"The encounter at Walwal was the signal bell of a situation that had been maturing for some time—a situation that imposes on Fascist Italy the fulfillment of inescapable duties. . . . Only men in bad faith, only hidden or open enemies of Fascist Italy can pretend to be stupefied or simulate protests for the military measures which we have taken or for those we are about to take."

And suiting words to action he ordered to Africa 20,000 officers and mechanics of the Class of 1912.

Thus the world came to know what the inner statesmen at Geneva already knew—that Mussolini's acceptance of conciliation was hollow gesturing. Dickering with Abyssinia would carry him through July 25th, through August 25th, possibly until September 25th. All of this was the rainy season. All this time, transportation across the trackless highlands of Abyssinia was impossible. All this time, Italian troop concentration could be perfected along the border.

Marking time in the council halls of Geneva had merely played into Mussolini's hands.

It is customary, when any delegate of the League of Nations departs from Geneva, for a group of fellow diplomats and members of the Secretariat to accompany him to the station. This has become a ritual never dispensed with.

After his hectic sessions with Captain Eden and Pierre Laval concluded at Geneva, Tecle-Hawariate, delegate of the independent Empire of Abyssinia, arrived at the railroad station, en route to Paris.

He was escorted by a Swiss porter. No one else was within sight.

THE WHO'S WHO OF OUR DIPLOMACY

AMERICAN DIPLOMACY

Cordell Hull came into office with the opportunity of being the most outstanding Secretary of State in years. But so far he had been a blank and an enigma. He has a benign manner, a kindly disposition, an unconquerable inability to express himself on any one point in less than a thousand words, and the vindictiveness of the Tennessee mountain clans from which he sprang.

Hull's father once was captured by Northern guerrillas during the Civil War, stabbed in one eye, and thrown over a low bank of the Tennessee River. Some years later, having identified his assailants, he traced the ring leader through the Southwest, eventually caught him, gave him time to make his peace with God, and killed him.

Cordell Hull, his son, is somewhat like his father. He has not forgotten his vendetta with Professor Moley, at one time Assistant Secretary of State; nor will he ever forget. It is one of the personal tragedies of his administration that he has been surrounded either by career diplomats or political appointees, whom the President has put in over his head.

Secretary Hull lives on the memories of the Pan-American Conference at Montevideo, where he was a hero. And any ambassador who comes to see him finds the conversation, sooner or later, drifting around to "the spirit of Montevideo." Most ambassadors, however, do not come to see Mr. Hull. They find him far too loquacious on the question of tariffs—but only on tariffs. When they want something done they see

Under-Secretary Phillips, or on Latin-American affairs, Sumner Welles.

William Phillips, Jr., Under-Secretary of State, is an accomplished diplomat. His clothes are well cut, his ties, shirt, and handkerchiefs harmonize, his voice is soft and agreeable. He can say nothing in several languages.

Phillips' chief characteristic is to take no responsibility under any circumstances. When he says, "I don't know," the cadences of his voice vary according to whether he is Acting Secretary of State or just the Under-Secretary.

Of human passions he knows nothing. Whatever feelings he may have are carefully suppressed by the dignity of his office.

While this fear of responsibility makes him incapable of showing any initiative, he is an excellent executive. There are few men in the State Department who can take orders with the same precision, and execute them as punctiliously.

Sumner Welles, Assistant Secretary of State, is the most forthright executive in the State Department. He has under his "suzerainty" the twenty republics of Latin-America, and the path in front of his door is worn with their goings and comings. Despite a conservative—almost Tory—background, Welles is a liberal and is opposed to championing the rights of American bankers and big corporations in the Western Hemisphere, whose destiny, in part, he controls. It was Welles who sold President Roosevelt on the "good neighbor" policy; and when it comes to Latin-American affairs, he is the State Department. Certainly, Mr. Hull would not think of overruling him, and on most policies this applies also to the President.

Wilbur John Carr, the oldest Assistant Secretary of State, is the only man in the Department who has worked his way up from a menial clerkship to a position of major importance. For nineteen years he supported an invalid wife on an infinitesimal salary and rose from Clerk to Chief Clerk, then to Director of the Consular Bureau. His wife died, and seven years later he married again, this time a lady of wealth. Wealth is the first requisite of success in the State Department, and from that time on Carr was made. Carr had not only wealth but experience and a reasonable amount of brains. The result is that he runs most of the administrative bureaus of the State Department and runs them fairly well. He is slow, meticulous to the last T, and has a habit of getting his desk piled so high with papers that the Under-Secretary of State once ordered him to clean them off. He is cursed from every side. It is Carr here and Carr there, and Carr's to blame for anything happening anywhere, but if he passed out of the picture the State Department would look years before it could replace him.

"*Judge*" *Walton Moore* accepted the position of Assistant Secretary of State at the age of seventy-six because his old friend, Secretary Cordell Hull, asked him to. He has one outstanding distinction. He is the only high official in the State Department appointed by Mr. Hull.

While in Congress, he was an interested, though innocuous, member of the House Foreign Affairs Committee; hence his dubious knowledge of international affairs. Moore is a modest man who would rather talk about the charms of the Virginia countryside or his trip to Europe in 1901 than about the intricacies of American foreign policy. But whenever his old friend Hull entrusts him with some job, he tries to do it thoroughly and generally succeeds.

He is the only high official in the State Department with a broad sense of humor. When his relative and former colleague in the House, Hamilton Fish, threatened to berate the Administration by radio, because it recognized Russia, Moore told him: "Ham, I always enjoy Amos and Andy on the radio and I know I shall appreciate you."

Joseph Clark Grew, American Ambassador to Tokyo, has recovered from the blight cast upon his reputation as Under-

Secretary of State, and is now ranked as one of the ablest of career men. A wealthy descendant of the Boston Cabots, related by marriage to the House of Morgan, Grew prepared for a diplomatic career by tiger shooting in Manchuria, elephant hunting in India, and a clerkship in the American Consulate in Cairo at the age of twenty-four. As Under-Secretary of State, Grew was in constant hot water, but as Ambassador to Japan he has handled a delicate diplomatic situation with consummate tact and skill.

Alexander W. Weddell has spent a lifetime in the Consular Service, and was not elevated to the important post of American Ambassador to Argentina until after he had married a wealthy St. Louis widow and contributed heavily to the Democratic Party. His wife he met while she was on a world cruise and he was Consul General at Calcutta.

Weddel has come in for indirect State Department censure on various occasions, one of them being when he arrived from Argentina and described Roosevelt as a "mystic." Also he predicted that Argentina would sell wheat to the United States—which was the last thing the Roosevelt Administration wanted the American farmer to think.

Hal Sevier was appointed by Jim Farley to be Ambassador to Chile, and the State Department has been regretting it ever since. Sevier's qualifications for office were the fact that his wife was a member of the Democratic National Committee from Texas, and that he had antagonized various Chileans while serving in that country as the representative of George Creel during the World War. Before his appointment, Sevier's name was not listed in *Who's Who*, though his wife's was. Following his appointment, his wife's sketch has been removed and his inserted.

Nelson Johnson, American Ambassador to China, is one of the few men in the career service who has reached the top without having his path plentifully lubricated with money. Johnson lives only on his salary, and now that after forty years of bachelordom he has married, he must live as meagerly as the Chinese. He has spent some twenty years among the latter, but unlike most people who have been close to the yellow race, he has not soured on it.

Before leaving Washington to become Minister, Lyle Wilson of the United Press showed Johnson an airplane which looped the loop, dipped, and circled automatically. Johnson was as pleased as a small boy. A few days later, Wilson went back to the store to get another plane, but the dealer was sold out. He explained that the new envoy to China had purchased his entire stock.

Dr. Stanley Hornbeck, the Chief of the State Department's Far Eastern Division, is more pedagogue than diplomat. He is pompous and didactic. When he looks in the mirror, he sees a man who never can be wrong. The secret is that he suffers from an inferiority complex—which makes him arrogant toward all those who are not his superior in rank. He has as few friends as he has enemies. To all with whom he comes in contact, he is just Dr. Hornbeck.

Pierrepont Moffat, Chief of the State Department's important Western European Division, is a born career diplomat.

Intelligent and hard-working, he would have made a success at selling insurance—but he prefers diplomacy. As a young man, Moffat was afflicted with a serious illness which made him an invalid for an interval. Instead of reading detective stories or light novels, he read philosophy and history. A conservative by birth and education, he is almost a liberal, but can't quite get there.

The only unfortunate thing in his life was his transfer from the field to the State Department, where he became contaminated with the "hush-hush" disease so prevalent among career men.

Michael McDermott, Chief of the Division of Current Information, is an amiable Irishman, naïve and idealistic enough to believe that the Hand of God guides the Secretary of State, which makes him suffer inward agonies in dealing with agnostic newspaper men. Despite the fact that under the New Deal some fifty or more skilled reporters have been hired by the Government to disseminate news to the press, McDermott remains probably the most efficient press relations officer of them all.

THE WASHINGTON DIPLOMATIC CORPS

ALBANIA

Faïk Konitza, charming Minister of Albania, occupies a much more prominent position in Washington than his country does in Europe. He is famous for his coffee, which he roasts, grinds, and brews himself. He is also an authority on Oriental cocktail recipes which he guards with great secrecy, the most famous being a mixture of crushed almonds and absinthe.

ARGENTINA

Felipe Espil, Ambassador of Argentina, sometimes is referred to as "the friendliest enemy" in the Diplomatic Corps. The description is derived from the fact that he has opposed the United States on almost every commercial policy it puts forth in Latin America and yet remains in the highest esteem of the State Department.

Espil came to the United States as a young lawyer twenty years ago and has virtually grown up here. He knows the United States as few foreigners—in fact, as few Americans—know it.

He has an American wife to whom he is so devoted that he will scarcely go out to lunch without her. And yet he continues to be an ever alert fighter for the rights of his country.

He walks four miles around the Speedway every afternoon, has his clothes tailored in London, and sometimes is called the Mona Lisa of the Pampas.

AUSTRIA

Edgar L. G. Prochnik, Austrian Minister, is likely to retain his job as long as he—or his wife—has money to finance it. For his government can scarcely afford to pay his passage home.

Prochnik is a diplomat of the *vieille noblesse;* has all the stiffness of the Imperial School of Pages, where he was educated. Never does he talk out of turn. He is the only member of the Diplomatic Corps who can keep a monocle in place while singing.

BOLIVIA

Dr. Don Enrique Finot, Minister of Bolivia, is one of the most hectic diplomats in the Capital. He spends much of his time trotting back and forth between the Legation and the State Department, where he is a constant pleader for the rights of his country in the war against Paraguay. Finot began life as a school teacher, is an able writer, and has a much broader vision than the militarists who actually guide the destinies of his country.

BRAZIL

Oswaldo Aranha is one of the few ambassadors Brazil has sent to this country in recent years who has cut any swath whatsoever. The others were famous for their hair dye, their pet cats, and their amours.

Aranha comes from the cattle-punching district of southern Brazil and punched his way into fame by leading the revolution which put the present Brazilian government in power. As a result his stomach is still full of lead. After that he was able to dictate the job he wanted, and became, first Minister of Finance—the hardest job of all—then Ambassador to Washington.

Although a comparative stranger and handicapped by his scanty knowledge of English, Aranha already stands out as one of the forceful diplomats in the Corps.

CANADA

William Duncan Herridge, Minister of Canada, probably knows the United States better than any other diplomat, . with the possible exception of Ambassador Espil. Members of the New Deal are constantly at his dinner table; and in Canada, where he is an important political power, he preaches a doctrine at times even more radical than that of President Roosevelt. Having become a ripe and somewhat seasoned old bachelor, he married the sister of Prime Minister Bennett and has become almost as important as his brother-in-law in guiding the political destinies of the Dominion. Immensely wealthy, he finances his brother-in-law's campaign expenses. Professor Tugwell helps with his speeches.

CHILE

The Chilean Ambassador, Don Manuel Trucco, is famous for having the hardest luck of any member of the Diplomatic Corps. Last year while flying to the deathbed of his wife, his airplane crashed at Lima and he spent two months in the hospital. After returning to the United States, he was operated on for appendicitis, following which pneumonia set in. Because of his long illness and his lack of a knowledge of English, he is almost unknown in Washington.

CZECHOSLOVAKIA

Ferdinand Veverka, Czechoslovak Minister, is a practical idealist. At the bottom of his heart he is a realist who has seen too much of the diplomatic ballyhoo to believe in it. But since he wants to keep his job and aspires to become

Foreign Secretary in his country—when Beneš becomes
President of Czechoslovakia—he must adopt official idealism.
This intellectual fight with himself has made the otherwise
gay and lively Czech almost a neurasthenic.

DENMARK

The chief worry of Otto Wadsted is that the Virgin Islands,
which his government sold to this country for $25,000,000,
be returned to Denmark. Otherwise his job in Washington
is pleasant and easy.

When a son was born to him two years ago he was also
worried as to his child's nationality. Having been born in a
hospital outside the Legation, his friends argued that the
boy was American. Finally Wadsted went to Professor James
Brown Scott, noted authority on international law, who
rendered a twenty-five-page opinion removing conclusively
the dread fear that the child was an American.

ECUADOR

Captain Colon Eloy Alfaro, Minister of Ecuador, was graduated from West Point and is the son of a former president.
Last summer, he also was offered the presidency of his
country, but decided it was more peaceful in Washington.

FRANCE

His Excellency *André de Laboulaye* is the scion of an ancient
family who in these trying days of democracy would much
prefer to live in the traditions of the past. Most ruefully he
adopts himself to the present.

M. de Laboulaye has the highest regard for constituted
authority and has never made a grave error. Also he has
never accomplished anything of note.

He was sent to Washington because he represented himself
to his Foreign Office as one who could call President Roosevelt "Franklin." This may have been true when Franklin

was a bumptious young Assistant Secretary of the Navy and André was an innocuous young counselor of the French Embassy. But times, at least on one side, have changed. Franklin is now the dynamic executive of a great nation; André is as innocuous as ever.

As Ambassador of France he is less known, less understood, less liked than any that have come this way in years.

GERMANY

Dr. Hans Luther owes his job as German Ambassador to the fact that super-zealous Nazi underlings tried to bump him off when he was President of the Reichsbank.

Instead of collapsing in the face of gun muzzles, Luther called up Hitler and asked whether it was the policy of the Chancellor thus to dispose of the President of the national bank of Germany. Hitler likes nerve, and next day offered Luther the ambassadorship to the United States. Washington is about five thousand miles away from Berlin. Luther accepted.

Since then he has been busy out-Nazying the Nazis. His hand leaps to the traditional salute at the slightest provocation. Everything the Führer does is sacrosanct. There is no stauncher defender of the Nazi doctrine than Luther—he does not want to return to Germany yet.

GREAT BRITAIN

Sir Ronald Lindsay, His Britannic Majesty's Ambassador to the United States, has a somewhat dull exterior under which he hides the abilities of a first-class diplomat.

He is dean of the Diplomatic Corps and the tallest ambassador Washington has ever seen. His trousers come almost to his armpits; he plays a snappy game of tennis; and is married to a schoolgirl friend of Mrs. Roosevelt.

Because he hates the limelight which other diplomats love, Sir Ronald is supposed to have more brawn than brain, which is not the case. He is cordial, simple, sometimes even frank. When embarrassed by an indiscreet question, he replies: "Well, really, I don't know anything about it. You know, these days ambassadors are nothing but the letter boxes of their respective governments."

HUNGARY

John Pelényi replaces the magnificent, snobbish, and inefficient Count László Széchényi as Minister of Hungary. The only thing these two have in common is American wives. Széchényi married a Vanderbilt and Pelényi a girl from Ohio. Széchényi selected his guests only from the *Social Register;* Pelényi, from the *Congressional Directory.*

In his anxiety to please the Horthy government, Pelényi emulates the former Italian Ambassador, Giacomo de Martino, and has become the greatest "protestant" in the Diplomatic Corps. An avid reader of newspapers, he catches everything written about Hungary, trots down to the State Department with formal protests on the slightest provocation.

IRISH FREE STATE

Michael MacWhite has no mission in the United States other than to exercise his personality, and this he does to the credit and glory of the Irish Free State. He performs exactly the duties which the Free State Government and the Irish-American Societies want an Irish Minister to perform, and, as a result, he is in great demand. He is one of the most popular diplomats in Washington.

ITALY

Dapper *Augusto Rosso* is the baby of the ambassadorial family, having just passed the forty-fourth milestone. Mussolini never takes into consideration length of service and age, hence Rosso's appointment to one of the prize posts in the Italian service.

A bachelor, despite Mussolini's orders for all men to get married, Rosso does not entertain lavishly. But his simple manner has gained him more friends in Washington than any other European representative. He loves a good game of bridge and between bids can draw more important political information from his fellow players than if he went to the State Department twice a day.

The New Deal interests him more than America's foreign policy, which he believes will remain as obscure in the present as it was in the past.

JAPAN

Hirosi Saito of Japan believes in blurting out the truth, even at the cost of becoming the most undiplomatic ambassador ever to sip a cocktail in the Capital. He is a great propagandist. No college, no matter how unimportant, no society or association, regardless of distance from Washington, ever has been denied the diminutive Ambassador's presence to explain Japanese-American relations.

Saito prides himself on his aggressiveness. He is the appointee of the Tokio military clique, and he must please his masters. His American nickname, "The Ambassador for War," pleases him more than all the honorary degrees he has been able to garner from all the colleges of the country. Yet, at the bottom of his heart, Saito is no jingoist. His thesis—though probably a mistaken one—is that the more Japan shows that it has no fear for the United States, the less chance there is of war.

MEXICO

Ambassador *Castillo Najera* is one of those rarities in Washington—a diplomat with both charm and brains. How he happened to become a diplomat is more than most of his colleagues understand. Once he was one of Mexico's leading surgeons; for a time served as Minister of Health.

He has written a volume of Mexican poetry; translated Belgian verse into Spanish. Of late years—as Minister to France and delegate to the League of Nations—he has served brilliantly as mediator in the Leticia dispute between Colombia and Peru and in the Chaco controversy between Bolivia and Paraguay. After a year of the Catholic anti-Mexican barrage in Washington it is predicted he will go back to poetry.

THE NETHERLANDS

Jonkheer H.M. van Haersma de With, wealthy scion of an old Dutch family and Netherlands minister to Washington, is a man whose chief claim to fame is a very pretty wife and six servants imported directly from Holland.

NORWAY

Were it not for the question of whale oil, *Wilhelm Munthe de Morgenstierne* would be happy. He came to Washington as Norwegian Minister with the chief ambition of negotiating a commercial treaty with the United States. But just as he saw his goal within sight, Congress slapped a three-percent tax on whale oil, one of Norway's largest exports to this country. The treaty is now in the fat.

Morgenstierne is one of the youngest ministers in the Corps and is too young, both in age and sojourn here, to count.

PANAMA

Dr. Ricardo J. Alfaro, Minister of Panama, once was president of his country and is a constant thorn in the side of the State Department, because of his demand that Panama throw off the political yoke of the United States. His favorite expression is: "If you throw a rock against an egg, the egg breaks. Or, if you throw an egg against a rock, the egg breaks. That is Panama and the United States. In either case Panama is broken." He is a collector of rock crystal but is bashful about admitting it.

PARAGUAY

The body of *Dr. Don Enrique Bordenave*, Minister of Paraguay, bears three wounds as mute testimony of the martial prowess of his countrymen. He is an extremely able envoy, the half-brother of the President of Paraguay, is married to a charming and wealthy Argentine lady, and carries tremendous weight with his government.

PERU

Although he has no very absorbing duties, *Don Manuel de Freyre y Santander*, Ambassador of Peru, is one of the ablest and most charming diplomats in Washington. His chief official concern is smoothing out war between his country and Colombia, and his chief private concern is the care of his children, with whom he invariably breakfasts and lunches. Señora de Freyre died while the children were young. The Ambassador arises at five-thirty and, no matter what the weather, goes for a long constitutional.

Although his country has been virtually at war with Colombia, the Colombian Government pays Freyre a regular pension in honor of the fact that one of his great-grandfathers fought as Chief of Staff with Bolívar, the Liberator.

POLAND

Polish Ambassador *Stanislaw Patek* boasts a record of having slept in more jails than any other diplomat. He is a famous revolutionary, has one of the best chefs in the Corps, and in his day he was a statesman.

SOVIET RUSSIA

Alexander Antonovich Troyanovsky, Ambassador of the Soviet Union, was destined by his father to be an officer in the Czar's army. But while in the military academy at Tula he became a Socialist and a revolutionary. Because he knew

Japan he was sent by Moscow as the first ambassador to Tokio, and because of Japanese-American relations he was later selected as the first U. S. S. R. ambassador to Washington.

Troyanovsky was warned that he would be snubbed by many here and came prepared for it. His military training taught him that the best defensive is the offensive. When he called at the State Department for the first time he was received by Under-Secretary William Phillips, Jr. Phillips was uneasy. In order to break the ice he volunteered the innocuous remark: "You are fortunate to have a nice embassy here, Mr. Ambassador."

"Why, yes," replied Troyanovsky, "I believe it is a very nice house for a private person, and I think that Mrs. Pullman must have been quite comfortable there. But for the embassy of a great power it is totally inadequate."

Troyanovsky's parties are lavish, probably more lavish than he would like to have them. But Soviet "face" considers this necessary.

The rumor of this has traveled rapidly, and even the most starched opponents of Moscow among Washington's social élite now are eager to obtain the little cardboard inviting them to dine with the Bolshevists.

SPAIN

Don Luis Calderon, thin and ascetic Ambassador of Spain, came to Washington flushed with the expectation of negotiating a commercial treaty with the United States. He has now been here over one year, and not until recently did the State Department deign to discuss commercial problems with him.

Calderon's predecessor, Ambassador Cardenas, was eased out of Washington because he was too friendly with Latin-American diplomats, thereby being accused of creating a Spanish-American Entente. Calderon remains rigidly aloof.